CRITICAL TERRITORIES
From Academia to Praxis

AA LANDSCAPE URBANISM

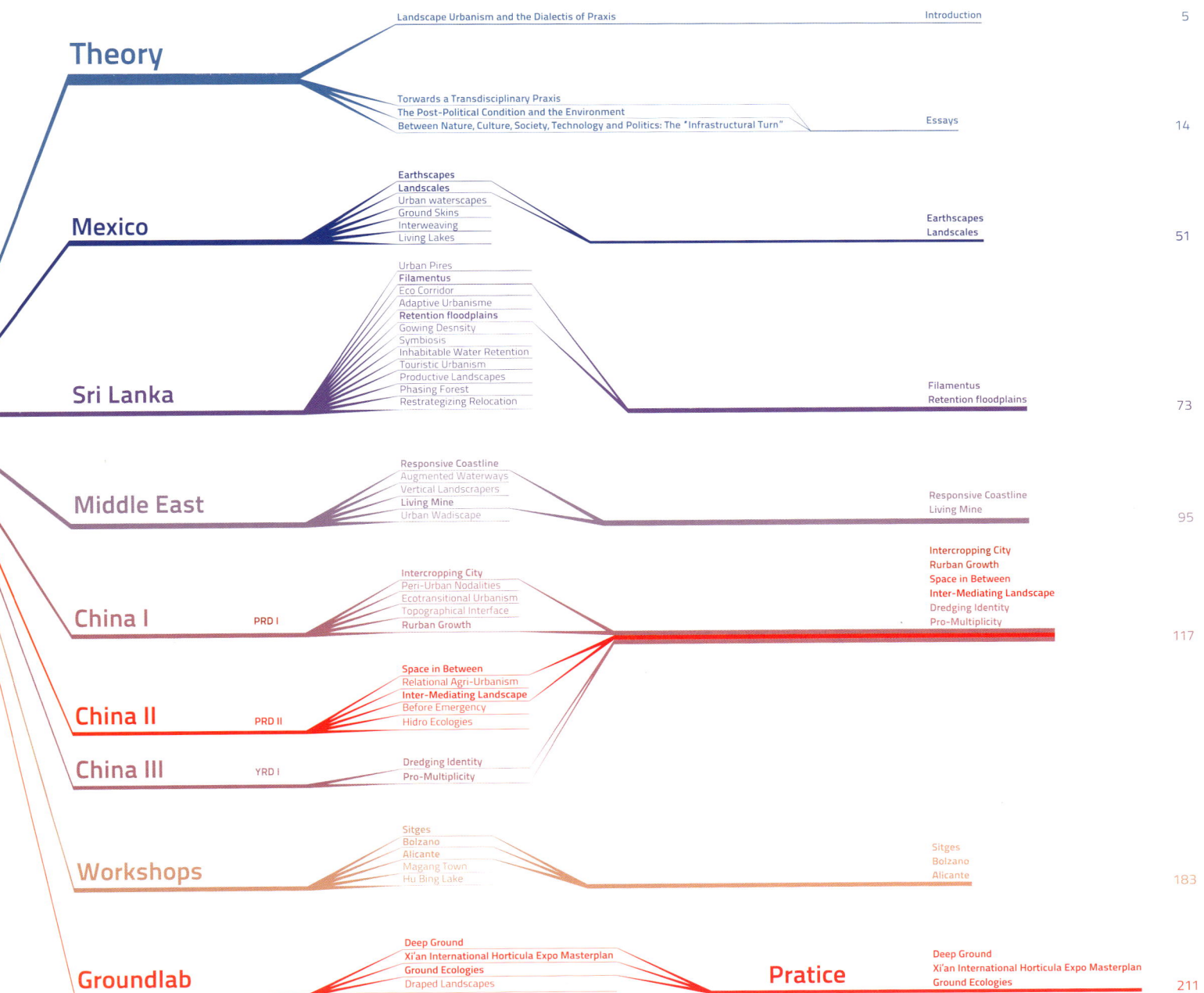

AALANDSCAPEURBANISM

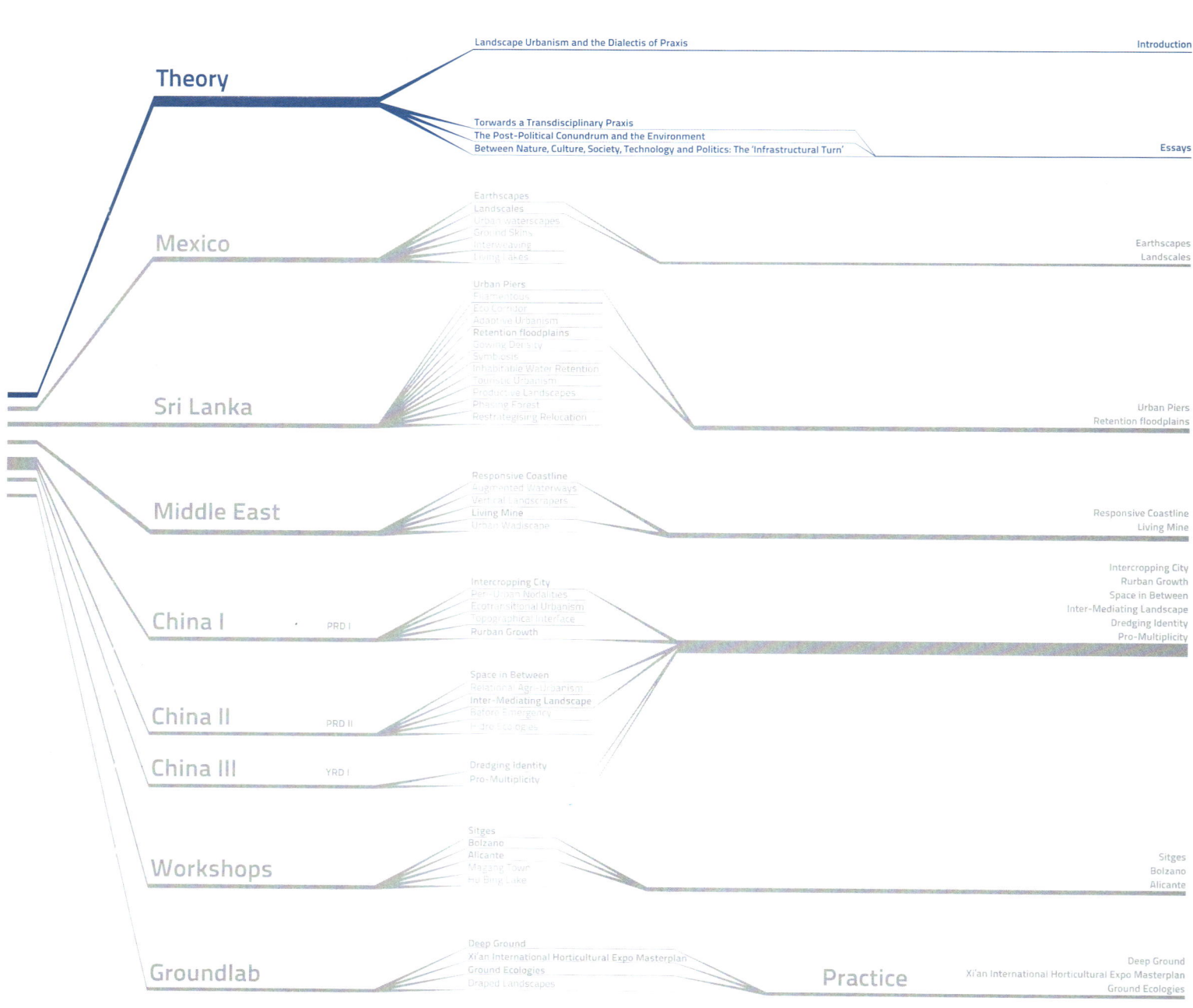

Introduction
Landscape Urbanism and the Dialectics of Praxis

EVA CASTRO, ALFREDO RAMIREZ, EDUARDO RICO, DOUGLAS SPENCER

This book records the current state of our practice, theory and teaching of Landscape Urbanism and its development in recent years. It describes the phases and processes through which we have arrived at a distinctive model of Landscape Urbanism and the movement, from academia to praxis, through which this has been achieved. To this end, *Critical Territories* opens with a series of contributions to the ongoing development of our theoretical perspectives before turning to elaborate, from within the academic framework of the Architectural Association, the work of our students and the agendas they have engaged with in Mexico, Sri Lanka, Dubai and China and the intensive workshops with which they have been involved in Europe. It then turns, finally, to the projects produced and realised by the Landscape Urbanist practice Groundlab, whose work both puts into practice our model of Landscape Urbanism and offers an opportunity to reflect upon its further development.

Our model of Landscape Urbanism – as Douglas Spencer outlines in the book's opening theoretical essay, 'Towards a Transdisciplinary Praxis' – is distinctive. Others have envisaged Landscape Urbanism as a means to decamp the depopulated western post-industrial city; to use *landscape* as the medium through which the *urban* can be reprogrammed for its post-fordist fate. Rather than looking to accommodate a post-urban condition, our agenda has turned to the problematics and possibilities of its future in what has been called the 'urban century'. Rapid urbanisation, mass migration from country to city, ecological and economic precarity, informal settlements, opportunistic urban entrepreneurialism and the wholesale reconfiguration of large-scale territories constitute the globalised conditions of contemporary urbanism with which we are concerned. These phenomena render the simple equation of post-fordism and postindustrialism with depopulation redundant for all but a rather limited set of specifically European and North American scenarios. The steep rise in urban populations occurring throughout much of the world is no longer exclusively linked to or de-

FRAMING THE MODEL

pendent upon economic or industrial growth. As Mike Davis has observed, we are now experiencing, globally, a '"perverse" urban boom' that has 'contradicted orthodox economic models which predicted that the negative feedback of urban recession should slow or even reverse migration from the countryside.'[1] Moreover, the territorial forms assumed by current processes of rapid urbanisation – 'rurban' hybrids of the rural and urban and rapid cycles of transformation between agricultural, industrial, post-industrial and leisure-based land use – pose a significant challenge to any project seeking to intervene within their complex dynamics. Landscape alone, particularly when simply conceived as the ameliorative greening of public space, cannot, as a discipline be considered adequate to this challenge.

Neither do we find those approaches to Landscape Urbanism that have been inflected through the discourse of critical regionalism apposite to the conditions of contemporary urbanisation. As Fredric Jameson wrote of this position some time ago,'Here not the emergent but the residual is emphasised (out of historical necessity), and the theoretical problem is at one with a political one, namely, how to fashion a progressive strategy out of what are necessarily the materials of tradition and nostalgia?' This theoretical and political problem is only exacerbated by the recent turn, within this current of Landscape Urbanism, to appeals for the restoration of 'indigenous traditions' in tune with 'natural rhythms' as its proper goal,[2] and the advocacy of 'traditional' techniques of geomancy, such as feng shui, as its instruments.[3]

Rather than proposing to substitute the discipline of architecture with that of landscape as the medium through which the urban should be engaged, we have developed a *transdisciplinary* methodology. Rather than approach contemporary conditions by reaching for tradition we have pursued a *praxis* through which research, theory and practice are continually developed through their interrelation. Hence a 'transdisciplinary praxis'. As Spencer explains in 'Towards a Transdisciplinary Praxis', engaging with the territories to which AALU (Architectural Association Landscape Urbanism) has addressed itself…requires not a 'disciplinary realignment' in which landscape replaces architecture but a transdisciplinary praxis in which both can be mobilised alongside and in concert with other fields of knowledge and practice.

Spencer's essay not only elaborates the development of this approach, placing it within the historical context of debates around urbanism, landscape and the

---

1. Mike Davis, 'Planet of Slums', *New Left Review* 26, March-April 2004, p. 9.

2. Kelly Shannon, 'South Asian Hydraulic Civilizations' in Kelly Shannon, Bruno De Meulder, Viviana d'Auria, Janina Gosseye, eds., *Water Urbanisms*, Amsterdam: Martien de Vletter, SUN, 2008, p. 57.
3. Kongjian Yu, 'Five Traditions for Landscape Urbanism Thinking', in *Topos*, 71, 2010, p. 58-63.

metropolis, but also itself exemplifies it. Here a range of critical positions – including Marxism, critical theory, poststructuralism, and urban political ecology – are drawn upon in order to explicate and critically address the issues at stake in our practice.

This approach is exemplified in the Longgang City Masterplan, 'Deep Ground', in which the method of 'thickening' the ground deployed in this project, we write, 'introduces high density and integration of functions as a mode of weaving an overall fabric. The strategy of the thickened ground also challenges the traditional opposition of building vs. landscape, and generates a higher density in areas which are currently under-used, increasing the overall value, open space usage and intensity of life at street level.'

In formal terms there is evident in this project, and throughout the work featured here, an exploration of the potentials of what Spencer describes as 'topographically oriented built form'. Rather than *formalist*, however, these 'artificial topographies' operate instrumentally, as 'a means through which existing typologies and urban programmes can be recomposed and rethought so that, for example, infrastructure may become inhabitable or architecture operate as a conduit for mobility.' Locating the origins of this approach within the obliquely-planed architecture and megastructural projects of Claude Parent and Paul Virilio's Architecture Principe, designed so as to reacquaint the modern subject with 'the physiological pleasures of self-locomotion through a renewed contact with gravitational force', Spencer explains how it has been developed, in the work of the students of AALU and of Groundlab, 'as a means to selectively channel, distribute, mobilise or stabilise the material, technological, social and environmental forces at play within a given territory.' In this sense the design of the built environment with which we are engaged aims to operate as a form of mediation between the natural, cultural, social, technological and political matters whose articulation Stephen Graham's contribution here identifies as the definitive function of infrastructure.

So, as opposed to the 'weak urbanism' often associated with Landscape Urbanism,[4] with its call for absolute flexibility, mobility and adaptability in urban design, our employment of form is concerned with the construction of determinate scenarios. Rather than service the imperatives of neoliberal urban entrepreneurialism, by providing it with smooth landscapes amenable to continuous reprogramming according to its shifting requirements, form, particularly archi-

---
4. See, for example, Charles Waldheim 'Notes Toward a History of Agrarian Urbanism' accessed April, 2011 at <http://urbanchoreography.net/2011/04/05/notes-toward-a-history-of-agrarian-urbanism-charles-waldheim/>, and Kelly Shannon, 'From Theory to Resistance: Landscape Urbanism in Europe', in Charles Waldheim, ed., *The Landscape Urbanism Reader*, New York: Princeton Architectural Press, 2006, pp. 141-161.

tectural form, enables us to achieve a critical agency, as designers, rather than operate as mere 'service providers'.

SOME NATURES RATHER THAN OTHERS

If Landscape Urbanism is to realise its potential to operate as an agent of intervention within the critical conditions of contemporary territorial transformation, it must move beyond the straightforward affirmation of the paradigms of mobility and flexibility which it shares with neoliberal urban entrepreneurialism. It is to a critique of both the *abstract* principles of contemporary urbanisation and their concrete manifestation in specific locales that Landscape Urbanism must turn. In order to do so, we believe that it must also now question and move beyond the simplistic rhetoric of 'environmentalism', 'sustainability' and 'eco-cities'; terms which are, more often than not, used to obscure or excuse the reproduction of social inequalities and purely commercial interests within urban development. In this context, the inclusion of Erik Swyngedouw's essay, 'The Post-Political Condition and the Environment' is both highly pertinent to our concerns, and points the way to their further development.

The target of Swyngedouw's critique in this essay is the consensual and commonsensical discourse of 'sustainability'. He describes the condition produced by this consensus as 'a post-democratic or post-political configuration, one that increasingly sutures the landscape of managerial-technocratic socio-environmental interventions.' Consensus, in this sense, refers to the subsumption of the properly political under the imperative of 'saving the planet'. In the process our active and political engagement in deciding *which* future we may want, and *which* particular configuration of 'nature' we are advocating, is suspended in favour of simply 'managing' the putative crisis of the environment within the given terms of the status quo:

> The key political question is one that centers on the question of what kind of natures we wish to inhabit, what kinds of natures we wish to preserve, to make, or, if need be, to wipe off the surface of the planet (like the HIV virus, for example), and on how to get there. The fantasy of 'sustainability' imagines the possibility of an originally fundamentally harmonious Nature, one that is now out-of-synch but which, if 'properly' managed, we can and have to return to by means of a series of technological, managerial, and organisational fixes.

Pertinent to the question of design as a practice of critical agency, rather than of servicing a dominant discourse of 'flexibility' or 'sustainability', Swyngedouw continues:

...the practice of planning interventions, when becoming concretely geographical or ecological, is of necessity a violent act of foreclosure of the democratic political (at least temporarily), of taking one option rather than another, of producing one sort of environment, of assembling certain socio-natural relations, of foregrounding some natures rather than others, of hegemonizing a particular metonymic chain rather than another...the legitimation of such options cannot be based on corralling Nature or Sustainability into legitimizing service.

The choice of one sort of environment over another, of one nature rather than others, as a constituent quality of design's agency, is registered throughout the projects featured in this book. Typically, the matter of urban infrastructures has been central to the formulation of such choices.

INTEGRATING INFRASTRUCTURE

Infrastructures, as Stephen Graham expresses it in the title of the essay included here on the 'infrastructural turn', operate 'Between Nature, Culture, Society, Technology and Politics'. As such, they play a fundamental, and increasingly significant, role as *the* apparatus through which the material, social and economic flows which constitute the territory of globalised capitalism are captured, processed, organised and (unevenly) distributed.

As Graham argues here – and as he has done at length with Simon Marvin in their *Splintering Urbanism: Networked Infrastructures, Technological Mobilities and the Urban Condition* – infrastructures, whilst globally connective, are often locally divisive. Whilst they service the globally privileged with power, sanitation, transportation and communication, they 'splinter' and segregate territories both spatially and economically, and in ways obscured by simplistic enthusiasms for mobility. Thus, for example:

...celebrations about the ways in which fast-rail networks speed up the circulation of people within Europe need to be tempered by attention to the ways that they can actually make intervening spaces less accessible from city cores because local train services are often sacrificed as a result of their development.
Similar logics of bypass are evident in the pipelines of potable water which thread across the surface of Mumbai, lacing together the gated communities of the affluent, whilst providing no access to the informal cities which they bisect. Indeed, tendencies to glorify new airport extensions or highway networks in Global South megacities need to be confronted with the way informal districts are often completely erased to make way for such projects.

Turning to the role Landscape Urbanism might play in addressing this tendency

Graham argues that:

In our world architecture increasingly melds into landscape and infrastructure, landscape increasingly is infrastructure, and 'nature' is increasingly a social and technological construction of gigantic proportions. The real challenge though is that the infrastructural turn reveals all this to be shot through with politics in ways that architectural theory in general, and the debates of landscape urbanism, has barely begun to consider, let alone address.

The point is well made. Landscape Urbanism has typically approached infrastructure *from the outside*, as an urban phenomenon to be smoothed into the urban fabric, 'greened' and 'naturalised', or endowed through ornamentation with a 'local identity'. Against this strategy of camouflage, we are committed to working *with* and *through* infrastructure, as an integral part of our practice, so as to address both the problematics identified by Graham and its potential to function otherwise.

MODELLING THE METHOD

There are three core elements to the methodology that reappear, with differing degrees of emphasis, throughout the projects shown in this book: indexing, prototyping and multi-scalarity. Their consideration in the projects is not sequential. Rather, each forms an essential component within a reciprocally informed assemblage. In presenting the works produced by the students of AALU and Groundlab, the book adopts a structure through which these three elements are reiterated within the analysis of each project. The periodic sequencing through which this reiterative structure is articulated – rendered tangible by the rhythmic punctuation of pages printed on graphite paper – serves as the basis for a dialogue between the projects through which their multiple affiliations can be mapped.

INDEXING, MAPPING AND THE DIAGRAM

We understand the index and the diagram, broadly, as forms of mapping that are both exploratory and propositional, and thus crucial to the design process. Indexing records the constitution of a given territory. It registers its topographical, geological, environmental, demographic and socio-economic conditions as processes, forms and parameters. From its reading of constituent elements it establishes a kind of common language that enables an understanding of their interrelated operations as a contingent whole. This, in turn, facilitates the generation of strategies premised upon an understanding of their impact upon the territory as a whole, as opposed to one focused upon the remediation of its 'problematic' parts. Following Deleuze, we describe the propositional dimension of mapping as diagrammatic, as a shift from the representational to the productive, 'setting up so many points of emergence of creativity, of unexpected conjunctures, of improbable continuums.'[5] In contradistinction to a previous generation of 'diagram architects', however, we do not seek to establish our autonomy, as designers, from the ground conditions identified in the index, but rather to identify their potentials.

5. Gilles Deleuze, *Foucault*, translated by Sean Hand, Minneapolis: University of Minnesota Press, 1988, p. 35.

PROTOTYPICALITY AND INFRASTRUCTURE

In order to address the infrastructural problematics revealed by Graham's analysis – its tendency to 'splinter' the lived environment along lines of class, race and gender – as well as to explore its capacity to operate beyond a narrowly defined functionality, our engagement with it moves beyond the established paradigm of scenographic treatment. Rather than approach the question of infrastructure as a cosmetic problem we treat it as an opportunity to engage with the machinic processes ranged across its sites. The critical role played by infrastructure in the organisation and management of the city's complex systems of movement, communication and exchange is recognised as the basis from which its operation can be further developed, can be pushed beyond its tendency to fragment and divide toward other possibilities. Thus, for example, a number of the projects represented here have sought, through infrastructure, to coordinate industrial development with the provision of public services; to configure networks through which the practice of urban agriculture and its products can be integrated within local economies; and to enable public circulation throughout the urban terrain.

These objectives, and others, are pursued through the formal and material articulation of infrastructure, coordinating its operations with the territorial processes, forms and parameters identified in the indexing of site, developing its relation to the ground, and elaborating its architectural composition. These exercises combine to form a prototypical methodology, where the prototype is understood as the mechanism through which the machinic operations of the site, including those of its infrastructure, are mediated by the intentions of the designer. Through the prototype these relations can be calibrated and their capacities tested. Further, from the side of design, the potential to push the functionality of the site beyond the trope of efficiency, to explore the possibility of generating a decoded space beyond the purview of urban 'management', resides in the malleable properties of the prototype. Rather than seeking to arrive at a single design solution optimised in terms of efficiency, to resolve, that is, the complexities and potentials of the site within a typical solution, the prototype is used to generate multiple outcomes. The exploratory deformation of the optimised type used to generate these outcomes, where its geometry is pushed and pulled along various axes, results in a catalogue whose iterations are more or less efficient in terms of their initially proposed purpose, but which reveals in the process differing valences, opportunities to explore further programmes and possibilities.

MULTI-SCALARITY AND GROUND MORPHOLOGIES

If many of the perspectives used in the mapping exercises of indexing and diagramming, with their bird's eye perspectives, appear to suggest the unengaged practice of perception from a distance, they represent, in fact, only one dimension of our engagement with the territories they depict. As is already suggested in the case of the prototype, our practice operates through multiple-scales that are always engaged in some way with the morphology of the ground. Each prototypical unit, for example, exists in its own right as a smaller-scale presence within its site. Through their proliferation throughout the site, however, the prototypical units emerge as large-scale multiplicity. Working in a multi-scalar fashion involves more, however, than the movement back and forth between the large and small scales. Each scale of operation engages with a different register of the site and its operations. Hence the mapping exercises can function as a prelude to addressing large-scale environmental forces such as marine oxygenisation or air pollution. At the scale of infrastructure, design interventions may register an impact upon a social ecology of transport, communication and access to resources. At the more intimate scale of built form the experiential qualities of space, the production of perspectives and the haptic encounters of bodies, for instance, acquire greater significance. At the smaller scale, where techniques such as terracing or 'cut and fill' are employed, their programmatic functions are immediately manifest, whilst their cumulative effect registers upon the totality of the environment thus articulating them, at the same time, within the large-scale.

Collectively, these different dimensions and registers of the site are coordinated through the morphology of the ground. It is especially through the treatment of the ground, through its *formation*, that AALU has sought a means to resist the tendency to conceive of site as, ideally, horizontally articulated, absolutely flexible, and infinitely reprogrammable. We would argue, against the grain of many of the arguments from which Landscape Urbanism originated, that it is through *form* that Landscape Urbanism attains one of its principal means of agency as a design practice concerned to commit itself toward *specific* urban scenarios:

Many of the sites with which AALU and Groundlab have been engaged, for example, particularly those in China, suffer from soil pollution and degradation requiring processes such as excavation, cutting, filling and capping in order to effect their remediation. More than a problem-solving exercise, however, this type of 'groundwork' also provides an opportunity to generate artificial topographies with the formal capacity to structure relations between environmental, social, cultural and economic factors on a given site. Whilst the techniques employed for this type of groundwork may be borrowed from those used in more conventional techniques of landscaping, however, it is through their *architectural* elaboration that these forms achieve the greatest potential to articulate determinate – though not deterministic – urban relationships. Architecture, like no other medium, is able to structure the city, its functional, cultural, social and even political implications, into a coherent assemblage.

The fashion in which the relations between the ground plane, architecture, and also infrastructural elements are configured – as an articulation between form and programme – holds the capacity to organise the relationships that the designer, as an active and critical agent, seeks to retain, reinforce, or reconfigure within the urban terrain.

FROM ACADEMIA TO PRAXIS

This book's structure aims to demonstrate, then, in its elaboration of our theoretical concerns, and its representations of our pedagogy and practice, a movement between academia and praxis. This movement is not linear but dialectically composed and continually evolving. It originates in our experiences of urban life in Europe, South America and China, and our work as designers, engineers, theorists and writers. It has been developed through our work as teachers and practitioners; through the research agendas pursued in Mexico, Sri Lanka, the Middle East and China; through a series of intensive workshops; through the practice of Groundlab; and through our exchanges with critical theorists, political ecologists and urban historians. It has evolved, we believe, into a distinctive and significant contribution to the development of Landscape Urbanism.

Towards a Transdisciplinary Praxis: AALU
DOUGLAS SPENCER

INTRODUCTION: A THIRD POSITION

Some years since the 'disciplinary realignment' identified by Charles Waldheim as 'Landscape Urbanism' was first announced, its practice has settled into two broad camps.[1] One, in North America, informed by a post-fordist teleology where post-urban territories are to be 'decamped' and dispersed within the landscape, the other adopting a critical regionalist position in which landscape is mobilised in the conservation of site and tradition against the encroachments of globalisation and its supposedly universalising technology. The post-urban variant of Landscape Urbanism, advocated and practised by figures such as James Corner and Stan Allen has been at least acquiescent, if not opportunistically instrumental, to a post-fordist spatial logic of socio-spatial transformation. The critical-regionalist strategy, proposed by Kenneth Frampton and pursued by practitioners such as Kelly Shannon, whilst clearly articulating a certain politics of landscape, has, in its strategies of resistance, focused upon a place-making approach through which such values as 'cultural difference' might be conserved.[2] A third position has been developed, within the Landscape Urbanism programme in the Graduate School of the Architectural Association, eschewing both the strategies of dispersal and the politics of conservative resistance. Since its inception under the directorship of Mohsen Mostafavi and Ciro Najle in 2000, and its subsequent development under Eva Castro's direction since 2004, this programme has pursued a distinctive approach to the practice and theorisation of Landscape Urbanism. On the one hand, the consistently international body of students and tutors that have been attached to the programme, combined with the range of locations and conditions that it has engaged with – Mexico, Sri Lanka, Dubai and China – for example, has rendered any straightforward adoption of the North American model of post-urban decampment incongruous to its concerns. On the other hand, the programme's theoretical orientation, drawing at its outset upon the poststructuralist thought of figures such as Michel Foucault, Gilles Deleuze and Félix Guattari, has placed it directly at odds with the phenomenological and humanist orientation of Frampton's critical regionalist position. Rather than operate under the dictates of a post-fordist teleology, or be guided by a phenomenological/humanist agenda, AALU has forged a distinctive framework of practical knowledge, responsive design instruments and theoretical perspectives developed in an ongoing dialogue with the conditions and locations it has addressed over the course of its existence. In this sense the programme has developed through a logic of praxis. Praxis, as famously defined by Marx in the 11th thesis of his critique of Feuerbach, and as later developed by Georg Lukács in his *History and Class Consciousness*, is concerned with the interrelationship of theory and practice, of thought to material existence, as a

---

1. Charles Waldheim, 'Landscape Urbanism: A Genealogy', in *Praxis*, no. 4, 2002, pp. 10-17.

---

2. Kenneth Frampton, 'Towards a Critical Regionalism: Six Points for an Architecture of Resistance', in Hal Foster, ed., *The Anti-Aesthetic: Essays on Postmodern Culture*, Seattle: Bay Press, 1983, pp. 16-30. Kelly Shannon, 'From Theory to Resistance: Landscape Urbanism in Europe', in Charles Waldheim, ed., *The Landscape Urbanism Reader*, New York: Princeton Architectural Press, 2006, pp. 141-161.

[3]. 'The philosophers have only interpreted the world, in various ways; the point is to change it', Karl Marx, 'Theses on Feuerbach', in Karl Marx and Frederick Engels, *Collected Works*, Vol. 5. London: Lawrence and Wishart, 1976. Georg Lukács, *History and Class Consciousness: Studies in Marxist Dialectics*, London: Merlin Press, 1971.

radical project through which their mutual transformation will follow.[3] It cannot, of course, be claimed that any design discipline can by itself produce such a project of transformation of thought and material existence. Yet it might be possible that it contribute to this process by refusing, on the one hand, the fatalistic subsumption of its own agenda to the productive logic of capitalist development and, on the other, the idealism which posits an immutable human nature defined by principles of attachment to place and tradition. It might be possible that through its own form of praxis it achieves the ability to critically rethink the conditions of subjective experience and social existence in relation to the production of space, and its ecological, economic and political dimensions, and that it defines projects through which these could be productively reconfigured. Rather than following the broader trajectory of Landscape Urbanism toward the post or ex-urban, the locus of praxis for AALU has in recent years gravitated toward new forms of large-scale and rapidly developing urbanism. The implications of this particular orientation, running against the grain of much other Landscape Urbanism, are significant.

TALKING DETROIT: A GENEALOGY OF LANDSCAPE AS URBANISM

Occupying a privileged place in the discourse of Landscape Urbanism, and forming the focus of the essays contained in the book *Stalking Detroit*, the arc of the Motor City's rise and fall has been neatly correlated with the arrival and departure of the automobile industry, and its post-fordist, post-industrial trajectory mapped onto the shifting articulations of 'property ownership, speculative development, and mobile capital' identified as its determining conditions.[4]

[4]. Charles Waldheim, Georgia Daskalakis and Jason Young, eds., *Sta!king Detroit*, Barcelona: Actar, 2001. See for example the essay 'Decamping Detroit' by Charles Waldheim and Marili Santos-Munné in this collection.
[5]. Patrik Schumacher and Christian Rogner, 'After Ford' in Charles Waldheim, Georgia Daskalakis and Jason Young, eds., ibid., p. 49.
[6]. ibid., p. 51.

In their essay 'After Ford', Patrik Schumacher and Christian Rogner argued that 'Detroit offers a paradigmatic case study of fordism as an organizational model'[5] and that the 'totalizing notion of fordism became instrumental to the underlying rationality of modern architecture and urbanism' in America and across Europe.[6] Inextricably bound to the logic of fordism, Detroit was amongst the first of cities to experience the depopulation that followed the dispersive urban-regional practices of the former's decentralising phase in the mid-twentieth century.

The responses to the prevalence of vacant sites and void spaces now left in the wake of Detroit's depopulation and decentralisation have, on the part of Waldheim and others been to propose a remediative strategy drawing upon landscape as its medium. In answer to the patterns of abandon and decay exemplified in Detroit they proposed an 'urbanism of landscape' which 'stages and choreographs the process of decommissioning, depopulating and [the] reconceiving' of its 'territories'.[7] As recounted by Graham Shane, Detroit's decommissioning is envisaged here as a four-part process comprised of the following stages: '*Dis-*

[7]. Charles Waldheim and Marili Santos-Munné, op cit., p. 110.

location' (disconnection of services), then 'Erasure' (demolition and jumpstarting the native landscape ecology by dropping appropriate seeds from the air), then 'Absorption' (ecological reconstitution of part of the Zone as woods, marshes, and streams), and then 'Infiltration' (the recolonization of the landscape with heteropic village-like enclaves).[8]

Both the broader applicability of the Detroit model outlined here and its politics, or lack thereof, are not unproblematic, however. As Graham Shane, in an essay otherwise broadly sympathetic to Landscape Urbanism, observes: *the problem is that the small scale, bottom-up, and eco-friendly moves advocated by Stalking Detroit do not address fundamental issues of social justice and equity that are also part of the foundations of a true urbanity. Other cities have not fallen prey to Henry Ford's myopia, racism, and antiurbanism. Other successful cities have moderated their dynamic and destabilizing tendencies with pushes for justice and equality, so that wealth and information are redistributed throughout the urban network in the interest of social reproduction, efficiency, and competitiveness in a global market.*[9]

Moreover, given the uniquely intimate relationship between the automobile industry and Detroit, the extent to which it can be claimed as a paradigm of anything other than its own particular history is questionable. But the wider applicability of this very particular model is nowhere problematised by Schumacher and Rogner. Their argument in fact suggests its more global validity: contemporary urbanism in general is subsumed under a single model of linear development which leads to an inevitably post-urban outcome. Whilst the correspondences between industrial and urban phases of development which the authors have argued for may offer a neatly deterministic formula, its precise telos is specific to certain features of the North American context, rather than universal, and is not equipped to address the multiple forces shaping contemporary urbanism or their manifold dynamics.

In the production of this telos Schumacher and Rogner follow an orthodox western Marxist theory of urbanisation recently analysed by David Cunningham as driven by arguments about the primacy of industrialisation and the factory – over any relatively autonomous processes of urbanisation – within the 'laws of motion' of capitalist development, as well as in the composition of the proletariat as a force opposing it.[10] More contemporary theories of urbanisation, attempting to account for the real complexities of its current formations, have come to focus instead, he continues, on the role of the logics of production, and of the social relations, specific to urbanisation – as logics that are not reducible to the 'industrial' – and their connection to the contemporary spatial structuration of

8. Graham Shane, 'The Emergence of Landscape Urbanism', in *Harvard Design Magazine*, Fall 2003/Winter 2004, pp. 4-5.

9. ibid., p. 7.

10. David Cunningham, 'The Concept of Metropolis: Philosophy and Urban Form', *Radical Philosophy*, no. 133, September/October 2005, p. 14.

increasingly globalised flows of money, information and people.

The post-urban orientation of much Landscape Urbanism derives not only from its alignment with the trajectory of post-fordism within North America and Europe, but also by a turn toward regional-scale planning through which longstanding antinomies between city and country are, it is proposed, to be overcome. As Waldheim observes in his essay 'Motor City'[11] Henry Ford himself proposed a decentralised system of industrial production through which its dependence on the existing city might be superseded: *The belief that an industrial country must concentrate its industry is, in my opinion, unfounded. That is only an intermediate phase in the development. Industry will decentralize itself. If the city were to decline, no one would rebuild it according to its present plan. That alone discloses our own judgment on our cities.*[12]

This 'judgement on our cities', as Waldheim also observes, was cited by Ludwig Hilberseimer within the context of the architect's *Cities and Defense* in 1945 where Ford's ambitions were seen to coincide with contemporary anxieties over the vulnerability of the centralised city to the atomic bomb. Waldheim's argument is that at this juncture modernist approaches to urban planning became redundant and new methods of low-density, regionally-oriented and infrastructurally-networked forms of planning emerged as their successors. Hilberseimer's *New Regional Pattern* of 1949, with its planning of dispersed settlements through which infrastructure would be rendered less vulnerable to attack, at the large scale, and his Lafayette Park project in Detroit at the smaller one, are for Waldheim the very models of a 'direct critique of modern urbanism' and prescient exemplars of the contemporary need to rethink and remodel urbanism as landscape.[13] The tendency toward regional planning and urban dispersal does however present a far denser palimpsest of contradictory and historically specific motivations than can be represented in this account of their sources. These motivations, and their particular origins, need to be teased apart, however briefly, in order to reflect upon the nature and viability of a regional orientation within the contemporary conditions to which Landscape Urbanism might address itself.

Hilberseimer's own ambivalence toward the modern city, or more specifically the metropolis, is already evident in his *Grostadtbauten* (translated as Big City Buildings) of 1925 where he writes: *The big city as an economic type is a creation of modernity (Neuzeit). It is the natural and economic consequence of the industrialization of the world. In the first instance, it appears as a creation of all-powerful big capital, as an expression of its anonymity. It is a type of city with singular socioeconomic and collective-psychological foundations. A thousand-times intensified life rhythm drives out the local individual in rapid tempo.*[14]

---

11. Charles Waldheim, 'Motor City', in Edward Robbins and Rodolphe El-Khoury, eds., *Shaping the City: History, Theory, and Urban Design*, London: Routledge, 2003, pp. 79–99.

12. As cited by Waldheim in 'Motor City', ibid., p. 85.

13. ibid., p. 87.

14. Ludwig Hilberseimer, *Big City Buildings*, Hanover: Aposs Verlag, 1925, p. 8.

There is in *Grostadtbauten* both a fascination with the new intensities and rhythms of the 'Big City' and a complaint against its lack of organisation. In the context of his later references to Henry Ford it is notable that Hilberseimer already posited here contemporary business practice as a model of organisational clarity to which architecture and planning could aspire: *The spirit of organization, as it is perhaps expressed in the business management of big industrial or commercial concerns, was completely disregarded in the layout and extension of the big cities. There the principle of the division of labor has organized the whole business according to plan, here everything goes in a motley jumble.*[15]

Whilst Hilberseimer's remedy for the city explores the potentials of its vertical growth, it includes too proposals for its dispersal into patterns of concentric satellite cities which will be more fully developed in his postwar work in America. However, the architect's broader engagement with the question of the city is not primarily motivated by the needs of business and any alignment with these ought to be understood as tactically motivated. Hilberseimer, like many on the left at the time, including anarchists, Marxists and socialists, understood the metropolis as the potential locus of new forms of socially transformative communality and, at the same time, the site of the most brutal exploitations and inequalities brought about by the rapid growth of industrial capitalism in the nineteenth and twentieth centuries. 'With surprising plenty', he writes, 'a set of powers rushed to big city formations, without being able to achieve control over these, to organize them, to make their vital excess usable by the commonality, the people entire.'[16]

His proposals to disperse the big city into a regional conurbation of small-scale cities were then motivated by the desire to bring to the 'commonality' the benefit of its productive capacities and, through studies of solar and wind patterns, these would be planned so as to grant to all the environmental qualities denied them in the unplanned metropolis. Regional dispersion was then to operate as a means to achieve equitable redistribution of the city's 'vital excesses'. Hilberseimer appears to be drawing here on the thought of the anarchist geographers of the late-nineteenth/early-twentieth century such as Peter Kropotkin, Élisée Reclus and Patrick Geddes. The echoes of Kropotkin's *Fields, Factories and Workshops* in the subtitle of Hilberseimer's *New Regional Pattern*, 'Industries and Gardens, Workshops and Farms", for instance, can be no coincidence. Neither can the emphasis in his thought upon the virtues of the regional as the essential focus of planning be understood outside of the influence of these figures. Arguments for regional planning also contain a Marxian dimension. In *The Manifesto of the Communist Party* Marx and Engels express their approval of utopian

15. ibid., p. 9.

16. ibid., pp. 8-9.

socialist ambitions for the 'abolition of the distinction between town and country'[17] and Engels writes, in *The Principles of Communism*, that the contradictions between the city and the country will wither away under communism.[18] Yet there is also within Marx a disdain for the 'idiocy of rural life' and, as David Cunningham has observed, a belief in Marx, also to be found within the *Manifesto*: that what he called 'enormous cities' might constitute one key condition of both a spatial concentration and social collectivity in which some new social class's strength could grow and it could feel 'that strength more'.[19] Such ambivalence is perhaps echoed in Hilberseimer's proposals in his *Grostadtbauten* both for the regional dispersal of the city's functions and population and for their intensification within a vertically oriented metropolis.

These same concerns over the city and the country were taken up too by the disurbanists working in the Soviet Union in the 1920s. Influenced in part by the Garden City movement as well as their own readings of Marx and Engels, the goal for this school of architects, planners and theorists was, in dialectical terms, to achieve a final synthesis of the agricultural and the urban through new forms of networked settlements which were, like those of Hilberseimer, typically oriented to a combination of social and environmental considerations.[20]

Yet deeply conservative currents of anti-urbanism have also informed arguments for the dispersal of the metropolitan population within the country. Henry Ford's proposals to decentralise industry were not argued solely on the grounds of efficient business practice, but informed too by his hatred of the city on moral and religious grounds. The city was for Ford an unsolvable problem that ought to be abandoned in the name of reestablishing the traditional values of the community: *we shall solve the City problem by leaving the City. Get the people into the country. Get them into communities where a man knows his neighbor, where there is a commonality of interest, where life is not artificial, and you have solved the City problem. You have solved it by eliminating the City. City life was always artificial and cannot be made anything else. An artificial form of life breeds its own disorders and these cannot be 'solved'. There is nothing to do but abandon the course that gives rise to them.*[21]

Ford's anti-urbanism was also, in a certain sense, an anti-modernism that derived from his opposition to the forms of modern life and social experience then emerging from the 'artifice' of the big city. Where the left found the metropolis problematic in terms of its economic equalities and environmental conditions, for its conservative opponents such as Ford, its corrupting influences, the radicalisation of the masses gathered in its factories, its sensual intoxications and its cosmopolitan mixing of races and creeds were the problem.[22] In projects such

---

17. Karl Marx and Friedrich Engels, *The Communist Manifesto*, London: Penguin, 1967, p. 116.
18. Friedrich Engels, 'The Principles of Communism', in *Selected Works, Volume One*, Moscow: Progress Publishers, 1969, p. 90.

19. David Cunningham, 'Metropolitics: Critical Theory, Collectivity and The Right to the City', unpublished transcript of public lecture at the Architectural Association, London, UK, March, 2009.

20. For an account of the disurbanists see, for example, Richard Stites, *Revolutionary Dreams: Utopian Vision and Experimental Life in the Russian Revolution*, Oxford: Oxford University Press, 1989, pp. 193-196.

21 Henry Ford, 'The Modern City - A Pestiferous Growth', in *Ford Ideals: Being a Selection from Mr. Ford"s Page in the Dearborn Independent*, Dearborn, Michigan: The Dearborn Publishing Company, 1922, p. 157.

as his Village Industries[23] and Greenfield Village museum[24] Ford attempted to rescue the city-dweller from the malign forces of city life and return him or her to a supposedly natural environment and traditional moralities. Decentralisation was for Ford, and others within this conservative current of anti-urbanism, a means of re-grounding the subject within the landscape, of relocating him or her back within the supposedly natural order of things.

The sources of the impulse toward decentralisation are then derived from multiple and sometimes contradictory motivations, and also from specific social, historical and geographic contexts which render it problematic to adopt as a general model for contemporary Landscape Urbanism. To be clear, Waldheim's argument for the prescience of Hilberseimer's regional planning, and particularly for his Lafayette Park project in Detroit is not being contested here. In the specific context of Detroit and its history his argument is compelling, particularly given the consideration to matters of ethnic diversity and social class by which it is informed (these are rarely discussed more broadly within Landscape Urbanism). The pertinent question for Landscape Urbanism more broadly, however, concerns the implications of pursuing the largely post-urban, if not anti-urban, direction suggested by adopting the models of decentralisation where, as Waldheim expresses it, landscape operates as urbanism, as its universal paradigm.

22. This is not to suggest that there was never some overlap between left and conservative arguments against the metropolis, only to identify the principal differences in their motivations.
23. John Robert Mullin 'Henry Ford and Field and Factory: An Analysis of the Ford Sponsored Village Industries - Experiment in Michigan, 1918-1941', accessed online at <http://works.bepress.com/cgi/viewcontent.cgi?article=1021&context=john_mullin>, May 28, 2010.
24. Peter Ling, 'Henry Ford's Greenfield Village', in *History Today*. Volume: 46. Issue: 1. January 1996.

THE URBAN CENTURY

Not least among the limitations of adopting this model, outside of certain specific conditions, is the fact that the global tendency of population movement is towards and not away from the urban. As Stephen Graham writes in his *Cities Under Siege*: *As we move into what has been called the 'urban century', there appears to be no end to this headlong urbanization of our world. In 2007, 1.2 million people were added to the world's population each week. By 2025, according to current estimates, there could easily be five billion urbanites, two thirds of whom will be living in 'developing' nations. By 2030, Asia alone will have 2.7 billion; the Earth's cities will be packed with 2 billion more people than they accommodate today. Twenty years further on, by 2050, fully 75 per cent of the world's estimated 9.2 billion people will most likely be living in cities.*[25]

Rural populations are in decline and urban ones, particularly in the Global South, are existing in ever more and not less densely packed conditions: 'Given the density of cities, more than half of humanity is currently squeezed onto just 2.8 per cent of our planet's land surface, and the squeeze is tightening every day.'[26]

As Mike Davis has exhaustively reported in *Planet of Slums*, the lives of many, over a billion, of these city-dwellers are lived in abject poverty within the make-

25. Stephen Graham, *Cities Under Siege: The New Military Urbanism*, London and New York: Verso, 2010, p. 2.

26. ibid., p. 1.

shift settlements, shanty towns and favelas that constitute their precarious niche in the neoliberal order of this 'urban century'.[27]

It is towards such conditions of rapid urban growth, population density and informal settlement that AALU has turned its attention in its work in the Pearl River and Yangtze River Deltas of China. In these massive 'urban corridors' post-reform economic boom, combined with mass rural to urban migration, has fueled a high-speed urbanism and produced new cities at a globally unprecedented pace. This intense urbanisation process has brought even the smallest villages into immediate and sudden proximity to the economic forces of globalisation, whilst producing circumstances in which disenfranchised migrants are forced to live and work within the densely-packed quarters of the city's informal and temporary settlements.[28]

These factors, alongside the pace and scale of development in the mega-cities of Beijing, Shanghai, Shenyang and Wuhan, and concerns over food security for their populations, has underscored for AALU the critical and urgent need to attend there to the interrelations between the phenomena of mass migration, pollution and the loss of arable land.

If landscape as urbanism is an appropriate model for 'decamping' a settlement after the economic forces which originally shaped it have moved on, it is clearly not applicable for the very different, in fact diametrically opposed dynamics of rapid urbanisation exemplified in China.

Here, as in much of the 'developing' world and elsewhere, the phenomenal transformations of social reality understood as the experience of modernity have not ceased, but have rather extended their global reach and intensified their operations. Even in Europe, with the growth of urban networks linked by high-speed transport, the tendency is towards the consumption of the landscape by the city and its connective infrastructures rather than of greening depopulated urban cores. As Pepe Barbieri notes in the Italian context of these developments, the reality of these phenomena must be properly grasped in order to comprehend the potentials for the formation of an adequate response to them: *Once we accept that we must overturn the traditional approach that we use to read the contemporary transformation of the city - not how to extend the city into the territory, but as an assimilation of the entire territory to the city - then we can change the role of systems of mobility and interchange.*[29]

In its own engagement with these contemporary urban-territorial dynamics AALU is extending and testing the capacities of Landscape Urbanism to address the intensities and intersections of the urban, architectural, agricultural, infrastructural and landscaped elements of which these sites are composed.

---

27. Mike Davis, *Planet of Slums*, London and New York: Verso, 2007.

28. See, for example, Zhang Li, *Strangers in the City: Reconfigurations of Space, Power, and Social Networks within China's Floating Population*, Stanford: Stanford University Press, 2002.

29. Pepe Barbieri, 'Evaluating Design Quality' in Alberto Clementi and Matteo Di Venosa, eds., *Infracity*, Barcelona: List, 2003, p. 49.

Whilst landscape in no way disappears from the concerns of the programme, it no longer assumes absolute primacy as the medium with which to engage with urbanism. By contrast, the landscaping strategies with which much Landscape Urbanism has been most often concerned, with their at times rather formulaic proposals for remediating post-industrial voids as parkland, appear to identify at some level, in their post-urbanism, with the anti-urban tradition of thought in which the condition of the metropolis is rejected outright and landscape-oriented alternatives, typically invoking the redemptive features of 'nature' are argued for. Key to Landscape Urbanism's particular inflection of this tradition is the notion of the 'non-site' and its use as a means to conceptualise the spaces left in the wake of post-urban decentralisation. These non-sites are indeterminate and unproductive zones without programme or function, spaces removed from the logic of production and development. 'Non-sites' are figured by Waldheim, borrowing from de Certeau, as analogous to the dying man who no longer functions as a 'site' for the disciplinary and productive regimes to which he would otherwise be subjected.[30] Detroit is thus figured by him as a 'non-site' since it cannot be subjected, in its decommissioned state, to the developmental and productive procedures of architecture or planning. It falls beyond the logic of their disciplinary operations. Only under these conditions of abandon, it is argued, can the 'non-site' be opened to other futures and its territory reconceived.

For Frampton too, from his critical regionalist perspective, the potential of the non-site is premised upon its abandoned state in order that it function as a compensatory, remedial or resistant other to the putatively homogenising logic of development. Despite their differences in approach, in both Waldheim's and Frampton's urban landscapes populations are largely defined by their departure and absence. The projects informed by these positions, whilst often imaginatively and rigorously oriented toward ecological concerns, and articulated in relation to the powers of mobile capital, are thus not required to think or engage with either the type of urban-territorial processes which prevail across much of the globe or with the transformative potentials of these.

Within both of these currents of Landscape Urbanism there is a sense in which landscape's primacy as a means of conceiving and producing territories, works to project the image of a future world which might come after the processes of transformation which have produced the metropolis have exhausted themselves – hence the post-industrial landscape of Tarkovsky's *Stalker* as a preferred point of iconographic reference. Landscape is proposed as a holding ground against development and in anticipation of a post-urban society. As Alan Berger has suggested of Frampton's proposals for undeveloped and voided zones, they await a

30. Charles Waldheim 'Ford's Fields', public lecture at the Architectural Association, London, UK, March 2008.

time 'when society comes to its senses and acknowledges the destruction it has caused with wasteful development practices'[31], a position echoed in the strategies of 'ecological reconstitution' to be followed by 'village-like enclaves' outlined in Stalking Detroit.

There is a further intimation here too of a desire to finally have done with modernity, with both the problems and potentials of its contradictions and with the continuous transformations and upheavals of its metropolitan spaces. Previous instances of this antimodernist position were lamented some time ago by Marshall Berman as indicative of a new pastoralism in his All That is Solid Melts Into Air. His argument, which has something to say still to Landscape Urbanism, was that an understanding of modernity in fact acquired a renewed relevance through the contemporary globalisation of its transformative effects, and the extension of the 'trauma of modernization' far beyond its western origins.

The continued relevance of comprehending the metropolis as the locus of intensive processes of social transformation, exchange, interaction and social experience is underlined too by Cunningham when he writes, in his 'Nine Theses on the Metropolis': 'The era of the metropolis is no more at a close than are modernity or capitalism themselves.'[32]

Describing the contemporary processes through which capital transforms the globe as continuous with earlier forms of modernity does not though prescribe that it be engaged with through modernism or modernist approaches. Rather the methods employed should be developed through a praxis which is in constant and close dialogue with the sites it is addressing. Nor should the overarching term modernity allow what is specific to these spaces to be obscured. The contemporary 'trauma of modernisation' does not straightforwardly replay and reproduce at a global scale the precise developmental logic of earlier and more specifically western forms of urbanisation. The growth of the metropolis now occurs at a speed and magnitude that produces historically unique conditions – huge informal settlements, new hybrid forms such as the urban-village and massive pressures on local ecologies – whilst contemporary infrastructural programmes produce networks of urban centres that pose new questions of regional-metropolitan scale, for example.

If landscape as urbanism is inadequate as a model with which to engage with the larger realities of global urbanisation on the grounds that it appears oriented to a post-urban condition, it is also problematic in its political implications. As with the case of Ford's anti-urbanism, calls to return to the village and the country are often marked by a deep conservatism, particularly where these propose the fixing of a 'people' within the supposedly natural order of the landscape. The

---

31. Alan Berger, Drosscape: *Wasting Land in Urban America*, New York, Princeton Architectural Press, 2006, p. 33.

32. David Cunningham, 'Nine Theses on the Metropolis' in Marina Lathouri, ed., *Positions on the City*, London: AA Publications, 2010.

identification of a 'people' with 'their' place in the world (of which there is an element too in Geddes' famous Valley Section diagram), typically implies the urban as a force of corruption through its promiscuous intermingling of ethnicities, nationalities, classes and creeds. Whilst this diversity cannot be superficially glossed as an ideal of consensual cosmopolitanism, given the stark divisions and inequalities existing in the metropolis, these same conditions, precisely because of what Ford termed their 'artifice', do still contain the potential to harbour new forms of collectivity capable of achieving the radical transformation of these very conditions.

The strategies of dispersal proposed or practised within much of Landscape Urbanism have not of course straightforwardly proposed the same 'return' to the land as that of Ford. Many of its projects have in fact been highly motivated by and oriented towards environmental concerns in their proposals for land remediation and the cultivation of wildlife ecologies, and also with the leisure functions of these. Yet such projects, when used as the sole means of engaging with the city, render Landscape Urbanism something of a post-political and post-philosophical discipline in the strict sense of the terms 'political' and 'philosophical'. This is so since the urban subject is largely absented, other than as a temporary visitor, from their spaces. As Cunningham observes in his 'The Concept of Metropolis: Philosophy and Urban Form', the practices and meanings of politics and philosophy are explicitly associated with the spaces and uses of the city: *...in its classical 'origins', philosophy itself is very precisely situated in the city (polis)...The city is the point at which Plato's philosophy as a whole converges, and not only in the Republic. The 'destiny of knowledge [of the truth] and that of communal [city] life' are inextricably linked. This means not only that it is philosophical thought that is entrusted with the foundation and government of a being-in-common that would constitute 'the unity of one and the same city', but that there can be no thought without the polis...Philosophy, in its classical Greek determination, is irreducibly urban. Thus, for Aristotle, similarly, man's unique nature as a political animal [politikon zoon] – a conception taken up later by Marx, among others – translates as he 'whose nature is to live in a polis".*[33]

In the absence of the polis there is literally no place in which to practise philosophy and no place from which to produce its politics. Cunningham notes elsewhere, however, that in this context the concept of the polis too may problematically invite the notion of a return to some idealised form of community which might be recovered through urban design.[34] This notion of recovering community is the principle that informs new urbanism, after all, and to the extent that it is able to sustain this it does so within enclaves which shelter it from both the sur-

---
33. ibid., p. 15.

---
34. This point is made by David Cunningham in his 'Metropolitics: Critical Theory, Collectivity and The Right to the City', op. cit.

rounding environment and the movement of history. For thinkers of the metropolis as a distinctly modern spatial formation Marx, Simmel, Benjamin, Kracauer, Tafuri, Cacciari, Lefebvre, and Harvey, for example in contrast, the gathering of the masses in the city, with its intensities of exchange and its production of new forms of experience and subjectivity, is both symptomatic of the transformative effects of capitalism and ripe with the potential to function otherwise: as the means to overcome capitalism itself. Within this current of urban critique, however problematic the conditions of the metropolis, their solution is not located in the return to some pre-modern social formation, or to a post-urban exodus. Rather the means through which social justice, or an end to exploitation and alienation are to be achieved are held to be already immanent to the forms and processes of the capitalist metropolis. If Landscape Urbanism is to engage with the metropolis in these terms, and also the territories through which it is networked, then landscape alone cannot, for the reasons given here, function as its sole or even primary medium, but as only one amongst a number of disciplinary practices on which it might draw.

TRANSDISCIPLINARITY

According to Charles Waldheim's now much-quoted definition: *Landscape Urbanism describes a disciplinary realignment currently underway in which landscape replaces architecture as the basic building block of contemporary urbanism. For many, across a range of disciplines, landscape has become both the lens through which the contemporary city is represented and the medium through which it is constructed.*[35]

Engaging with the territories to which AALU has addressed itself in recent years, however, requires not a 'disciplinary realignment' in which landscape replaces architecture but a transdisciplinary praxis in which both can be mobilised alongside and in concert with other fields of knowledge and practice. In this context, the place of architecture maintained within AALU at its inception by the programme's first director, Mohsen Mostafavi is significant: *As a framework for the imagination, landscape produces new insights in response to the contemporary urban situation. It allows one to describe the territory in terms of an equal, though artificial, dialogue between buildings and landscapes. Yet this dialogue is not limited by the traditional definition of the terms 'building' and 'landscape': it allows for the simultaneous presence of the one within the other, buildings as landscapes, landscapes as buildings. And in this lies the potential to redefine the parameters of each discipline – architecture and landscape architecture in relation to one another.*[36]

---

35. Charles Waldheim, 'Introduction: A Reference Manifesto', in Charles Waldheim, ed., op. cit.

36. Mohsen Mostafavi, 'Landscapes of Urbanism', in Landscape Urbanism: A Manual for the Machinic Landscape, London: AA Publications, 2003, p. 7.

Mostafavi's conception of the disciplinary relations intrinsic to Landscape Urbanism differs significantly from Waldheim's. Rather than a 'disciplinary realignment', where landscape achieves hegemony over architecture in its claims to offer a model of practice for urban design, both disciplines are reconfigured through their interrelationship. Landscape Urbanism is conceived by Mostafavi as a transdisciplinary practice, one in which buildings are landscaped and landscape becomes architectural. It is worth noting too, in reference to the 'urban situation', that this is not posited as a site for the remediative strategies of landscape, but as a territory in which the mutual redefinition of landscape and architecture can be productively mobilised.

For architecture, then, the model of landscape outlined here suggests, rather than an eco-pastoral or ex-urban condition, a model through which built form becomes topographic. Rather than the figure-ground relations through which the urban fabric has traditionally been produced, with architecture as the static, and at times monumental figure accommodating and enveloping fixed programmes, and the street as the ground through which movement between these is channelled, an architecture as landscape suggests the capacity to produce more complex articulations within the urban fabric. A topographically, even topologically, directed architecture also provides the means through which to recompose and invent new configurations of infrastructure, agriculture, inhabitation and mobility within urban space and across the wider territories in which these are networked. In his 1995 essay 'Toward an Urban Landscape', Kenneth Frampton, himself drawing upon Peter Rowe's *Making a Middle Landscape*, appears to advance a similar argument for a landscaped architecture: *two salient factors may be derived from Rowe's thesis...first, that priority should now be accorded to landscape rather than to freestanding built form and second, that there is a pressing need to transform certain megalapolitan types such as shopping malls, parking lots and office parks into landscaped built forms.*[37]

Whilst the proposal Frampton presents here has often been drawn upon within the discourse of Landscape Urbanism (the essay in question is referenced in texts by Waldheim, Shannon and Richard Weller in the *Landscape Urbanism Reader*, for example), his 'landscaped built forms' actually bear little resemblance to the models of practice developed within AALU. Frampton's position is primarily formal in its strategy since it is addressed to existing typologies' shopping malls, parking lots and office parks' which he argues ought now to assume a landscape form so as to minimise the impact of development within existing landscapes. The role of this formal landscaping is understood by Frampton to be remedial and compensatory, whereas within AALU the topographically ori-

37. Kenneth Frampton, 'Toward an Urban Landscape', *Columbia Documents* no. 4, 1994, p. 91.

ented built form is both responsive and inventive. Formal complexity becomes a means through which existing typologies and urban programmes can be recomposed and rethought so that, for example, infrastructure may become inhabitable or architecture operate as a conduit for mobility.

In this sense the practice of AALU is closer to that of certain moments in the practice of Koolhaas disparaged by Frampton as 'avant-gardist', as exemplified in projects such as his unrealised project for Parc de la Villette. Here the promise of programmatic cross-fertilisation, to be realised through the proximity of the project's stripped orientations, suggests a desire to work inventively with programme with which AALU is itself similarly concerned. Perhaps more significant as a precedent though, in terms of the articulation of built form, is the work of Paul Virilio and Claude Parent as the short-lived architectural practice Architecture Principe of the 1960s.

Through their articulation of the ground as an oblique gradient, as both floor and partition, Architecture Principe proposed a mediation of the strict division between the vertical, as a boundary-support function, and the horizontal, as the plane of inhabitation and mobility. Virilio and Parent's drawings of the period picture large-scale urban environments of intermeshing ramps and planes, of megastructures inhabited by figures reacquainted with the physiological pleasures of self-locomotion through a renewed contact with gravitational force. The potentials of the 'function of the oblique', as it was termed by Architecture Principe, have been further developed, across a range of scales, by AALU director Castro both in her architectural practice, Plasma Studio, and collaboratively with other tutors and former students of the AALU programme, in the design group Groundlab. In this body of design work the potentials of the oblique function in architecture are extended beyond the production of physiological qualities and explored as a means to selectively channel, distribute, mobilise or stabilise the material, technological, social and environmental forces at play within a given territory.

This is achieved not, as in Frampton's model, through some process of landscaping architecture so that its forms are simply smoothed into the landscape, nor indeed through rendering it visually symbolic of the 'natural' by having its contours conform to the curvilinear and blob-like image of the organic to which so much contemporary architecture is attached. Rather, through the development of responsive prototypes, a tectonic strategy through which the forces shaping the territory might be differently articulated is produced. This process of articulation has often been pursued through addressing the role of infrastructure within and between the spaces of the urban territory.

Infrastructures, as Stephen Graham and Simon Marvin have argued in their seminal account of the subject, *Splintering Urbanism: Networked Infrastructures, Technological Mobilities and the Urban Condition*, now play a major role both in connecting certain privileged zones and their occupants within a globalised network whilst, at the same, fragmenting local urban space and effectively disenfranchising certain of its considerably less privileged inhabitants.[38] Alberto Clementi, in the European context, has explored how urban and peri-urban space tends to be divided into two distinct territories, those of the network and those of the area, by these developments. We need now to consider, he argues, 'not only the familiar territory-area dictated by the principle of spatial proximity, but also the territory-interchange between the networks of trans-national and spatial flows that are locally stratified.'[39] Engaging with these problematics through architecture has meant exploring the means through which infrastructure might operate not divisively, but instead as a productive hinge through which the different scales and speeds of the territory can be mediated. Hence strategies of 'thickening' infrastructure through architecture so as to accommodate multiple programmes, of reshaping it as a platform for local patterns of social use, have typically been developed within AALU's programme.

Wenwen Wang's project for the Pearl River Delta, 'Space In Between', for example: ...*criticises national planning regulation in terms of its tendencies toward social and environmental fragmentation, which refer to generating homogeneous single land use block and large-scale infrastructures without responding to local conditions, as a result creating barriers in terms of public circulations between top-down planned fabric and informal rural villages. It elaborates, as an alternative, informal growth processes in terms of continuity of public circulation, diversity and complexity of public activities and strong linkages and responses to the surroundings (or infrastructures, such as the street), as the main conditions around which emergent forms of resistance to top-down planning are articulated*. The role of architecture is then reconceived, rather than replaced, within the transdisciplinary model which AALU has developed, and so too is that of landscape. Landscape, understood as a medium possessed of scalar and temporal sensibilities, qualities now more relevant to the contemporary city than those of conventional planning, is a model common to North American and European variants of Landscape Urbanism and also to those of AALU. Yet since the beginnings of the AALU programme this understanding has had a distinct inflection of its own. Where other approaches to Landscape Urbanism have drawn heavily upon the discipline of Landscape Architecture, this relationship has never really been as strongly established within the AA's graduate programme. Rather,

38. Stephen Graham and Simon Marvin, *Splintering Urbanism: Networked Infrastructures, Technological Mobilities and the Urban Condition*, London and New York: Routledge, 2001.

39. Alberto Clementi, 'Introduction', in Clementi and Di Venosa, eds., op. cit.

landscape been understood within AALU, since the programme's inception in 2000, more in accordance with a 'machinic' model largely drawn from the thought of Deleuze and Guattari. Through this model landscape has been understood as an organisational medium through which the topographic, agricultural, infrastructural or architectural elements of a territory may be synthesised. This conception of landscape as a synthetic organisational medium corresponds, in significant ways, with one that predates by some centuries the modern understanding of the term. As J.B.Jackson observed in his *Discovering the Vernacular Landscape*: *...landscape is not a scenery, it is not a political unit, it is really no more than a collection, a system of man-made spaces on the surface of the earth. Whatever its shape or size it is never simply a natural space, a feature of the natural environment; it is always artificial, always synthetic, always subject to sudden or unpredictable change.*[40]

40. John Brinckerhoff Jackson, *Discovering the Vernacular Landscape*, New Haven: Yale University Press, 1984, p. 156.

Jackson, in his schematic historiography of the landscape, termed the pre-modern vernacular landscape which organised the territory for agriculture on this basis 'Landscape One'. 'Landscape Two' describes the formal and centrally-planned construction of the territory as 'landscape' as a largely scenographic practice prevailing from the Renaissance to the 19th century. 'Landscape Three' describes the contemporary return to the ad hoc organisation of the land, but one now produced by the processes and requirements of global modernity. The iconography of 'Landscape Three' is an endless sprawl of industrial plants, shopping malls, car parks and highways. Jackson's 'Landscape Three' corresponds to some degree, then, with the model of landscape understood by AALU: as a large-scale and complex assemblage of infrastructural elements, built fabric and urban processes as well as its agricultural and topographic features.

The adoption of this understanding of landscape by no means infers a lack of concern for what is more conventionally understood as the 'land' such as, for example, the importance of agriculture within a number of the sites addressed by AALU. Certain projects set in the Pearl River Delta, for instance, explore the possibilities for agriculture to perform as a means both of securing food for the local population and also as a space of associative social practice. The forms of geologically and topographically informed practice and expertise commonly employed within Landscape Architecture or Landscape Design are also utilised by AALU in a number of its projects such as those engaged with post-tsunami conditions in Sri Lanka.

The larger point to be made here is, though, that agricultural or ecological concerns cannot be addressed in isolation, but only in terms of their relations with the infrastructural and built fabric of the urban environment, its social and political dimensions, and the globalised flows of exchange, information and populations that comprise contemporary forms of territorial composition. In order to adequately engage with these a properly transdisciplinary praxis is required.

PRAXIS: SRI LANKA, DUBAI AND CHINA

AALU has addressed its transdisciplinary praxis to such territories in a series of research and design projects in Mexico, Sri Lanka, Dubai and the 'urban corridors' of the Pearl River and Yangtze Deltas of China. In Sri Lanka, for example, the programme engaged with the aftermath of the 2004 tsunami and its subsequent social, economic and environmental impact upon a region especially vulnerable, in these terms, to 'natural disasters'. The rebuilding and reoccupation of the affected areas of Sri Lanka required clear identification of hazard zones to avoid future loss of life and property. At the same time, the new sociopolitical configurations generated as an immediate consequence of the local death toll called for a reinterpretation of the traditional patterns of spatial inhabitation, both at the macro and micro scales. In the aftermath of the tsunami, the regions' newly established urban organisation – in part artificially generated by new policies responding to the perception of the urgent need to develop tourism – enforced the regional dislocation of underprivileged communities, put the economic future of these in jeopardy, and, in the process, caused drastic changes to the local ecosystem. The projects produced in this programme, such as Zoe Spiegel's 'Urban Piers' explored the means through which foreign capital could be engaged in the region so as to fund development that, whilst still providing for tourism, could also accommodate the existing local fishing economies and work to mitigate the threat of future flooding.

In Dubai the dynamics of urban growth, in which billions were to be spent on the development of infrastructures supporting tourism and financial economies, were addressed in terms of their environmental implications and tendency to physically and socially segregate the urban fabric. Then hosting around 6 million tourists a year, and engaged in the creation of the artificial topographies of the palm islands, Dubai's massive infrastructural projects were reconceived, as in the 'Responsive Coastline' by Alejandra Bosch, as mechanisms through which financial, technical and environmental forces could be productively reconfigured so as to obviate their negative impact upon social and ecological conditions. AALU has more recently turned the focus of its attention to China, whose post-reform economic boom, combined with its mass rural to urban migration, is fuelling a high-speed urbanism and producing new cities at a globally unprecedented pace. This intense urbanisation process has brought even the smallest villages into immediate and sudden proximity to globalisation, foreign capital and the generic architecture that serves to accommodate it, and as a consequence, produced new hybrid spatial formations such as the 'urban village' and 'rurbanism' (closely-articulated patterns of rural-urbandevelopment). Alongside these factors, in many of the country's megacities the absence of a coherent urbanisation policy means that there are no existing mechanisms of negotiation between economic interests, existing social formations, developmental pressures and environmental ecologies. Working within this scenario AALU projects for the region, as represented by Katya Larina's 'Rurban Growth' have sought to develop prototypical models of urbanism, often through the close articulation of architecture, infrastructure and agriculture, seeking to grasp and redirect both the complexities and the possibilities immanent to these phenomena away from their otherwise detrimental social and environmental outcomes.

CONCLUSION

AA Landscape Urbanism has demonstrably eschewed any straightforward mobilisation of landscape, in its established sense, as means of pastoral remediation, resistance, cultural identification or developmental amelioration of the type to be found within other currents of Landscape Urbanist practice. It operates rather on the basis of a transdisciplinary praxis, necessarily engaged, given the territories with which it is concerned, with conditions which are simultaneously and complexly social, political, ecological and economic, and with the transformative possibilities of these. Its proposals and interventions are derived from critical reflection not only upon such territorial conditions but also upon the means through which it engages with these. In this context it has developed hybrid forms of 'material organisation' drawing not only from landscape" to "In this context it has developed synthetic models of operation drawing not only from landscape and architecture, rethought and reconfigured through their mutual interference, but also from infrastructure and engineering, and has done so in order adequately to respond to the phenomena that define contemporary urban and regional problematics. This response is one that searches for and is prepared to invent the specific means at the disposal of a design-based practice, not so as to assume control over these conditions, but, on the basis of comprehending their implications in social and environmental terms, so as to identify the potentials to inflect, perhaps even detour, these toward becomings which challenge the purely capitalist valorisation of social space and its attendant production of social and environmental injustice.

The Post-Political Conundrum and the Environment [1]
ERIK SWYNGEDOUW

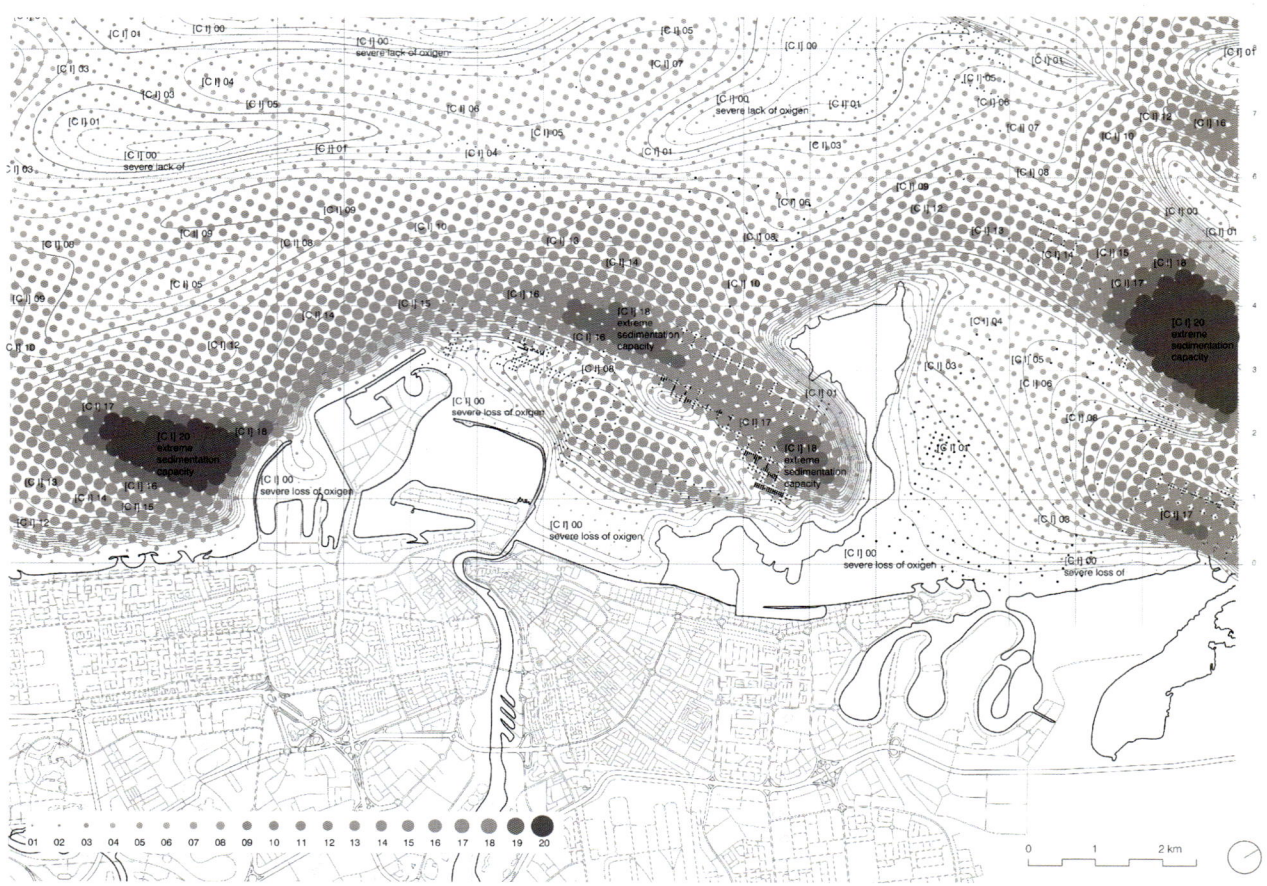

URBAN ENVIRONMENTS: POST-POLITICAL AND POST-DEMOCRATIC

There is now a widespread consensus that the environmental condition needs to be taken seriously. Moreover, environmental processes, locally and globally, are to a large extent conditioned by the spiraling growth of cities. Indeed, growing environmental concerns are marked by a series of emerging metaphors like eco-urbanism, eco-cities, sustainable planning and design. They each relay a sense of urgency that signals recognition of the ecologically disastrous situation the world is in. The few remaining detractors are relegated to the margins of social and political respectability. There is also a consensus that appropriate managerial-technological apparatuses should and can be innovated and negotiated to avoid the socio-ecological predicament we are in to sink into catastrophe, possibly announcing the disintegration of civilisation as we know it.

At the same time, of course, there is hegemonic consensus, further re-inforced in the aftermath of the global financial crisis, that no alternative to liberal-global hegemony is possible, that the market, albeit tempered by humanitarian and ecological concerns, offers the proper institutional and economic configuration to manage our ecological predicament, to retrofit Nature to a more stable and benign – sustainable – condition.

This paradoxical situation, whereby decisive action in environmental matters is called for but whereby the modalities, technologies and institutional-managerial apparatuses are consensually framed within a given political-economic configuration that is in itself beyond dispute, is the theme of this contribution. This paradox is defined as a post-democratic or post-political configuration, one that increasingly sutures the landscape of managerial-technocratic socio-environmental interventions.

Post-Democracy, which we have elsewhere defined as organised through new institutional forms of autocratic Governance-beyond-the-State,[2] reconfigures the act of governing to a stakeholder-based arrangement of governance in which the traditional state forms (national, regional, or local government) partake together with experts, NGOs, and other 'responsible' partners or stakeholders[3] in the pursuit of environmentally sustainable socio-ecological practices, articulated around a set of specific symbolisations of what Nature is or ought to be.[4]

Not only is the political arena evacuated from radical dissent, critique, and fundamental conflict, but the parameters of democratic governing itself are being shifted, announcing a new form of what Foucault called governmentality, a rationality and practice of good governing. These new forms of 'governance', operative at a range of articulated spatial scales, are expressive of the post-political configuration:[5] *Governance entails an explicit reference to 'mechanisms' or 'organized and coordinated activities' appropriate to the solution of some specific problems.*

---

1. This chapter is partly based on arguments developed in a number of earlier papers, in particular Erik Swyngedouw, 'The Antinomies of the Post-Political City. In Search of a Democratic Politics of Environmental Production', in *International Journal of Urban and Regional Research* 33, 2009, pp. 601-620, and Erik Swyngedouw, 'The Trouble with Nature: Ecology as the New Opium for the Masses' in P. Healey and J. Hillier, eds., *Conceptual Challenges for Planning Theory*, Aldershot: Ashgate, 2010, pp 299-320.

2. Erik Swyngedouw, 'Governance Innovation and the Citizen: The Janus Face of Governance-beyond-the-State' in *Urban Studies* 42, 2005, pp. 1-16.

3. See Colin Crouch, *Post-Democracy*, Cambridge: Polity Press, 2004.

4. For details, see Swyngedouw, 'The Trouble with Nature' op. cit.

5. Chantal Mouffe, *On The Political*, London:

Unlike government, governance refers to 'policies' rather than 'politics' because it is not a binding decision-making structure. Its recipients are not 'the people' as collective political subject, but 'the population' that can be affected by global issues such as the environment, migration, or the use of natural resources.[6]

In this sense, environmental and other politics are reduced to the sphere of the police, to the domain of governing and polic(y)ing through allegedly participatory deliberative procedures, with a given distribution of places and functions. Consensual policy-making in which the stakeholders (i.e. those with recognised speech) are known in advance and where disruption or dissent is reduced to debates over the institutional modalities of governing, the accountancy calculus of risk, and the technologies of expert administration or management, announces the end of politics, annuls dissent from the consultative spaces of policy making and evacuates the proper political from the public sphere.

Slavoj Žižek and Chantal Mouffe, among others, define the post-political as a political formation that actually forecloses the political, that prevents politicisation.[7] In Europe and the US, in particular, such post-political arrangements are largely in place. Post-politics reject ideological divisions and the explicit universalisation of particular political demands. It disavows the constitutive lack or excess that splits the social and prevents saturation, as it insists on the 'democratic' inclusion of all, thereby suturing the totality of the social, and precluding the political moment to arise. Such configuration succumbs to the 'totalitarian' temptation of democratic institutions.[8]

Post-politics is thus about the administration (policing) of environmental, social, economic or other domains, and they remain of course fully within the realm of the possible, of existing social relations, they are 'the partition of the sensible'. 'The ultimate sign of post-politics in all western countries', Žižek argues, 'is the growth of a managerial approach to government: government is reconceived as a managerial function, deprived of its proper political dimension'.[9] The consensual times we are currently living in have thus eliminated a genuine political space of disagreement. However, consensus does not equal peace or absence of contestation.[10] Under a post-political condition, '[e]verything is politicized, can be discussed, but only in a non-committal way and as a non-conflict. Absolute and irreversible choices are kept away; politics becomes something one can do without making decisions that divide and separate. When pluralism becomes an end in itself, real politics is pushed to other arenas'.[11] Difficulties and problems, such as re-ordering the urban or re-shaping the environment, that are generally staged and accepted as problematic, are dealt with by means of compromise, managerial and technical arrangement, and the production of consensus: *consensus refers*

---

6. Routledge, 2005, p. 103.; Erik Swyngedouw, 'The Post Political City' In BAVO, ed., *Urban Politics Now. Re-imagining Democracy in the Neoliberal City*, Rotterdam: Netherlands Architecture Institute NAi Publishers, 2007, pp. 58-76.; Erik Swyngedouw, 'Civil Society, Governmentality and the Contradictions of Governance-beyond-the-State' In J. Hillier, F. Moulaert and S. Vicari, eds., *Social Innovation and Territorial Development*, Aldershot: Ashgate, pp. 63-78.

6. Nadia Urbinati, 'Can Cosmopolitan Democracy be Democratic?' in D. Archibugi, ed., *Debating Cosmopolitics*, London: Verso, 2003, pp. 67-85.

7. Slavoj Žižek, *The Ticklish Subject - The Absent Centre of Political Ontology*, London: Verso, 1999; Slavoj Žižek, *The Parallax View*, Cambridge, Mass: MIT Press, 2006; Mouffe, *On The Political*, op. cit.

8. Claude Lefort, *L'Invention Démocratique: Les limites de la Domination Totalitaire*, Paris: Fayard, 1994.

9. Slavoj Žižek, *Revolution at the Gates - Žižek on Lenin - The 1917 Writings*, London: Verso, 2002, p. 303.

10. Jacques Rancière, *Chroniques des Temps Consensuels*, Paris: Seuil, 2005, p. 8.

11. Bülent Diken, Carsten Bagge Laustsen '7/11, 9/11, and Post-Politics', 2004 <http://www.comp.lancs.ac.uk/sociology/papers/diken-laustsen-7-11-9-11-post-politics.pdf> Accessed 15 September 2005.

to that which is censored ... Consensus means that whatever your personal commitments, interests and values may be, you perceive the same things, you give them the same name.

But there is no contest on what appears, on what is given in a situation and as a situation. Consensus means that the only point of contest lies on what has to be done as a response to a given situation. Correspondingly, dissensus and disagreement don't only mean conflict of interests, ideas and so on. They mean that there is a debate on the sensible givens of a situation, a debate on that which you see and feel, on how it can be told and discussed, who is able to name it and argue about it ... It is about the visibilities of the places and abilities of the body in those places, about the partition of private and public spaces, about the very configuration of the visible and the relation of the visible to what can be said about it ... Consensus is the dismissal of politics as a polemical configuration of the common world.[12]

The key feature of consensus is 'the annulment of dissensus ..... the end of politics'.[13] Of course, this post-political world eludes choice and freedom (other than those tolerated by the consensus). And in the absence of real politicisation, the only position of real dissent is that of either the traditionalist (those stuck in the past who refuse to accept the inevitability of the new global neo-liberal order) or the fundamentalist (ecological or otherwise). The only way to deal with them is by sheer violence, by suspending their 'humanitarian' and 'democratic' rights. The post-political relies on either including all in a consensual pluralist order and on excluding radically those who posit themselves outside the consensus. For them, as Agamben argues,[14] the law is suspended; they are literally put outside the law and treated as extremists and terrorists.

Late capitalist urban environmental governance and debates over the socio-ecological arrangement of the city are not only perfect expressions of such a post-political order, but in fact, the debate over the policing of sustainable urban environments, or more generally the environmental debate, is one of the key arenas through which this post-political consensus becomes constructed, when 'politics proper is progressively replaced by expert social administration'.[15] The post-political environmental consensus, therefore, is one that is radically reactionary, one that forestalls the articulation of divergent, conflicting, and alternative trajectories of future (urban) environmental possibilities and assemblages. There is no contestation over the givens of the situation, over the partition of the sensible; there is only debate over the technologies of management, the arrangements of policing, and the configuration of those who already have a stake, whose voice is already recognised as legitimate.

12. Jacques Rancière, 'Comment and Responses', in *Theory & Event* 6, 2003, § 4-6.

13. Jacques Rancière, 'Ten Theses on Politics' in *Theory & Event* 5, 2001, p. 32.

14. Giorgio Agamben, *State of Exception*, Chicago: The University of Chicago Press, 2005.

15. Slavoj Žižek, 'Against Human Rights' in *New Left Review*, 2005, p. 117.

In this post-democratic post-political era, adversarial politics (of the left/right variety or of radically divergent struggles over imagining and naming different socio-environmental futures for example) are considered hopelessly out of date. Although disagreement and debate are of course still possible, they operate within an overall model of elite consensus and agreement, subordinated to a managerial-technocratic regime.[16] Environmental concerns, whether expressed in the search for local sustainability, the quest for a more equitable distribution of ecological goods or bads, or the management of the climate, the properly political becomes evacuated from the disembedded polic(y)e configurations through which these concerns become articulated.

The barrage of apocalyptic warnings of the pending catastrophes wreaked by climate change and environmental degradation and the need to take urgent remedial action to engineer a retro-fitted 'balanced' climate and 'sustainable' environment are perfect examples of the tactics and configurations associated with the present post-political and post-democratic condition.[17]

Indeed, a politics of sustainability, predicated upon a radically conservative and reactionary view of a singular – and ontologically stable and harmonious – Nature is necessarily one that eradicates or evacuates the 'political' from debates over what to do with natures.

The key political question is one that centres on the question of what kind of natures we which to inhabit, what kinds of natures we which to preserve, to make, or, if need be, to wipe off the surface of the planet (like the HIV virus, for example), and on how to get there. The fantasy of 'sustainability' imagines the possibility of an originally fundamentally harmonious Nature, one that is now out-of-synch but which, if 'properly' managed, we can and have to return to by means of a series of technological, managerial, and organisational fixes. As suggested above, many, from different social, cultural, and philosophical positionalities, agree with this dictum. Disagreement is allowed, but only with respect to the choice of technologies, the mix of organisational fixes, the detail of the managerial adjustments, and the urgency of their timing and implementation. Nature's apocalyptic future, if unheeded, symbolises and nurtures the solidification of the post-political condition. As Žižek argues, ecology and the ecological imperative are becoming the new opium for the masses.[18]

A revived democratic intervention in socio-environmental conditions is of vital importance today. Exposing the infernal process of de-politicisation marked by the dominance of empty signifiers like Nature or Sustainability, and reviving democratic planning and design, mark the contours of what needs to be thought today. The claim made above that Nature or Sustainability are empty signifiers

---

16. Crouch, *Post-Democracy*, op. cit.

17. Erik Swyngedouw, 'Apocalypse Forever? Post-Political Populism and the Spectre of Climate Change' in *Theory, Culture & Society* 27, pp. 213-232.

18. Slavoj Žižek, 'Nature and its Discontents' in *SubStance 37*, pp. 37-72.

AVOWING THE VIOLENCE OF PLANNING: DEMOCRATISING THE PRODUCTION OF NATURE

in no way suggests ignoring, let alone forgetting, the reality of natures or, more precisely, the diverse, multiple, whimsical, contingent and often unpredictable socio-ecological relations of which we are part.[19] The claim we make is about the urgent need to question legitimising all manner of socio-environmental politics, policies and interventions in the name of a thoroughly imagined and symbolised Nature or Sustainability, a procedure that necessarily forecloses a properly political frame through which such imaginaries become constituted and hegemonised, and disavows the constitutive split of the people by erasing the spaces of dissensual encounter. We have to accept the extraordinary variability of natures and insist on the need to make 'a wager' on natures, to force to choose politically between this rather than that nature. We have to dare to plunge into the relatively unknown, expect the unexpected, accept that not everything can be known, and, most importantly, fully endorse the violent moment that is inscribed in any concrete or real socio-environmental intervention.

Indeed, the ultimate aim of planning or design is intervention, to change the given socio-environmental ordering in a certain manner. Like any intervention, this is a violent act, erasing at least partly what is there in order to erect something new and different. Consider, for example, the extraordinary effect the eradication of the HIV virus would have on sustaining livelihoods (or should we preserve/protect the virus in the name of biodiversity?). In ways comparable to how private decisions, like buying a car, or business decisions like recycling computers in the socio-ecological wastelands of Mumbai's shantytowns, are violent intrusions in the socio-ecological order, planning interventions are also irredeemably violent engagements that re-choreograph socio-natural relations and assemblages, both distant and nearby. The recognition that planning acts are singular interventions, that any form of spatialisation/environmentalisation closes down, at least temporarily, the horizon of time, inverts the dialectic of becoming over being, is of central importance. Such a violent encounter, of course, always constitutes a political act, one that can be legitimised only in political terms, and not – as is customarily done – through an externalised legitimation that resides in a fantasy of Nature or Sustainability. Any political act is one that re-orders socio-ecological co-ordinates and patterns, reconfigures uneven socio-ecological relations, often with unforeseen or unforeseeable, consequences.

Such interventions signal a totalitarian moment, the temporary suspension of the democratic, understood as the presumed equality of each and all as speaking beings. The dialectic between the democratic as a political given and the totalitarian moment of planning intervention as the suspension of the democratic needs to be radically endorsed. While a pluralist democratic politics, founded on

19. See Swyngedouw, 'The Trouble with Nature' op. cit.

a presumption of equality, insists on difference, disagreement, radical openness, and exploring multiple possible futures, concrete spatial-ecological intervention is necessarily about closure, definitive choice, a singular intervention and, thus, certain exclusion and silencing. The democratic planning process dwells, therefore, in two worlds simultaneously. As discussed above, Jacques Rancière[20] and others[21] define these spheres respectively as 'the political' and 'the police' (the policy order). The (democratic) political is the space for the enunciation and affirmation of difference, for the cultivation of dissensus and disagreement, for asserting the presumption of equality of all and everyone.[22] In contrast, the practice of planning interventions, when becoming concretely geographical or ecological, is of necessity a violent act of foreclosure of the democratic political (at least temporarily), of taking one option rather than another, of producing one sort of environment, of assembling certain socio-natural relations, of foregrounding some natures rather than others, of hegemonising a particular metonymic chain rather than another. And the legitimation of such options cannot be based on corralling Nature or Sustainability into legitimising service.

In conclusion, while Nature and Sustainability do not exist outside the metonymic chains that offer some sort of meaning, there are of course all manner of environments, assemblages of socio-natural relations. Environments are specific historical results of socio-physical processes.[23] All socio-spatial processes are indeed invariably also predicated upon the circulation, the metabolism and the enrolling of social, cultural, physical, chemical, or biological processes, but their outcome is contingent, often unpredictable, immensely varied, risky. These metabolisms produce a series of both enabling and disabling socio-environmental conditions.[24] Indeed, these produced milieus often embody contradictory tendencies. Processes of metabolic change are, therefore, never socially or ecologically neutral. For example, the unequal ecologies associated with uneven property relations, the commodification of all manner of natures, the impoverished socio-ecological life under the overarching sign of the commodity and of money in a neo-liberal order, and the perverse exclusions choreographed by the dynamics of uneven eco-geographical development at all scales, suggest how the production of socio-ecological arrangements is always a deeply conflicting, and hence irrevocably political, process. All manner of social power geometries shape the particular social and political configurations as well as the environments in which we live. Therefore, the production of socio-environmental arrangements implies fundamentally political questions, and has to be addressed in political terms. The question is to tease out who gains from and who pays for, who benefits from and who suffers (and in what ways) from particular processes of metabolic

---

20. Jacques Rancière, *Disagreement*, Minneapolis: University of Minnesota Press, 1998.
21. See, for example, Oliver Marchart, *Post-Foundational Political Thought - Political Difference in Nancy, Lefort, Badiou and Laclau*, Edinburgh: University Press, 2007, for a review.
22. See Erik Swyngedouw, 'The Antinomies of the Post-Political City. In Search of a Democratic Politics of Environmental Production' in *International Journal of Urban and Regional Research* 33, 2009, pp. 601-620.

23. Nik Heynen, Maria Kaika, and Erik Swyngedouw, eds., *In the Nature of Cities - The Politics of Urban Metabolism*, London: Routledge, 2005.

24. Erik Swyngedouw, 'Circulations and Metabolisms: (Hybrid) Natures and (Cyborg) Cities' in *Science as Culture* 15, 2006, pp. 105-121.

circulatory change. These flows produce inclusive and exclusive ecologies both locally and in terms of the wider uneven socio-ecological dynamics and relations that sustain these flows. Democratising environments, then, becomes an issue of enhancing the democratic content of socio-environmental construction by means of identifying the strategies through which a more equitable distribution of social power and a more inclusive mode of producing natures (of producing metabolic circulatory processes) can be achieved. This requires reclaiming proper democracy and proper democratic public spaces (as spaces for the enunciation of agonistic dispute) as a foundation for and condition of possibility for more egalitarian socio-ecological arrangements, the naming of positively embodied ega-libertarian socio-ecological futures that are immediately realisable.[25] In other words, egalitarian ecologies are about demanding the impossible and realising the improbable.

25. Maria Kaika and Erik Swyngedouw, 'The Urbanization of Nature: Great Promises, Impasse, and New Beginnings' in G. Bridge and S. Watson, eds., *The New Blackwell Companion to the City*, Oxford: Wiley/Blackwell, 2010.

Between Nature, Culture, Society, Technology and Politics: The 'Infrastructural Turn'

STEPHEN GRAHAM

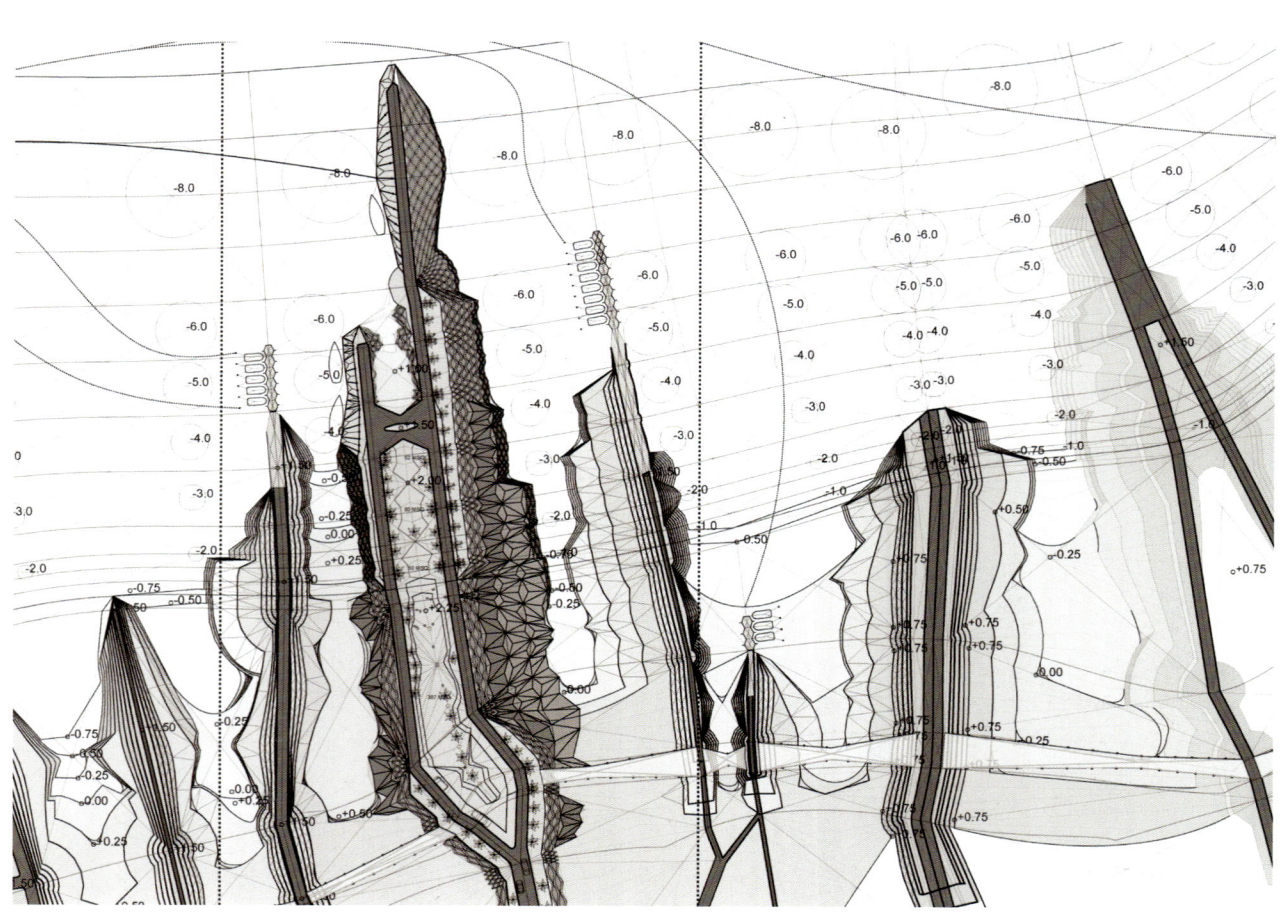

Recent research on urban infrastructure networks underlines their precarious and vulnerable nature and helps undermine assumptions of their necessary stability or permanence. This work is the result of a remarkable growth in critical social scientific discussions about urban infrastructure, of which this book is one part. Indeed, it is now possible to speak of an 'infrastructural turn'[1] in recent social scientific discussion about cities, which has paralleled the more well-known, but closely related, mobilities turn.[2] Work within the urban infrastructural turn has emphasised three key points.

1. Colin McFarlane and Jonathan Rutherford 'Political Infrastructures: Governing and Experiencing the Fabric of the City', *International Journal of Urban and Regional Research*, Volume 32.2 June, 2008, pp. 363–74.
2. John Urry, *Mobilities*, Cambridge: Polity, 2007; Tim Cresswell, *On the Move*, London: Routledge: London, 2006.

INFRASTRUCTURE AS ASSEMBLAGE

First, urban infrastructures are much more than a collection of technical 'things' working collectively. Rather, recent work has demonstrated convincingly, inspired largely by the work of Bruno Latour and Actor-Network Theory,[3] that it is best to describe urban infrastructures as complex 'assemblages' bringing all manner of human, non-human, and natural agents into a multitude of continuous liaisons across complex temporalities and geographic space.[4]

An excellent example of such a perspective comes from Jane Bennett's discussion of the US electrical power grid as such an assemblage. To Bennett, the electricity grid is best understood as 'a material cluster of charged parts that have indeed affiliated, remaining in sufficient proximity and coordination to function as a (flowing) system'. Burning hydrocarbons, falling rain, rivers spinning turbines in dams, atmospheric weather systems, turning wind turbines, transformers, wires, sockets, microprocessors, electrical consumer appliances – all relate together and gain agency alongside a myriad of social and cultural practices. 'The electrical grid', Bennett writes, is a volatile mix of coal, sweat, electromagnetic fields, computer programs, electron streams, profit motives, heat, lifestyles, nuclear fuel, plastic, fantasies of mastery, static, legislation, water, economic theory, wire, and wood – to name just some of the actants.'[5]

Such a perspective underlines that any 'coherence' that the electrical assemblage achieves as an 'infrastructure' must never be assumed, or taken as permanent and inviolable. Rather, as was made clear in the 2003 blackout in the Northeastern part of the USA, the grid is always a precarious achievement ready to untangle at a moment's notice through a myriad of possible causes. The electrical grid thus 'endures alongside energies and factions that fly out from it and disturb it from within. While they include humans and their constructions, they also include some very active and powerful nonhumans: electrons, trees, wind, electromagnetic fields.'[6]

3. Bruno Latour, *We Have Never Been Modern*, London: Harvester and Wheatsheaf, 1993, and John Law and John Hassard, editors, *Actor Network Theory and After*, London: Wiley, 1999.
4. Aihwa Ong and Stephen Collier, eds., *Global Assemblages: Technology, Politics, and Ethics as Anthropological Problems*, Oxford: Blackwell, 2005. Following Gilles Deleuze, Jane Bennett emphasizes that 'an assemblage is, first, an ad hoc grouping, a collectivity whose origins are historical and circumstantial, though its contingent status says nothing about its efficacy, which can be quite strong. An assemblage is, second, a living, throbbing grouping whose coherence coexists with energies and countercultures that exceed and confound it. An assemblage is, third, a web with an uneven topography: some of the points at which the trajectories of actants cross each other are more heavily trafficked than others, and thus power is not equally distributed across the assemblage. An assemblage is, fourth, not governed by a central power: no one member has sufficient competence to fully determine the consequences of the activities of the assemblage. An assemblage, finally, is made up of many types of actants: humans and nonhumans; animals, vegetables, and minerals; nature, culture, and technology.' Jane Bennett, 'The Agency of Assemblages and the North American Blackout'.
5. Ibid., p. 445.

6. Ibid., p. 446.

CYBORG CITIES: TECHNOLOGICAL MEDIATIONS OF SOCIETY, NATURE, CULTURE

7. Nik Heynen, Maria Kaika and Erik Swyngedouw, eds., *In the Nature of Cities: Urban Political Ecology and the Politics of Urban Metabolism*, London: Routledge, 2006.

8. Maria Kaika and Erik Swyngedouw, 'Fetishising the modern city: The phantasmagoria of urban technological networks', *International Journal of Urban and Regional Research*, 24(1), 2000, pp. 122.

9. Maria Kaika, *City of Flows*, London: Routledge, 2004.

10. Heynen, et al, *In the Nature of Cities* op. cit.

11. Matthew Gandy, 'Cyborg urbanization: Complexity and monstrosity in the contemporary city,' *International Journal of Urban and Regional Research*, Volume 29.1 March, 2005, pp. 26-49. See also Matthew Gandy, *Concrete and Clay: Reworking Nature in New York City*, Cambridge, MA.: MIT Press, 2002.

Secondly, and relatedly, recent work on the political nature of ecology has demonstrated convincingly that infrastructure networks, as well as blending the social and technical, also operate, in effect, to continually transform the natural into the cultural.[7] 'Technological networks (water, gas, electricity, information etc.) are constitutive parts of the urban', write Maria Kaika and Erik Swyngedouw. 'They are mediators through which the perpetual process of transformation of Nature into City takes place.'[8]

Thus, water systems draw water from distant biospheres, aquifers and hydrological systems and bring this into the metabolism of urban life which in turn supports the complex modern hydrological cultures of the body and the modern city.[9] Sewerage and solid waste infrastructures radically shape urban biospheres whilst metabolising waste matter from urban bodies, systems or industries. Energy systems bring fossil fuel, nuclear, hydro, wind, and solar energies into the city which in turn sustains the complex electrical cultures of modern urban life. Urban car cultures, meanwhile, are sustained by violent conflicts over distant fossil-fuel reserves and transnational pipeline systems and in turn play a major role in generating greenhouse gas emissions which tend to impact most negatively on far-off people and places through their contribution to sea-level rises and climate change.

Such perspectives demonstrate that infrastructural assemblages are involved in the active social production of urban natures, for example when the hydrological systems of entire continents are shaped over centuries by practices of urban water engineering and river management, or through the ways in which capitalism sustains long-distance resource-grabs – for food, energy or water – that add to the power of political or economic urban elites. Such productions of nature are profoundly political, even though these politics are often obfuscated by conventional ways of thinking about infrastructures as being wholly technical, separated from the entirely different and equally asocial domain of 'nature'.[10] Crucially, such a perspective underlines the cyborg nature of contemporary urbanisation: the ways in which the technological circulations sustained by infrastructural assemblages inseparably blend together the social relations of urban life and the relations between cities and the natural and biospheric processes upon which they rely.[11] Thus far, discussions on the blending of the biological and the social into 'cybernetic organisms' or cyborgs have most often focused either on sci-fi future dystopias or utopias; on the intimate blending of human and technological within military or space programmes; or on experiments within which bodies are artificially engineered or individual human bodies are blended seamlessly with individual technical or electronic systems or prosthetics.[12] However, Matthew Gandy and Antoine Picon,[13] amongst others, have suggested that cities and urbanisation can also be viewed profitably as cyborg processes themselves. The advantage of this approach is that it works to destabilise conventional notions that technologies somehow impact autonomously on the social world. In asserting that the cyborg materiality of a city's infrastructural circuits necessarily blends bodies, technologies, social relations and biospheric systems, cyborgian ideas of the city also help us to assert that notions of urban politics must now move far beyond the conventional physical limits of the city. Matthew Gandy, for example, asserts that 'the modern urban home, in particular, has become a complex exoskeleton for the human body with its provision of water, warmth, light and other essential needs. The home can be viewed as prosthesis and prophylactic in which modernist distinctions between nature and culture, and between the organic and the inorganic, become blurred.'[14]

'Study a city and neglect its sewers and power supplies (as many have), and you miss essential aspects of distributional justice and planning power.'[15]

Finally, and again relatedly, the recent profusion of critical research on infrastructure networks has sought to overcome the widespread tendency within popular discourse and social science alike to cast these systems as apolitical, 'boring' or merely 'technical' domains that can satisfactorily be partitioned off within the worlds of specialist engineers. A starting point for this work has been the criticism that, in both popular and academic discourses about cities and urban life, infrastructure networks have 'too often [been] relegated infrastructures to an apolitical context or backdrop, as not worthy of attention, too hidden from view.'[16] In order to assert the highly politicised nature of infrastructure it is necessary to get to grips with what Susan Leigh Star has called the 'hidden mechanisms subtending those processes more familiar with social scientists.'[17] A key starting point here is that the construction of spaces of mobility and flow for some always involves the construction of barriers for others.[18] The construction, maintenance and operations of a transport, water, energy or communications grid tends to privilege certain more powerful spaces and users over others. The material assemblages involved have to be immobilised in geographic space in order to facilitate mobilities and circulations for selected users, populations and economic groups.[19]

Infrastructure networks are thus thoroughly political constructions which tend instead to embody 'congealed social interests.'[20] This perspective emerges more easily when they are seen as messy assemblages or cyborgian complexes rather

12. See Chris Hables Gray, *The Cyborg Handbook*, New York: Routledge, 1995; Donna Haraway, 'A manifesto for cyborgs: science, technology, and socialist-feminism in the late twentieth century'. In D. Haraway (ed.), *Simians, Cyborgs and Women: The reinvention of Nature*. New York: Routledge, 1991, pp. 149-181.
13. See Matthew Gandy, 'Cyborg urbanization: Complexity and monstrosity in the contemporary city,' *International Journal of Urban and Regional Research*, Volume 29.1 March, 2005, pp. 26-49, and Antoine Picon, *La Ville Territoire de Cyborgs*, Paris: L'Imprimeur, 1998.
14. Gandy, 'Cyborg urbanization', op. cit. See also Maria Kaika, 'Interrogating the geographies of the familiar: domesticating nature and constructing the autonomy of the modern home', *International Journal of Urban and Regional Research*, 28(2), 2004, pp. 265-286.

POLITICAL INFRASTRUCTURES

15. Gregory Bateson, *Steps to an Ecology of Mind*, New York: Ballantine, 1978, p. 249.

16. Colin Mcfarlane and Jonathan Rutherford, 'Political Infrastructures: Governing and Experiencing the Fabric of the City', *International Journal of Urban and Regional Research*, Volume 32.2, June 2008, p. 363.
17. Leigh-Star, S., 'The ethnography of infrastructure', *American Behavioral Scientist*, 43(3), 1999, p. 377.
18. See David Harvey, *The Urbanization of Capital*, Blackwell: Oxford, 1985, and Eric Swyngedouw, 'Communication, mobility and the struggle for power over space', in Giannopoulos, G. and Gillespie, A. *Transport and Communications in the New Europe*, London: Belhaven, 1993, pp. 305-325.
19. David Harvey, *The Urbanization of Capital*, op. cit.
20. Wiebe Bijker, 'Do not despair: There is life after constructivism', *Science, Technology and Human Values*, 18(1), 1993, pp. 113-138.

than merely the 'technical' domain of engineers. (A key theme in cyborg science fiction, of course, has been the vulnerability of urban life to an increasingly automated, 'intelligent' or biologically engineered technics out of control).[21]

'For the person in the wheelchair, the stairs and door jamb in front of a building are not seamless subtenders of use, but barriers. One person's infrastructure is another's difficulty.'[22] Indeed, social biases have always been designed into urban infrastructure systems, and their abilities to respond to crises, collapse or disruption, whether intentionally or unintentionally. However, the lustre of highly symbolic infrastructure mega-projects, in particular, tends to obfuscate this point. Thus, celebrations about the ways in which fast-rail networks speed up the circulation of people within Europe need to be tempered by attention to the ways that they can actually make intervening spaces less accessible from city cores because local train services are often sacrificed as a result of their development. Similar logics of 'bypass' are evident in the pipelines of potable water which thread across the surface of Mumbai, lacing together the gated communities of the affluent, whilst providing no access to the informal cities which they bisect. Indeed, tendencies to glorify new airport extensions or highway networks in Global South megacities need to be confronted with the way informal districts are often completely erased to make way for such projects. Finally, suggestions that the opportunities of people are always improved by access to Internet computers need to be tempered by research into the ways in which software-code is being used by corporate service providers to automatically sort, prioritise, and even dump, electronic traffic within internet, call-centre and e-commerce systems, as they are organised to allow privileged groups to bypass the congestion caused by the sheer weight of traffic and so enjoy a premium service.[23]

On other occasions the negative effects of infrastructural construction and use are rendered invisible by geographic or temporal distance between use and effect. The costs and risks associated with the construction of a global airport system for the kinetic elites 'who most benefit from, or control, corporate globalisation, tends to fall on poorer groups, 'kinetic underclasses',[24] or distant countries facing the most cataclysmic and immediate consequences of airport expansion or climate change. Discussions about peak oil and the dependence of urban energy and transport infrastructures on fossil fuels, rarely encompass the catastrophic impacts that climate change and rising sea-levels are already having on many marginal and peripheral people and spaces in the contemporary world.[25] The violence, destabilisation and insecurity experienced by many oil-rich regions, as imperial scrambles and wars centre on appropriating the world's remaining fossil fuel reserves to feed burgeoning, largely urban, demands, are also

---

21. Gandy, 'Cyborg urbanization', op. cit.

22. Leigh-Star, 'The ethnography of infrastructure' op. cit.

23. Stephen Graham 'Software-sorted geographies', in *Progress in Human Geography*, 29(5), 2005, pp. 562-580.

24. Mark Salter, 'The Global Visa Regime and the Political Technologies of the International Self: Borders, Bodies, Biopolitics', *Alternatives 31*, 2006, pp. 167–189.

25. James Garvey, *The Ethics of Climate Change: Right and Wrong in a Warming World*, London: Continuum, 2008.

apposite here.²⁶ Similar quasi-imperial scrambles to buy up prime agricultural land in the Global South, to feed either the human mouths of northern cities in the future,²⁷ or, through biofuel production, the growing populations of automobiles, are crucial to any discussions about ecological sustainability or food security in a world of rapid urbanisation.²⁸ With global trends toward privatisation and liberalisation over the past three decades, many infrastructures built within the contexts of public or private monopolies and aspirations toward universal services for all, now operate according to imperatives of profit maximisation and the prioritisation of privileged users and markets. This 'splintering' of infrastructures can involve the construction of new premium spaces or networks such as TGV lines, electronically-tolled highways, skywalk city streets, privatised streets, or broadband communications networks, which bypass or become removed from the legacies of the inherited infrastructures.²⁹ More subtly, it may encompass the withdrawal of essential services from poorer or less profitable groups or spaces, as efforts concentrate on addressing the more profitable market segments.³⁰ It may also be associated with tendencies to privilege selected premium infrastructures whilst reducing essential public investment and maintenance from the wider inheritances of infrastructure converging entire cities, regions or nations.

Finally, the resilience of infrastructures may be severely compromised as they are actively reorganised to maximise profit or return, or absorbed wholesale within predatory models of neoliberal financial capital. The short-termism, predatory tendencies and risk of asset-stripping which attend the progressive merging of infrastructural and finance capital in many cases have been a notable element of the current collapse of neoliberal financial capitalism.³¹ Often, indeed, speculative finance capital has not only preyed on, and profited from, crises and disruption, it has constituted political economic conditions necessary to generate such crises, whether they be wars, postwar reconstruction efforts, financial meltdowns, or predatory disaster relief operations.³² The spectacular financial collapse of 2008-9, of course, has brought its own debilitating disruptions as bankruptcies and frozen credit markets have left a multitude of projects to build, ameliorate or improve infrastructural networks cancelled or on ice. In the UK, for example, the construction of new schools is now almost paralysed because it relies so heavily on neoliberal development models based entirely on private finance capital. Sparked by the collapse of California's deregulated electricity system in 2001, Gene Rochlin argues that this example, along with other notable cases such as the notoriously disastrous privatisation of the UK rail system, or the often chaotic trajectories of US airline or phone systems, demonstrates that

26. Stephen Graham, *Cities Under Siege: The New Military Urbanism*, London: Verso, 2009, Chapter 10.

27. Sue Branford, 'Food crisis leading to an unsustainable land grab', *The Guardian*, Saturday 22 November 2008, at <http://www.guardian.co.uk/environment/2008/nov/22/food-biofuels>

28. Stephen Graham, *Cities Under Siege*, op. cit.

29. Stephen Graham and Simon Marvin, *Splintering Urbanism: Networked Infrastructure, Technological Mobilities and the Urban Condition*, London: Routledge, 2001.

30. Stephen Graham, 'Constructing premium networked spaces: Reflections on infrastructure networks and contemporary urban development', *International Journal of Urban and Regional Research*, 24 (1), 2001, pp. 183-200.

31. See Morag Torrance, 'Forging Glocal Governance? Urban Infrastructures as Networked Financial Products' in *International Journal of Urban and Regional Research*, 32(1), 2008, pp. 1-21.

32. See Naomi Klein, *The Shock Doctrine: The Rise of Disaster Capitalism*, Penguin, 2007.

regulatory shifts in infrastructure development, legitimised by the dogmatic application of neoliberal economic dogma, can be as disruptive to reliable services as any natural disaster or terrorist attack.[33] In many cases, at least in the Global North, he suggests that liberalised infrastructure models have in many cases involved an abandonment of social regulations sustaining progressive cross-subsidies and universal distribution of services built up through Keynesian economic regulation and the development of welfare states.

Whilst they were far-from perfect and extremely varied, Rochlin suggests that the widespread replacement of socialised models of long-term, Keynesian infrastructure regulation with models privileging short-term or speculative profit, the role of finance capital, and individualised notions of consumption, have actually often worked to increase risks of failure and disruption in many cases. The shift from relatively coherent and equitable assemblages, based on ideas that infrastructures are economic 'natural monopolies', to a baroque complexity of fragmented institutional providers, certainly seems to underline that many infrastructure regulators do not seem to understand that complex infrastructural assemblages are not simple 'commodities' distributed to consumers within mythically perfect private markets. In the California electricity and UK rail cases, in particular, Rochlin argues that the result has been a startling increase in user prices, a rapid growth of disruptions, vulnerability and volatility, an over-reliance on the short-term volatilities of financial markets and a growth of predatory corporate behaviour where operators work to amass their own quasi-monopolistic powers whilst sucking in more and more hidden subsidy from Governments.[34]

Jane Bennett, though, reminds us that the technical elements of infrastructural assemblages have their own agency within infrastructural disruptions, and that it is inadequate to merely read-off the frequency or nature of disruptive events from political economic or regulatory transformations. This makes the post-mortems that follow major collapses like the 2003 US blackout especially interesting. 'A distributive notion of agency does interfere with the project of blaming', Bennett writes. 'But it does not thereby abandon the project of identifying [ ] the sources of harmful effects. To the contrary, such a notion broadens the range of places to look for sources.'[35] In this case, Bennett urges us to look to 'selfish intentions and energy policy that provides lucrative opportunities for energy trading while generating a tragedy of the commons'; at 'the stubborn directionality of a high-consumption social infrastructure'; and at 'the unstable power of electron flows, wildfires, ex-urban housing pressures, and the assemblages they form'.[36] Within such a context, the degree to which infrastructures are resilient to all manner of disruption is equally both socially constructed and

33. Gene Rochlin, 'Networks and the subversion of choice: An institutionalist manifesto', in *Journal of Urban Technology*, 8(3), 2001, pp. 65-96.

34. Ibid.

35. Jane Bennett, 'The Agency of Assemblages and the North American Blackout', op. cit., p. 463.

36. Ibid., pp. 463-464.

politically contested.[37] Infrastructures, and the way they are maintained (or not maintained) through continuous, often hidden, work, distribute risks unevenly. Despite the proliferation of state critical infrastructure policies since September 11th, 2001,[38] extremely uneven resources and effort are put into establishing back-up systems or alternative sources of supply for different portions of the population served by a system. As Julian Reid has argued, these policies reveal much about the way western political thought stresses infrastructural circulation as the very means of life – the key biopolitical basis of political power. 'The defence of critical infrastructure', he writes, 'is not about the mundane protection of human life from the risk of violent death at the hands of terrorists'. He sees it, rather, as a more profound defence of the combined physical and technological infrastructures on which global liberal regimes have come to depend for their sustenance and development in recent years. 'Quality of life' is deemed inextricably dependent in these documents on the existence of critical infrastructures. Terrorism is a threat to these regimes precisely because it targets the critical infrastructures which enable the liberality of their way of life rather than simply the human beings which inhabit them.[39]

Critical infrastructure response plans, moreover, are often extremely biased towards the needs of hegemonic elites or capital groups. Crises often bring unerring focus on glaring biases. Eric Klinenberg's ground-breaking research on the infrastructural and institutional response to Chicago's devastating 1995 heat wave, for example – which killed a crisis over 700 people – demonstrated systematic failures to address the extreme vulnerabilities of the city's poorest African-American neighbourhoods.[40]

Indeed, in many cities around the world, instead of addressing the needs of vulnerable groups and communities, major state and corporate investments go into sustaining continuities of flow and circulation, by providing back-ups to key electrical, communication, data processing, transport or other infrastructures that sustain the main nodes and enclaves of the globalised corporate economy. (The geographical organisation of corporate systems based on the seamless digital and material inter-linking of globally-stretched nodes with their 'just-in-time' logistics flows only adds to the imperatives here). Indeed, a key part of the spatial production of extra-judicial or extraterritorial free trade zones, export processing 'zones, or special economic zones' that are so central to global economic geographies these days, is the installation of systems that secure the circulation of capital even during times of crisis, whilst undermining labour and environmental controls at the same time.[42] Just beyond the borders of such nodes, however, service interruptions and disruptions often expose a stark lack of alternatives.

---

37. Lawrence Vale and Thomas Campanella, eds., *The Resilient City: How Modern Cities Recover From Disaster*, Oxford: Oxford University Press, 2005, and John Coaffee, David Murakami Wood and Peter Rogers, *The Everyday Resilience of the City: How Cities Respond to Terrorism and Disaster*, London: Palgrave Macmillan, 2008.

38. For a review, see Andrew Lakoff, 'Preparing for the next emergency', *Public Culture*, 19(2), 2007, pp. 247-271. Julian Reid, 'Open Source Destruction, Weak Discipline, War Infrastructure.' In Jordan Crandall, ed., *Under Fire*, at <http://underfire.eyebeam.org/?q=node/462> accessed February 1st 2009.

39. Ibid.

40. Eric Klinenberg, *Heat Wave: A Social Autopsy of Disaster in Chicago*, Chicago: University of Chicago Press, 2002.

42. See Keller Easterling, *Enduring Innocence: Global Architecture and Its Political Masquerades*, Cambridge, MA: MIT Press, 2007.

43. Gregory Squires and Chester Hartman, eds., *There Is No Such Thing as a Natural Disaster: Race, Class and Hurricane Katrina*, New York: Routledge, 2006.
44. Phil Steinberg and Rob Shields, eds., *What is a City? Rethinking the urban after Hurricane Katrina*, Athens and London: University of Georgia Press, 2008; Lakoff, 'Preparing for the next emergency', op. cit.; Julian Reid, 'Open Source Destruction', op. cit.

The final key point to stress is that the political nature of infrastructure disruption is often rendered invisible by media discussions of such events as mere 'technical' malfunctions or environmental 'Acts of God'. The notion that urban natures are actually produced through the long-term agency of political infrastructural assemblages renders such perspectives unhelpful, however. Such understandings hammer home the key point that, in infrastructurally-mediated natures, there is no such thing as a natural disaster.[43] Such problematisations still rarely encroach into popular discussions. Coverage of the impacts of Hurricane Katrina on New Orleans in 2005, for example, often failed to attend to the ways in which 'nature' in this case was actively produced by the long-term engineering of the mouth of the Mississippi by the US Army Corps of Engineers. Over centuries, the flood protection and river engineering systems, as well as coastal denudation in and around the mouth of the Mississippi worked to produce highly uneven geographies of exposure to flood risk, which were racially biased in ways that were only fully exposed by the disaster itself.[44]

LANDSCAPE URBANISM AND THE INFRASTRUCTURAL TURN

In helping to render the vast skein of systems, networks and material edifices that continually work to constitute the contemporary city as process, the infrastructural turn outlined above provides a dramatic challenge to conventional architectural perspectives of urbanity. But it also throws down a major opportunity: to re-imagine the connections between urbanity, nature, technology, politics and culture in highly creative and promising ways that help build on the progress already made within recent debates about Landscape Urbanism (and elsewhere). In our world, architecture increasingly melds into landscape; infrastructure, landscape increasingly *is* infrastructure, and 'nature' is increasingly a social and technological construction of gigantic proportions. The real challenge though is that the infrastructural turn reveals all this to be shot through with politics in ways that architectural theory in general, and the debates of Landscape Urbanism, have barely begun to consider, let alone address.

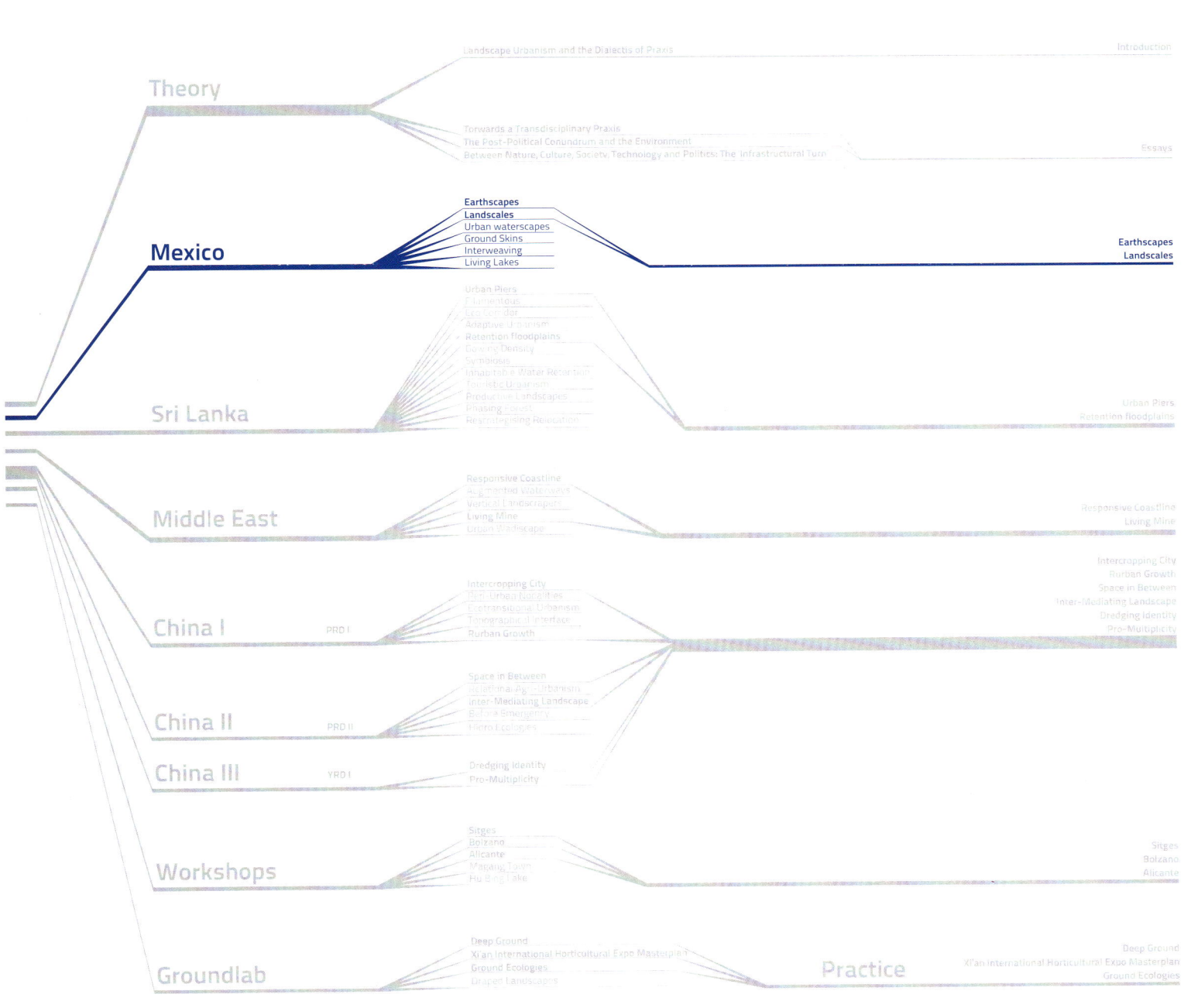

AA Landscape Urbanism 04/05
Diffusion-Mexico City

AGENDA Mexico city offered Landscape Urbanism the chance to explore ways in which the work of the course could serve to operate in the complex conditions emerging in one of the largest urban agglomerations on earth. The unplanned growth of some of the suburbs has left large tracts of the city devoid of basic services and quality urban space. But at the same time it has laid the basis for new forms of inhabitation, which deal with other processes and infrastructural problems, such as soil subsidence and depletion of water resources. The works of Landscape Urbanism in this year focused on the exploration of voids within a semi-continuous urban fabric, looking for potentials of development and exploring the ways in which local conditions and infrastructural constraints could work as a starting point for new urban organisations. The students studied processes of infilling within the street network, expansions, centralities and connectivity strategies in an exploration of the ways to work within the city fabric. The course combined the visit to Mexico City with the realisation of an on-site workshop, lectures by scholars from the National University and a series of technical lectures from Arup infrastructure. An initial bibliography was provided and further investigation was developed during the course through contact with local authorities, non-governmental agencies, developers, industrial sector practitioners, academic institutions, and members of the local population.

AALU Mexico City 04/05

Earthscape

Date **2004/05**
Location **Mexico**
Author **Sarah Majid**

Project description

Mexico City is one of the largest urban centres in the world with an estimated population of 22 million living within a surface area of 100,000 hectares [1], resulting in uncontrolled urban expansion and environmental deterioration. [2] As one moves outward from the historic centre and into the periphery, rapid growth of informal settlements begins to occupy Mexico City's empty voids, leaving little room for planned social spaces. Any forms of open space within this area of expansion, have proved to perform poorly because of an unorganised structure.

The project is located on the periphery zone mediating the federal district city centre and the expanding surrounding suburbs, occupying a derelict site inside a military camp. While this area is classified as an ecological reserve, it is neither maintained nor open to the public. The project aims to connect the fragmented spaces through the utilisation of an existing border condition, reinterpreting it as a distributed network which would form the infra-structural base of an 'event-surface', responding to the current sociological condition.

Urban strategy

The main strategy is to disperse the centralised pattern of services within the city centre and allow for a more polycentric distribution of resources by a counteraction of re-intensifying events on the periphery zone. The remaining open space would be retained as an urban park that would embed programmes such as sports and leisure, park and recreation, and culture and market exhibits.

The surrounding neighbourhoods are mainly mixed and commercial housing which are linked to the park via a series of land bridges that vary in width. The spaces above and below the bridges are appropriated for recreational, commercial and leisure facilities.

The neighbouring green areas and ecological reserves are annexed to the area of intervention as green anchors allowing for a continuous green structure extending throughout the urban fabric.

The proposed connections link the site to Chapultepec Park, existing informal markets, other nearby ecological reserves and gardens, and bus stops. The linear connections are also designed to pass through existing collection pools and the remaining forestation patches.

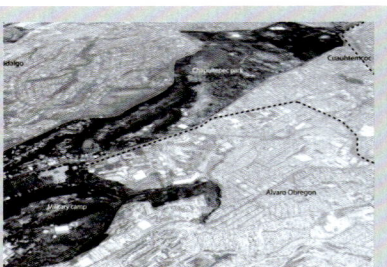

1. Site location
2. Site: military camp
3. Site: adjacent events

Mexico City is one of the largest urban centres in the world with an estimated population of 22 million living within a surface area of 100,000 hectares. Mexico City is an acute example of uncontrolled urban expansion and environmental deterioration.

The steep topography of the site is acting as a barrier for pedestrian movement as well as vehicular traffic. This has led to a clear disjuncture in the city fabric, with degraded edges around the ecological reserve which make the area inaccessible within the urban fabric.

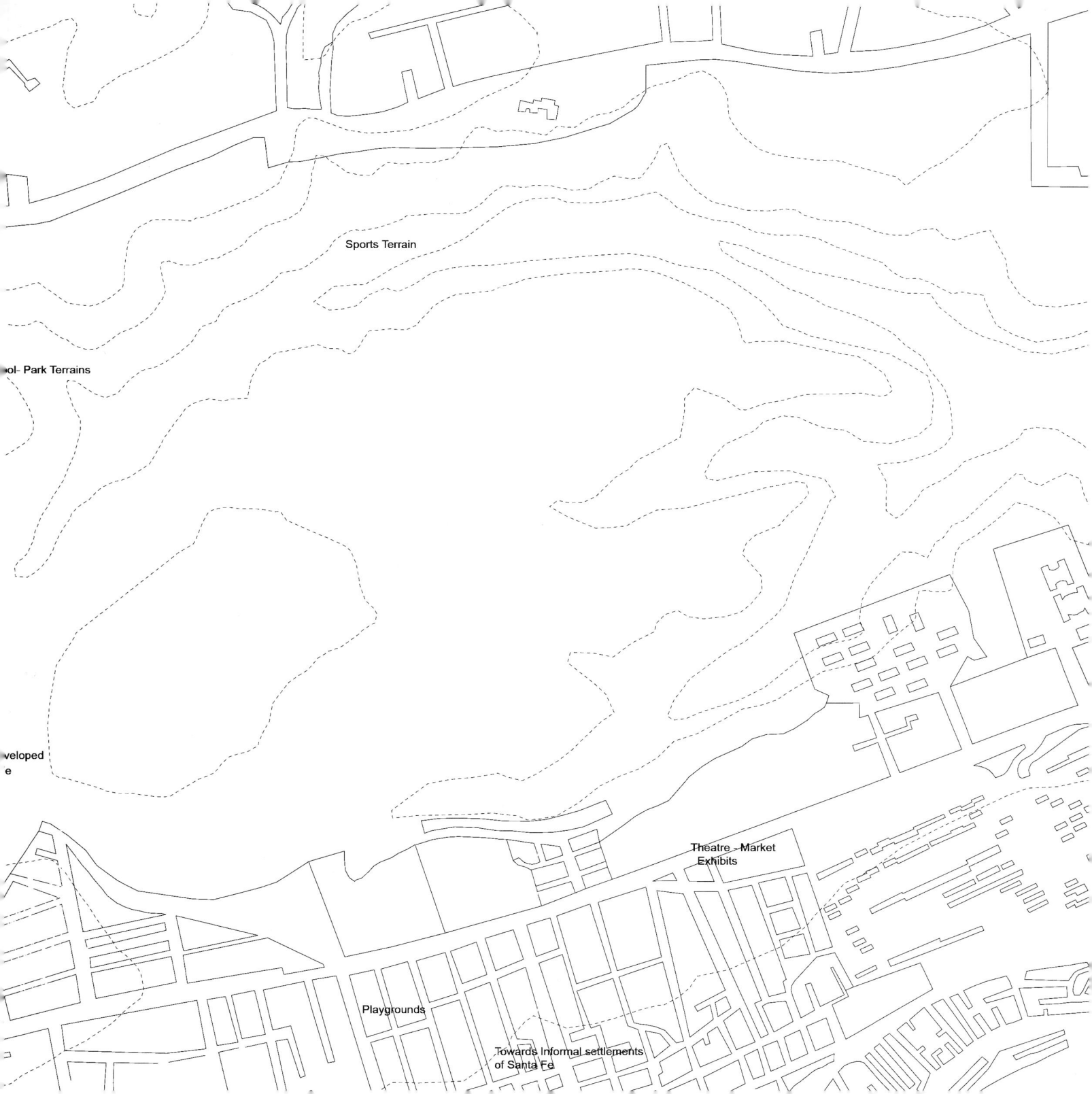

Detail of development

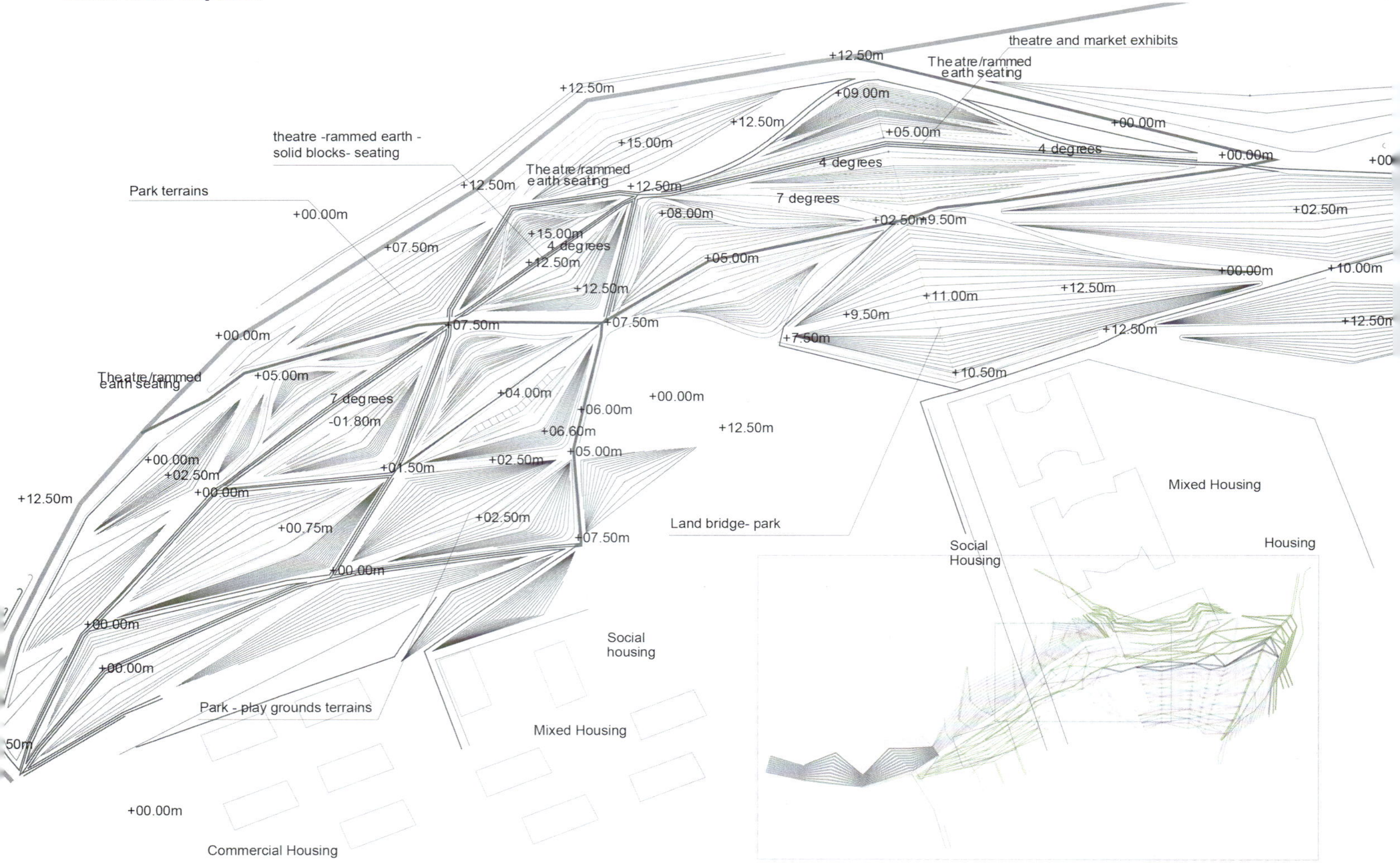

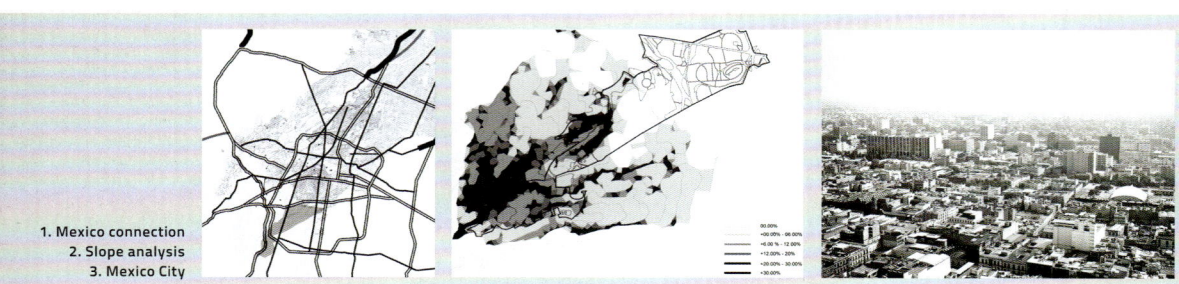

1. Mexico connection
2. Slope analysis
3. Mexico City

The three parts of the site are connected via a series of land formations derived from a prototypical definition of activated land bridges. These prototypes form a differentiated topography which hosts different activities while serving as water collection infrastructure.

The land forms grow outwards and towards each other, regularly weaving around the main circulation loop which ultimately organises the site itself.

Prototype proliferation on site according to steepness of slope

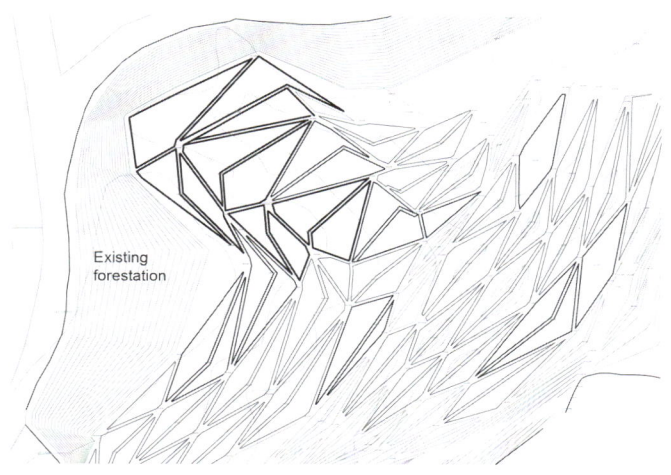

Natural convex and concave zones

Concaved
Convexed
Critical islands

Collection pools and water route

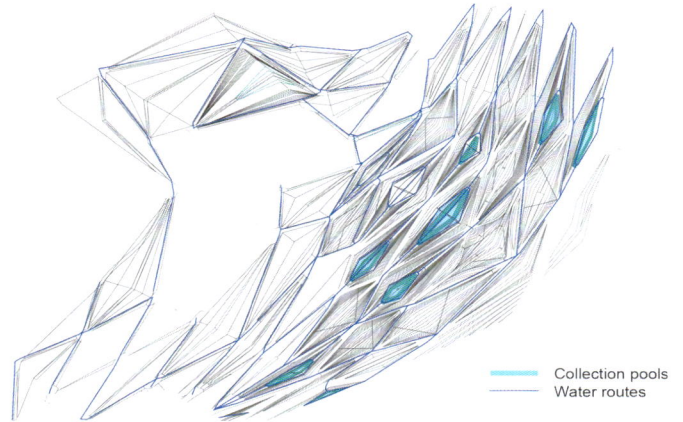

Collection pools
Water routes

Movement network routes

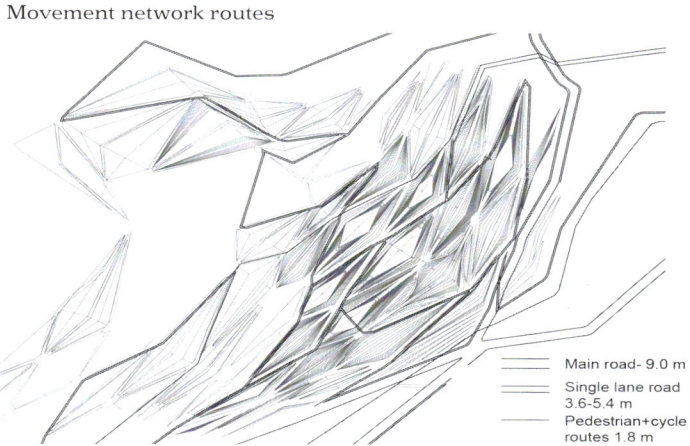

Main road- 9.0 m
Single lane road 3.6-5.4 m
Pedestrian+cycle routes 1.8 m

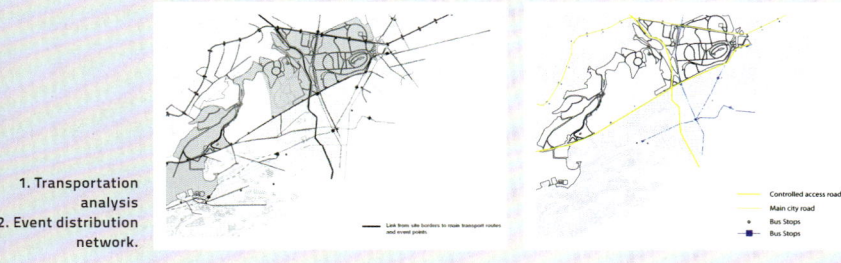

1. Transportation analysis
2. Event distribution network.

Instance 1: 'park-pool' terrains
The pockets function as collection pools during the rainy season. The water is collected through canals and inclined solid surfaces and reused within the park.

Instance 2: the 'theatre-park' and 'theatre-market' exhibits
This particular terrain is directly connected to the adjacent neighbourhoods linking social and commercial housing to the park and playgrounds. This takes place through land bridges that are occupied for cultural and recreational use. The surrounding neighbourhoods are mainly mixed and commercial housing which are linked to the park via a series of land bridges that vary in width. The spaces above and below the bridges are appropriated for recreational, commercial and leisure facilities.

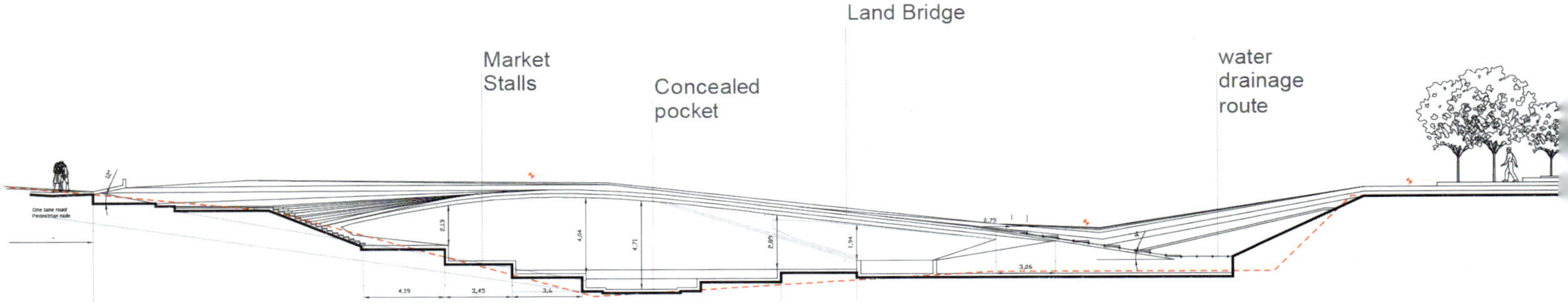

Site sections

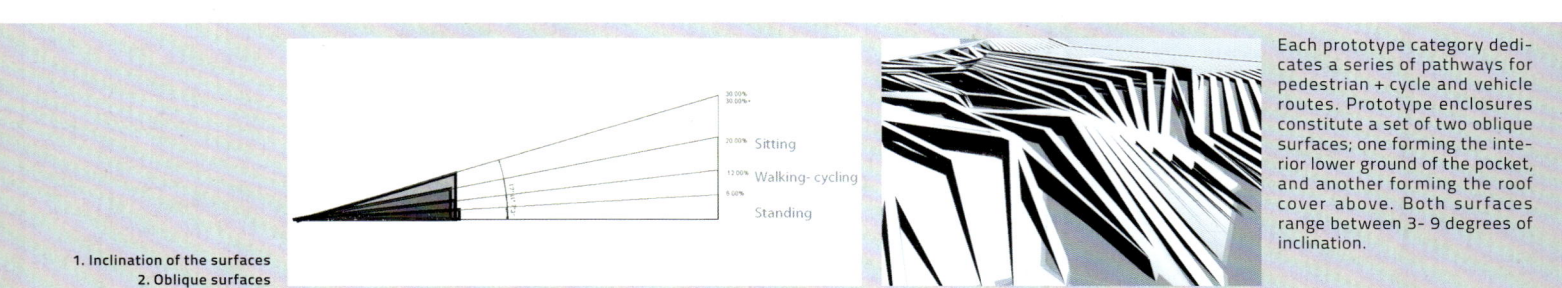

1. Inclination of the surfaces
2. Oblique surfaces

Each prototype category dedicates a series of pathways for pedestrian + cycle and vehicle routes. Prototype enclosures constitute a set of two oblique surfaces; one forming the interior lower ground of the pocket, and another forming the roof cover above. Both surfaces range between 3- 9 degrees of inclination.

Surface connections: land bridges

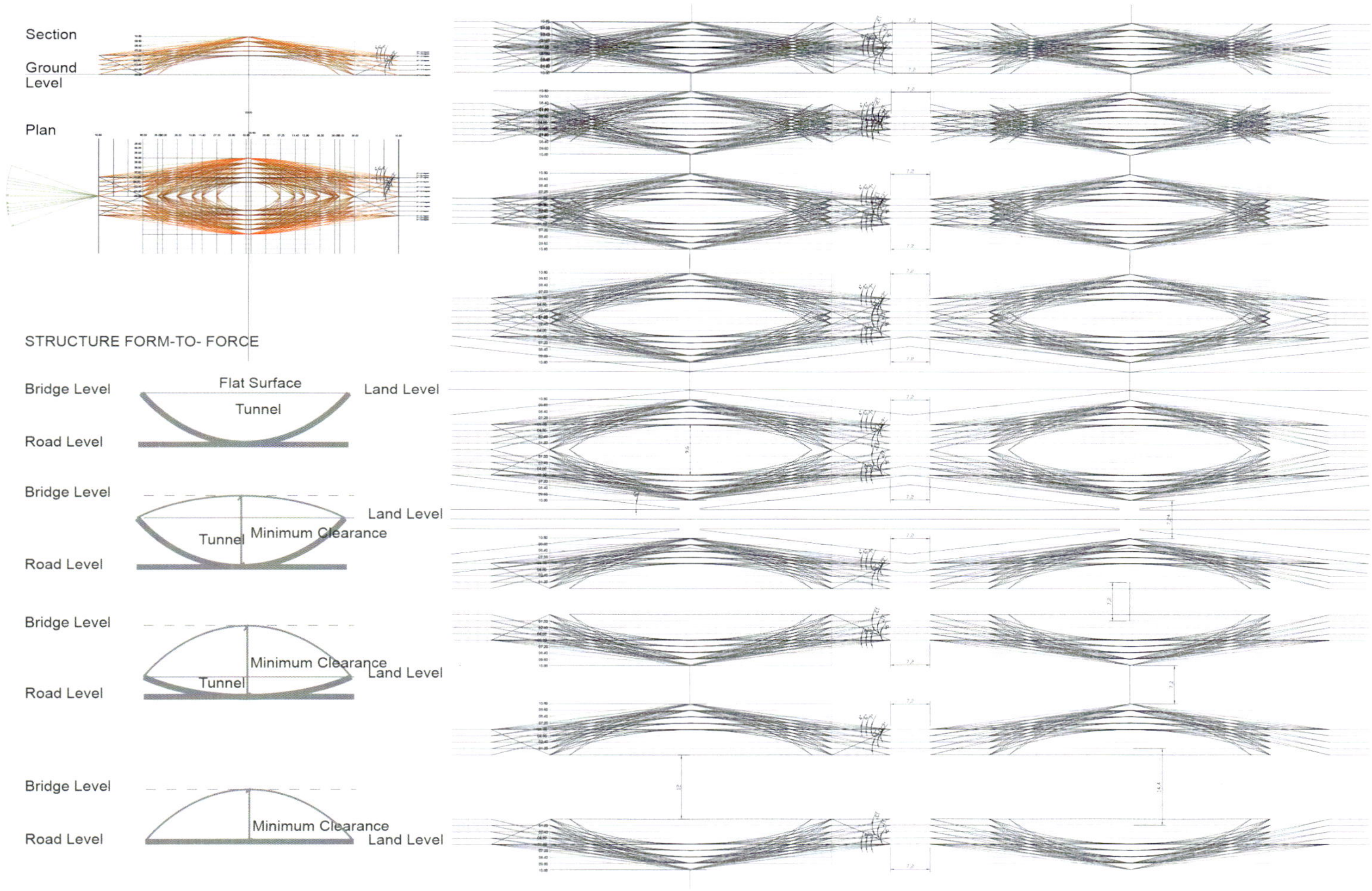

Section
Ground Level

Plan

STRUCTURE FORM-TO-FORCE

Bridge Level — Flat Surface — Land Level
Tunnel
Road Level

Bridge Level
Tunnel — Minimum Clearance — Land Level
Road Level

Bridge Level
Tunnel — Minimum Clearance — Land Level
Road Level

Bridge Level
Minimum Clearance — Land Level
Road Level

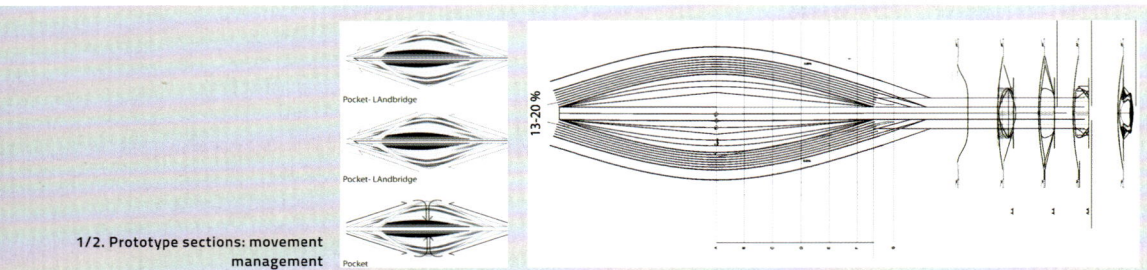

1/2. Prototype sections: movement management

Pocket- LAndbridge
Pocket- LAndbridge
Pocket

The catalogue above illustrates the geometric and infrastructural strategy in order to appropriate the different slopes of the site. It starts with flat land, moving to a steep slope of 30°. Each category defines one prototypical element of the catalogue. The prototypes differ in their width, depth and slope - to ramped or stepped area. The steeper the slope the wider and deeper the prototype becomes, with a denser pattern of ramps and steps.

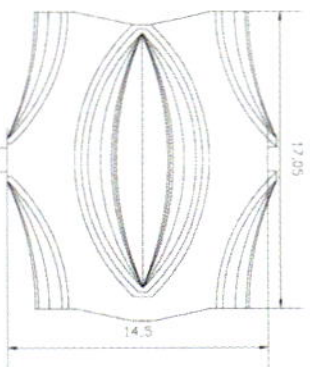

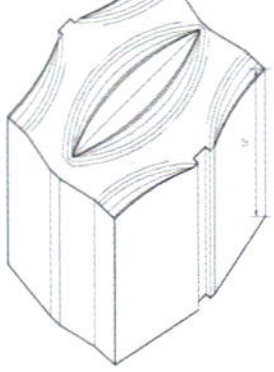

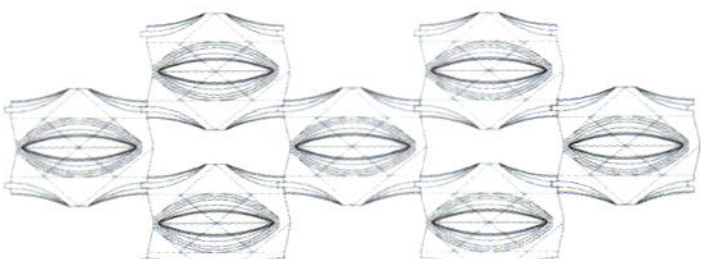

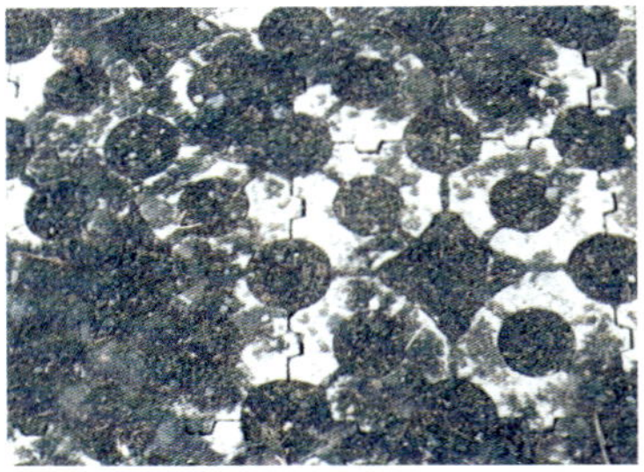

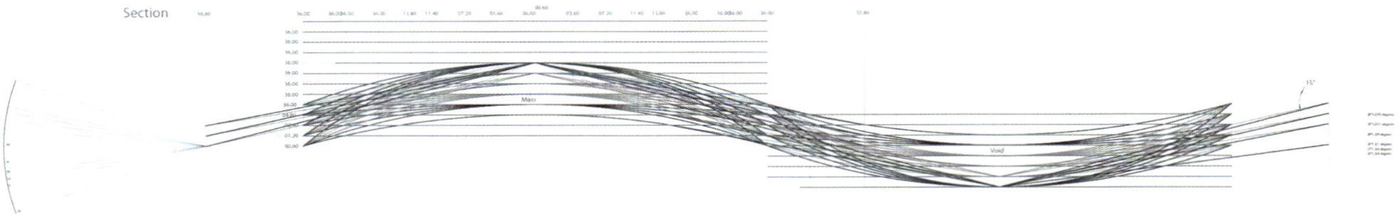

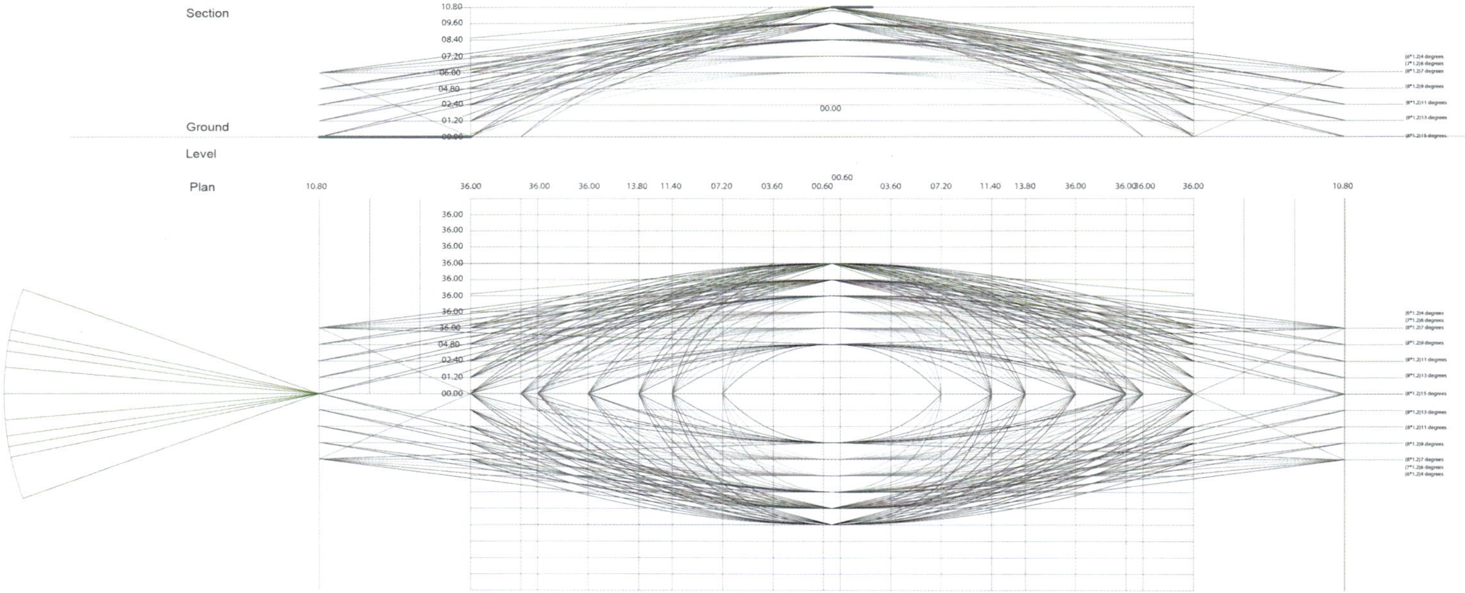

1. Instance 2: The theatre market
2. Green space distribution network

The prototypical unit also incorporates a modular skin ground cover that inhabits the surface as a dynamic progressive materialisation system. The repetitive units are formed from pre-cast rammed earth blocks which are designed with voids for top soil and slope retention purposes.

The modular tiling system varies in density and frequency in its organisations, allowing for a smooth progression from whole green cover into whole solid-scapes.

Instance 2: The theatre-park

Instance 1: Park-pool terrains

AALU Mexico City 04/05
Landscales

Date **2004/05**
Location **Mexico**
Author **Eva Tsouni**

Project description

'Landscales' is an artificial landscape of earth retention structures that derives from the geo-morphological and hydrological conditions of an ecologically preserved site in Santa Fe, Mexico City. The land formations perform as water-catchments that protect the hillsides and the ravines from progressive erosion. At the same time, they generate ease of movement across the terrain for the formation of a cohesive, multi-cultural public space. The 'landscales' project addresses an existing pattern of urbanisation that was founded on the abandonment and subsequent opportunistic resettlement of the hillside that is repeatedly taking place within the context of Mexico City. This pattern has resulted in the deterioration of the natural ecosystem, the segregation of the urban fabric and, consequently, of the decline in the quality of the urban space.

The proposed urban landscape acquires its geometry from the traditional terracing system and derives the resources required for its maintenance from the practice of urban agriculture. While the terracing system functions as a tool for constructing the urban landscape, urban agriculture serves as a means of structuring and sustaining the urban landscape by securing its land-tenure stability and management. The density of the system of land formations is heterogeneous. Its variability permits the structures to define degrees of resistance to the erosive forces and constitute the ground for multiple recreational activities and agricultural production according to their distribution within the site.

As the proposal deals with a sustainable reappropriation of the slope, it is based on an understanding of the minimal technical requirements, namely, the infrastructure needed for the stabilisation of the land in order to generate the basis for urban continuity and social cohesion.

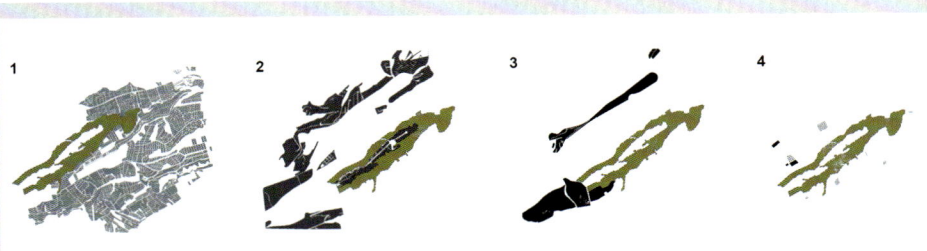

1. Housing with commerce - informal settlements
2. Private enclave - rich enclaves
3. Mixed housing - work and live
4. Existing park facilities

Initial analysis of existing urban infrastructures was undertaken in order to assess potential needs and service shortages. The project tries to fill in the programmatic gaps around the area while generating a robust infrastructure serving population needs and stormwater attenuation requirements.

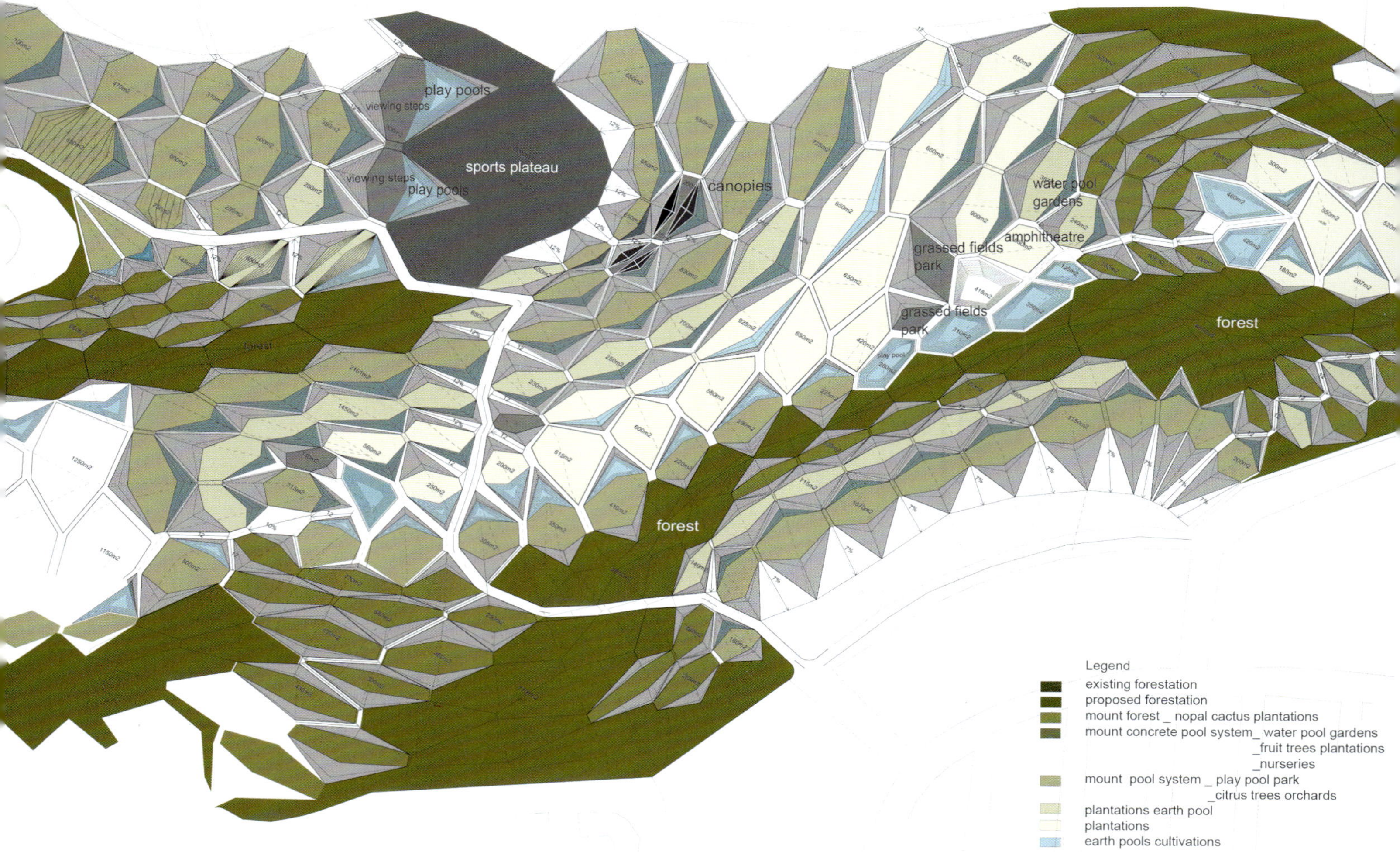

Detail of development

Legend
- existing forestation
- proposed forestation
- mount forest _ nopal cactus plantations
- mount concrete pool system _ water pool gardens
  _ fruit trees plantations
  _ nurseries
- mount pool system _ play pool park
  _ citrus trees orchards
- plantations earth pool
- plantations
- earth pools cultivations

1. Site location
2. Site photo

The site is located in the area of Santa Fe in the west of the Federal District of Mexico City. It is a derelict site and is the property of the government. 81.4% of the total area is covered by the urban fabric whilst the remaining 18.6%, including the site, was designated in 1997 under the ecological rescue and preservation regulations that encourage any recreational use and activities that will enhance and maintain the character and value of the area.

Terracing system as a tool for constructing the Urban Landscape
Additional manipulation of the terracing system and its geometries can generate a flexible way of dealing with the slope in order to create ease of movement and to accommodate different agendas for diverse social groups.

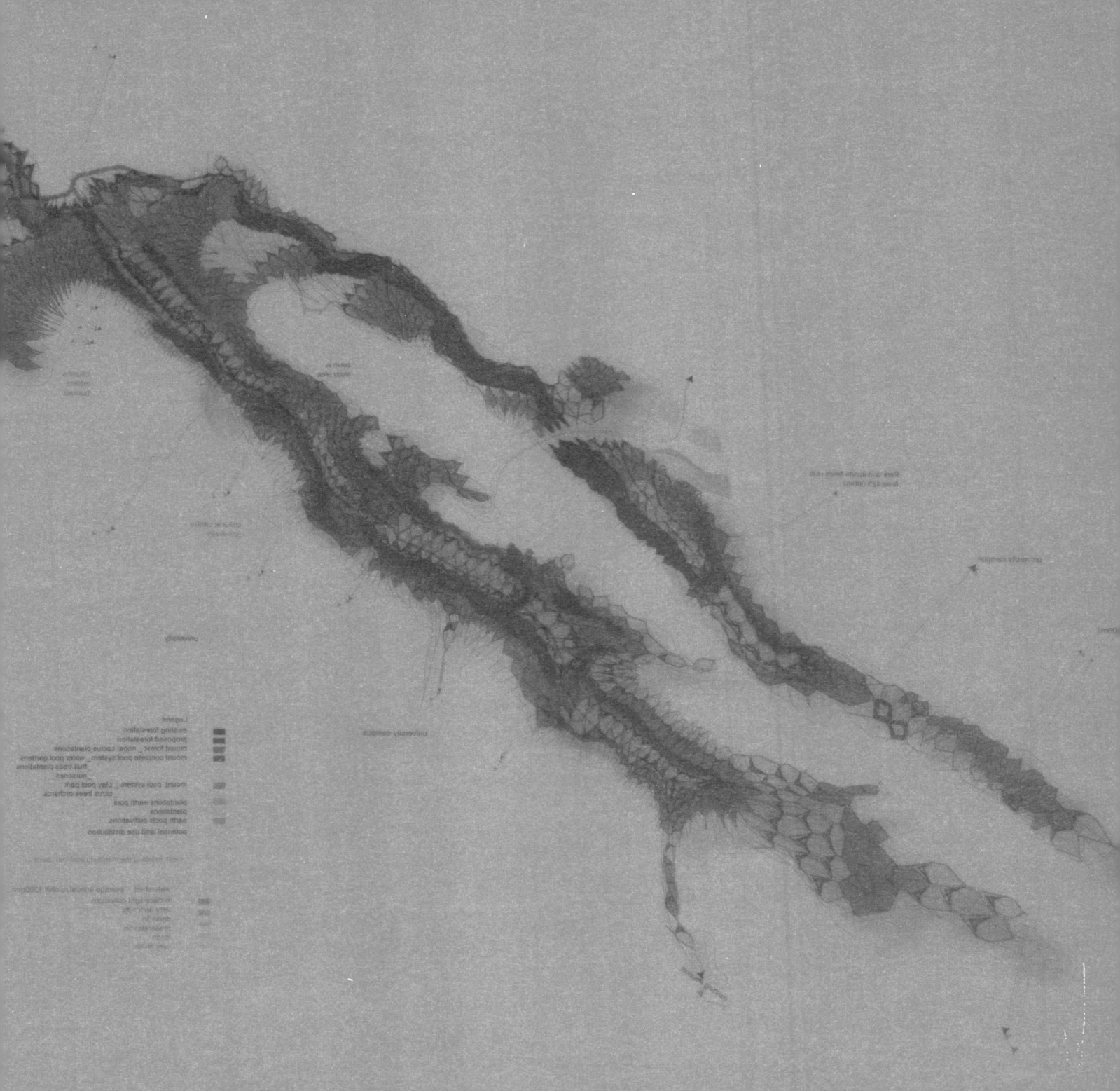

Site conditions

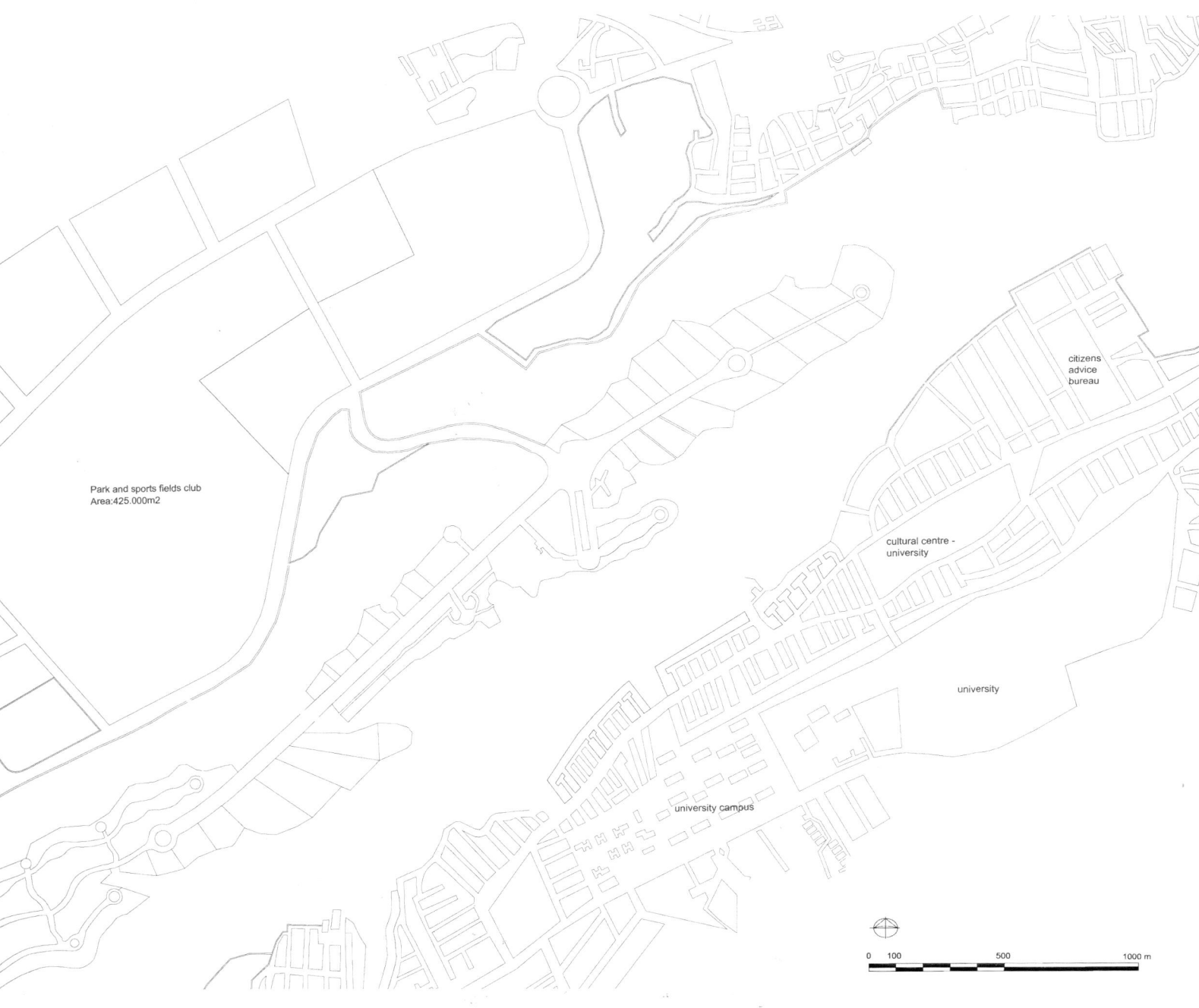

Typology development

slope of repose (%)	25°-40%	20°-35%	18°	17°	16°	15°	14°	13°	12°	11°-20%	10°	9°	8°	7°-12%	6°	5°	4°	3°	2°-3%
min. terrace width (m)	0.9	1.8	1.8	1.8	1.8	1.8	1.8	1.8	1.8	1.8	1.8	1.8	1.8	1.8	4.6	7.1	9.8	12.	15.
max. terrace width (m)	1.8	3.6	3.6	3.6	3.6	3.6	3.6	3.6	3.6	3.6	3.6	3.6	3.6	3.6	8.9	14.	19.	24.	30.
length of section (m)	5.4	25	32	34	36	39	39	40	41	42	43	46	75	90	105	120	133	150	165	177

land use distribution	forests or engineered solution	mount system terrace: nopal cactus slope: stepped greenery urban agriculture association	concrete pool and mount system terrace: gardens, recreation, canopies (the angle of the slope is steep enough to host a structure that will merge with the proposed landscape) slope: bioretention greenery university in coordination with urban agriculture	earth pool and mount system terrace: cultivation, recreation slope: cultivation, earth pool plantations, play pool park urban agriculture association	earth pool system rain season: water harvesting in earth pools dry season: recreation urban agriculture assoc.
management	governmental bodies				

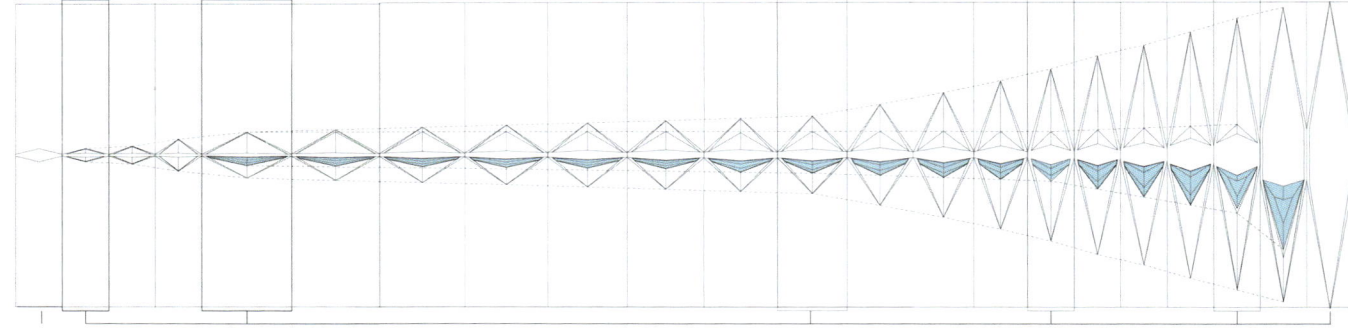

1. Objective: crop management
2. Bench terraces built in a single operation

Technical Parameters

A. Watershed management for controlling erosion, infiltration into the aquifer and irrigation;
B. Slope length and angle retained by bioengineering techniques for controlling erosion;
C. Width and length of terrace platforms on the hillside for planting and future development;
D. Movement on the oblique surface of the slope for generating easy public access and service routes on the landscape.

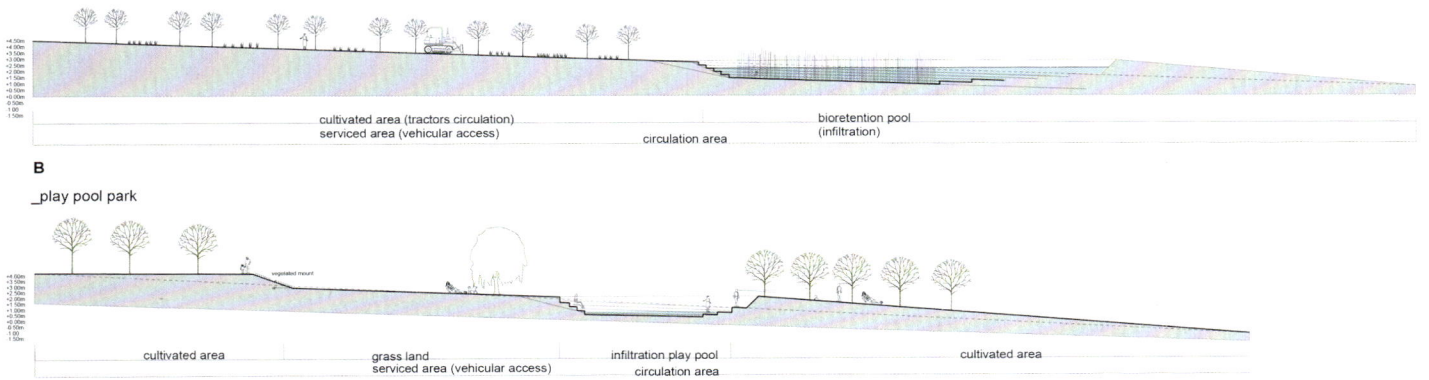

B
_play pool park

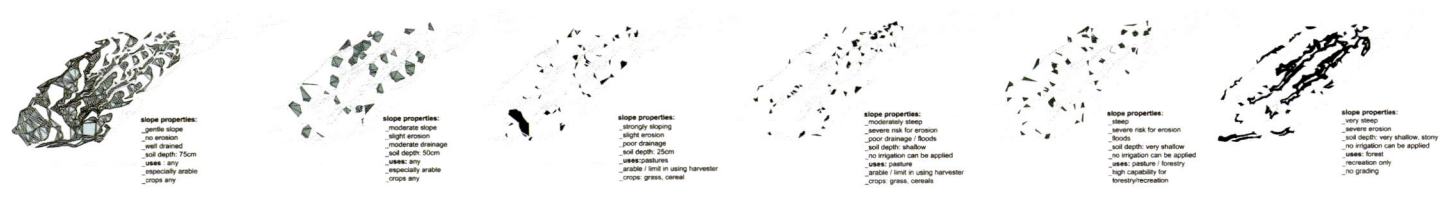

1/2. Rain absorption
3. Control run-off

Definition of the typology of the landscales

The landscale prototype is based on the study of existing techniques and geometries that appear on the slope. The understanding and adaptation of the minimal technical requirements produces the infrastructure necessary for stabilising the hillside, percolating water, generating ease of movement, and practising urban agriculture while providing a social space for the city and its inhabitants. The definition of the prototype reveals a process of transforming the derelict and deteriorated landscape into resurfaced lateral segments that deliver measured amounts of water into a carefully planned drainage and percolation system. The length of each lateral terrace is determined by the adjacent surface area and its resultant water run-off. The terraces drain into pools which detain the water in order to prevent soil erosion and flooding, enabling the vegetation to establish and restabilise the surface of the landscape to allow secondary use.

Details of development

A. cut and fill ratio for the generation of land formations

- earth pools, amphiteatre
- concrete pools
- mounts
- main waterways
- indicative irrigation system

secondary footpaths access to slope and waterways 1m
main cycle routes and footpaths 3.6m
and auxiliary circulation of goods
secondary cycle routes and footpaths 1.8m

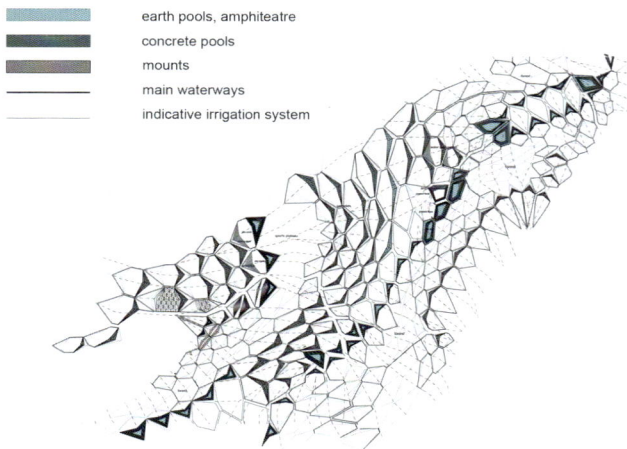

B. water control and distribution

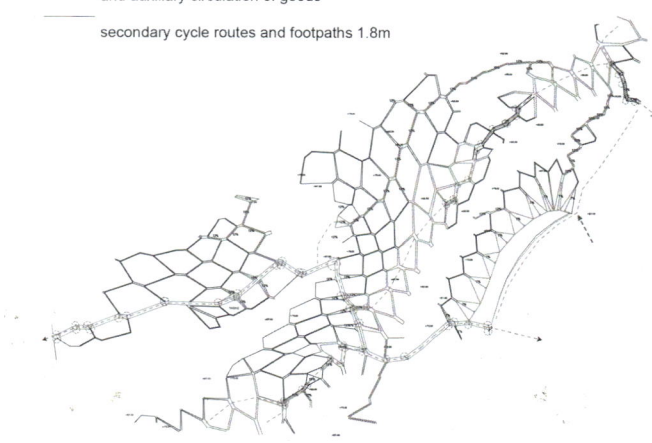

C. circulation pattern

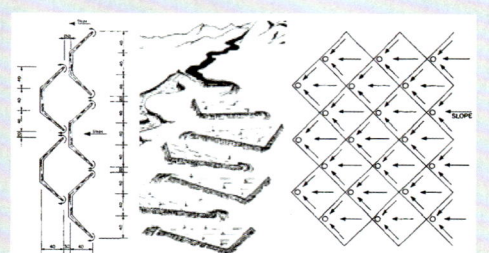

1. Objective: crop management
2. Water harvesting standard system

Case study of terracing system

Additional manipulation of the terracing system and its geometries can generate a flexible way of dealing with the slope in order to create ease of movement and to accommodate different agendas for diverse social groups.

Component development and prototype proliferation on site

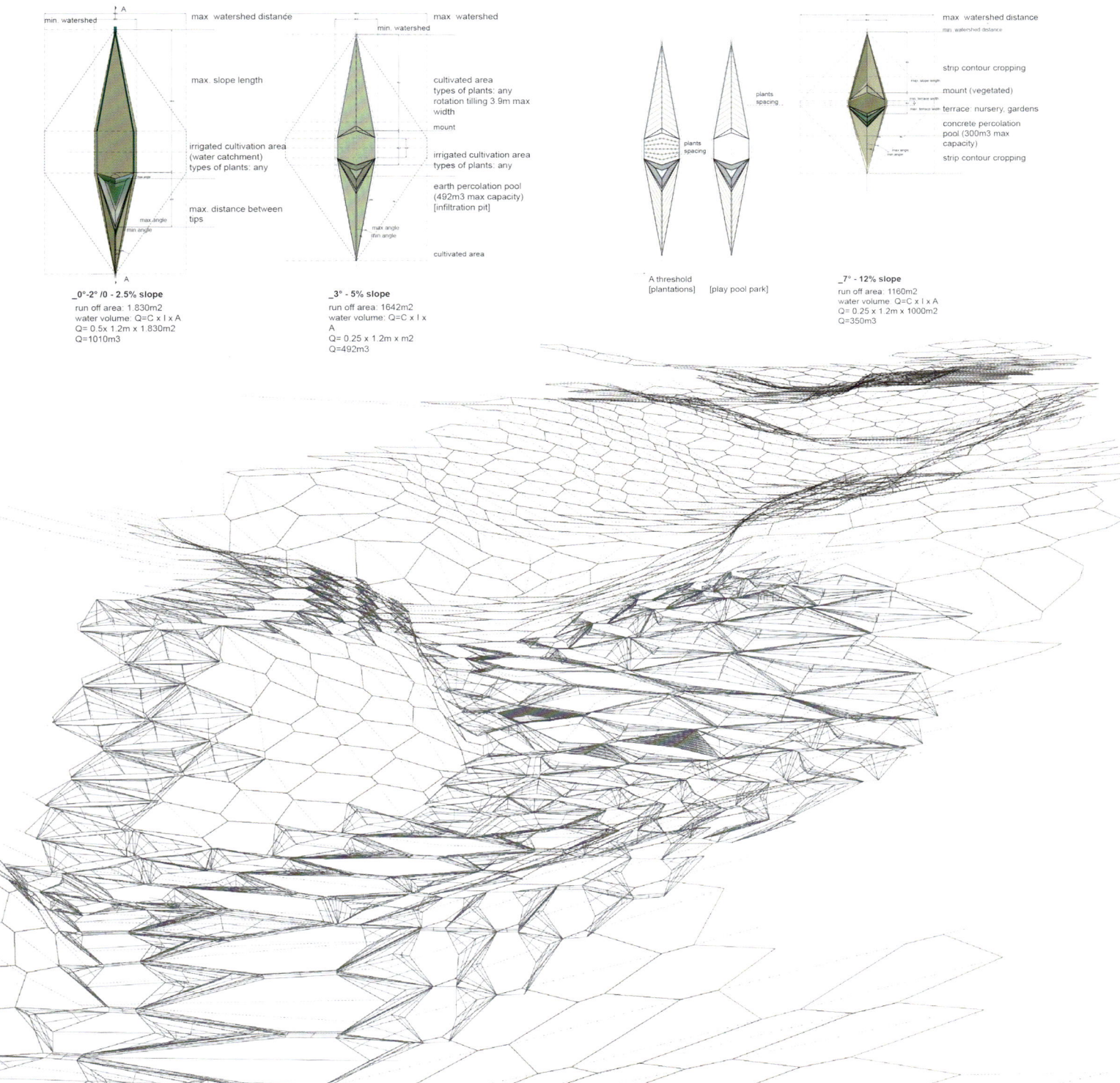

_0°-2° / 0 - 2.5% slope
run off area: 1.830m2
water volume: Q=C x I x A
Q= 0.5x 1.2m x 1.830m2
Q=1010m3

_3° - 5% slope
run off area: 1642m2
water volume: Q=C x I x A
Q= 0.25 x 1.2m x m2
Q=492m3

[A threshold / plantations]   [play pool park]

_7° - 12% slope
run off area: 1160m2
water volume: Q=C x I x A
Q= 0.25 x 1.2m x 1000m2
Q=350m3

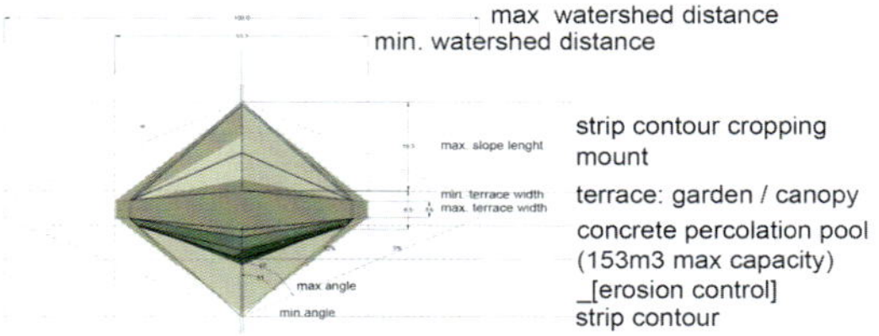
max watershed distance
min. watershed distance
max. slope lenght
min. terrace width
max. terrace width
max angle
min.angle
strip contour cropping mount
terrace: garden / canopy
concrete percolation pool (153m3 max capacity)
_[erosion control]
strip contour

_11° - 20% slope

run off area: 640 253m2
water volume: Q=C x I x A
Q= 0.2 x 1.2m x 640m2
Q=153 216m3

C threshold
[ornamental gardens]

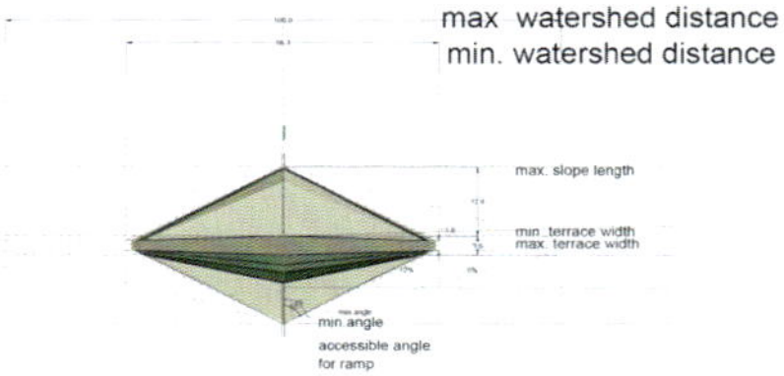
max watershed distance
min. watershed distance
max. slope length
min. terrace width
max. terrace width
min.angle
accessible angle for ramp

_18° - 30% slope

run off area: 640m2
water volume: Q=C x I x A
Q= 0.1 x 1.2m x 640m2
Q=76m3

C threshold
[water pool gardens]

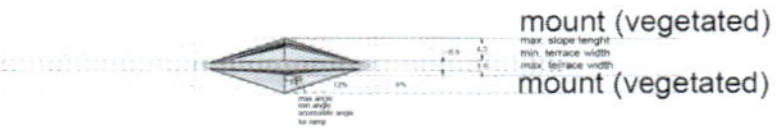
mount (vegetated)
mount (vegetated)

_25° - 40% slope

run off area: 179m2
water volume: Q=C x I x A
Q= 0.06 x 1.2m x 179m2
Q=12.8m3

D threshold
[cactus plantations]

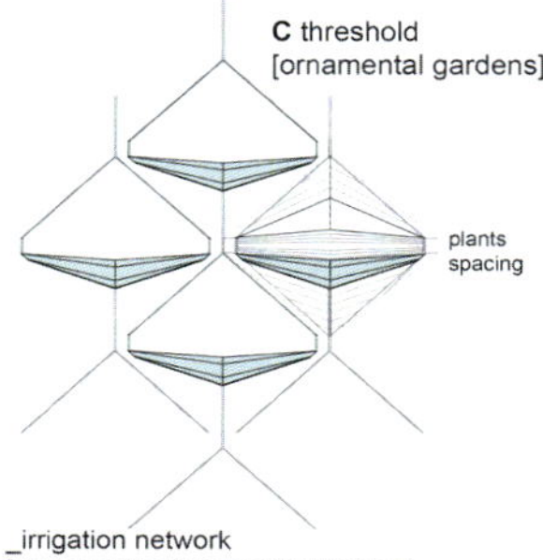
plants spacing

_irrigation network
[water collection and distribution]

_ gardens in combination with plantations

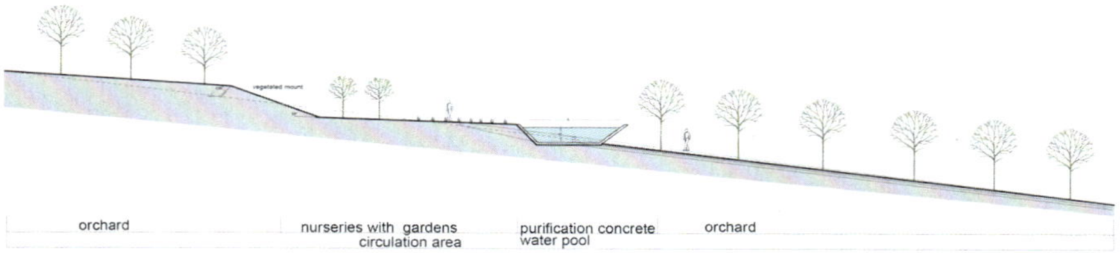
orchard
nurseries with gardens
circulation area
purification concrete water pool
orchard

_7° - 12% slope

AA section

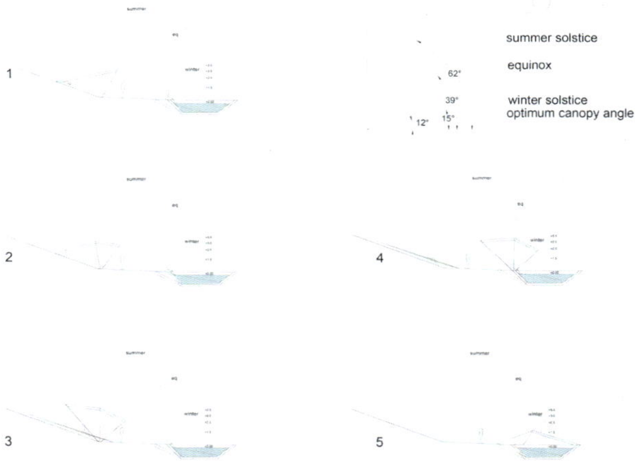
1
2
3
4
5
summer solstice
equinox
winter solstice
optimum canopy angle
62°
39°
15°
12°

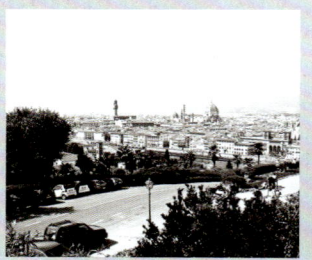

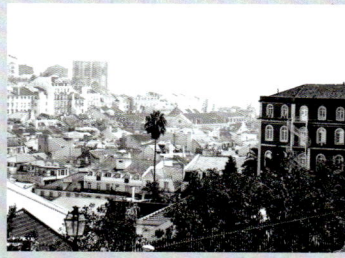

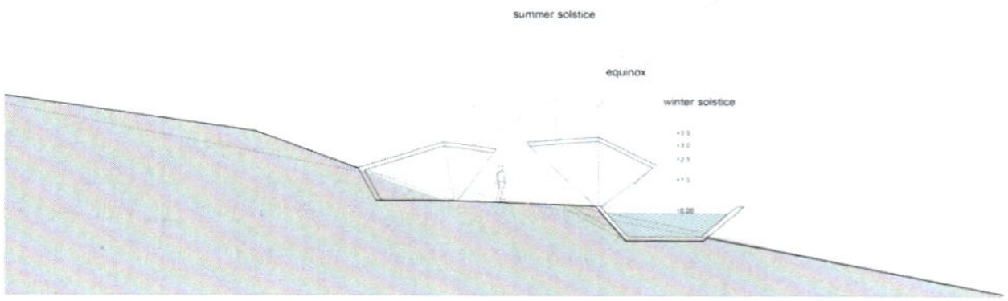
summer solstice
equinox
winter solstice

1. Case studies of terracing systems
2. Lisbon case study

Case studies of urban patterns on the hillside in Lisbon

A series of public terraces used as parks or viewing platforms on the hillside enrich the quality of the urban space and constitute the ground for public activities. The apparent configurations of this urban pattern reveal the importance of respecting and preserving the existence of the natural element within the urban fabric.

Perspective view 1

Perspective view 2

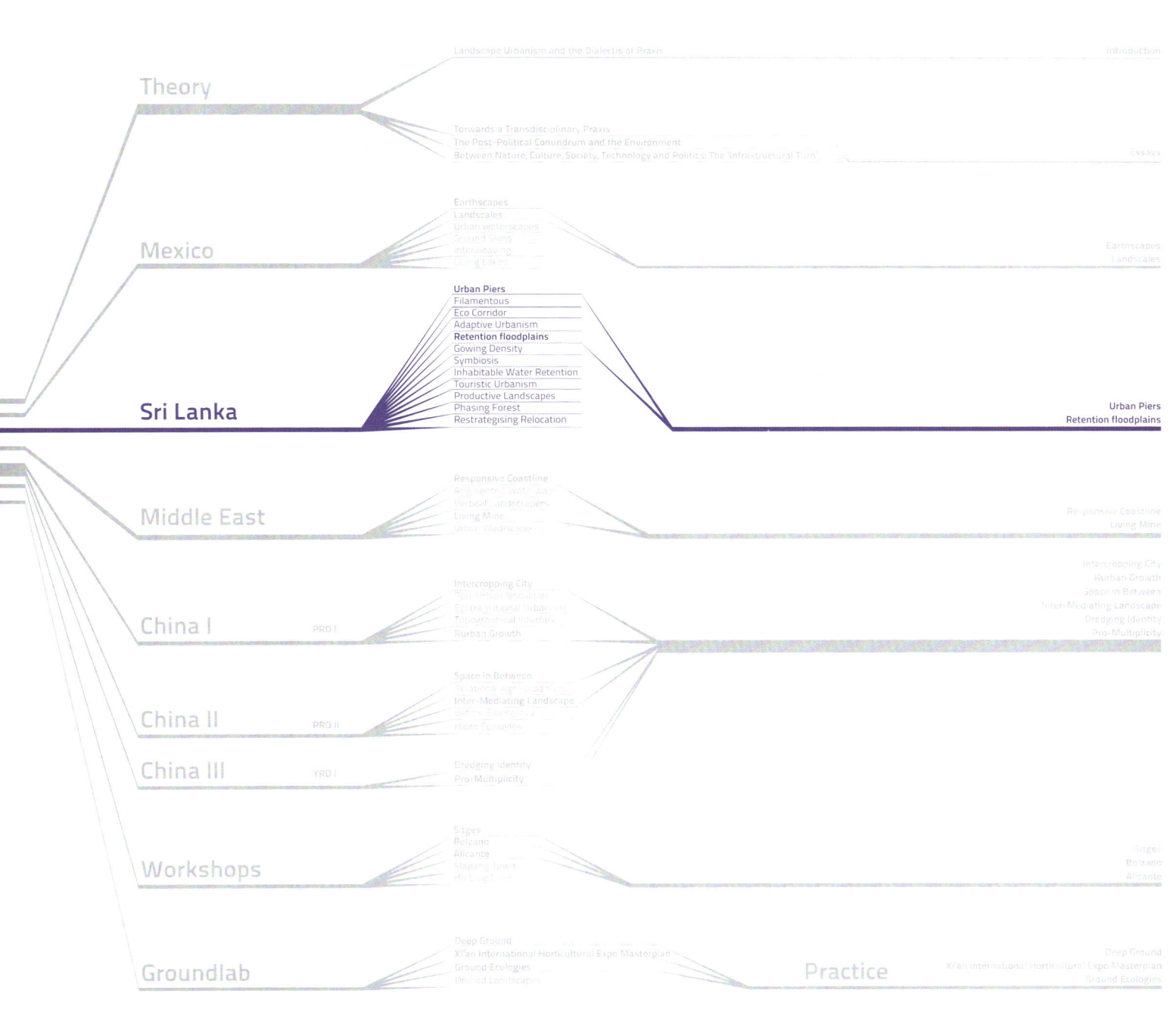

AA Landscape Urbanism 05/06
Post Tsunami Reconstruction - Sri Lanka

AGENDA At 00.59 GMT on 26 December 2004, a magnitude 9.3 earthquake ripped apart the seafloor off the cost of northwest Sumatra. Over 100 years of accumulated stress was released in the second biggest earthquake in recorded history.

It unleashed a devastating tsunami that travelled thousands of kilometres across the Indian Ocean, taking the lives of more than 200,000 people in countries as far apart as Indonesia, The Maldives, Sri Lanka and Somalia. This year we focused on the development of the studio's work in Sri Lanka. Rebuilding and reoccupation of these areas required careful determination of potential hazard zones to avoid future loss of life and property. At the same time the new sociopolitical configurations generated as an immediate consequence of the local death toll called for a reinterpretation of the traditional pattern of spatial inhabitation, both at the macro and micro scale. The new ground configuration – partly artificially generated by new policies which are responding to the pressure and perceived need to develop tourism – enforced the regional dislocation of underprivileged communities, in the process causing serious concern for their economic future and drastically changing the local human urbanism. We sought to seize the opportunity which presented itself: that of engaging foreign capital while negotiating the needs of the local population to improve their conditions in what ought to become a sustainable regenerative process.

AALU Sri Lanka 05/06

Urban Piers

Date **2005/06**
Location **Sri Lanka**
Author Zoe Spiegeli

Project Description

The Government of Sri Lanka is to commence the construction of an international shipping port in the Karagan Lewaya - coastal lagoon, immediately adjacent to the southern city of Hambantota. In response to the port development, this project, Urban Piers, is situated in the interface between the city and the port harbour. It is opportunistic by nature, taking advantage of the port infrastructure development. The project establishes an overlap between city and port called the urban apron, which is a zone of experimentation in port urbanisation. Urban Piers project explores the potential relationship between a contemporary city and port which share a waterfront.

In contrast to the mono function of the traditional container port, a mixed use waterfront, the urban/port interface has the potential to serve a diverse range of programmes and account to environmental, social and economic concerns. Through material and ground organisation the proposed urban/port landscape is configured into a series of earthen piers.

The piers are differentiated in profiles and skin conditions, from hard concrete piles to soft vegetated mangrove slopes. It is the modulation between hard and soft material/landscape throughout the zone which differentiates the edge condition. The variation in edge condition develops variation in potential programmes. Furthermore the project takes advantage of one of the by-products of port construction, which is earth from dredging operations. The earthen piers provide a local use for the material dredged to develop the harbor basin. Overall, the proposed landscape on the southern side of the port harbor is juxtaposed against the government's shipping port on the northern edge of the harbour, as an alternative treatment of a working waterfront. The proposed landscape or urban apron, addresses both the needs of the existing urban areas, for a mixed use waterfront and ecological concerns on the foreshore. The primary ecological concerns addressed throughout the proposal are flood mitigation, which is critical to developing a waterfront immediately adjacent to existing urban fabric and the sustenance of an intertidal zone, which is vital for promoting biodiversity along the waterfront.

1. Site location
2. Coastal lines

Local conditions

The urban apron is the interface between the port harbour and the city. The primary infrastructure of earthen piers is distributed along the waterfront to create the urban apron. In this zone a working relationship between city and harbour is developed. The piers are organised by the existing urban fabric and topographic conditions. Additional manipulation of the terracing system and its geometries can generate a flexible way of dealing with the slope in order to create ease of movement and to accommodate different agendas for diverse social groups.

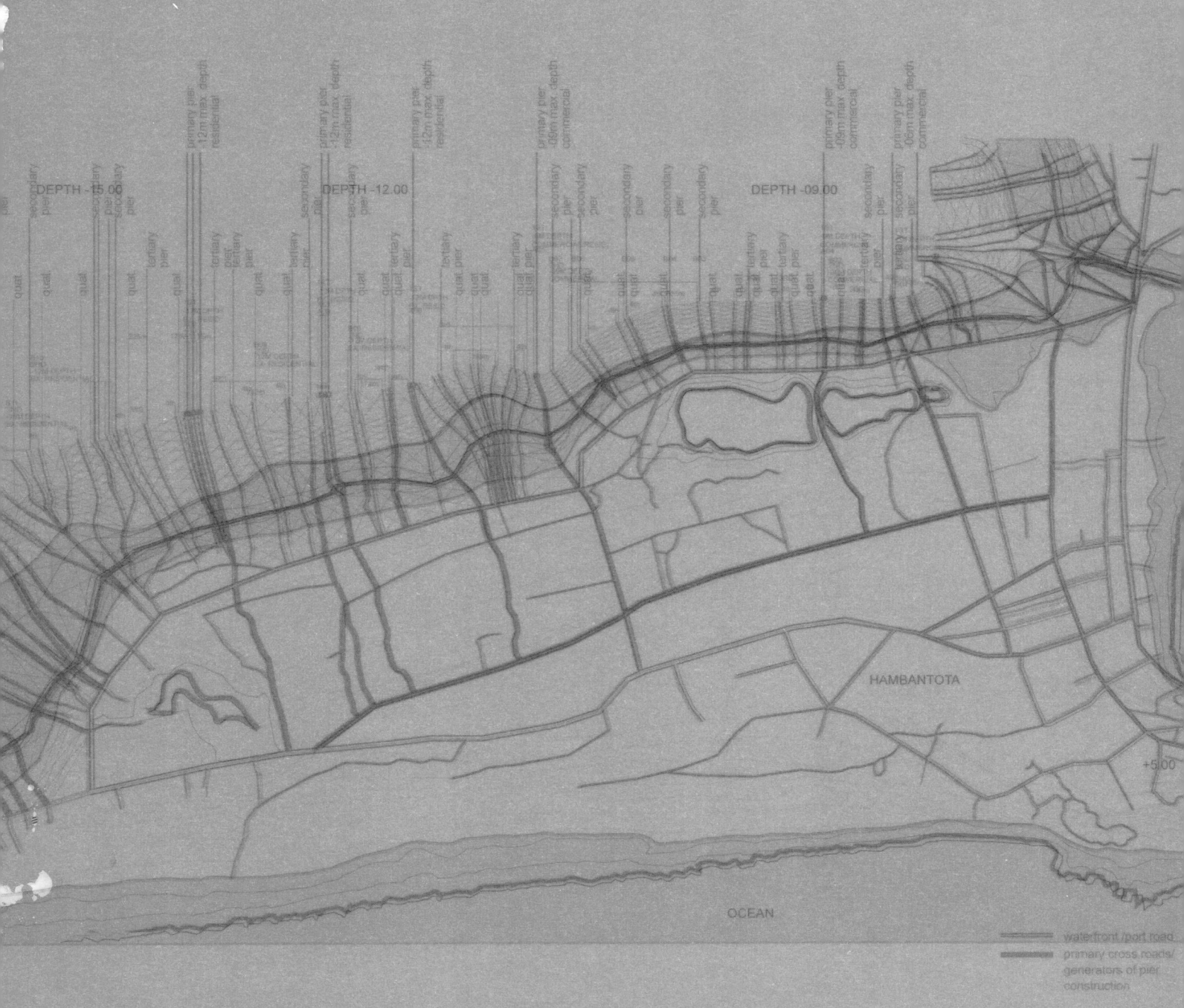

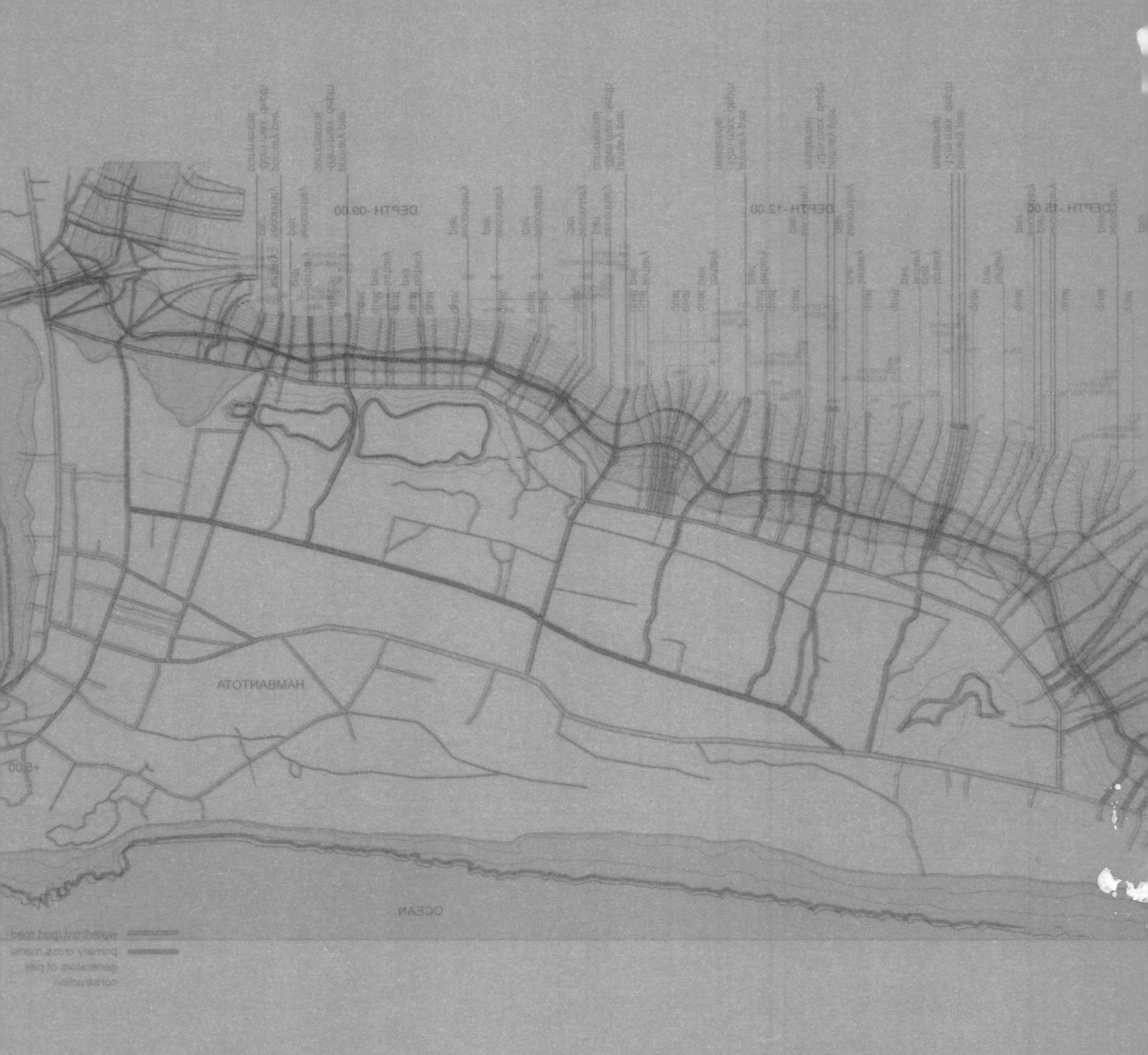

Site condition

Detail of development

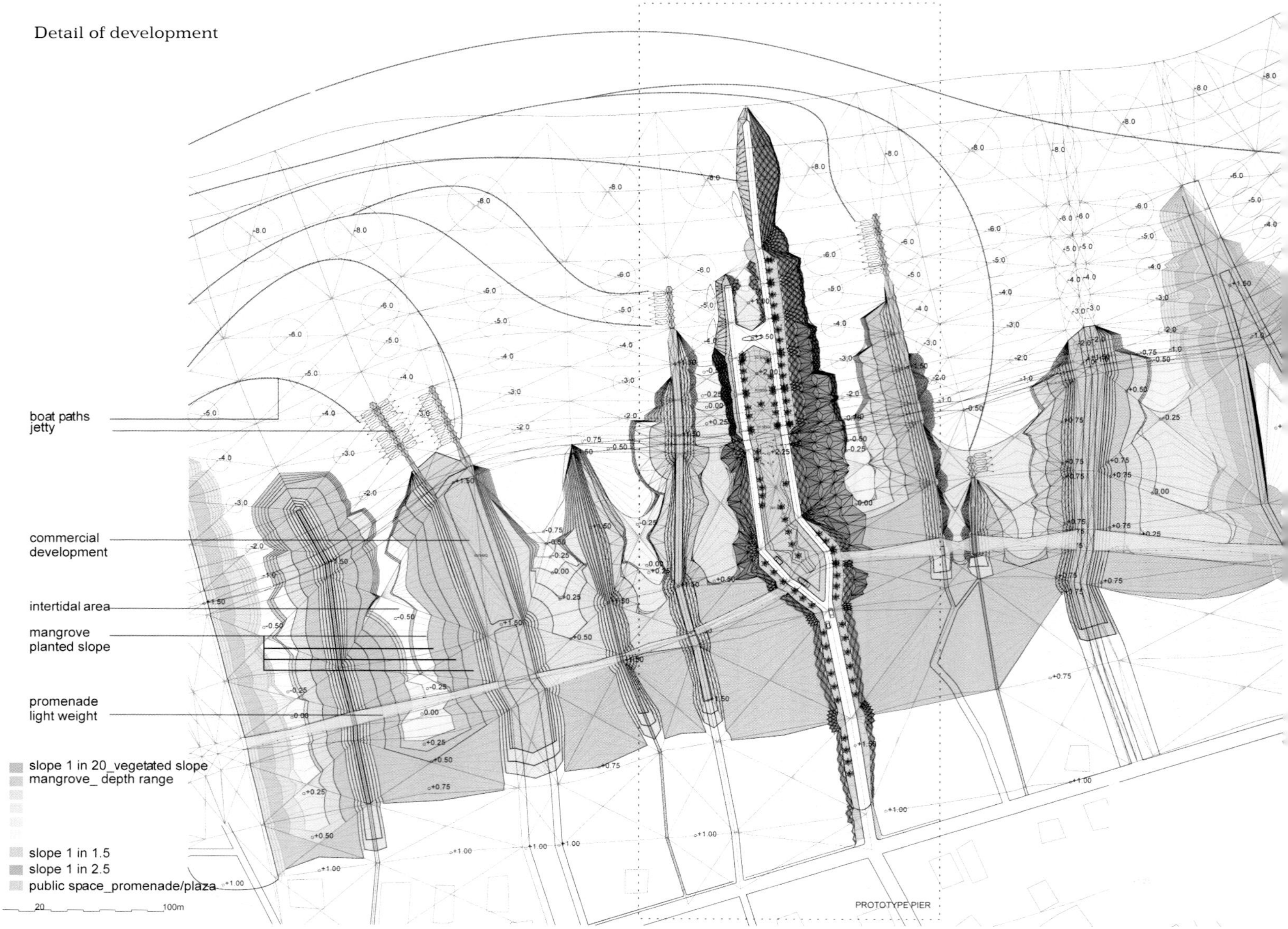

- boat paths
- jetty
- commercial development
- intertidal area
- mangrove planted slope
- promenade light weight

- slope 1 in 20_vegetated slope
- mangrove_ depth range
- slope 1 in 1.5
- slope 1 in 2.5
- public space_promenade/plaza

20   100m

CASE STUDY AREA

PROTOTYPE PIER

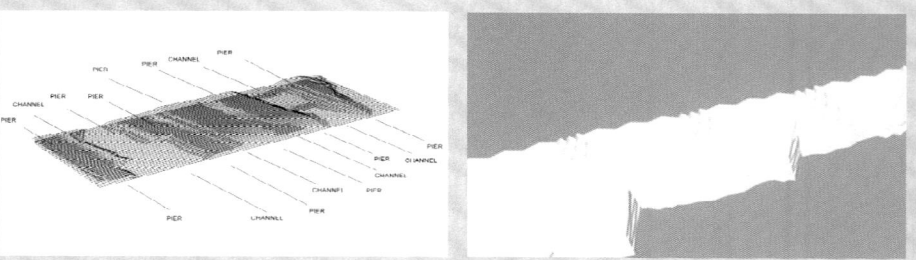

1. Topographic details
2. 3D pier skin

Component types

While a series of piers will define the space of the waterfront, these will subsequently be defined by modular components which articulate the overall inhabitable surface, differentiating slope into varying materiality, gradients and terraced surfaces. Through this variation, different conditions are produced and varying programmes can take place along the edge.

Detail of development

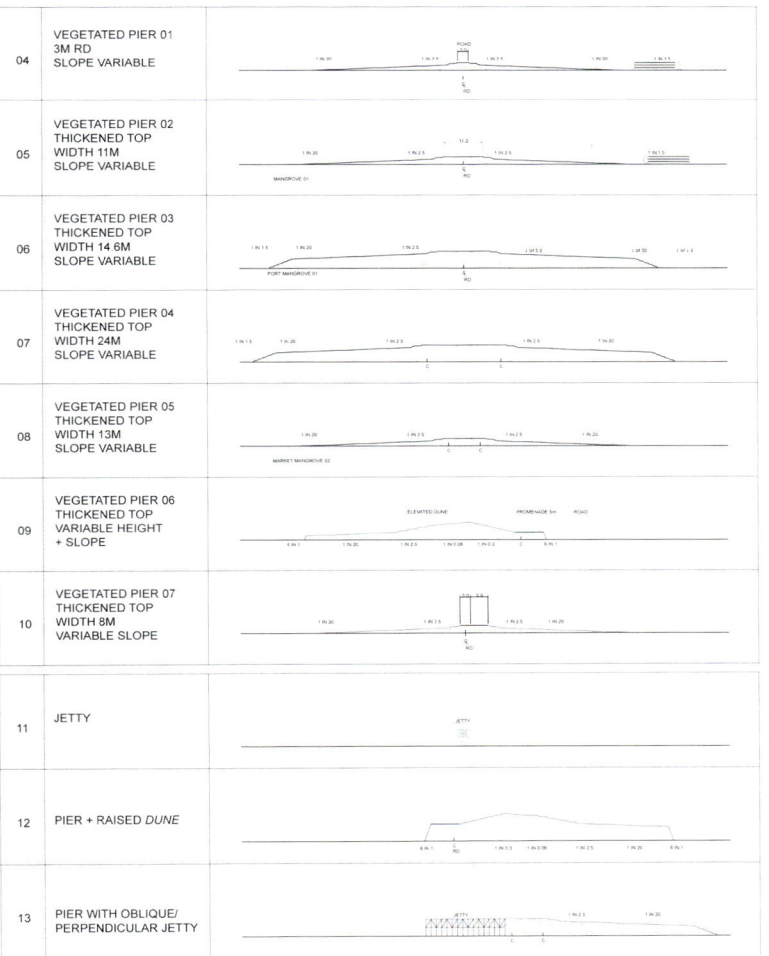
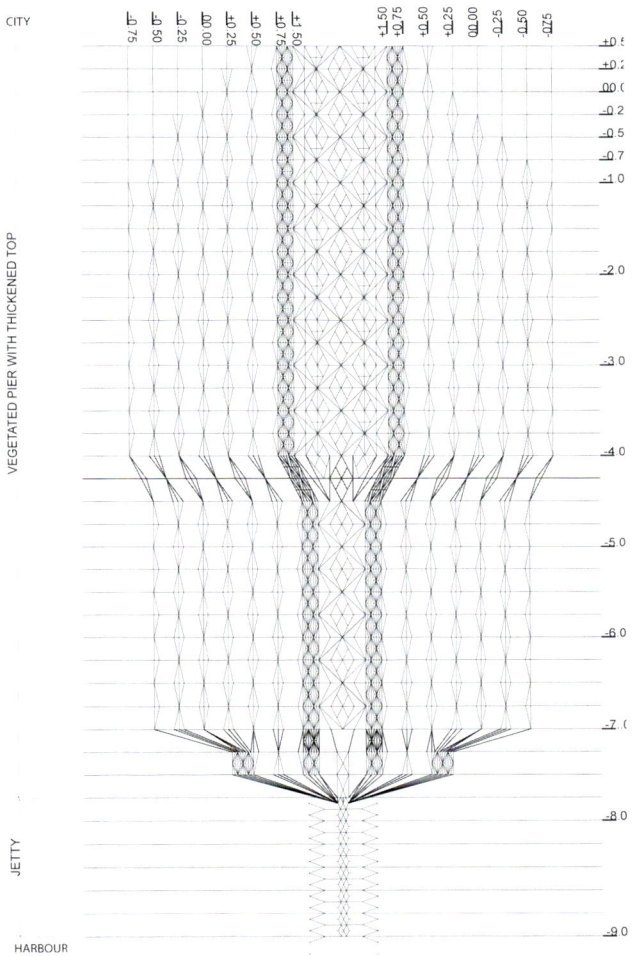

04	VEGETATED PIER 01 3M RD SLOPE VARIABLE	
05	VEGETATED PIER 02 THICKENED TOP WIDTH 11M SLOPE VARIABLE	
06	VEGETATED PIER 03 THICKENED TOP WIDTH 14.6M SLOPE VARIABLE	
07	VEGETATED PIER 04 THICKENED TOP WIDTH 24M SLOPE VARIABLE	
08	VEGETATED PIER 05 THICKENED TOP WIDTH 13M SLOPE VARIABLE	
09	VEGETATED PIER 06 THICKENED TOP VARIABLE HEIGHT + SLOPE	
10	VEGETATED PIER 07 THICKENED TOP WIDTH 8M VARIABLE SLOPE	
11	JETTY	
12	PIER + RAISED *DUNE*	
13	PIER WITH OBLIQUE/ PERPENDICULAR JETTY	

1. Steel sheet pile surface
2. Wood surface
3. Concrete surface

Catalogue of pier types

The reference section of a groyne is used as the basic type on which a catalogue of pier types is developed. The catalogue explores the variations in the slope, width and elevation of the piers. The reference catalogue has to incorporate both consistency and diversity, such that its distribution along the coastline generates a rich environment both in terms of its social inhabitation, and its ecological performance.

The component also indexes the tidal range, in the form of contour depths from -0.75m to +0.75m. By articulating the surface of the pier, different slopes and areas of terraced surface can be proliferated. Through this variation different conditions are produced and varying programmes can take place along the edge.

Phasing earthen pier construction

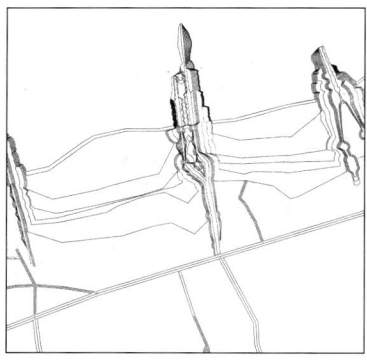

PHASE 1
This is generated by the main cross streets which link the two waterfronts. Construction is coordinated with the dredging of the port basin.

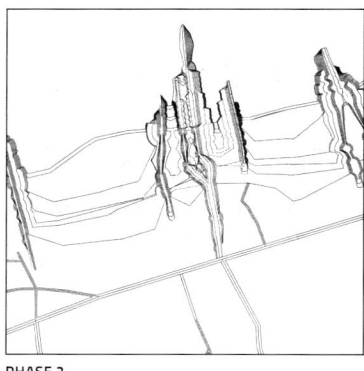

PHASE 2
This is generated by existing street access to the harbour. The secondary piers constructed as a by-product of port dredging.

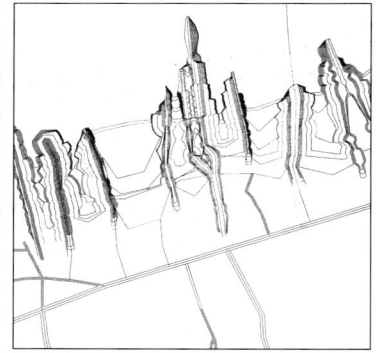

PHASE 3
These infill piers are located by the maximum width of a mangrove pier.

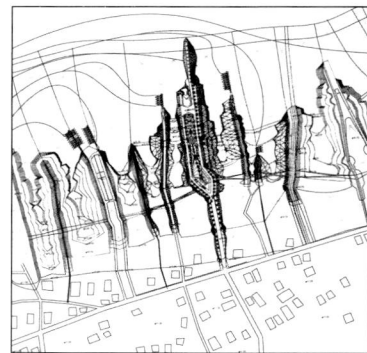

PHASE 4
This is related to the smallest scale pier. These are local projects to cater to the specific needs of the waterfront to which they are attached. In the case of residential areas, the fourth phase piers form small jetties to be used by shallow canoes, typical to the area.

Topography

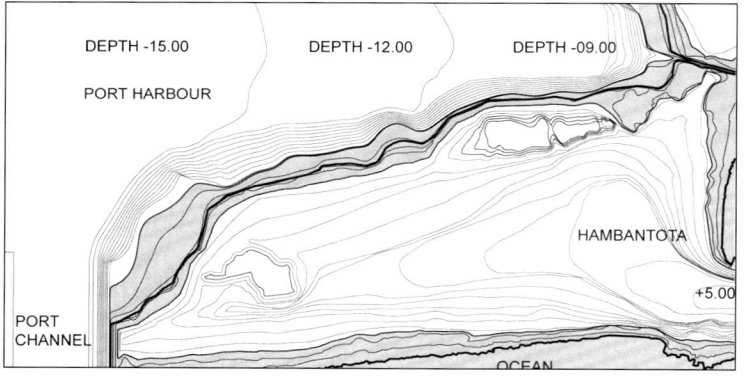

Extension of the street network

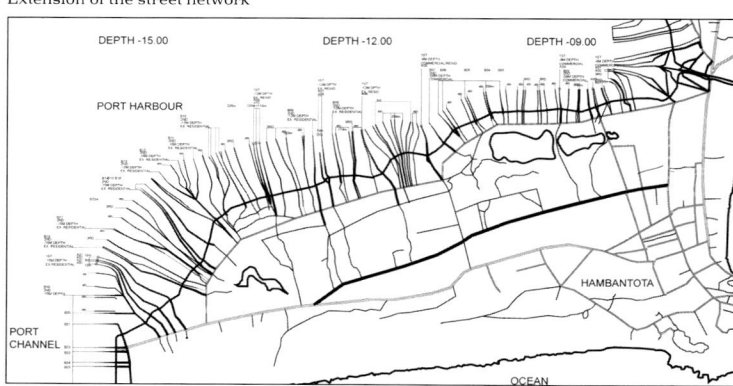

Beyond existing limits, into the harbour as per pier type organisation of the waterfront

1. The working mesh

The working mesh

The street network and topographic conditions generate a primary mesh which helps organise the location of piers, distribution of programmes and ultimately the general attributes of the spatial proposal. It functions as the primary ground organisation on which prototypycal piers are configured. This organisation is then fed further information relating to accessibility and the provision of urban infrastructure nearby.

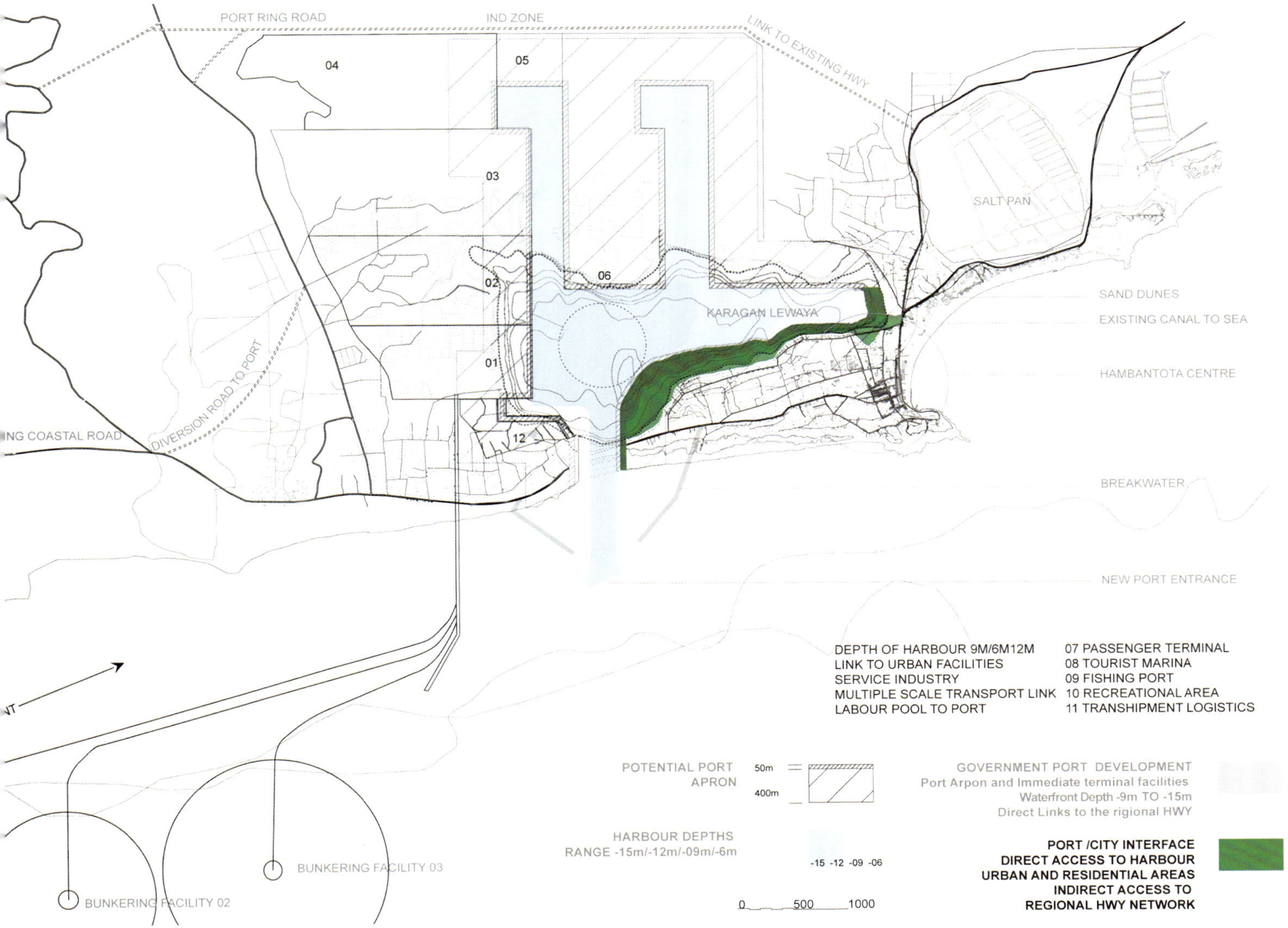

PORT RING ROAD
IND ZONE
LINK TO EXISTING HWY
04
05
03
02
01
06
12
SALT PAN
KARAGAN LEWAYA
SAND DUNES
EXISTING CANAL TO SEA
HAMBANTOTA CENTRE
BREAKWATER
NEW PORT ENTRANCE
NG COASTAL ROAD
DIVERSION ROAD TO PORT
DEPTH OF HARBOUR 9M/6M12M
LINK TO URBAN FACILITIES
SERVICE INDUSTRY
MULTIPLE SCALE TRANSPORT LINK
LABOUR POOL TO PORT
07 PASSENGER TERMINAL
08 TOURIST MARINA
09 FISHING PORT
10 RECREATIONAL AREA
11 TRANSHIPMENT LOGISTICS
POTENTIAL PORT APRON
50m
400m
GOVERNMENT PORT DEVELOPMENT
Port Arpon and Immediate terminal facilities
Waterfront Depth -9m TO -15m
Direct Links to the rigional HWY
HARBOUR DEPTHS
RANGE -15m/-12m/-09m/-6m
-15 -12 -09 -06
PORT /CITY INTERFACE
DIRECT ACCESS TO HARBOUR
URBAN AND RESIDENTIAL AREAS
INDIRECT ACCESS TO
REGIONAL HWY NETWORK
BUNKERING FACILITY 03
BUNKERING FACILITY 02
0 500 1000

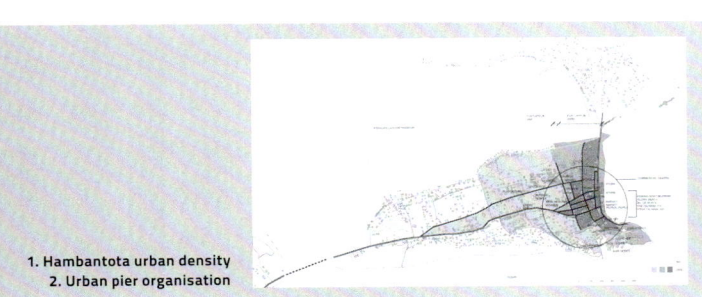

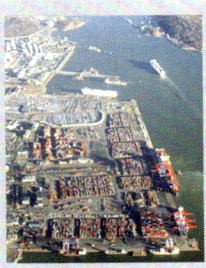

1. Hambantota urban density
2. Urban pier organisation

City and port development in Hambantota

As ports grew mainly due to containerisation, the port demanded more ground area, ports reclaimed land, or moved to the periphery of the city. The split between city and port created areas of vacant land in the city centre on the waterfront. The situation in Hambantota is one where a contemporary port development is located adjacent to the city-centre, city and port will have a common waterfront.

The port apron is prime real estate, and the critical area which allows the port to function. The first 50m around the water's edge is used for loading and unloading of freight, followed by the next 400m, which allows for storage and transport access.

Prototype proliferation

Prototype development initial clusters

Initial geometric manipulations
These basic studies develop the geometric parameters by which the component functions.

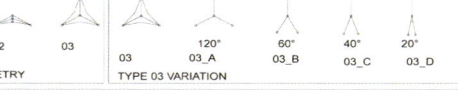
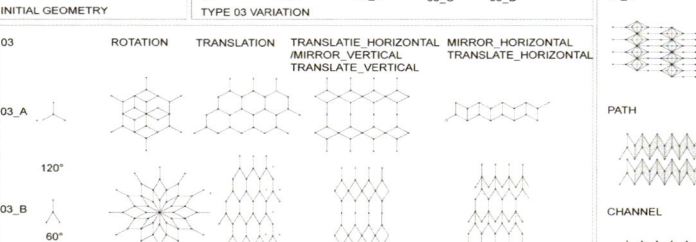
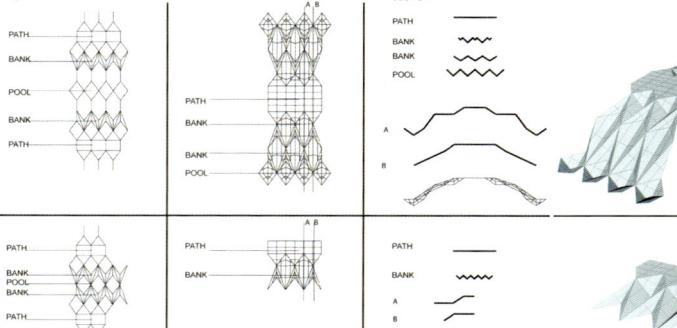
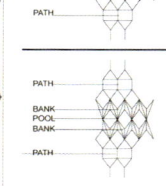
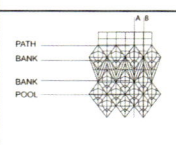
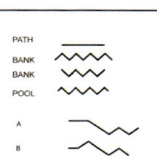

Geometric Relationship

The initial geometry and diamond grid is loselybased on a field of sand dunes.
Dunes stabilised by vegetation create a buffer condition along the coast.
A field of coastal sand dunes, form an arrangement alternating between depressions and dunes (mounds), perpendicular to the wind direction.

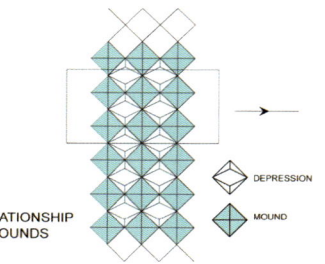

PLAN_THE ALTERNATING RELATIONSHIP BETWEEN DEPRESSIONS + MOUNDS

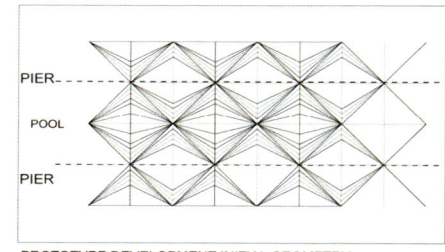

PROTOTYPE DEVELOPMENT INITIAL GEOMETRY

1/2. Component in sequence - 3D

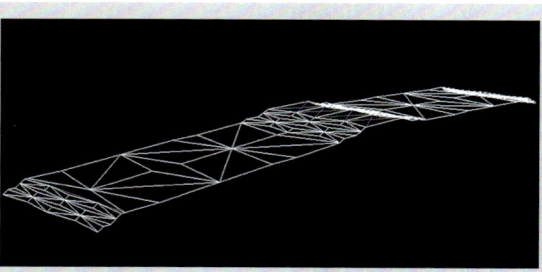

The earthen piers are a hybrid coastal infrastructure. Their performance range between the types of a pier/seawall and groyne. The piers are constructed from material dredged out of the lagoon basin to achieve required port draft.

Its geometry is organised by height above mean sea level, incorporating variations according to the local tidal range, and the slope variation. The varying slopes allow for different materials to be used as a stabilising skin on the piers, ranging from hard to soft scape, from gently sloping vegetation to vertical concrete piles, ultimately generating spatial diversity and allowing for a variety of conditions and programmes.

Perspective view

Perspective view

AALU Sri Lanka 05/06

Retention flood plains

Date **2005/06**
Location **Sri Lanka**
Author **Eduardo Carranza**

Project description

The project focuses on Matara, one of the coastal cities which suffered from the tsunami's catastrophe. This city is built around the Nilwala River, which divides the city into two parts. While the city traditionally has based its economy on the river, it has also suffered from the threats it poses, both serving as a gateway for tsunami waves to enter the mainland, but also causing massive seasonal floods during the periods of the monsoon. This natural process regularly damages the urban landscape of Matara, hampering its growth and development.

A masterplan strategy to develop an urban park was proposed within the agricultural areas, undeveloped open space and dispersed settlements along the river. The plan did not address the river in its broader scale nor as a systemic principle and considered it from a zoning perspective. The project took this plan as an opportunity to explore a different strategy in response to the complexity of Matara's urban development and the embedded natural processes of the river. Retention floodplains is a bottom-up scheme which proposes to build a territorial strategy to mediate the seasonal flooding of the Nilwala River with Matara's urban fabric reconstruction and development. Through the assemblage and performance of SUD (Sustainable Urban Drainage) landscape techniques, the project generates a robust landscape of proliferated ponds and swales to create areas for flow attenuation. These landscape elements negotiate strips of urban park with a new network of road infrastructure and pedestrian paths. They define higher areas for urban consolidation, lower areas for drainage and evacuation corridors along the river and into the city.

Retention floodplains is a diagrammatic response to negotiate the development of local activities for a potential sustainable relocation of Matara's fishermen. Rainwater harvesting, permaculture and river markets are considered in this new spatial strategy to regenerate the affected livelihood of fishermen after the tsunami.

1. Site conditions; Nilwala River

Site strategy

The site is a 2km² area located within the centre of the city which runs along the floodplain of the Nilwala River. The strategy proposes an organisational system linked to the existing built conditions, the location of agricultural areas and its connection to the transport networks. These territorial elements will define the basis of an operative ground for new patterns of urban infrastructure, occupation and programmed activities along the river.

The final aim is to inform the relationship between open space and the existing dispersed settlements within the site. It develops as a geometric and spatial tool that negotiates the relation between length and proximity.

Detail of development

Cluster 03
Comercial area
+ Market area
+ Housing
Raised level of the ground

New Area for Housing

New Area for Housing

Cluster 01

Section 01 - 02

Cluster 02

500m x 500m

Nilwala River

Cluster 04

New Area for Housing

Section 03

Local Train Station + Housing

Zoom in

1. Site conditions

A combination of two skeletons is generated as an initial site structure to organise the spatial outcome of the project. The existing settlements are grouped and allow ways of accessibility within the open space, defining a geometric pattern with equidistant points between each building and generating a right of way through the open space. This initial skeleton starts to suggest potential connections and road layouts. A second iteration of the same geometric tool produces a new collection of midpoints, which is the base for a second skeleton defining drainage lines. This second skeleton mediates between the existing settlements and the first skeleton.

Based on these two skeletons, a new striated topography is proposed. The skeleton of accessibility defines a set of high-level contours for site-wide circulation, while the drainage skeleton defines the lower level contours for new floodplains that could be developed over time.

Site conditions

Prototype proliferation – urban parks topography

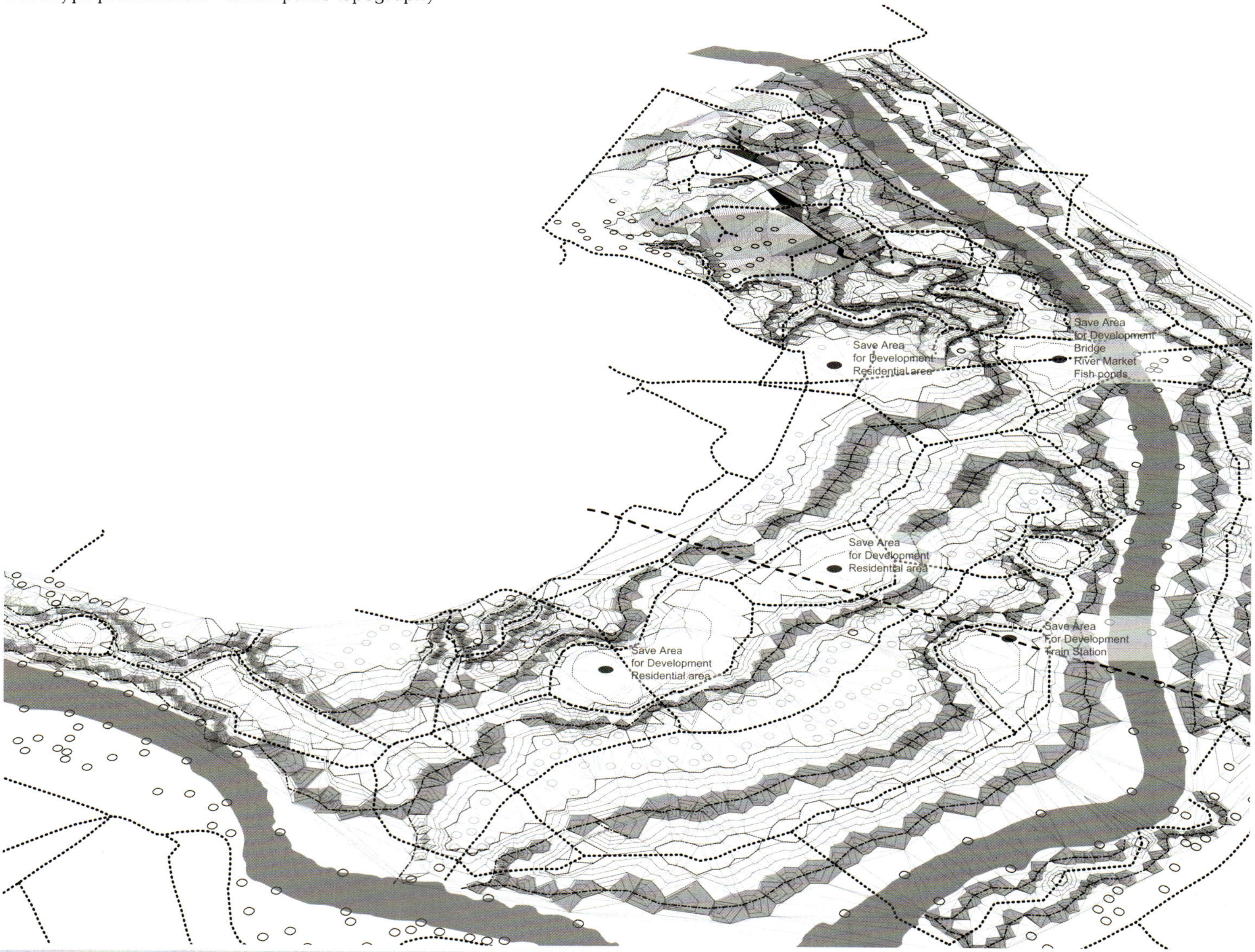

1. Agricultural lands
2. Coastline market

Through a last iteration of the voronoi geometry, the limits of the buffer areas are traced into another collection of points to incorporate the proliferation of drainage areas and consolidate the flood basins.

The tessellated mesh is the base for a new topography where the prototypical section of the SUDS technique can be proliferated to create the strips of urban parks and where safe areas are generated for potential urban development.

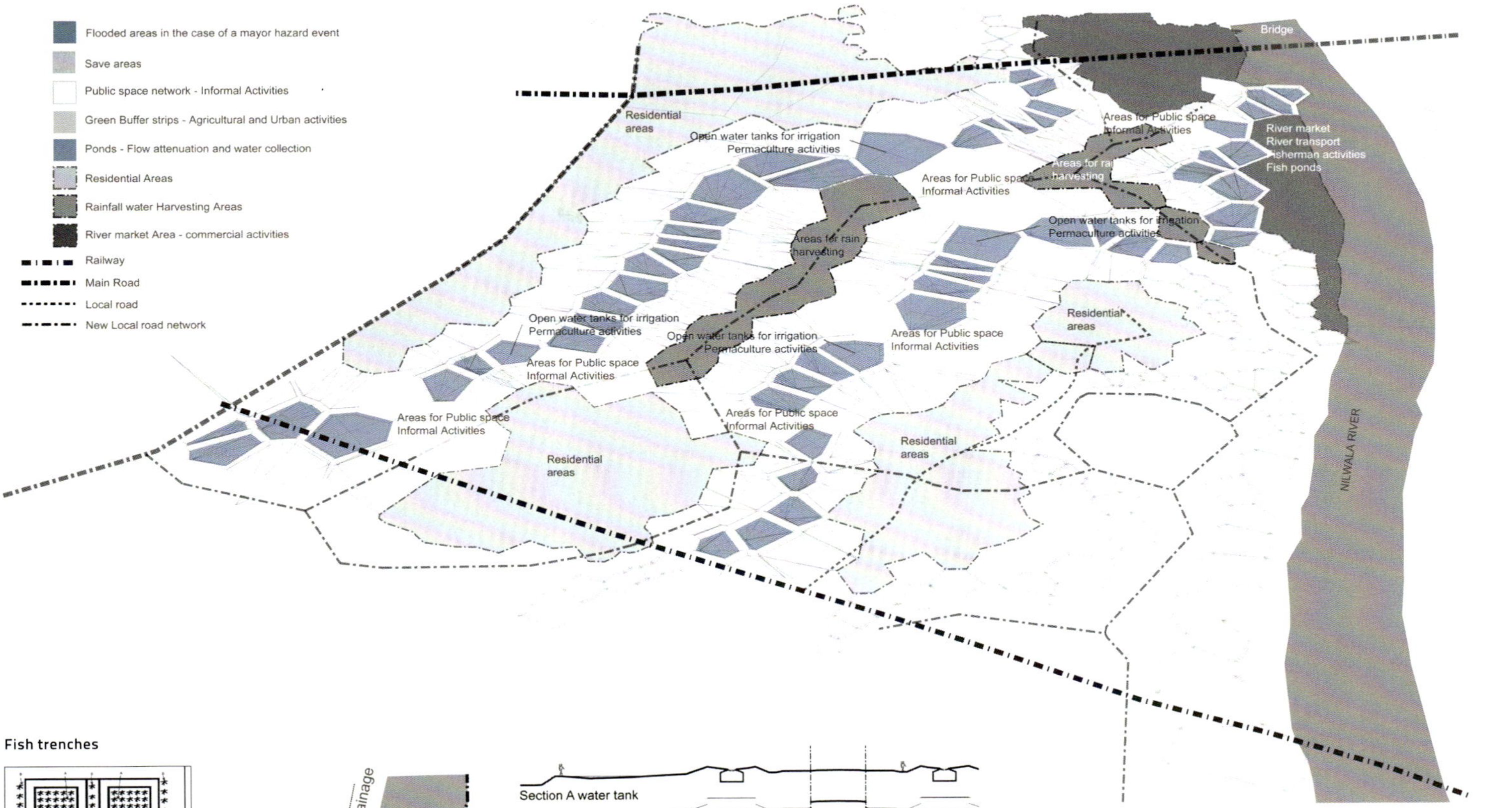

Flooded areas in the case of a mayor hazard event
Save areas
Public space network - Informal Activities
Green Buffer strips - Agricultural and Urban activities
Ponds - Flow attenuation and water collection
Residential Areas
Rainfall water Harvesting Areas
River market Area - commercial activities
Railway
Main Road
Local road
New Local road network
Bridge
Residential areas
Open water tanks for irrigation
Permaculture activities
River market
River transport
Fish ponds
Open water tanks for irrigation
Permaculture activities
Open water tanks for irrigation
Permaculture activities
Areas for Public space
Informal Activities
Areas for Public space
Informal Activities
Areas for Public space
Informal Activities
Residential areas
Residential areas
Residential areas
NILWALA RIVER

Fish trenches

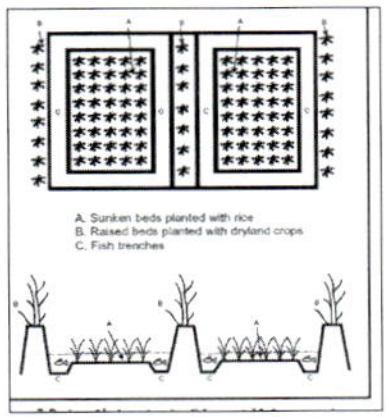

Indonesian rice-fish-vegetable farm:
- Refuge if water level drops
- A path for fish to have better access for feeding in the rice field.
- Catch basin during harvesting.

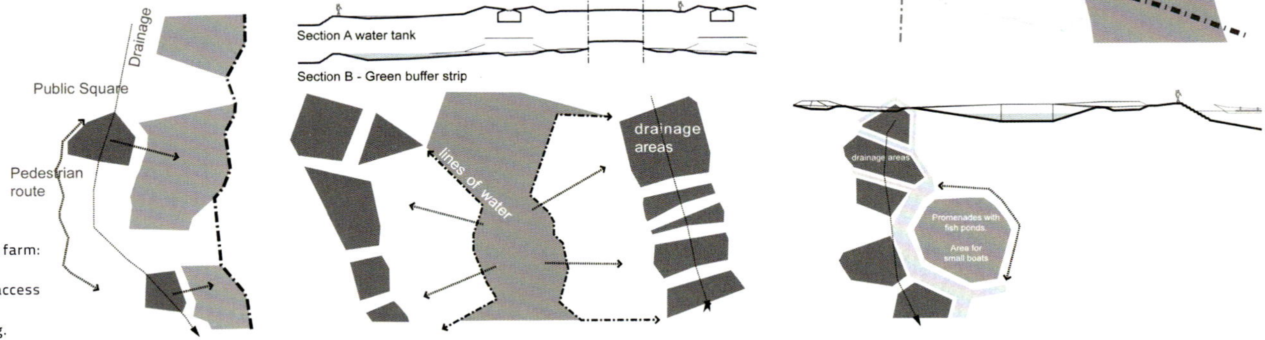

Drainage
Public Square
Pedestrian route
Section A water tank
Section B - Green buffer strip
lines of water
drainage areas
drainage areas
Promenades with fish ponds.
Area for small boats

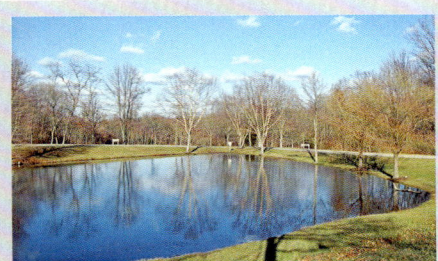

1. Landscape materiality: ponds

Urban park 01 - Permaculture
Rice Fish farming is a practice in Asian countries in which fish are bred and harvested in rice fields.

Urban park 02 - Rainwater harversting
The rainwater tanks are on a domestic scale, and can store about 10,000 litres of rainwater at a time, sufficient to irrigate a quarter or half an acre of land, to successfully grow 35-40 perennial crops such as `Jak`, coconut, pomegranate, orange and mango.

Urban park 03 - River markets
The Nilwala River is a natural feature within the city of Matara. It is a means by which relocated fishermen can have access to the sea, thereby becoming a potential way of transport.

Prototype detention pond – sedimentation basin

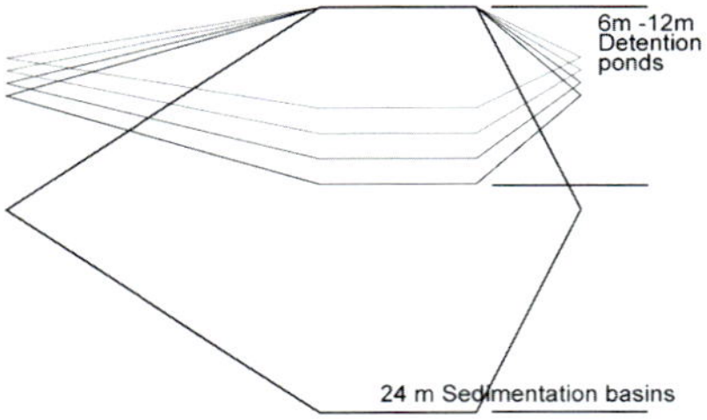

Site area = 2 km²
Rainfall December 1999 = 720 mm
Average rainfall intensity = 23 mm/day
Detention ponds = Storage within 48 hrs
Maximum depth = 3m

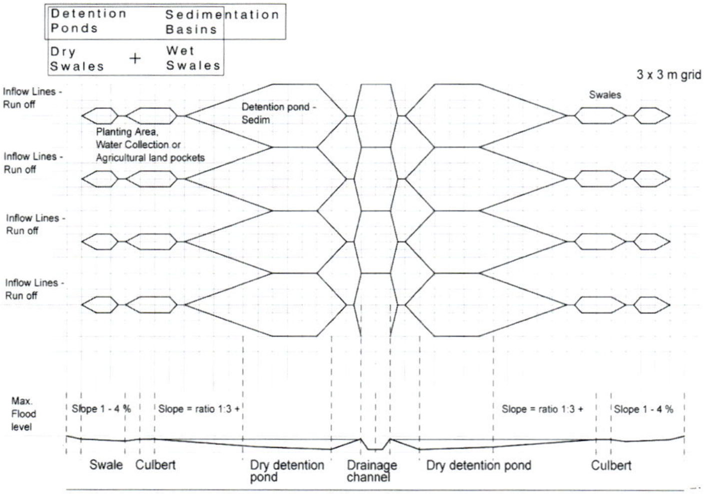

6m – 12m Detention ponds
24 m Sedimentation basins

Sustainable urban drainage – landscape technique

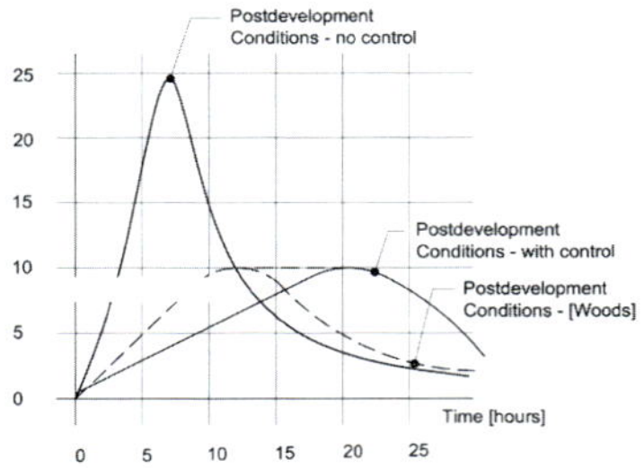

Component 01 - Swales
Water storage within 24 hrs

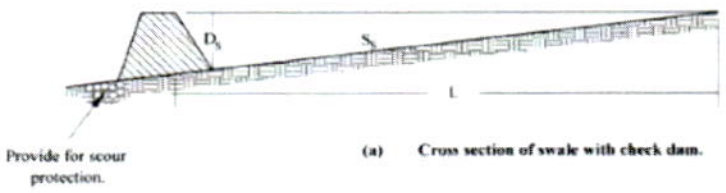

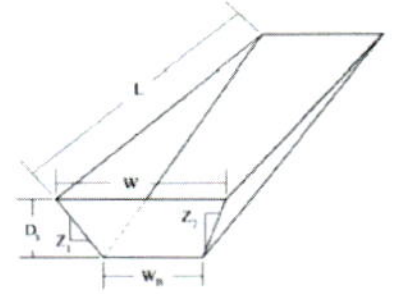

Component 02 - Ponds
Water storage within 48 hrs

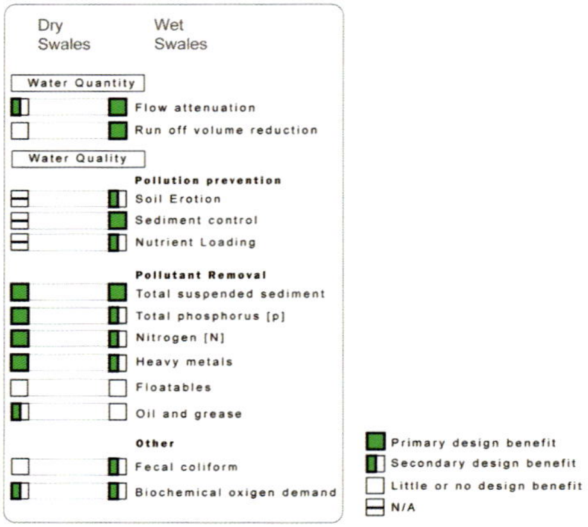

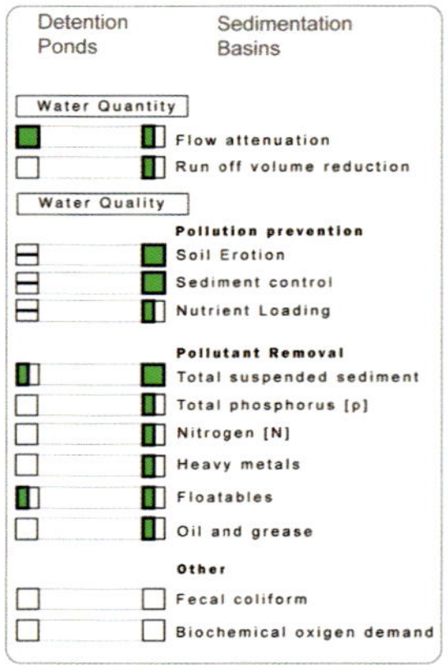

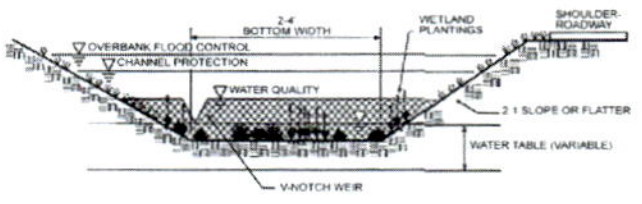

Figure 3. Wet Swale Cross Section
Source: Center for Watershed Protection, 2001

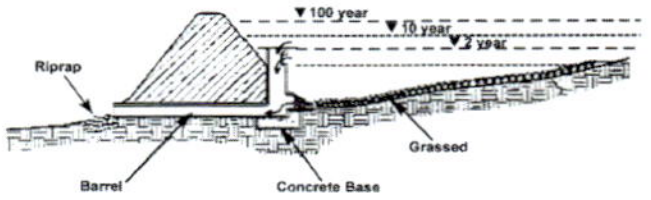

Figure 1: Typical Dry Pond
Source: NVPDC, 1992

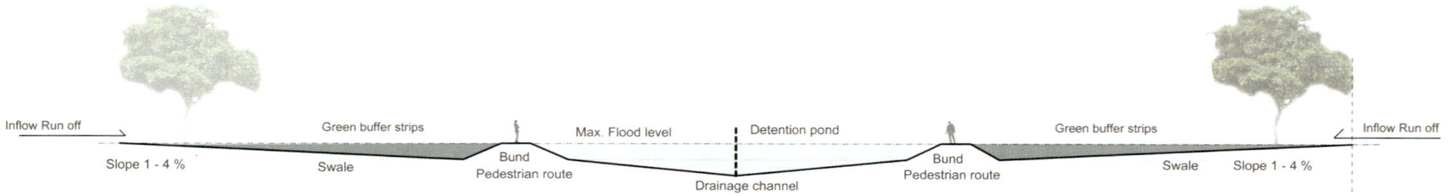

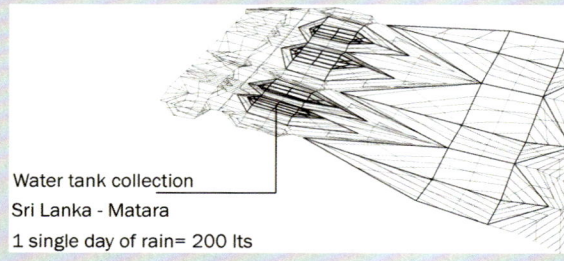

1. Water tank collection

Water tank collection
Sri Lanka - Matara
1 single day of rain = 200 lts

Prototype development (I)

A prototype is designed incorporating physical parameters and constraints from stormwater management and flood control systems.

In the case of detention ponds and sedimentation basins a retention period of 48 hours is assumed, while in the case of grassed channels, dry swales and wet swales, this retention period comes down to 24 hours.

Through the process of proliferation, the aim is to build an armature of ponds and swales which can bring along clusters of local activity to diversify the urban conditions of the landscape as well as its performance as stormwater retention infrastructure.

Prototype development

Design constraints

Slopes, depth, distance and ratios are indexed to condition the capaties of both acomponents and also avoid problems of erosion .

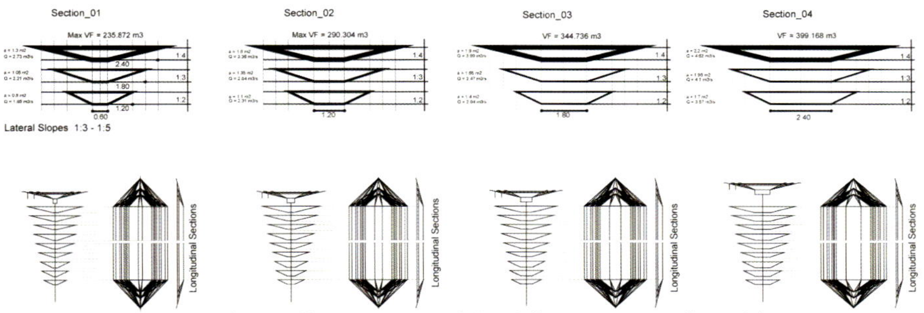

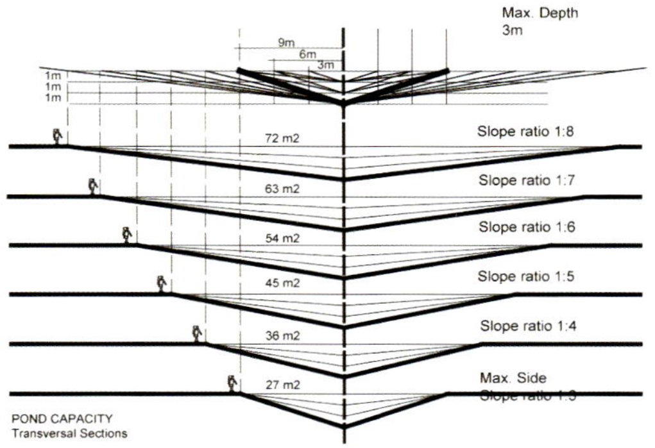

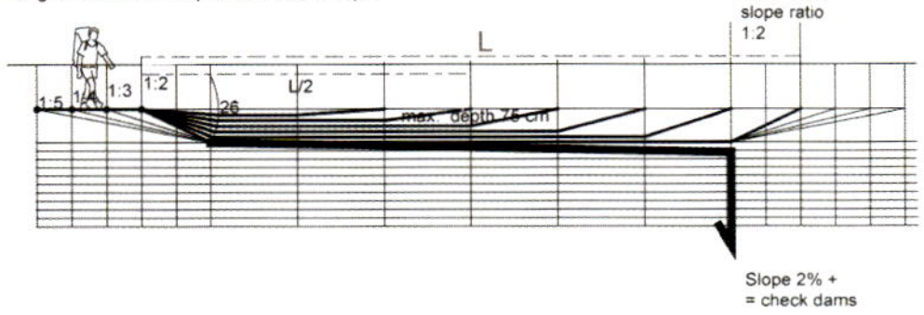

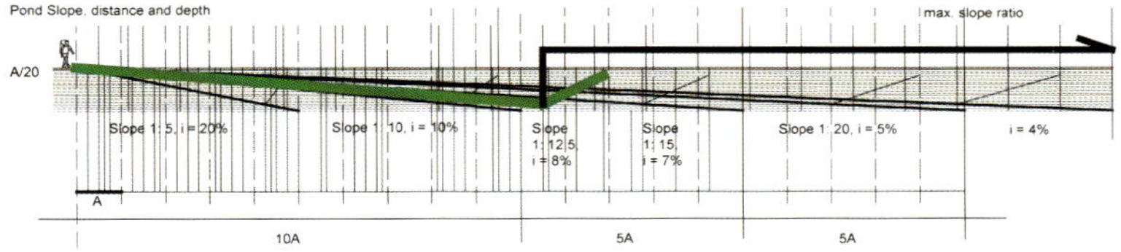

Prototype

Along the drainage areas detention ponds will be proliferated based on its technical design constraints. Swales will be deployed within the buffer zone areas to drain water into the ponds where the slopes are less than 5%.

performance 01

Stormwater detention area

performance 02

Stormwater detention area

performance 03

Stormwater detention area

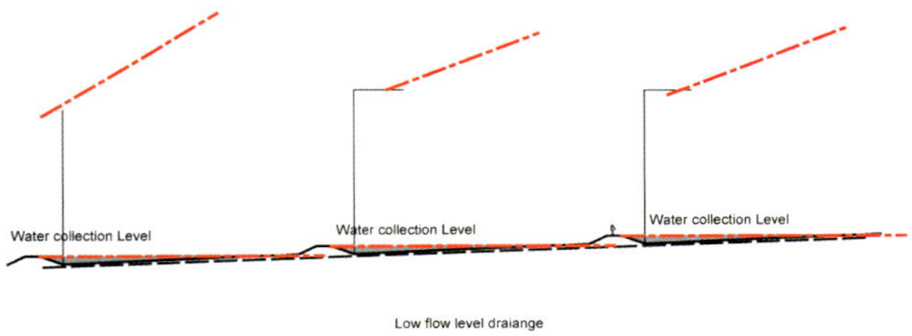

Longitudinal Section_Cascade System_Flow attenuation

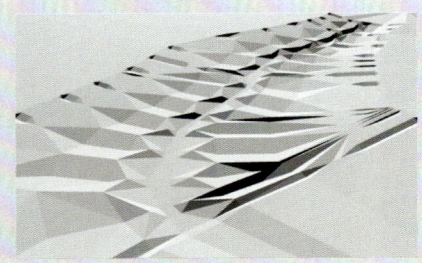

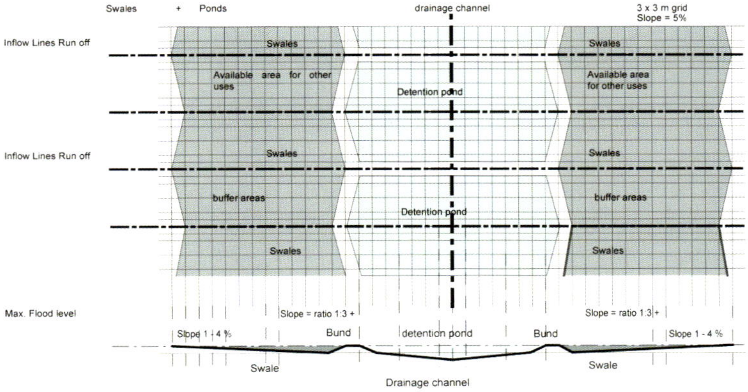

Storm water and Flood control prototype

1. System proliferation

Prototype deployment (II)

Along the drainage skeleton, a parameter of 5° of slope for people accessibility is applied. This creates continuous strips of swales and ponds, defining buffer zones between the drainage skeleton and the existing settlements.

The result of this material performance is proliferated in order to consolidate strips of urban park that will articulate public space with private space. The diversity and material richness embedded in the definition of the prototype becomes a key factor in the generation of a spatially rich environment.

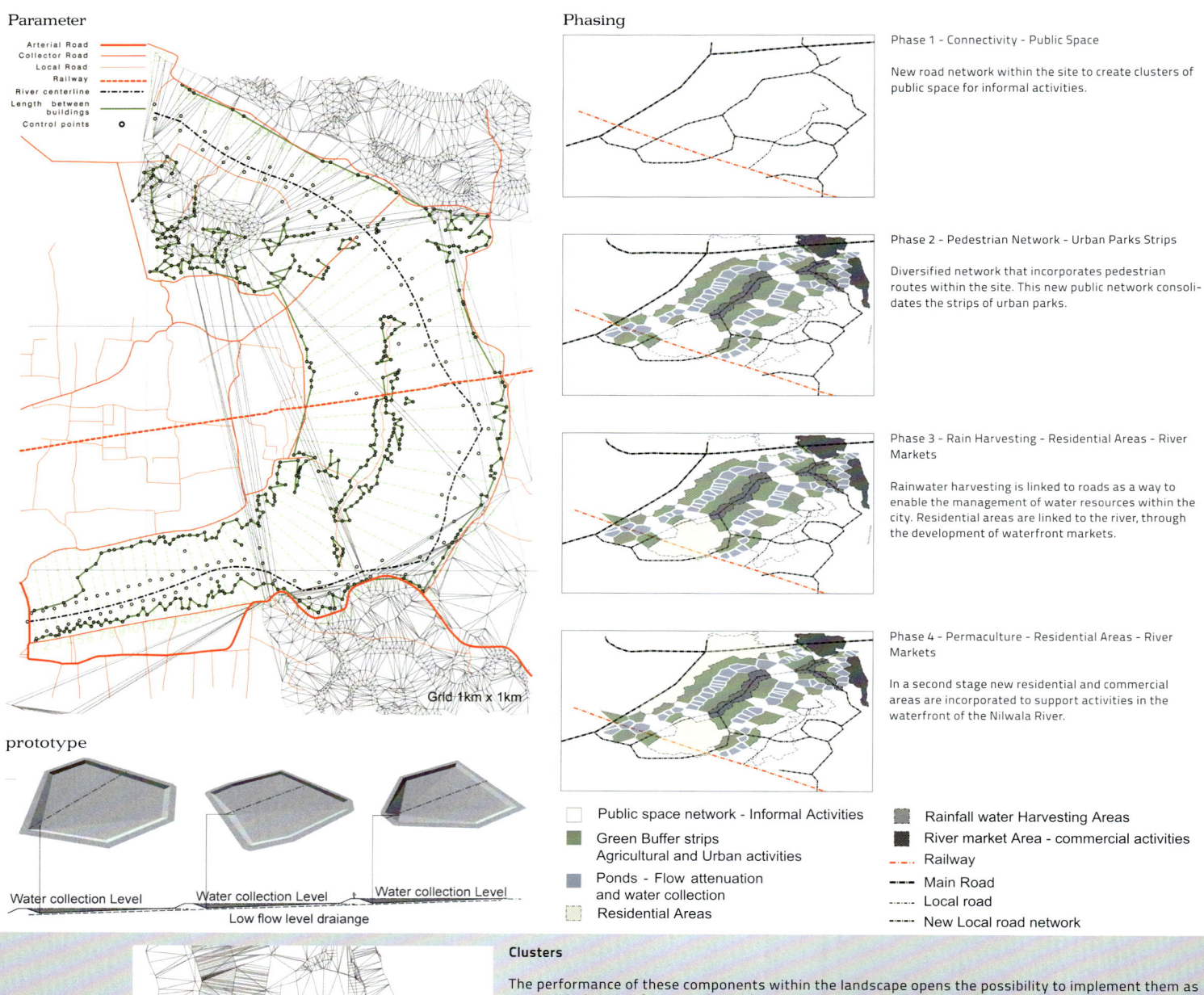

Parameter

- Arterial Road
- Collector Road
- Local Road
- Railway
- River centerline
- Length between buildings
- Control points

Grid 1km x 1km

prototype

Water collection Level — Water collection Level — Water collection Level
Low flow level draiange

Phasing

Phase 1 - Connectivity - Public Space

New road network within the site to create clusters of public space for informal activities.

Phase 2 - Pedestrian Network - Urban Parks Strips

Diversified network that incorporates pedestrian routes within the site. This new public network consolidates the strips of urban parks.

Phase 3 - Rain Harvesting - Residential Areas - River Markets

Rainwater harvesting is linked to roads as a way to enable the management of water resources within the city. Residential areas are linked to the river, through the development of waterfront markets.

Phase 4 - Permaculture - Residential Areas - River Markets

In a second stage new residential and commercial areas are incorporated to support activities in the waterfront of the Nilwala River.

- Public space network - Informal Activities
- Green Buffer strips — Agricultural and Urban activities
- Ponds - Flow attenuation and water collection
- Residential Areas
- Rainfall water Harvesting Areas
- River market Area - commercial activities
- Railway
- Main Road
- Local road
- New Local road network

1. Tessellated mesh

Clusters

The performance of these components within the landscape opens the possibility to implement them as prototypical spaces for a new form of urbanity. Urban parks become a more operative landscape, allowing the combination and deployment of cultural activities that can help support urban life together with the provision of urban infrastructures. It aims to build a public and transport network within the site that could encourage the local economy of the city.

Retention floodplains is a prototypical strategy that creates a particular rugosity in the landscape to respond not just to flood control, but to a variety of other ancillary activities.
The deployment of this hybridised prototype remains in the landscape as a pre-physical infrastructure for flood control that could work as design guidelines for further development.

Prototype proliferation.

Prototype proliferation

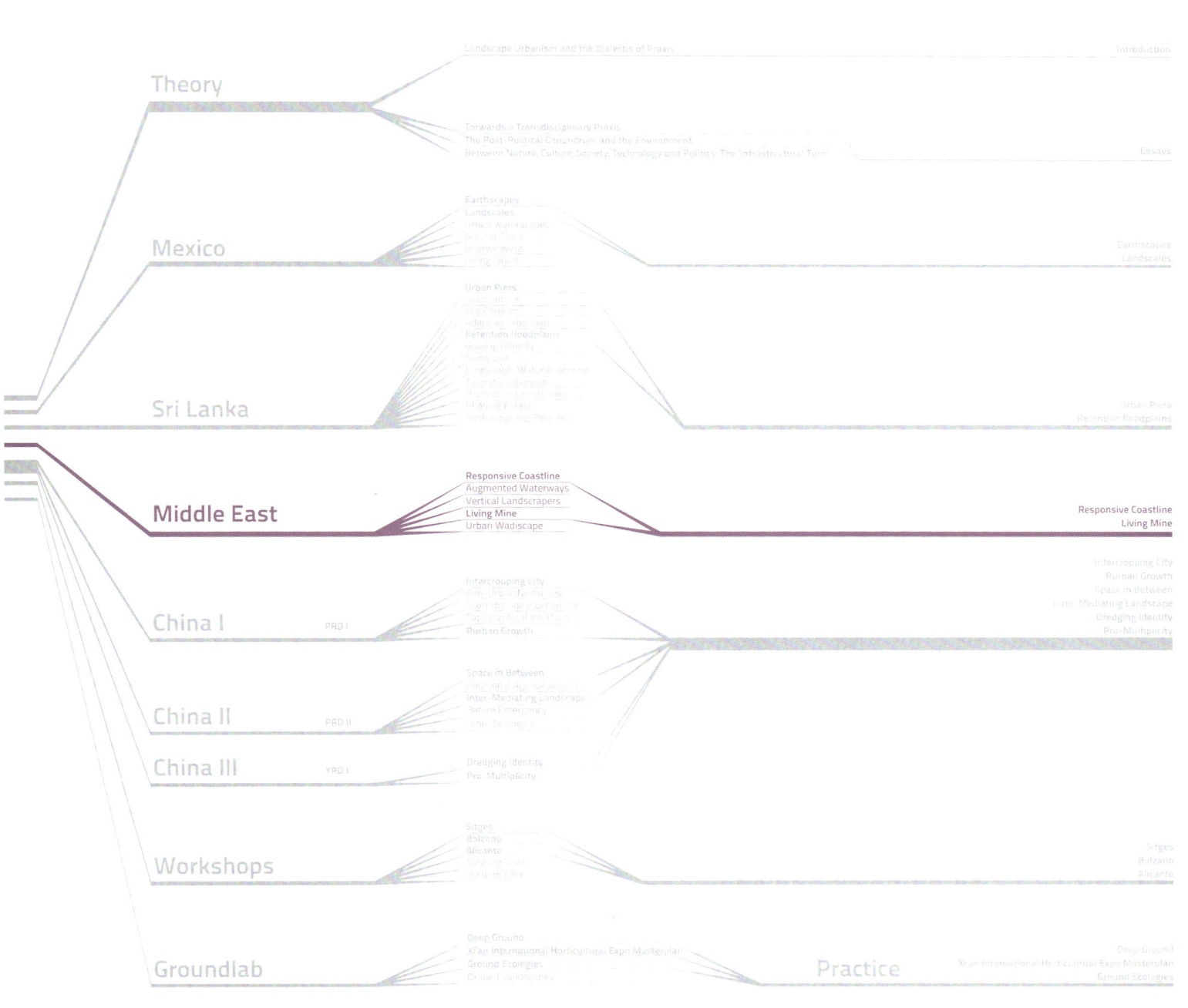

AA Landscape Urbanism 06/07
The Politics of Environment – Dubai

AGENDA The tight relationship between the environment, its natural resources, and the modern history of the Middle East is unavoidable; this simple, albeit powerful equation has, over the past fifty years or so, fuelled a series of major developments with implications ranging from the global to the regional and the local scales. In this case it seems appropriate to extend the characterisation of an 'extreme environment' – often assigned to the desert – to embrace and describe also local economic, social and political conditions, resulting in a concoction whose degree of excess and intensity generates an acute state of fragile equilibrium. Despite the environmental implications, human dependence on non-renewable energy resources continues to increase. In the UAE, for example, the oil consumption (per capita) is 1.21 barrels per day per 10 people (ranked 6th of 2070), a growing dependency that has largely annihilated the further development of alternative industries. At the same time, a high population growth, together with the rising participation of women in the labour force, is translating into a rapidly growing national labour force, which, given the limited room for further employment in the government sector, is generating an unemployment trend that has started to increase in most GCC countries. The governments, not oblivious to this fact, are engaging with a sustained pick-up in non-oil growth, exemplary of which is Qatar, committed to invest over $15 billion in R&D.

AALU Dubai 06/07

Living Mine
Fang Chun-Chien

Date **2006/07**
Location **Dubai**
Author **Fang Chun-Chien**

Project Description

The growing export of aggregates to neighbouring Dubai has fuelled a massive transformation of the surrounding hills into a degraded mix of spaces leftover from open cast mining activities. This is driving Muscat to turn its back on its surrounding landscape and to miss an opportunity to fabricate a new form of meaningful urban landscape which recognises the need for further expansion. The project tries to use the potential opened by the mining activity to think about the way in which urban growth relates to primary economies of mineral extraction, looking for opportunities for creating new synergies in terms of economies of scale and spatial outcomes.

The expansion of tourism and urban growth is ultimately organised by the mining technique through mass-produced pit formations accommodating specific programmatic requirements that converge from a central mining methodology structure system. A series of new public programmes was strategically distributed by responding to new artificial topographies generated during the mining extraction, maximising its tourist potential and residential use to host the city's growing population. The mining organisation provides different phases which respond to the urban infrastructure growth and inform the urban typology and layout of subsequent residential developments.

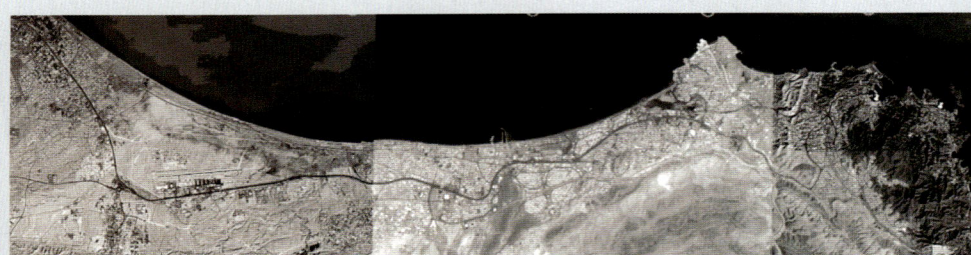

1. Muscat and its surroundings

Site location
Muscat is one of the fastest-growing cities in the Middle East and also the capital city of Oman.
The city is sited in between the hills and the sea. It attracts 9.2% tourist growth each year, but has failed to provide feasible tourist infrastructure and also lacks housing planning to accommodate its fast-growing population. Current urban growth is oriented toward the hill side of the city boundary, and is set to move further up its slopes.

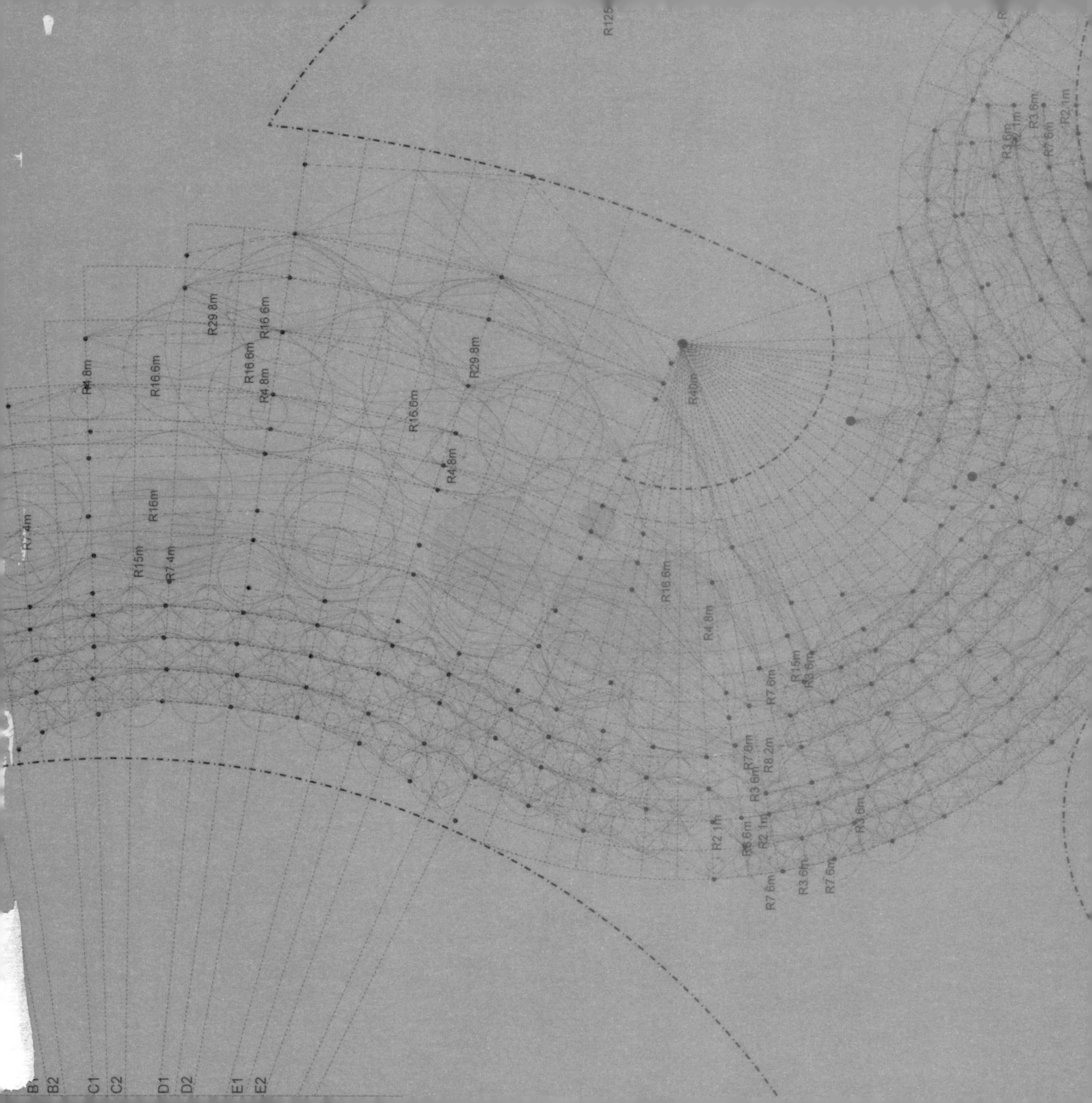

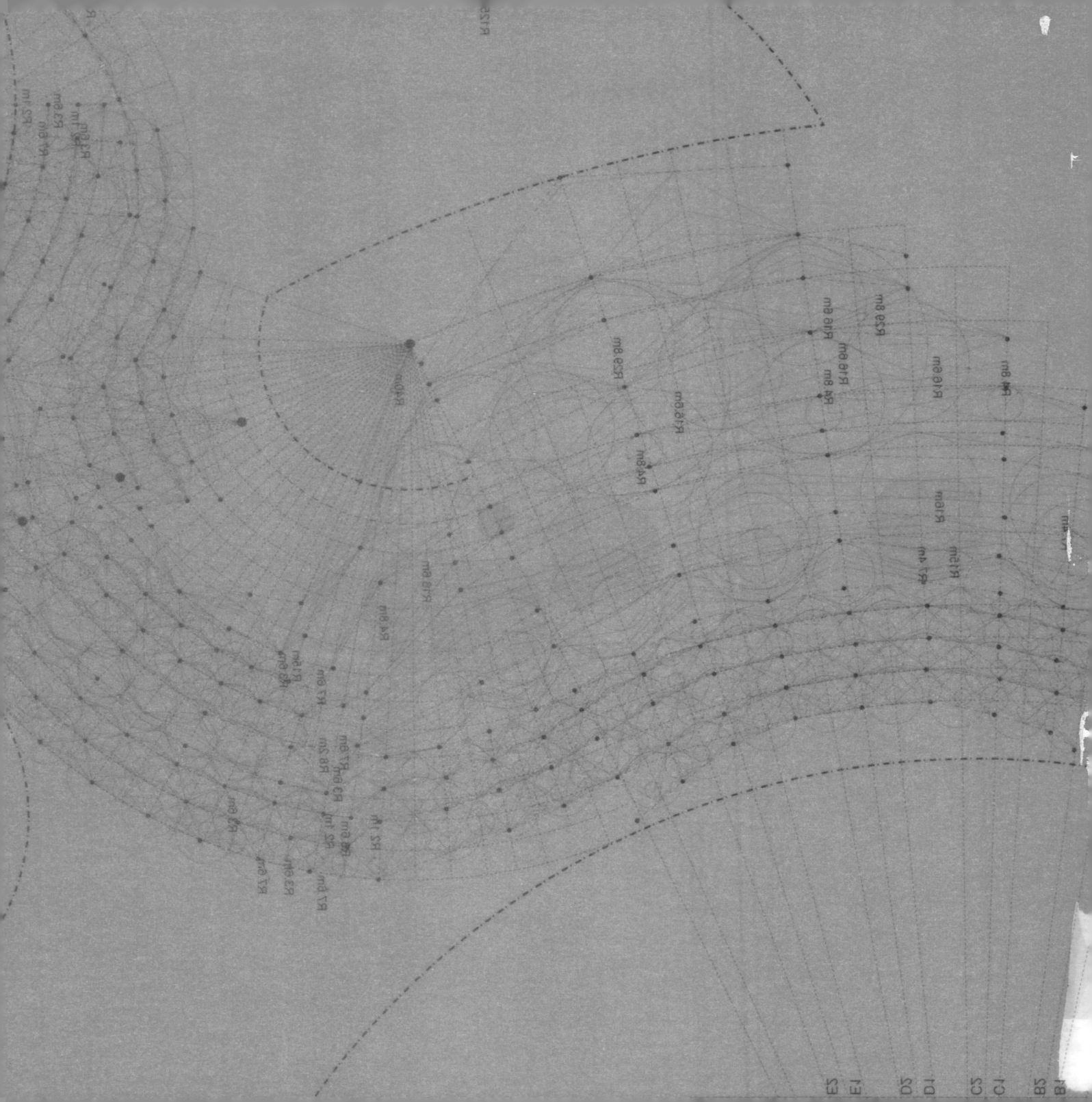

Site conditions

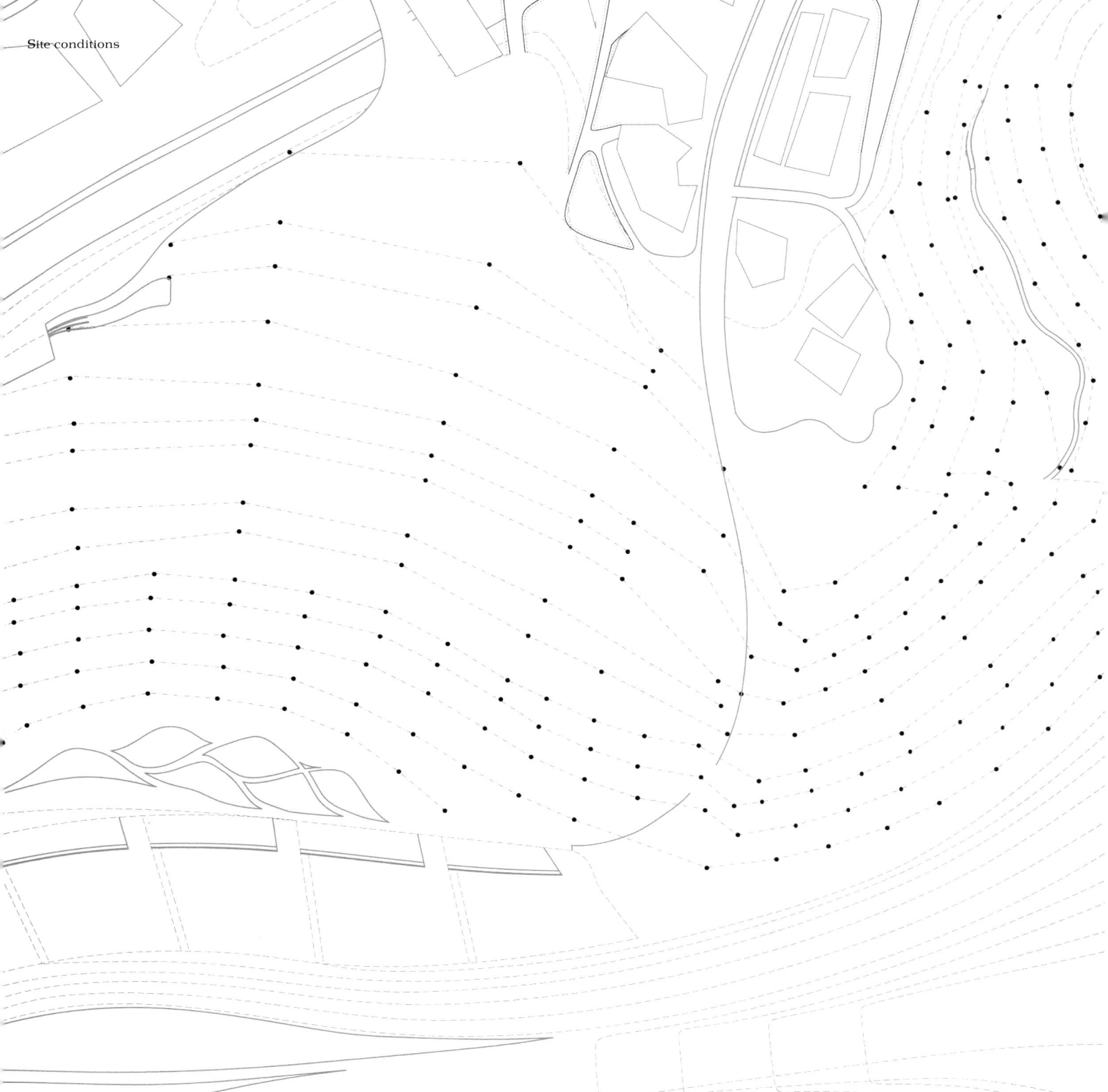

Overall proposal

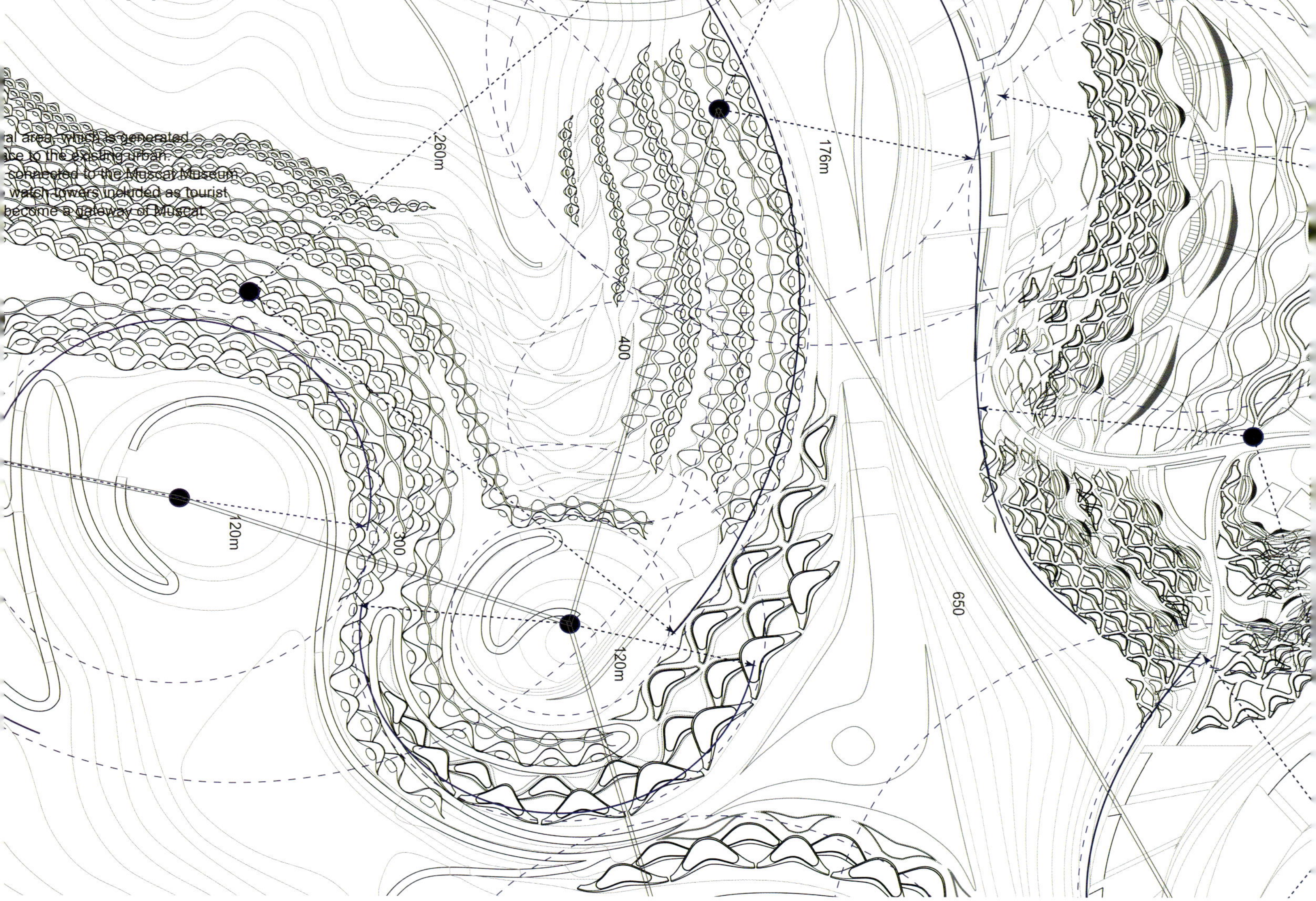

al area, which is generated
ace to the existing urban
connected to the Muscat Museum
watch towers included as tourist
become a gateway of Muscat
260m
176m
400
120m
300
120m
650

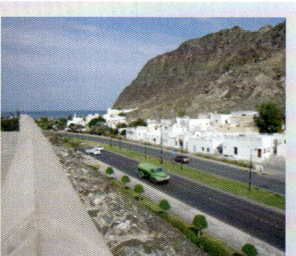

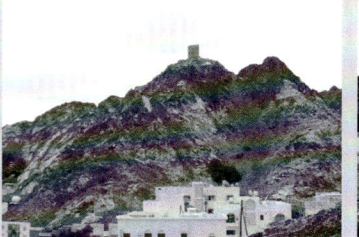

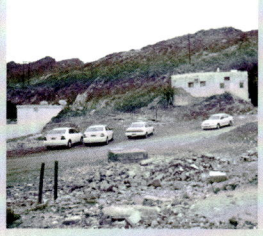

1/2/3. Muscat surroundings, existing conditions

The mining industry is one of the main sources of economic revenue for the country, fuelled by the demand for aggregates from Dubai. However, traditional open cast mining techniques leave large areas of the territory derelict after the period of exploitation which has to be remediated or 'landscaped over. The idea of the project would be to explore ways of reformatting the techniques of mining in such a way that the spatial results of the extraction process link to further appropriation of these spaces for urban growth.

Geometry study (pit type)

A : negative pit
B : positive pit

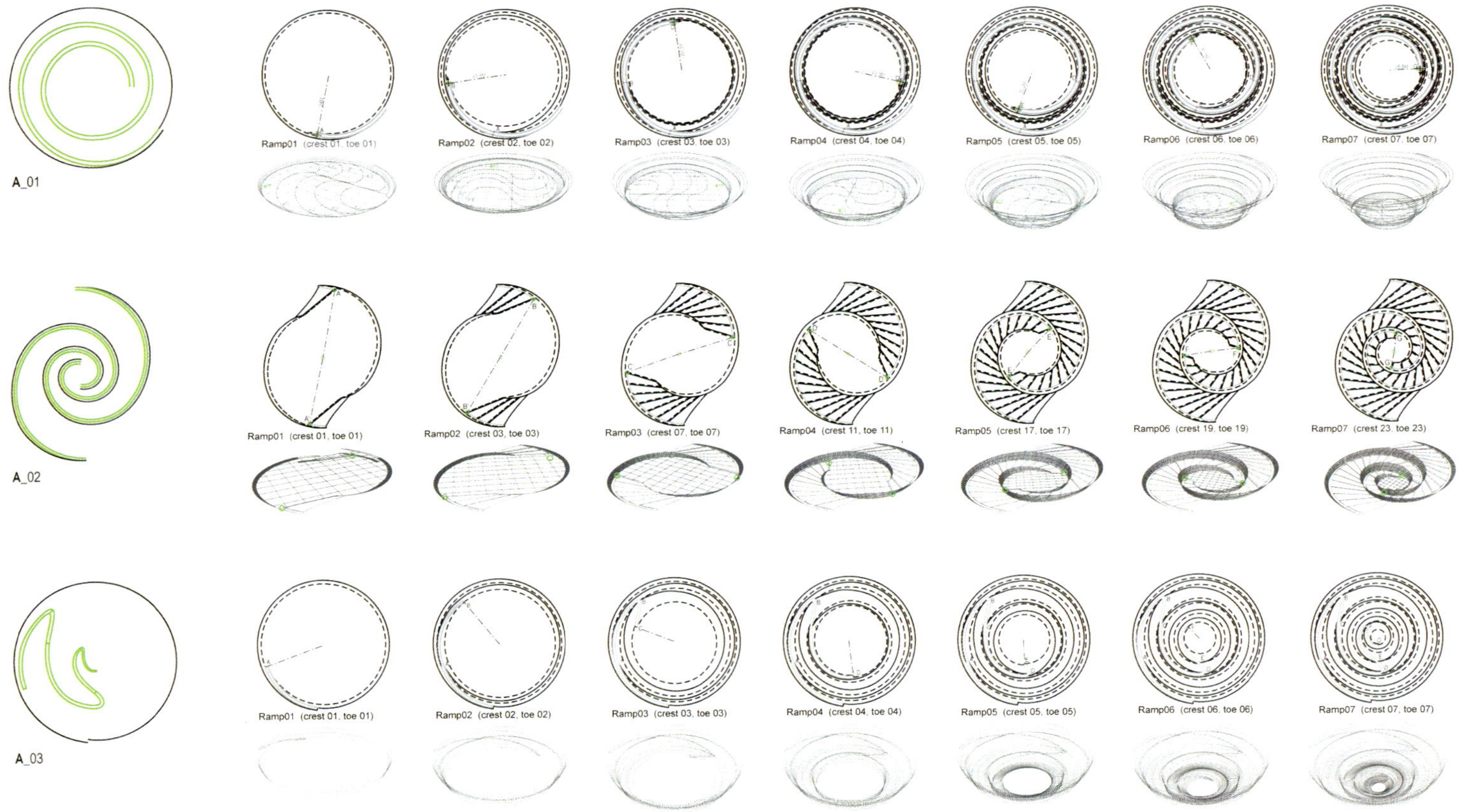

A_01

Ramp01 (crest 01, toe 01) Ramp02 (crest 02, toe 02) Ramp03 (crest 03, toe 03) Ramp04 (crest 04, toe 04) Ramp05 (crest 05, toe 05) Ramp06 (crest 06, toe 06) Ramp07 (crest 07, toe 07)

A_02

Ramp01 (crest 01, toe 01) Ramp02 (crest 03, toe 03) Ramp03 (crest 07, toe 07) Ramp04 (crest 11, toe 11) Ramp05 (crest 17, toe 17) Ramp06 (crest 19, toe 19) Ramp07 (crest 23, toe 23)

A_03

Ramp01 (crest 01, toe 01) Ramp02 (crest 02, toe 02) Ramp03 (crest 03, toe 03) Ramp04 (crest 04, toe 04) Ramp05 (crest 05, toe 05) Ramp06 (crest 06, toe 06) Ramp07 (crest 07, toe 07)

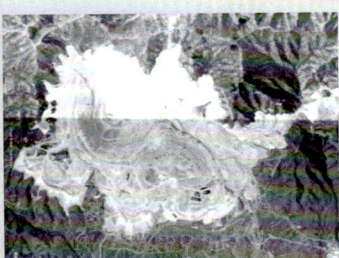

1/2/3. Existing open air mines close to Muscat

Such an exploration requires a multi-scalar approach, starting from a local understanding of the material techniques involved in open pit mining and then assessing how the proliferation of these operations across the territory can produce spatial effects relevant for other purposes. The understanding of these interlocking scales can be linked to the search for new scales of inhabiting the city and forms the base of the future potential of this type of project.

Prototype proliferation

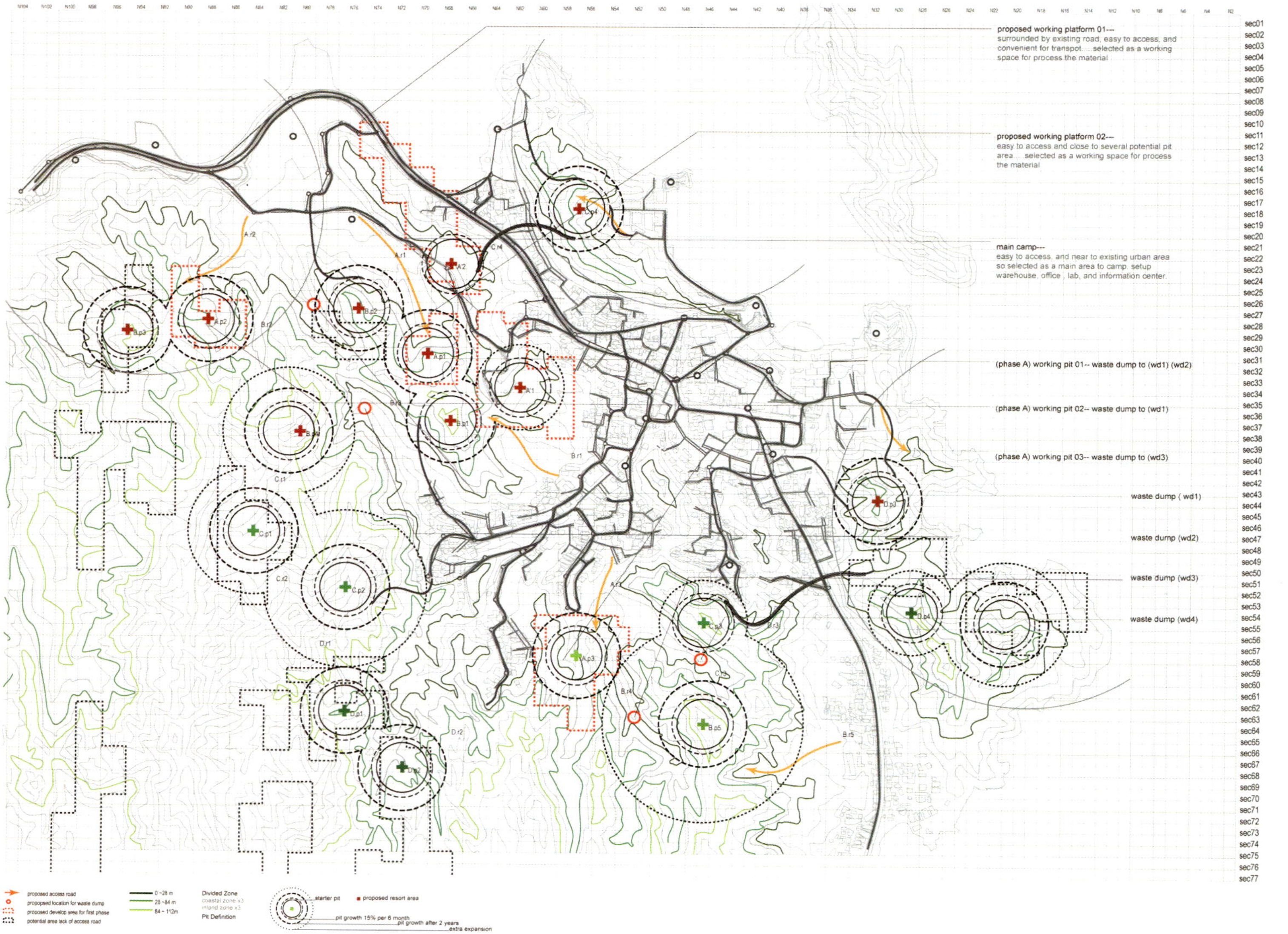

[Large map/diagram with labeled annotations:]

- proposed working platform 01 — surrounded by existing road, easy to access, and convenient for transport... selected as a working space for process the material
- proposed working platform 02 — easy to access and close to several potential pit area... selected as a working space for process the material
- main camp — easy to access, and near to existing urban area so selected as a main area to camp, setup warehouse, office, lab, and information center.
- (phase A) working pit 01 — waste dump to (wd1) (wd2)
- (phase A) working pit 02 — waste dump to (wd1)
- (phase A) working pit 03 — waste dump to (wd3)
- waste dump (wd1)
- waste dump (wd2)
- waste dump (wd3)
- waste dump (wd4)

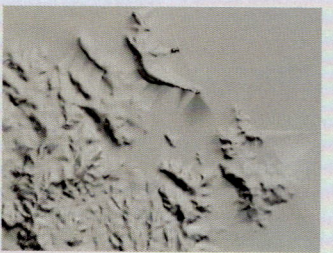

1. Existing topography around Muscat
2. Wind analysis for prevailing directions
3. Muscat Fort

Territorial networks and potential growth patterns

The project starts by studying the location of the open air quarries in the surroundings of Muscat. The intention is to understand the existing patterns of land use and define areas of potential growth both of the mining industry but also the urban fabric. This potential for growth is based on accessibility from the centre but also the presence of coastal winds that may serve as a cooling system for the urban environment.

Prototype proliferation

A - B) __ PIT COMBINATION

A : negative pit (A01, A02, A03)
B : positive pit (B01, B02, B03)
typology study by 3 "A" types and
3 "B" types pit geometry

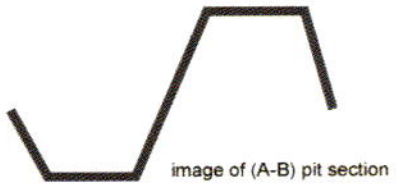

image of (A-B) pit section

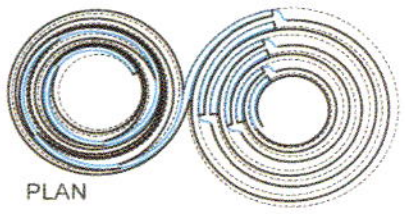

PLAN

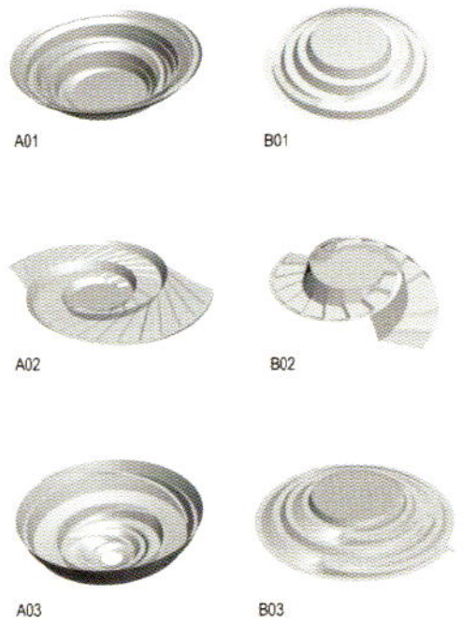

A01 B01
A02 B02
A03 B03

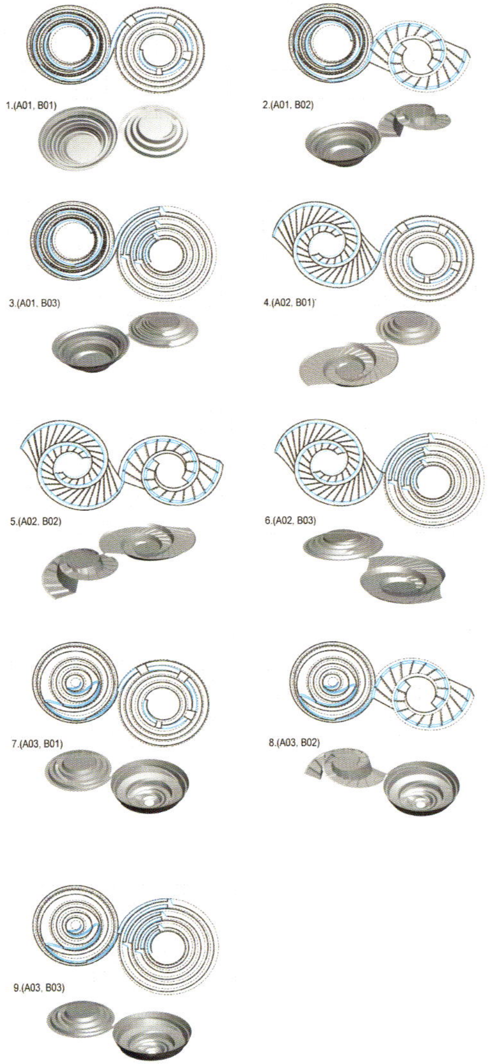

1.(A01, B01) 2.(A01, B02)
3.(A01, B03) 4.(A02, B01)
5.(A02, B02) 6.(A02, B03)
7.(A03, B01) 8.(A03, B02)
9.(A03, B03)

(A - B) __ PIT COMBINATION
example 3.(A01, B03)

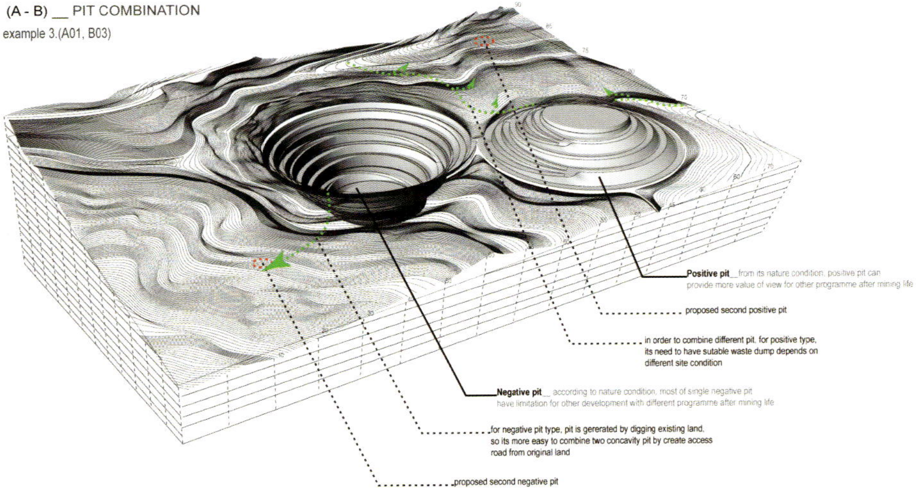

Positive pit __ from its nature condition, positive pit can provide more value of view for other programme after mining life

proposed second positive pit

in order to combine different pit, for positive type, its need to have suitable waste dump depends on different site condition

Negative pit __ according to nature condition, most of single negative pit have limitation for other development with different programme after mining life

for negative pit type, pit is generated by digging existing land. so its more easy to combine two concavity pit by create access road from original land

proposed second negative pit

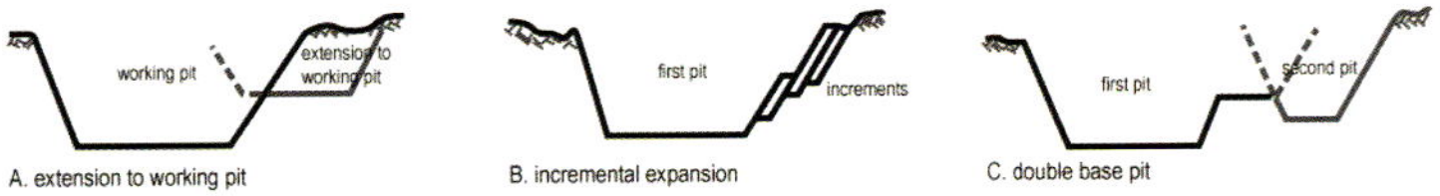

A. extension to working pit   B. incremental expansion   C. double base pit

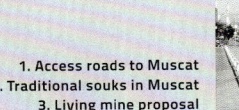

1. Access roads to Muscat
2. Traditional souks in Muscat
3. Living mine proposal

Single spiral open pit mining

Single spiral mining form is generated by the working ramp. The main road plan is set up with a maximum radius of 60m and minimum radius of 30m at the pit bottom.

Start point from centre : 60m
End point from centre : 30m
Ramp turns: 2
Number of arcs: 5
Operating angle: 137.5
Expansion parameter: 30 -- 34 -- 39 -- 45 -- 52 -- 60
                               4   5   6   7   8

 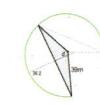 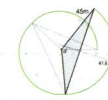 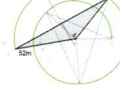 

STAGE 01 (30 – 34) STAGE 02 (34 – 39) STAGE 03 (39 – 45) STAGE 04 (45 – 52) STAGE 05 (52 – 60)

Double spiral open pit mining

Double spiral mining form is generated by the working ramp. The main road plan is set up with maximum radius of 210m and minimum radius of 30m at the pit bottom.

Start point from centre: 210m
End point from centre: 30m
Ramp turns: 1.5
Number of arcs: 4
Operating angle: 137.5
Expansion parameter: 30 -- 50 -- 80 -- 130 -- 210
                             20   30   50   80

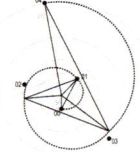  

STAGE 01 (30 – 50) STAGE 02 (50 – 80) STAGE 03 (80 – 130) STAGE 04 (130 –210)

Phasing

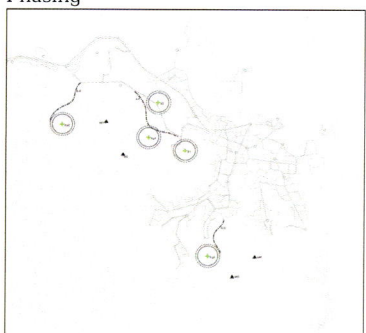 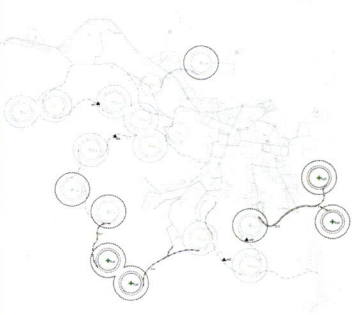 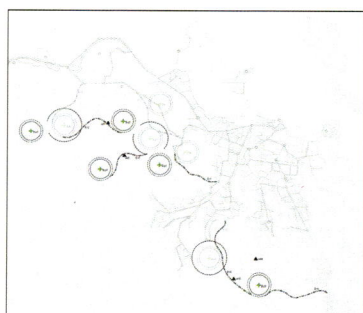

PHASE A

Working platform A' 1 - platform for process material
Main camp A'2 - zone for setup office

Working pit A.p1 - waste dump to wd1, wd2
Working pit A.p2 - waste dump to wd1
Working pit A.p3 - waste dump to wd3

Access road A.r1 - to approach A.p1
Access road A.r2 - to approach A.p2
Access road A.r3 - to approach A.p3

PHASE B

Working pit B.p1 - waste dump to wd2 merge A.p1
Working pit B.p2 - waste dump to wd1 merge A.p1
Working pit B.p3 - merge with A.p2
Working pit B.p4 - dump to create C.r1
Working pit B.p5 - waste dump to wd4

Access road B.r1 - to approach B.p1
Access road B.r2 - to connect A.p2 and B.p2
Access road B.r3 - to connect B.p4 and A.p1+B.p1
Access road B.r4 - to connect A.p3 and B.p5
Access road B.r5 - to approach B.p5

PHASE C

working pit C.p1 - Dump to create C.r2
working pit C.p2 - Dump to create D.r1
working pit C.p3 - Dump to create D.r3

access road C.r1 - To connect B.p4 and C.p1
access road C.r2 - To connect C.p1 and C.p2
access road C.r3 - To connect C.p3 and B.p5
access road C.r4 - To connect C.p4 and A'2

PHASE D

Working pit D.p1 - merge D.p2
Working pit D.p2 - merge D.p1 dump to create D.r2

Access road D.r1 - to connect D.p1 and C.p2
Access road D.r2 - to connect D.p2 and A.p3
Access road D.r3 - to connect C.p3 and D.p3 and D.p4

1. Overall proposal
2. Prototype development

 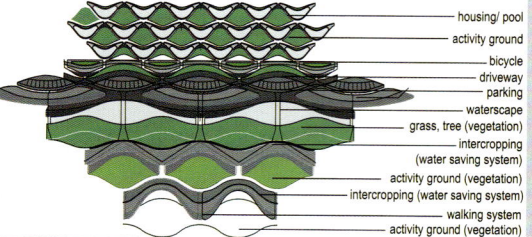

The material techniques used to shape the mine in the most efficient way are turned into a mechanism which produces spaces which satisfy both the mining operation criteria and also the requirements to host residential and recreational programmes. In this sense the time-based development of the spatial formation of the mine also corresponds with a process of inhabitation and reappropriation of these spaces back to the city.

Perspective view

Responsive Coastline

Date **2006/07**
Location **Dubai**
Author **Alejandra Bosch**

Project description

Dubai is experiencing an explosive growth and has been transformed into an immense tourist attraction, receiving an average of 6.3 million tourists per year. The coast is the major selling attraction of the city and therefore the strategy has been the exponential multiplication of the waterfront, reshaping and creating new urban coastlines involving substantial land reclamation and also diverting water channels inland. This topographic change has generated a segregated growth of the city and caused a major impact on the environment. The proposal consists of an alternative topographic configuration and strategy of growth for the coastline of Dubai. The aim of the project is to define the spatial configuration of the coastline in relation to the ecological demands and its articulation with an urban development that responds to the urban dynamic.

This will inform the relationship between the coastline and an integrated urban fabric. To test this proposal the case of the Palm Deira will be used, which is the third and biggest of the three Palm islands along the coastline of Dubai.

Pneumatic stabilised platform technology

In terms of construction technique of the islands, a hybrid system of land reclamation and floating structures was developed. The existing reclaimed land will be expanded with a pneumatic stabilised platform that allows additional coastline and developable land to be added while allowing the marine life and the local currents to maintain their natural status. The pneumatic stabilised platform is composed of a number of cylindrical-shaped components packed together in a rectangular pattern to form a module. Each cylinder is sealed at the top, open to the ocean at its base, and contains air at a pressure slightly above atmospheric pressure. This system utilises indirect displacement of water for its flotation, in which the platform rests on trapped air that displaces the water. The primary buoyancy force is provided by air pressure acting on the underside of the deck. The assembly process produces a series of enclosed interstitial regions between cylinders, which may be filled with air, foam or other material. These regions are isolated from the air pockets within the cylinders to provide additional buoyancy and righting moment. In comparison to conventional floating platforms, the pneumatic platform allows the distribution of the flotation force to be modified as needed to minimise the hogging moment or in response to large concentrated loads on the deck.

1/2/3/4. Land reclamation techniques along Dubai coastline

The exponential increase in real estate value of the land on the water's edge has fuelled the construction of an increasing number of artificial islands which have the effect of multiplying the contact of the city with the water. State of the art techniques for dredging have been imported with the objective of generating archipelagos of capricious shapes and forms. However this phenomenon of the extension of the coastline has been accompanied by an increasing privatisation of public space, turning the city into a disjointed set of enclosed environments with little left to give a sense of coherence to the city. The project tries to address these issues, generating alternative plot scenarios and edge details which will multiply the possibilities of urban interaction while bringing value to the overall developments.

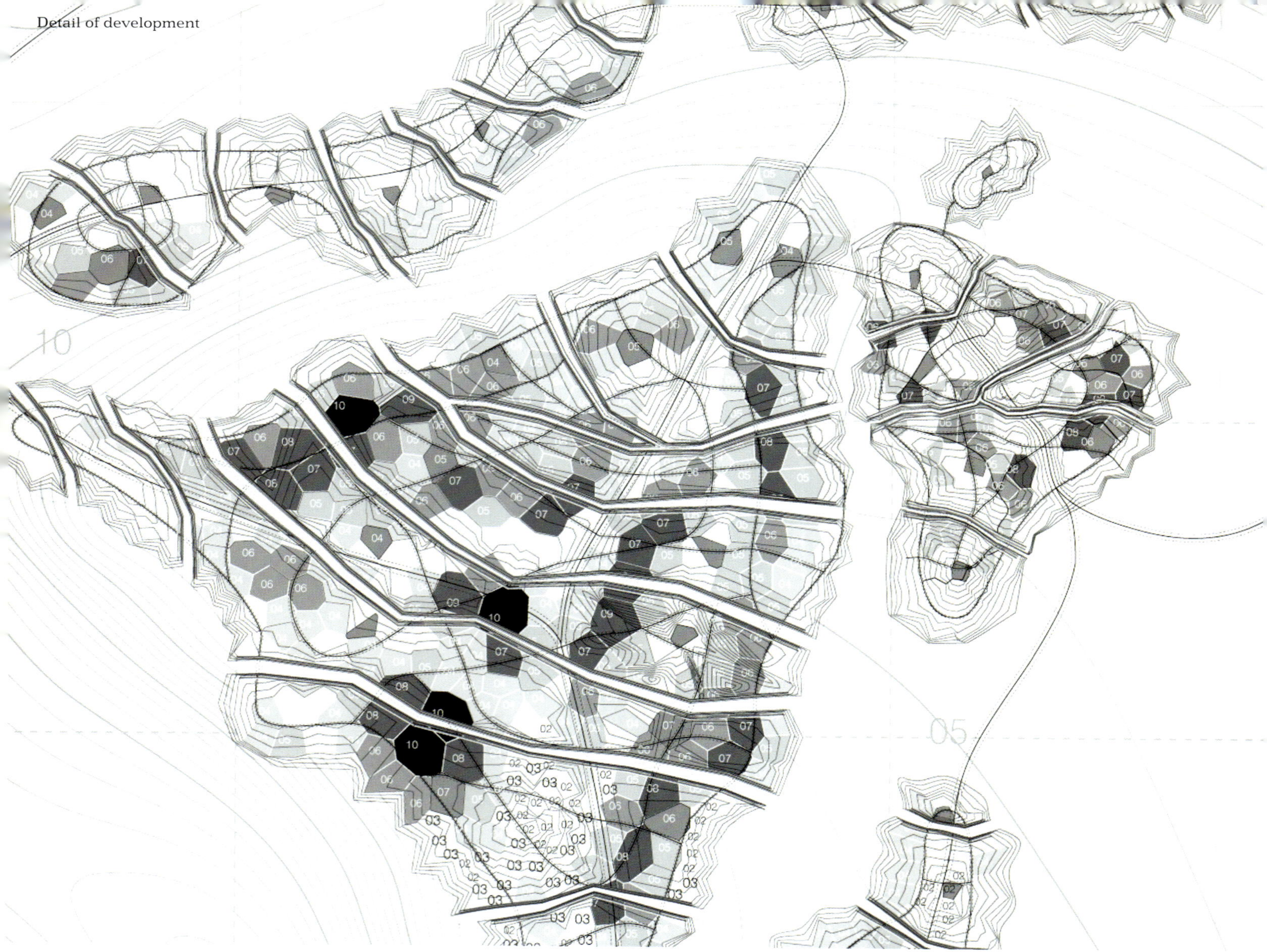

Detail of development

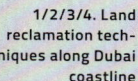

1/2/3/4. Land reclamation techniques along Dubai coastline

Advantages over traditional land reclamation:

-Easy and fast to construct. Components can be made at shipyards and then be transported and assembled at the site.
-Easy to relocate expand or remove
-Position of structure is constant with respect to the water surface
-Construction is not affected by the depth of water disadvantages
-Only suitable to use in calm waters associated with naturally sheltered coastal formations.
(Solution: use of breakwaters, antimotion devices, anchor or mooring system)

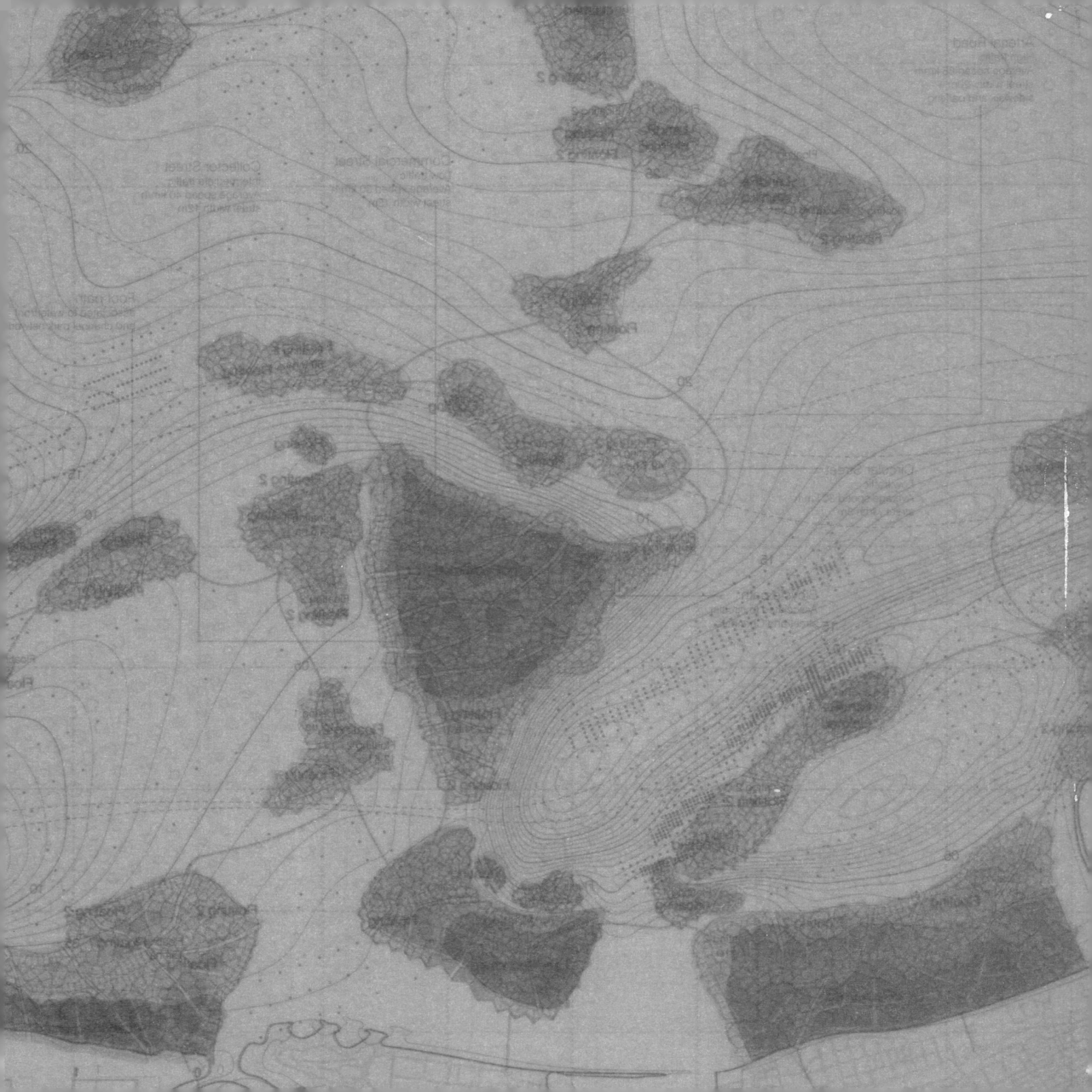

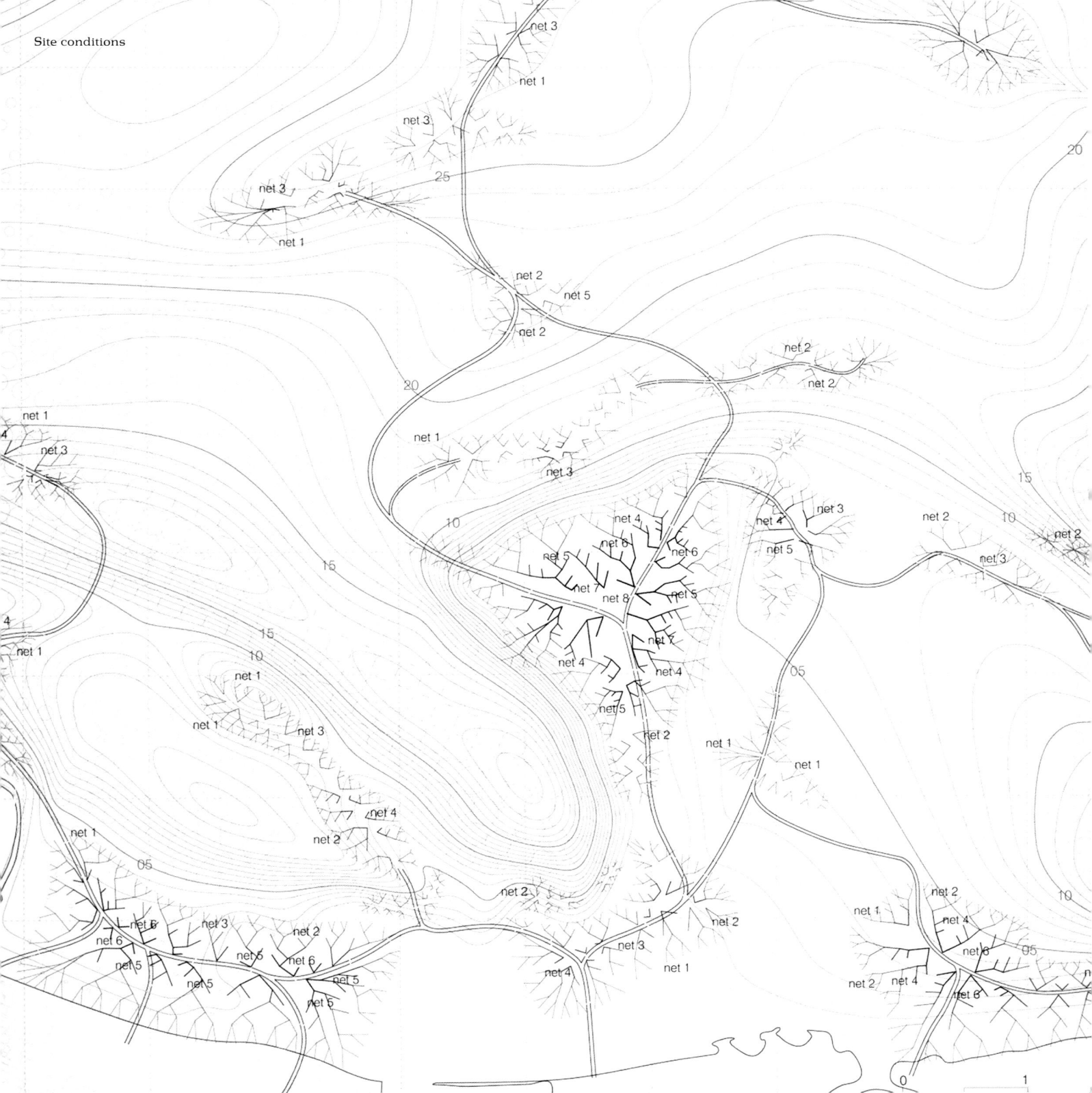
Site conditions

Palm Deira programme and local networks

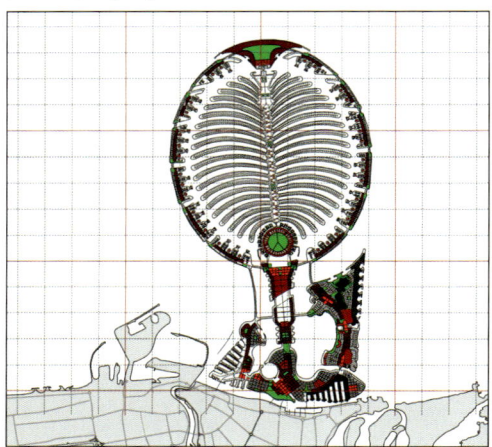
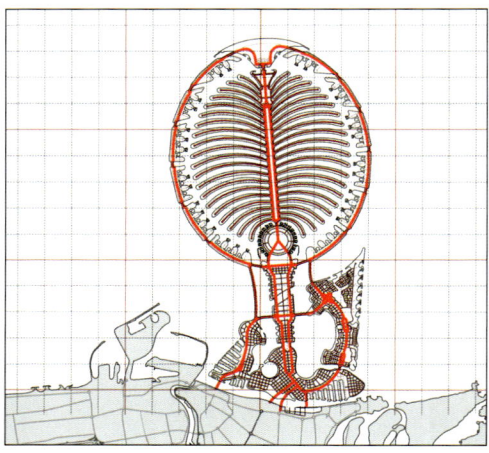
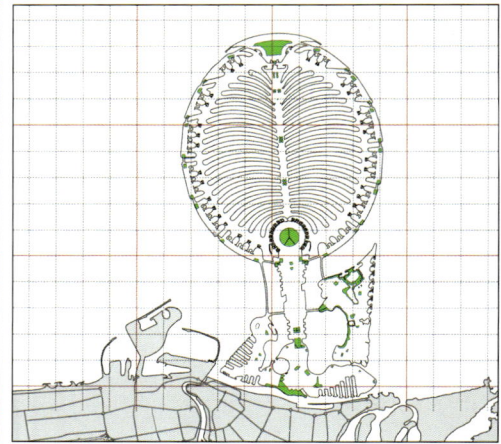

PROGRAMME DISTRIBUTION
Does not generate a mixed-use urban fabric but selected clusters of housing with no service programme. The programme allocation doesn't take into consideration the exisitng urban fabric of the old city.

INFRASTRUCTURE NETWORK
Is not integrated to the existing one and promotes the spatial segregation of the different programmes.

GREEN SPACE LOCATION
Doesn't generate a network of public space. These areas are residuals of the programme distribution with no connection to the housing areas or public programmes.

Local currents study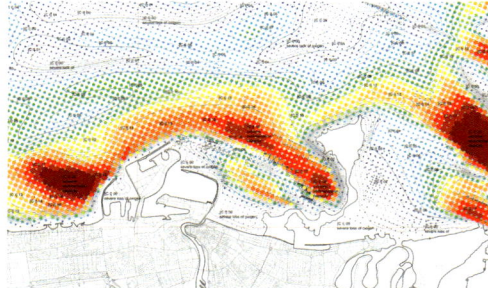

Prevailing currents direction and coral location

Responsive coastline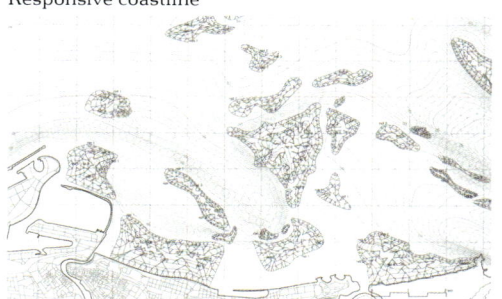

1. Waterfront Profile
2. Moll de la Fusta, Barcelona

Responsive coastline

One of the main problems that the Palm projects have caused in Dubai is a great impediment to coastal drift, blocking currents and sediment and having a negative impact on coral reefs. A series of current simulations were undertaken in order to understand water-flow regimes along the coastline. The outcome of these studies was used in order to propose a more porous system of smaller islands that would allow water to move freely causing minimal impact to the overall current system. The images above show studies of the existing condition (initial phases of Palm Deira) and the current scenario with Responsive coastline proposal.

Plot distribution and street layout

- Arterial Road — High traffic — Average speed 65 km/h — street width 20m + sidewalk and parking.
- Collector Street — Intermediate traffic — Average speed 40 km/h — street width 12 m
- Circular Street — Low traffic — Average speed 30 km/h — street width 8m
- Commercial Street — Low traffic — Average speed 30 km/h — street width 15m
- Bicycle path — Associated to circular street and channels
- Foot path associated to waterfront and channels park network

Banding analysis

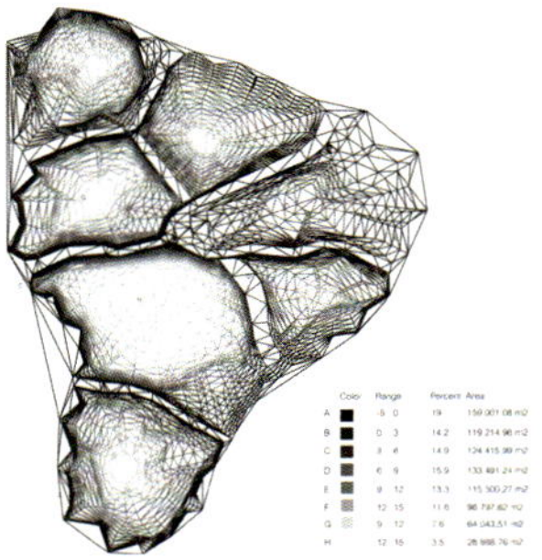

Slope analysis

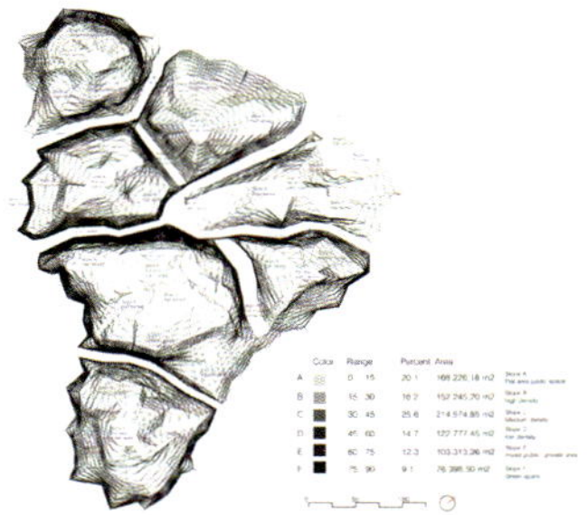

1. Frames for biorock reef structures
2/3. Biorock reef structures

A Biorock system is explored in order to encourage arrival of coral structures into the edges of the island. This system works via the application of low voltage current into metal structures, which greatly encourages the settlement of coral ecologies around the metal bars. This ecologic structure acts as a foundation for artificial floating topographies generating sub islands and ultimately informing a block typology and urban connectivity.

Water recycling

Cluster 1
Water-recycling pond: 1052 m²
Persons per cluster: 263
Water for irrigation: 1.2 L per m² per day
Irrigation area: 438 m²

Cluster 2
Water recycling pond: 1563 m²
Persons per cluster: 390
Water for irrigation: 1.2 L per m² per day
Irrigation area: 438 m²

Cluster 3
Water recycling pond: 1109 m²
Persons per cluster: 426
Water for irrigation: 1.2 L per m² per day
Irrigation area: 535 m²

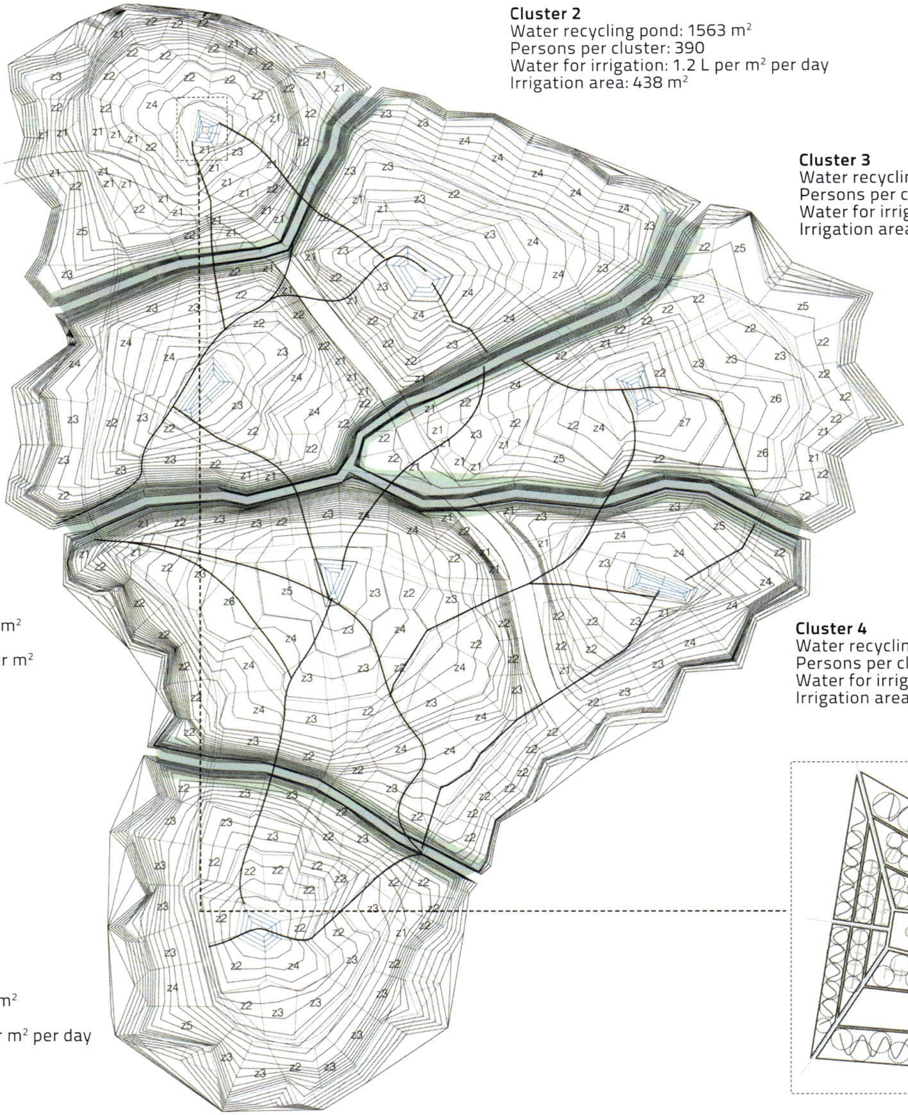

Cluster 5
Water-recycling pond: 1759 m²
Persons per cluster: 439
Water for irrigation: 1.2 L per m² per day
Irrigation area: 622 m²

Cluster 4
Water-recycling pond: 1789 m²
Persons per cluster: 447
Water for irrigation: 1.2 L per m² per day
Irrigation area: 722 m²

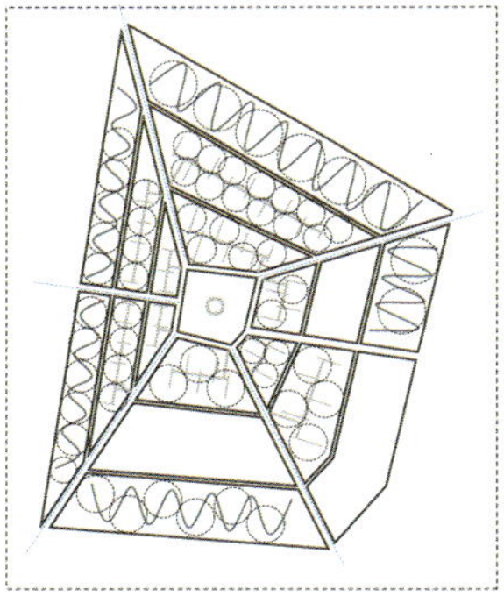

Cluster 6
Water-recycling pond: 1002 m²
Persons per Cluster: 526
Water for irrigation: 1.2 L per m² per day
Irrigation area: 485 m²

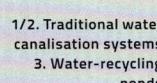

1/2. Traditional water canalisation systems
3. Water-recycling ponds

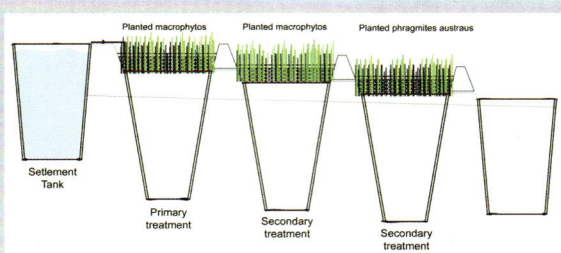

Water-recycling ponds

A system of plot by plot ponds is proposed in order to reuse water locally. Water is recycled for irrigation of public space:

1 treatment plant for each cluster.
1 cluster = average of 40 plots.
2 m² of treatment plant per inhabitant.

Planting strategy

Definition of irrigation area
Plant water requirements in litres per day for an area with several plants
LPD = 1.3 ETO x KL x A(3)
where
LPD = litres per day
KL = KS x Kmc x KD
KS = adjustment factor for a particular plant species
Kmc= Adjustment factor for shade or microclimate
Kd = Adjustment factor for plant density

Drought resistant plants 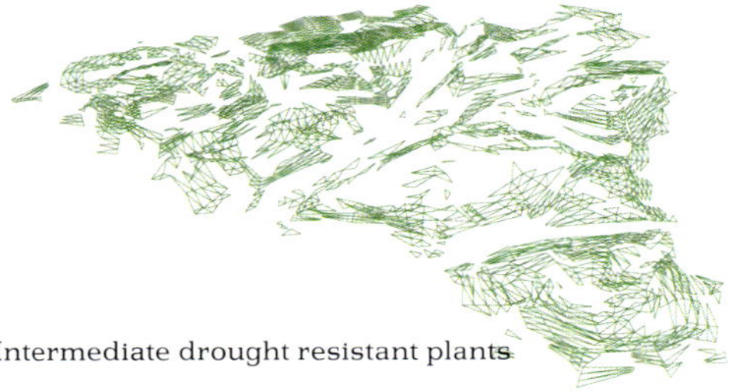   Intermediate drought resistant plants 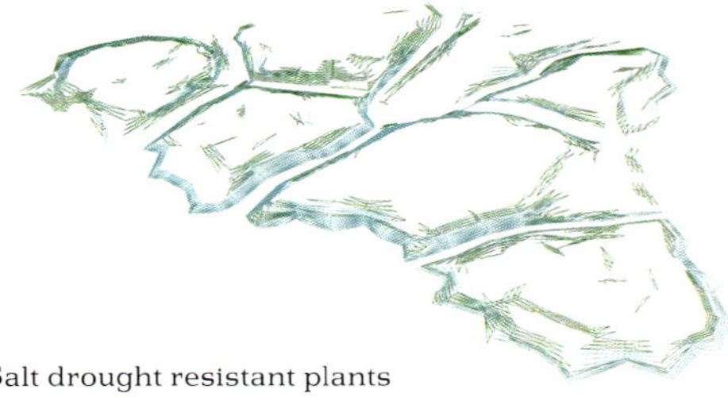   Salt drought resistant plants

1. Hymenache amplexicaulis
2. Stipagrostis plumosa
3. Salicornia
4. Groundlabia australis
5. Chrisantemoides monilifera
6. Trees casuarina

Planting strategy

Salt tolerant plants are used in the area of the channels and along the coastline. In the rest of the area, the planting types are defined by its proximity to the irrigation network.

Prototype development

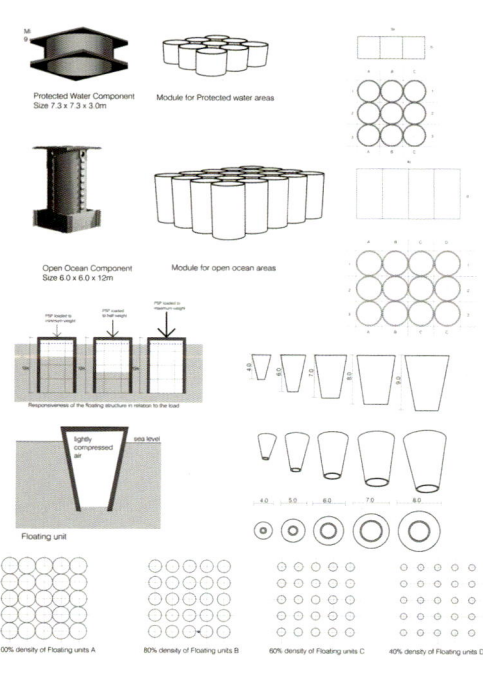
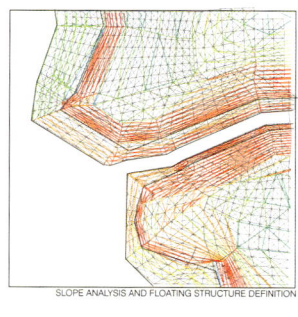
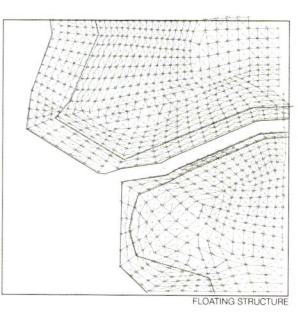
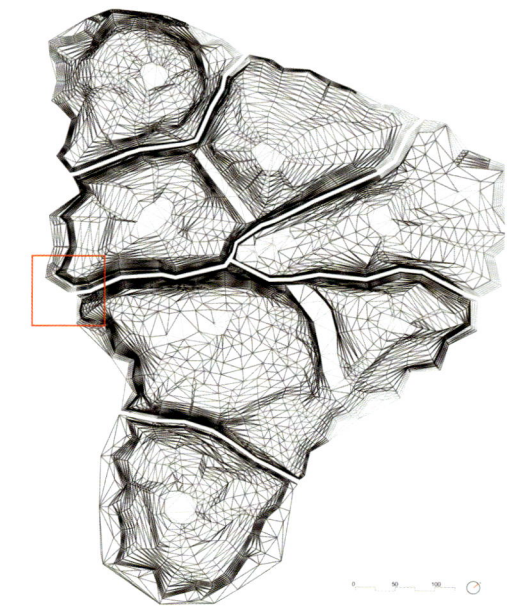
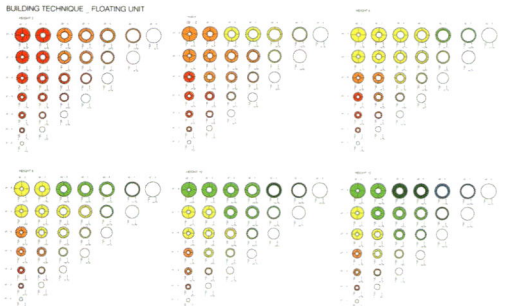
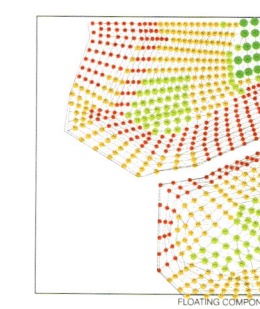
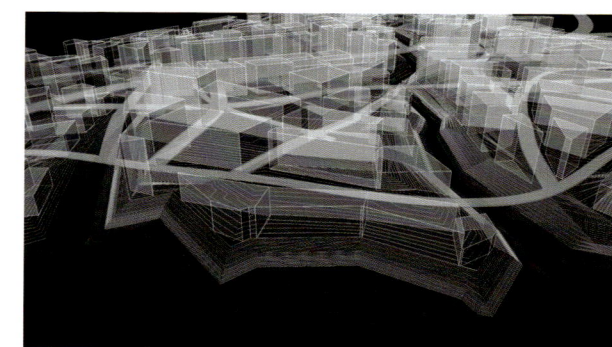

1/2/3/4. Local commerce in Dubai centre

The basic construction method is to wet-cast the individual cylinders with an integral top slab and assemble them into modules. These modules can then be joined with other modules to form a complete platform structure. The number of components in a module depends on the selected construction and launching environment. A nine-component module is considered adequate for maintaining stability during deployment. Generally, the larger the module, the lower the offshore labour cost. All joining of the manufactured units is with post-tensioned cables resulting in a monolithic structure. Pneumatic stabilised platforms normally have a substantially shallower draft than semisubmersibles, which would allow the marine currents to maintain their main direction.

Overall massing

Overall massing

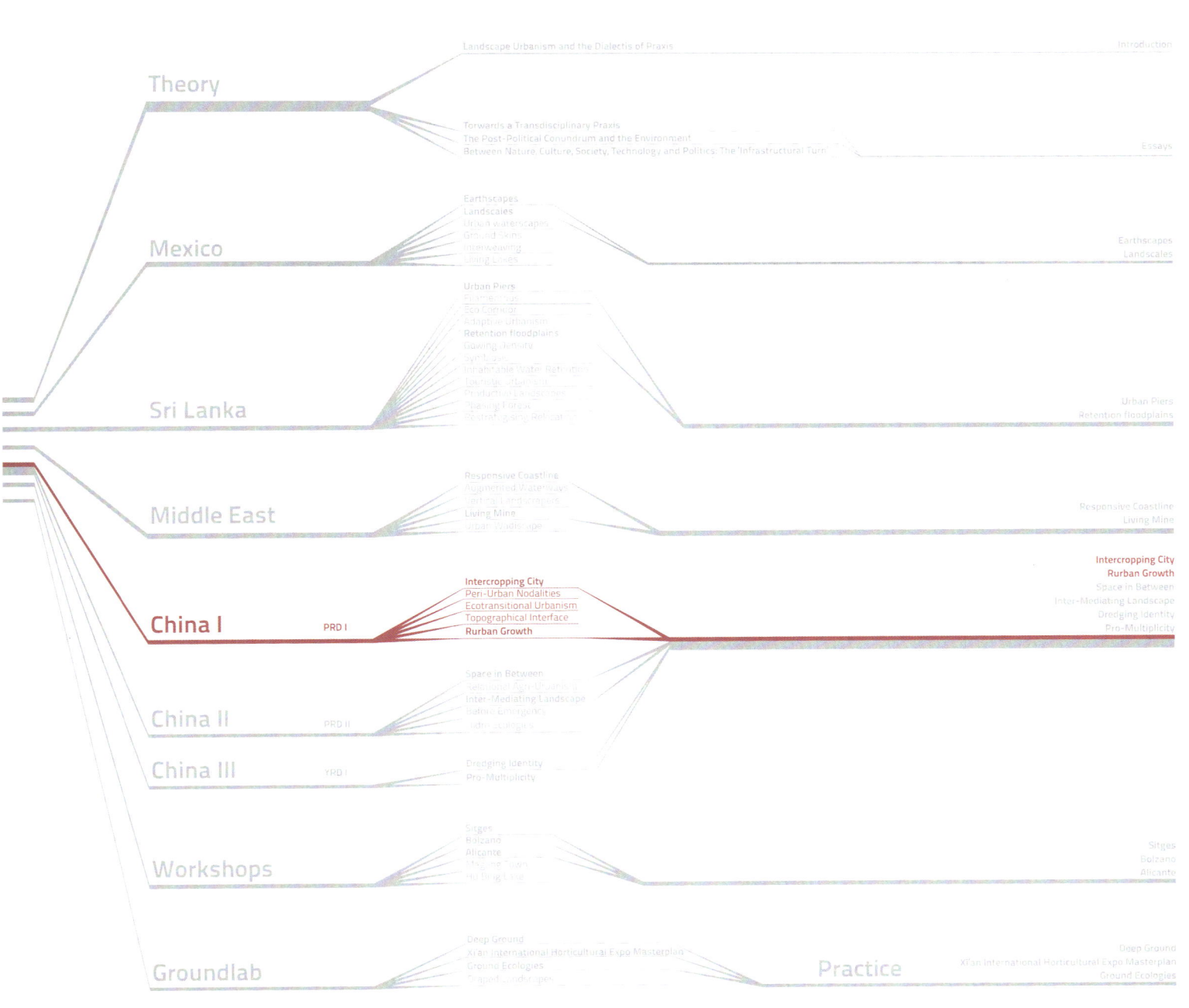

AA Landscape Urbanism 07/08
Prototypical Urbanities - PRD China

AGENDA China's economic boom, combined with migration from the rural areas, is fuelling a high-speed urbanism that is producing new cities in the shortest imaginable time and completely changing the face and character of the country's older towns. This directional urbanisation, propelled from within the coastal zones into the countryside, has brought even the smallest villages face to face with the phenomena of globalisation, foreign capital and generic architecture. At the same time, the pace and scale of development, particularly in the mega-cities of Beijing, Shanghai, Shenyang and Wuhan, has highlighted the interrelated problems of mass migration, pollution and the loss of arable land. The lack of an overarching urbanisation policy means that there are no mechanisms of negotiation between economic interests, cultural traditions, developmental pressures and existing ecologies. At a larger scale, China risks seeing its urban identity swamped by a generic pattern of indiscriminate urban sprawl.

400 NEW CITIES In 2000 the former civil affairs minister, Doje Cering, formulated a plan to build 400 new cities by the year 2020, to accommodate the migration from the countryside into urban conglomerations. According to this plan, 20 new cities need to be established each year. LU took this formulation as the framework for the year's research, testing the applicability of our methodology to the limit, then adjusting and reformulating it. The resulting work generated 'protostrategies' for new large-scale agglomerations as a way of critically addressing the phenomenon of mass-produced sprawl urbanisation. The test-bed for the year's project was Pingshan and the brief was the documentation recently provided by Chinese planning authorities, requesting its change of status from county to a new city. We operated critically, seeking to produce alternative templates of urbanisation based on strategies that stemmed from embryonic processes seeking the integration of cultural tradition, regional ecological systems and economic globalisation.

AALU China 07/08
Rurban growth

Date **2007/08**
Location **China**
Author **Katya Larina**

Project description

The project aim was to elaborate 'protostrategies' for new large-scale agglomerations, as a way of critically addressing the phenomenon of mass-produced sprawl urbanisation in the Pearl River Delta region, China.
The project uses the capacity of the rural self-industrialisation process, so-called TVE (Town Village Enterprise), as an instrument to form new urban tissue. In a context of such complex and dynamic process the urban model has to be spatially and programmatically readjustable.
The new flexible mode of urban development is going to happen by means of the introduction of self-sufficient urban clusters, which attach to the villages and contain a combination of plots with residential and manufacturing programmes.
The specificity of a material organisation of the cluster is an effect of hybridising the green engineering infrastructure with social and public services within one loop structure; this structure represents a backbone of each urban cluster and shares water, energy, and social resources between the different programmes of a cluster. Complex social and environmental data analysis allows spatial and programmatic elements to be built-in to the proposal within the dynamic context of industrial sprawl. The main design algorithm of the project allows for the simulation of diverse scenarios of urban development and for finding the right strategy for the preferable result. In the simulation of urban growth of the agglomeration within clusters, the important factors are the relations of the time of their appearance and the strategy applied to each cluster. The combination of programmes within each cluster is dependent upon the programs in adjacent clusters and the current stage of industrialisation of the adjacent villages. Thus the overall level of industrialisation of territory changes instantly, generating a timeline where the spatial character of each of the clusters is affected by its programmatic filling.

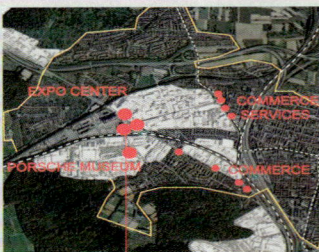
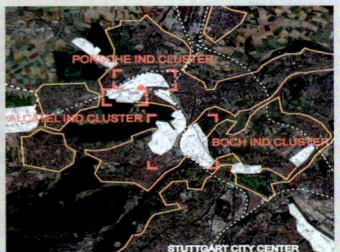
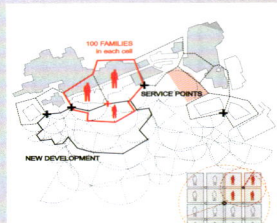

1. Urban analysis
2. Stuttgart city centre analysis comparison
3. Population density map

Population density map according to a site parcelation system that allocates an equal number of people in each cell (100 families in each unit). This has been done in order to recognise the points of location of social services shared between the village and the new development. Nodes of the infrastructural 'plug in' have also been defined. Social and infrastructural nodes are the starting points for attaching the new pattern of the development cluster plots, preferable scenario of urban development / simulation of spatial and programmatic organisation of the fabric.

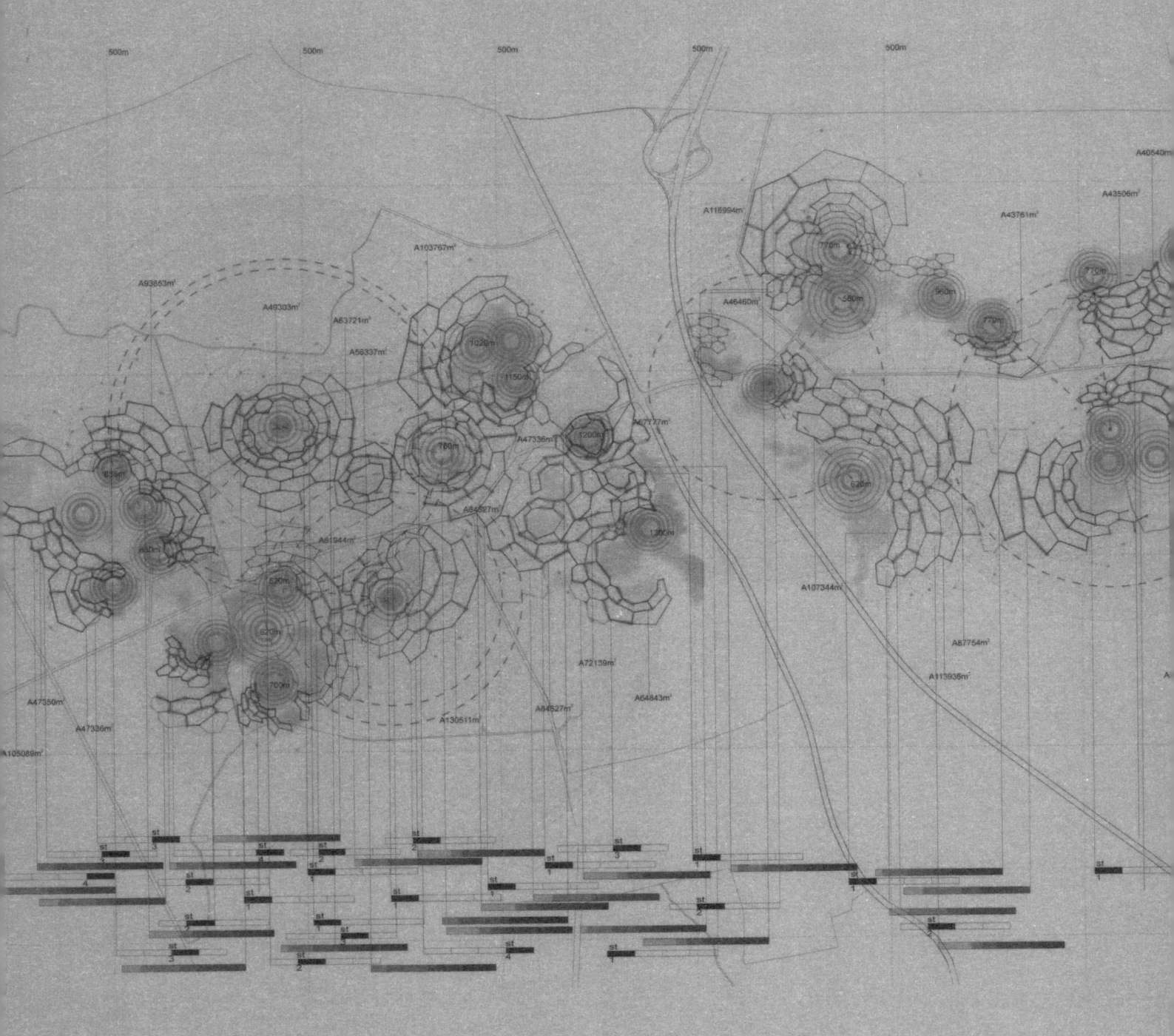

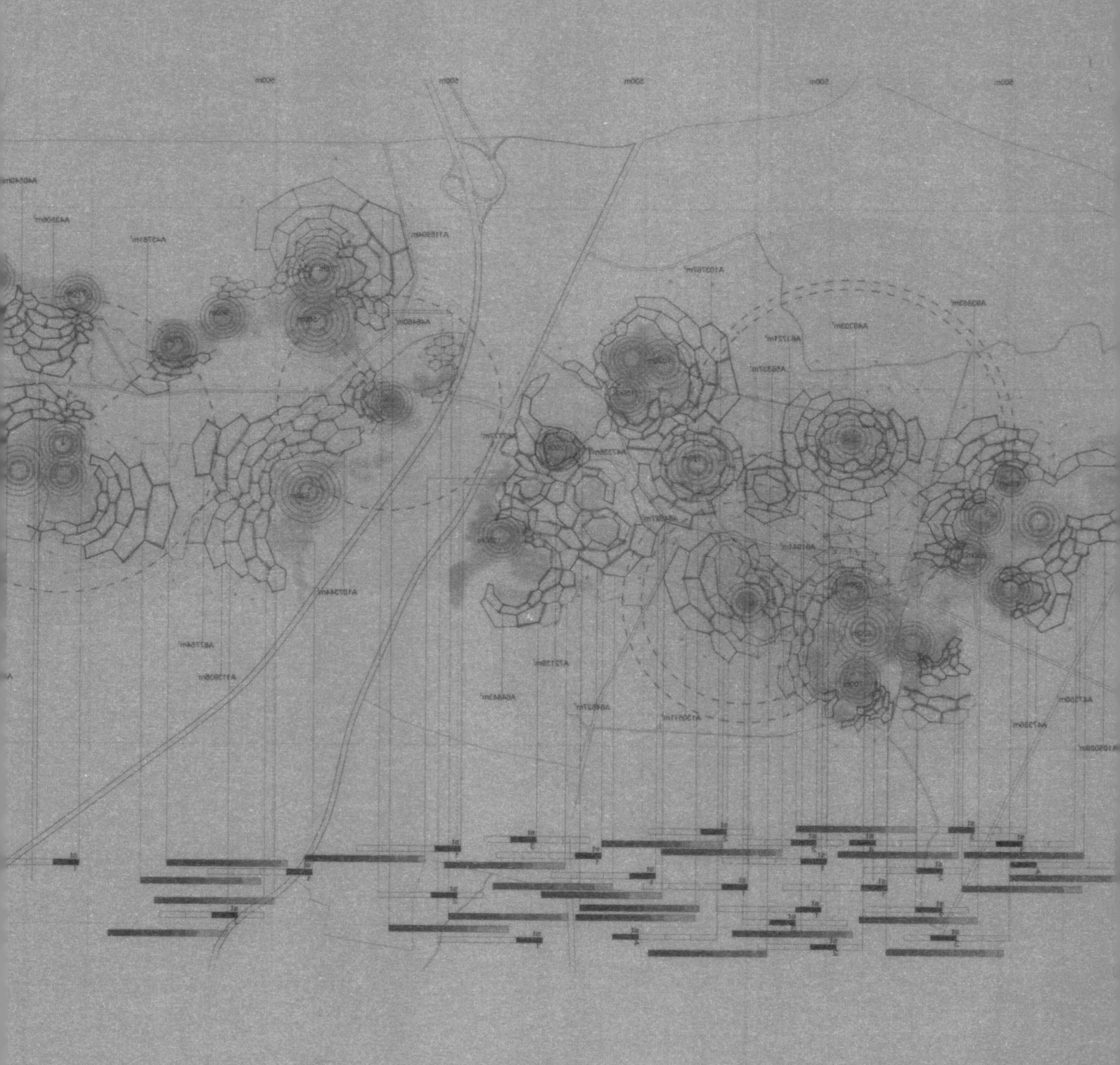

Simulation of urban development of the agglomeration site mapping

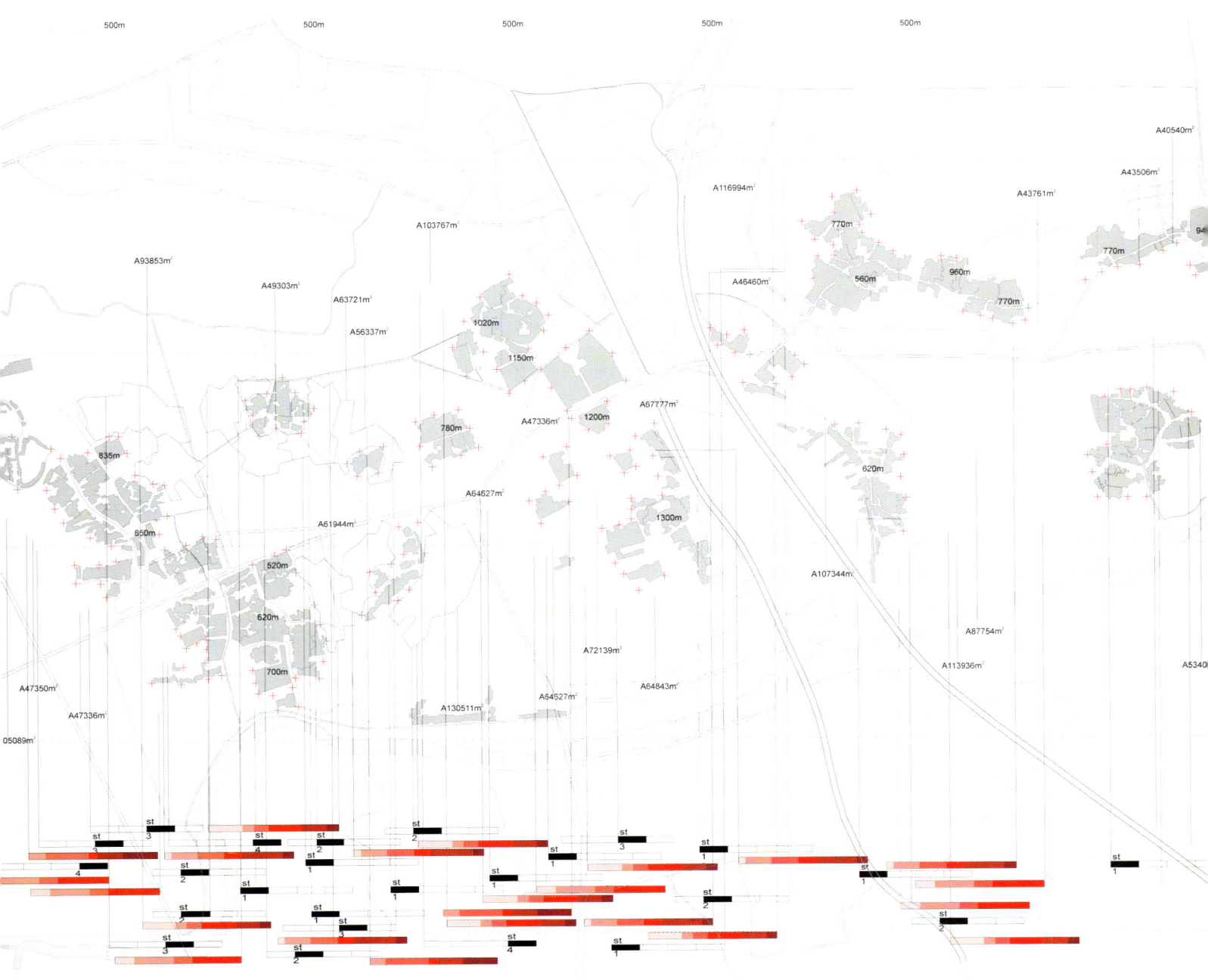

Programme filling adjustment

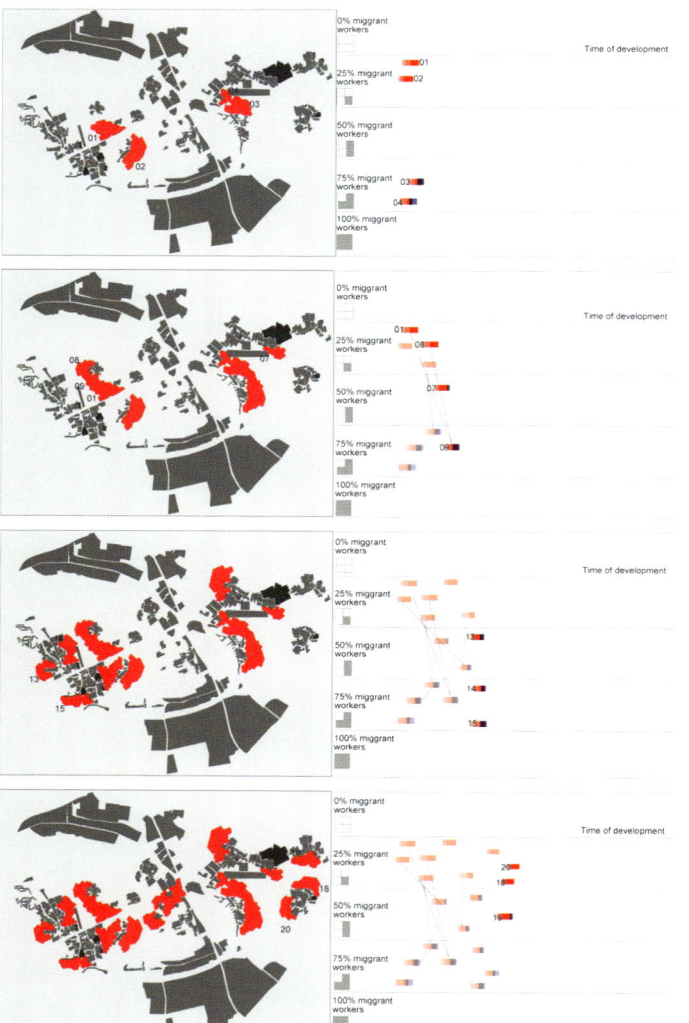

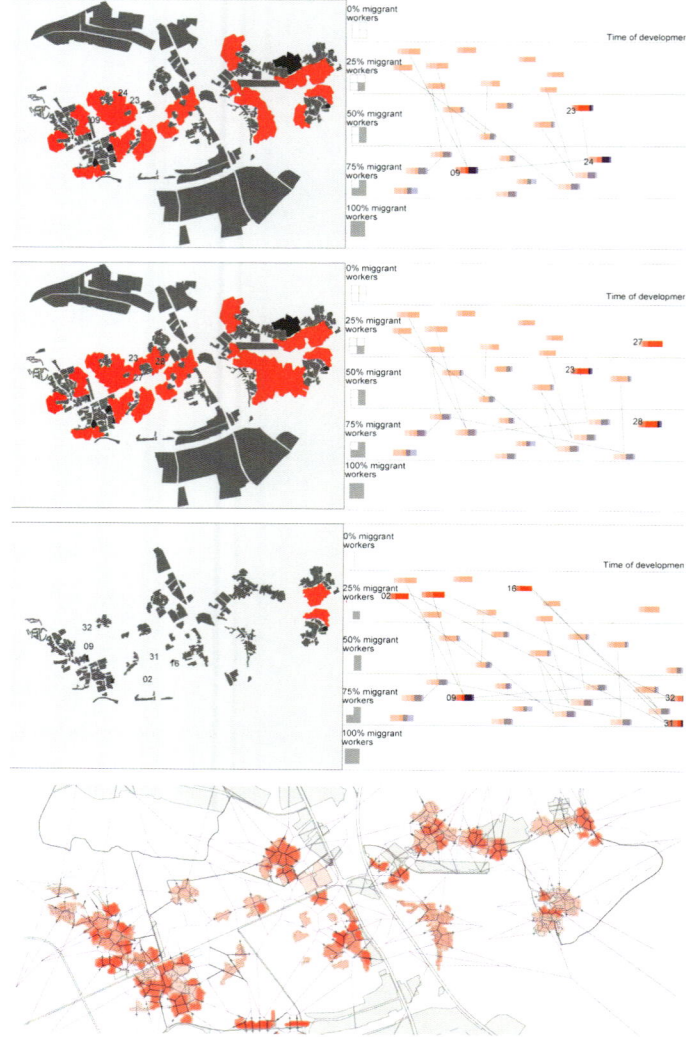

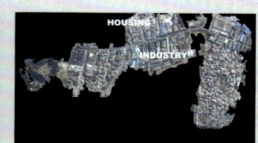

1. TVE's 0 stage / initial agricultural area
2. TVE's first stage
3. Introduction of industry to the village

TVE (Town Village Enterprise) evolution

Is a bottom-up process of the self-industrialisation of rural territories. It takes place as villages organise cooperatives and convert their farmland to industrial sites. Peasants become workers of those industries or landlords of the houses for migrant workers.

- Stage 0: Initial agricultural area. In rural settlements, groups of people mobilise to bring in industry.
- Stage 1: Introduction of industry to the village. Conversion of the village to Town Village Enterprise, conversion of peasants to industrial workers. The introduction of industry increases revenue for the settlement and reinvestment into the urban infrastructure.
- Stage 2: State Compensation of farm land reduction. Privatisation of land plots and building of the dwellings for the immigrant workers.

Application of four strategies to villages with different TVE stages

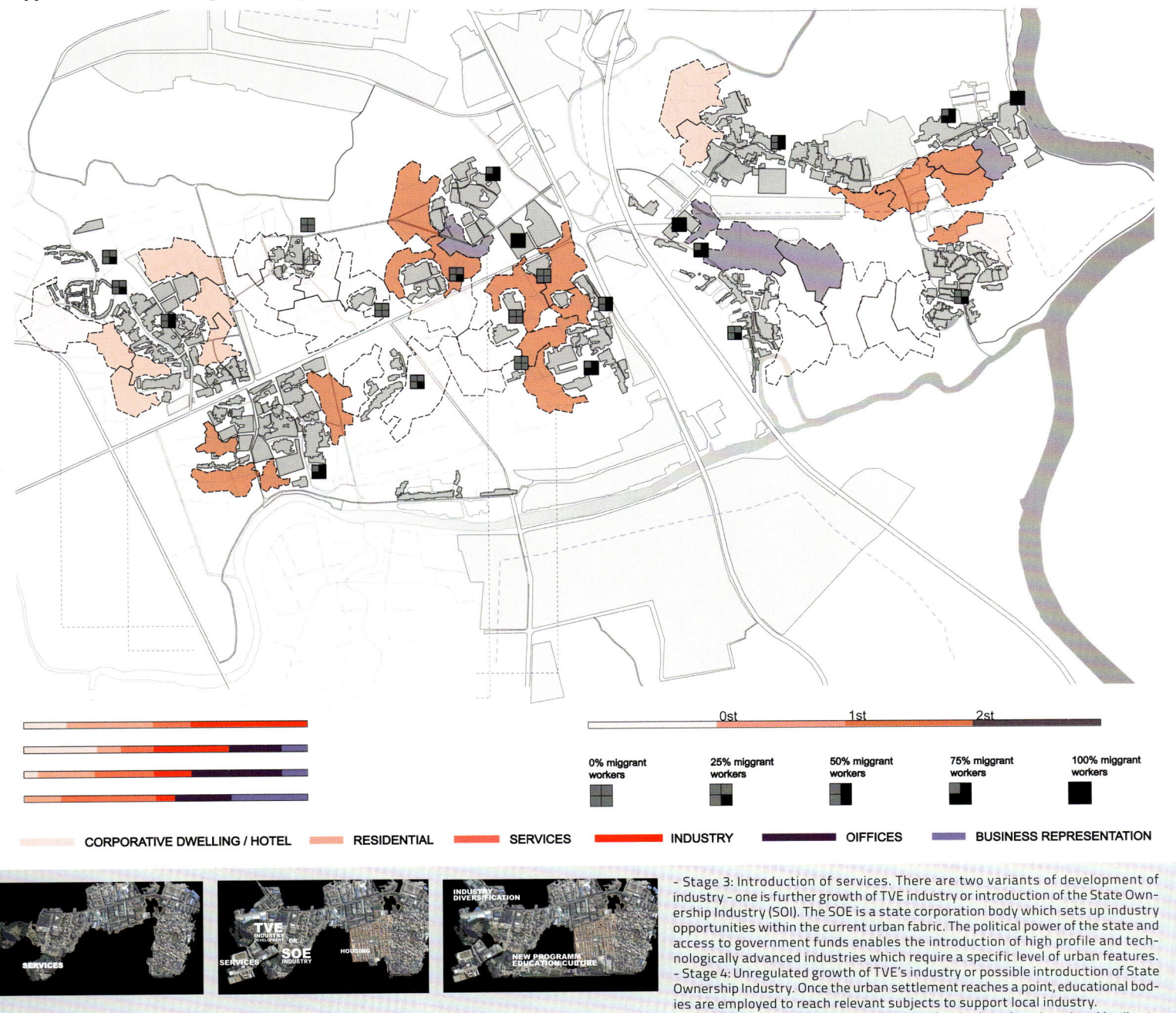

| | CORPORATIVE DWELLING / HOTEL | RESIDENTIAL | SERVICES | INDUSTRY | OFFICES | BUSINESS REPRESENTATION |

1. TVE's 3 Stage / Introduction of services
2. TVE's 4 Stage / Unregulated growth of TVE's industry
3. TVE's 5 Stage / Industry diversification and research sectors emerge

- Stage 3: Introduction of services. There are two variants of development of industry - one is further growth of TVE industry or introduction of the State Ownership Industry (SOI). The SOE is a state corporation body which sets up industry opportunities within the current urban fabric. The political power of the state and access to government funds enables the introduction of high profile and technologically advanced industries which require a specific level of urban features.
- Stage 4: Unregulated growth of TVE's industry or possible introduction of State Ownership Industry. Once the urban settlement reaches a point, educational bodies are employed to reach relevant subjects to support local industry. When high-end industries are introduced they look to the educational bodies to supply educated personnel, and they begin to support the research.
- Stage 5: Industry diversification and research sectors emerge.

Schema of ecology organised between new housing development industry and existing village

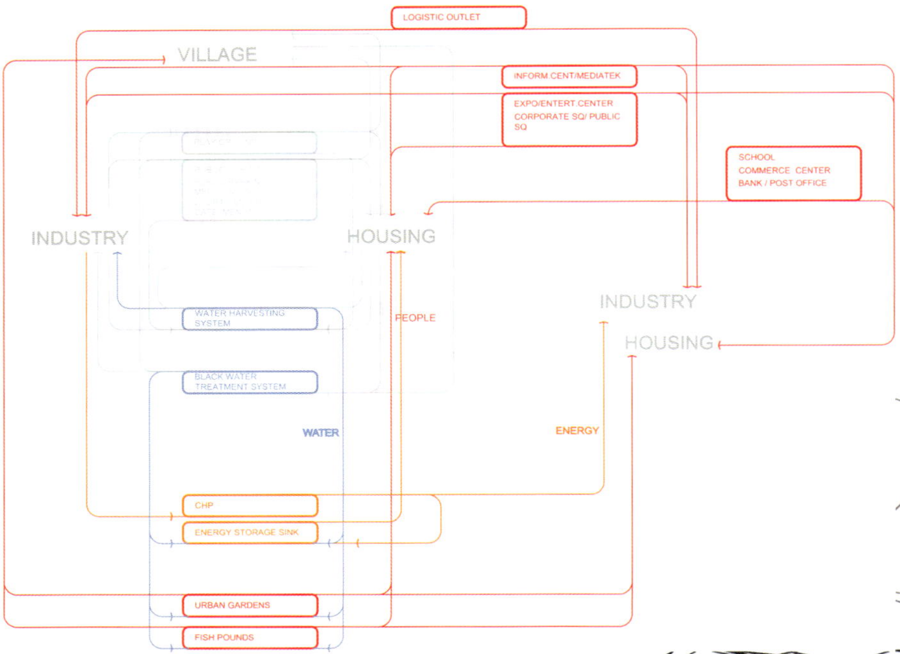

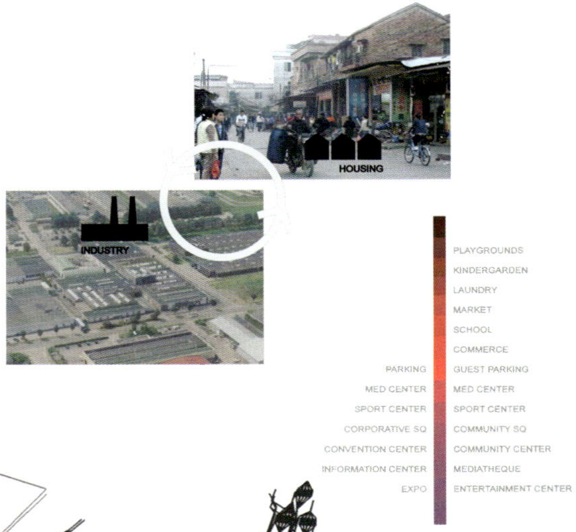

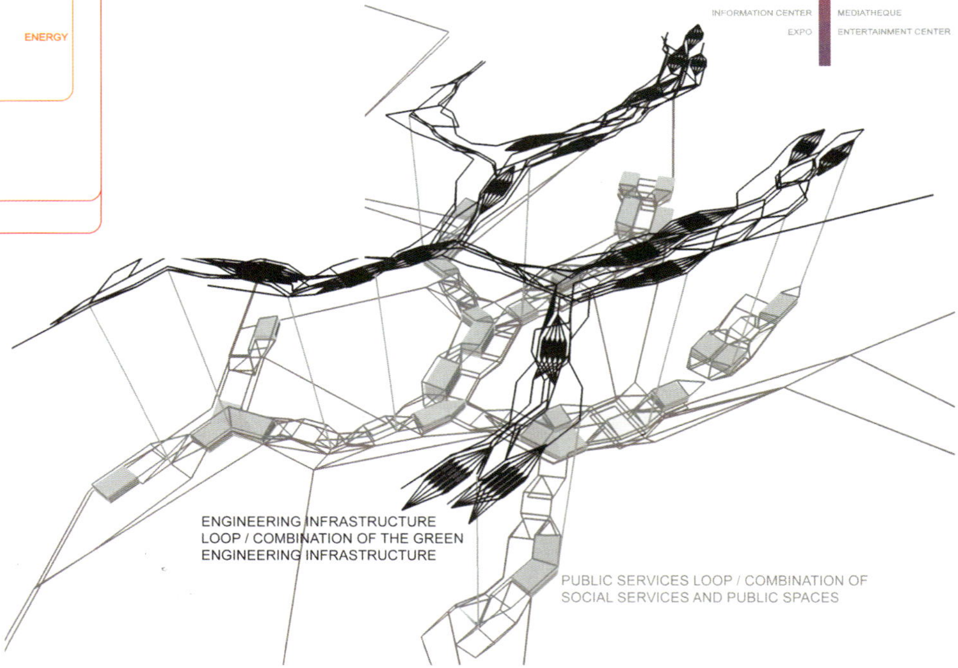

ENGINEERING INFRASTRUCTURE LOOP / COMBINATION OF THE GREEN ENGINEERING INFRASTRUCTURE

PUBLIC SERVICES LOOP / COMBINATION OF SOCIAL SERVICES AND PUBLIC SPACES

1. Industrial development in rural areas
2. Development of fragmented environment on the urban fringe

The 3-dimensionalisation of the engineering infrastructure, apart from the advantages of using gravity in the irrigation, water collection and heat distribution systems, creates the unique urban landscape, which is also used as the public space. This landscape creates a multi level public way, which allows a hierarchy of public and semi-public spaces. Building development of the plots connected to the branches can be attached to this multi-level public space.

Design instrument / catalogue of sections for different engineering systems

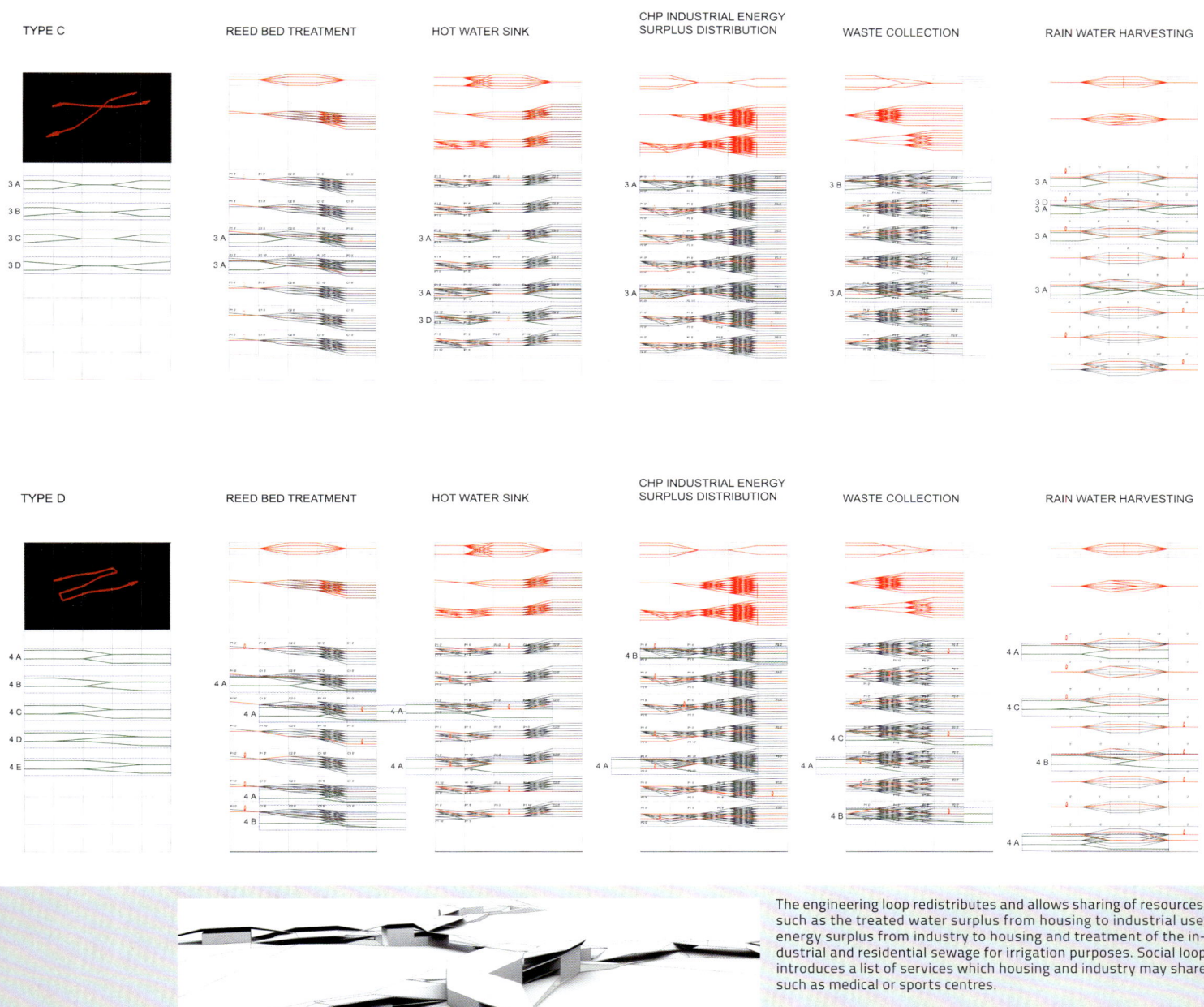

1. Engineering infrastructure loop

The engineering loop redistributes and allows sharing of resources, such as the treated water surplus from housing to industrial use, energy surplus from industry to housing and treatment of the industrial and residential sewage for irrigation purposes. Social loop introduces a list of services which housing and industry may share such as medical or sports centres.

In the material organisation of the cluster the project focused on the effects of the hybridisation of the engineering infrastructure with social and industrial services within one structure which I call a 'branch'. This branch organises a synergy between the plots with different programmes inside each cluster on the scale of the urban unit and between clusters at the regional scale.

Urban design guidelines

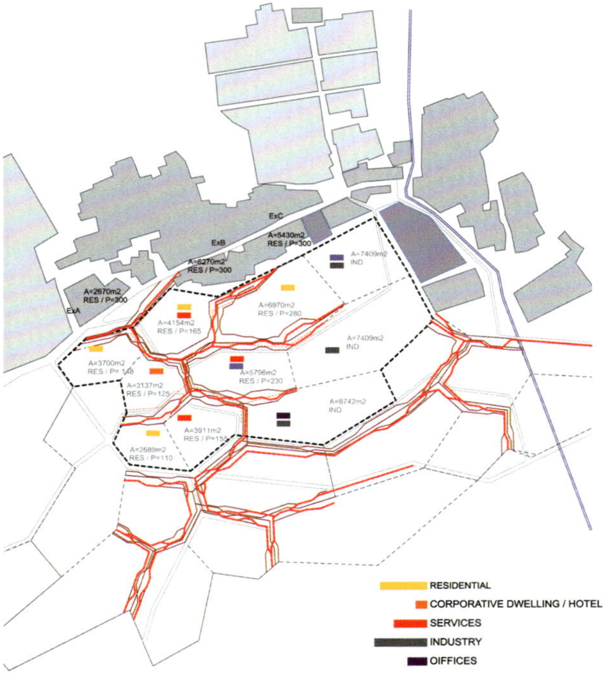

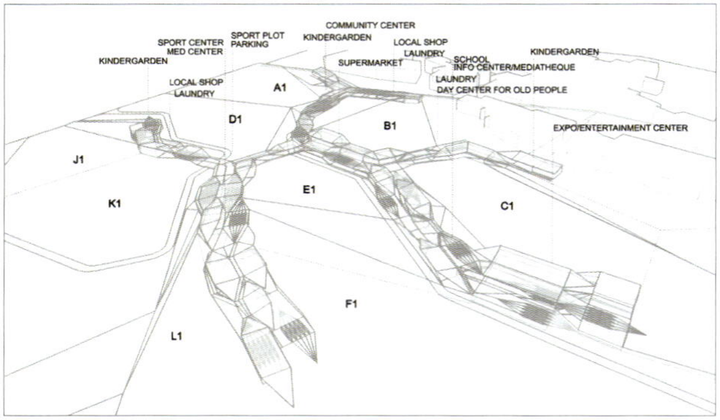

Examples of combination of engineering systems with different spatial organisations

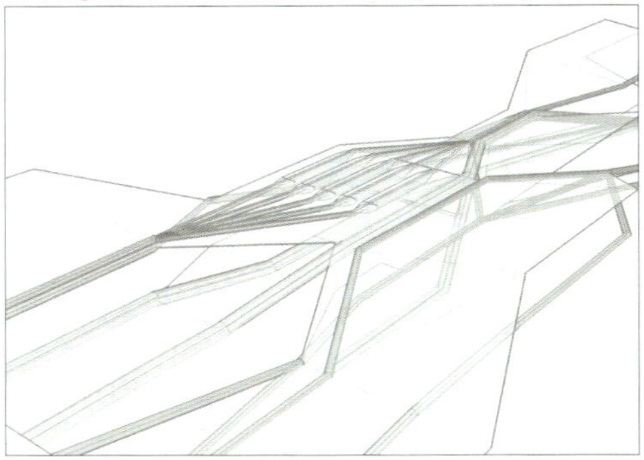

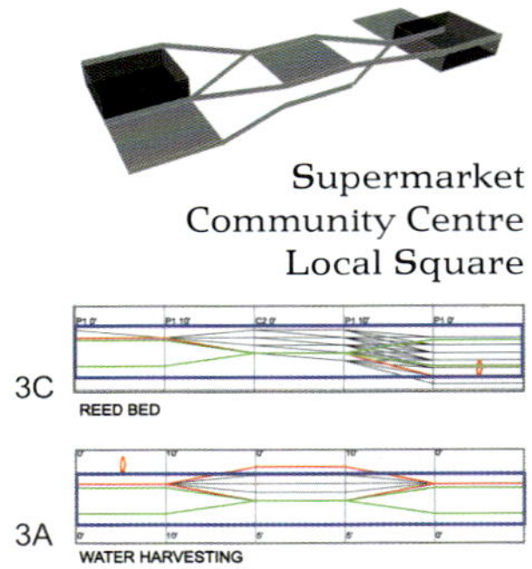

Supermarket
Community Centre
Local Square

3C REED BED
3A WATER HARVESTING

Example A

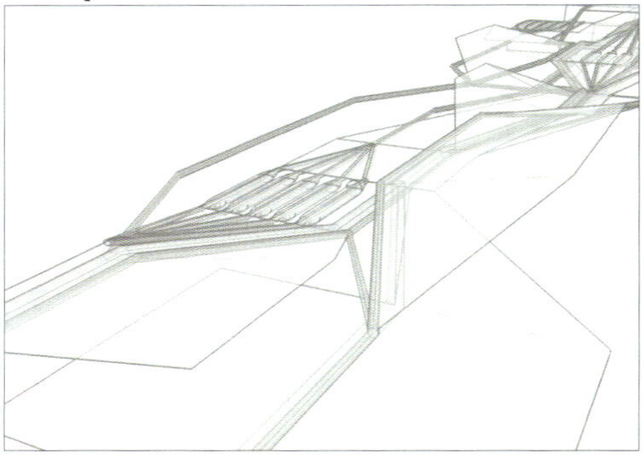

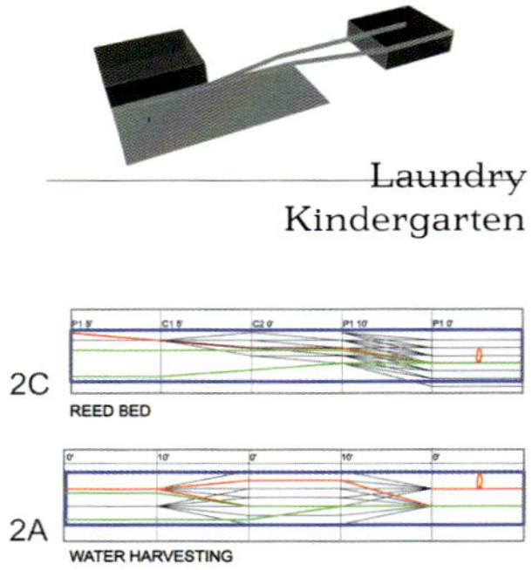

Laundry
Kindergarten

2C REED BED
2A WATER HARVESTING

Example B

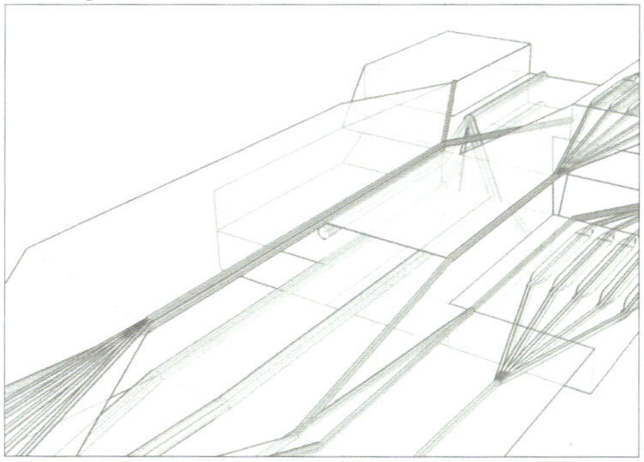

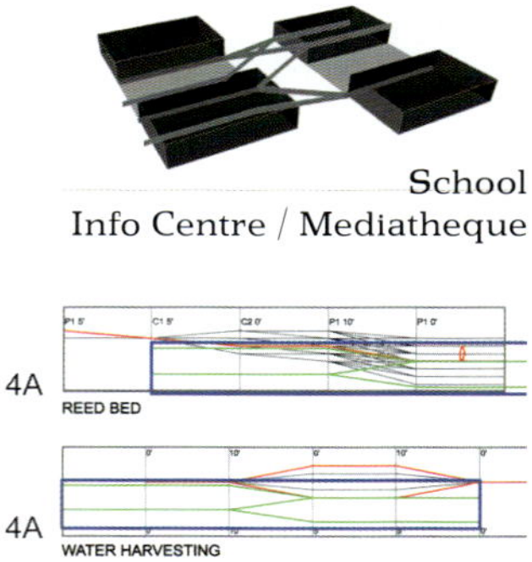

School
Info Centre / Mediatheque

4A REED BED
4A WATER HARVESTING

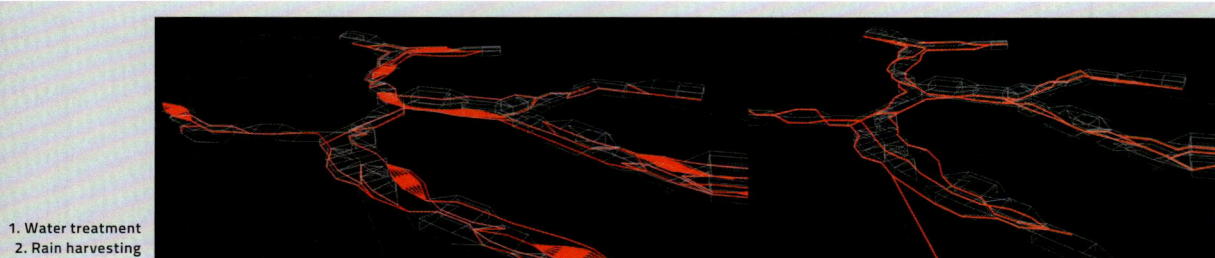

1. Water treatment
2. Rain harvesting

Infrastructural provision is not only a 'limiting factor' for the site capacity, but a tool for the spatial definition of the blocks themselves and the spatial proposal for a new network of public space. In order to explore how this can be implemented, a series of guidelines is generated describing the density of the plots, the range of programmes, open space requirements, and areas where it is possible to attach new building development to the 'branch'.

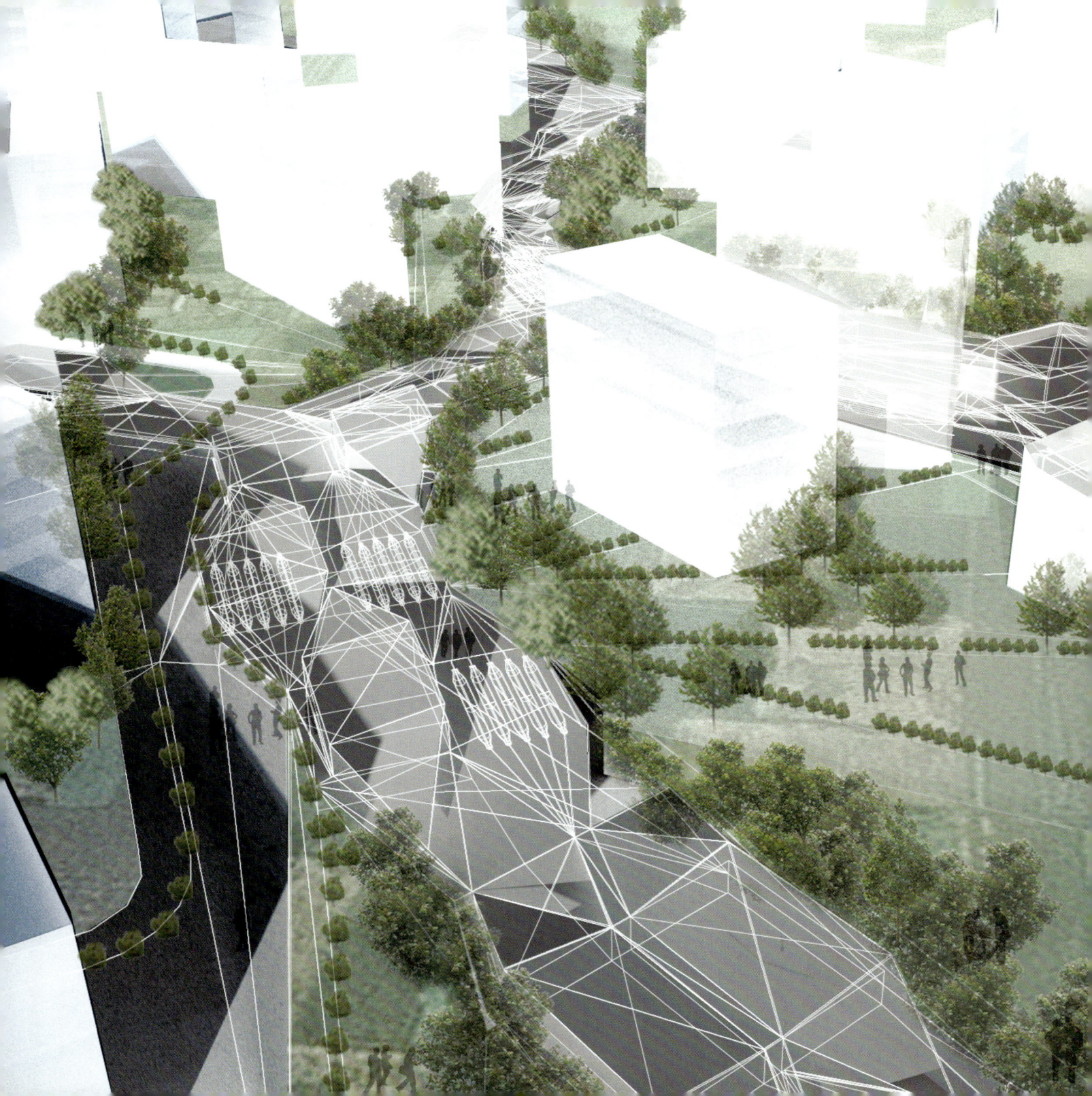

AALU China 07/08

Intercropping city

Date **2007/08**
Location **China**
Author **Hossein Kachabi**

Project description

Despite being located in one of the most stunning corners of the Pearl River Delta, most of Zhuhai's tourist development is focused on a small stretch of land in coastal areas, ignoring a rich hinterland of agrarian landscapes and its associated cultural heritage. Although there is an increasing number of voices recognising the potentials of this territorial asset, development trends do not seem to be taking much notice. Casino tourism and new technological parks are not currently showing much interest in a system of coevolution which would share benefits and responsibilities with the surrounding rural matrix, instead fuelling an urban sprawl which imports aesthetic and spatial formulas more akin to theme parks and occidental suburbia.

Gated developments targeting the upper middle class are starting to dot a landscape that will soon lose the quintessential characteristics that initially drove those developments to settle, in the search of a pristine environment. In this sense, the model of urbanisation, if taken to its limits (which is what is actually happening) is inherently contradictory and self-defeating, where developments currently under construction promise the enjoyment of a landscape that they are themselves destroying.

The project reevaluates the role of agriculture and its relationship with urbanism in order to redefine territorial regimes which are not alien to their own spatial production. Concepts of ground control and income sharing are therefore crucial in order to start using the dichotomy city – nature in a productive way, avoiding political correctness, weak compromise and an approach to landscape as a mere 'greening' postproduction.

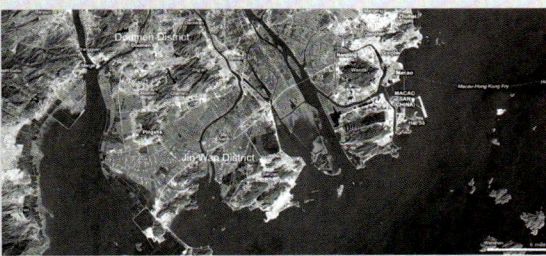

1. Zhuhai province

Zhuhai / Pearl River Delta

Situated in the southern part of Guangdong Province, China, Zhuhai city is a well-known garden-like coastal city occupying an area of 7,650 square kilometres with a population of 1.15 million. Founded in 1979, Zhuhai city set up its Special Economic Zone in 1980. As a harbour city, Zhuhai has five Grade-I and 20 Grade-II harbours and ports with 94 various productive berths completed and docks of 6,500 metres long, with an annual freight throughout of over 20.15 milion tons and annual volume of passenger transport of 8.45 million persons. Gaolan port is a major hub harbour in the coastal area of China, which is the only deep water harbour on the west bank of the PRD.

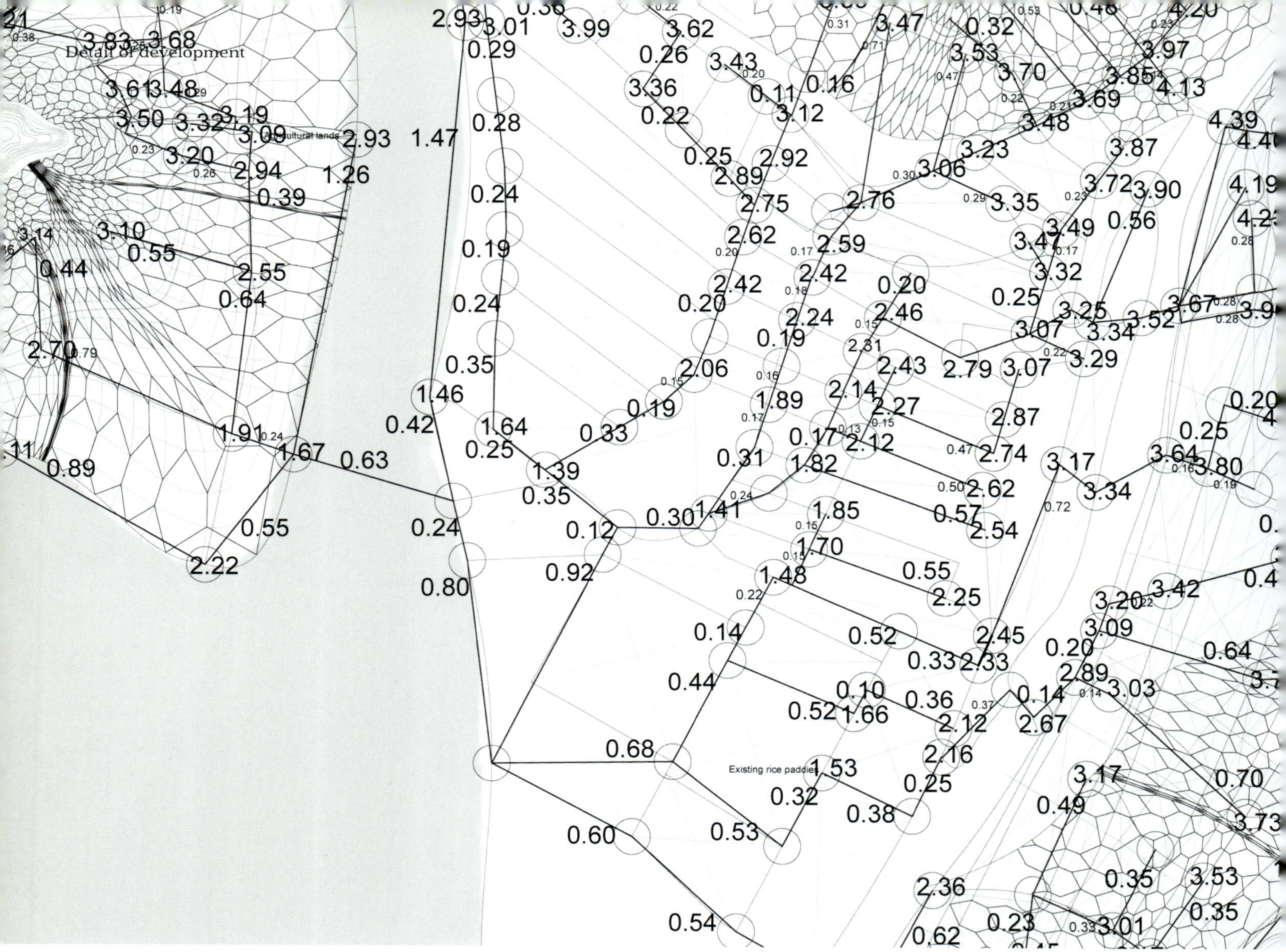

1/2. Landscape consumption

Generic landscape consumption

Topography and the series of mountain ranges around Zhuhai are one of the most valuable assets of the city. However, this is not always recognised with a number of developments 'levelling' hills and geographical features in a tabula rasa approach with the intention to generate the conditions for a perfect import of alien models of urbanism. The analysis of topography, water movement and its relations with the existing agricultural production system is the first step in the project.

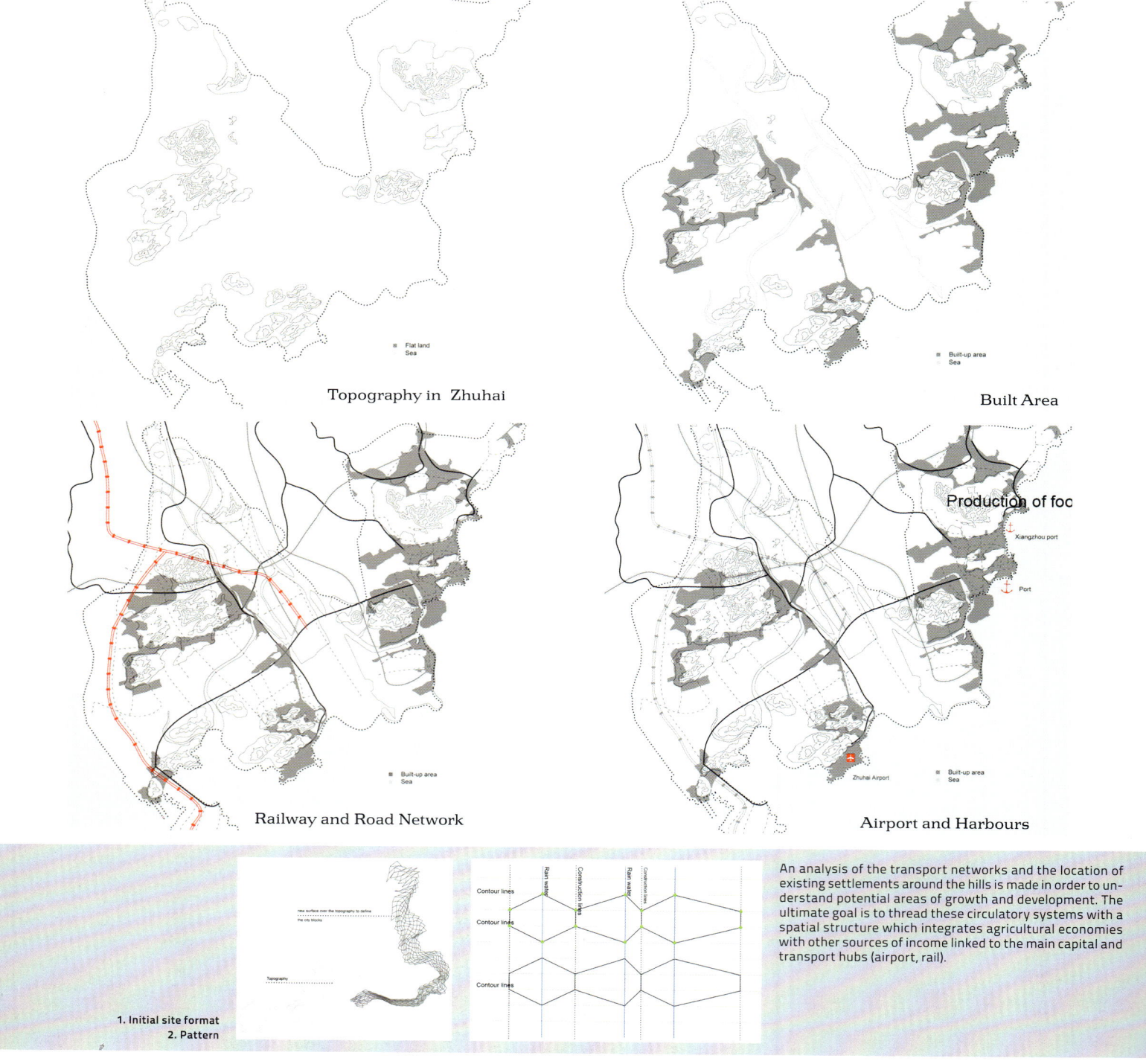

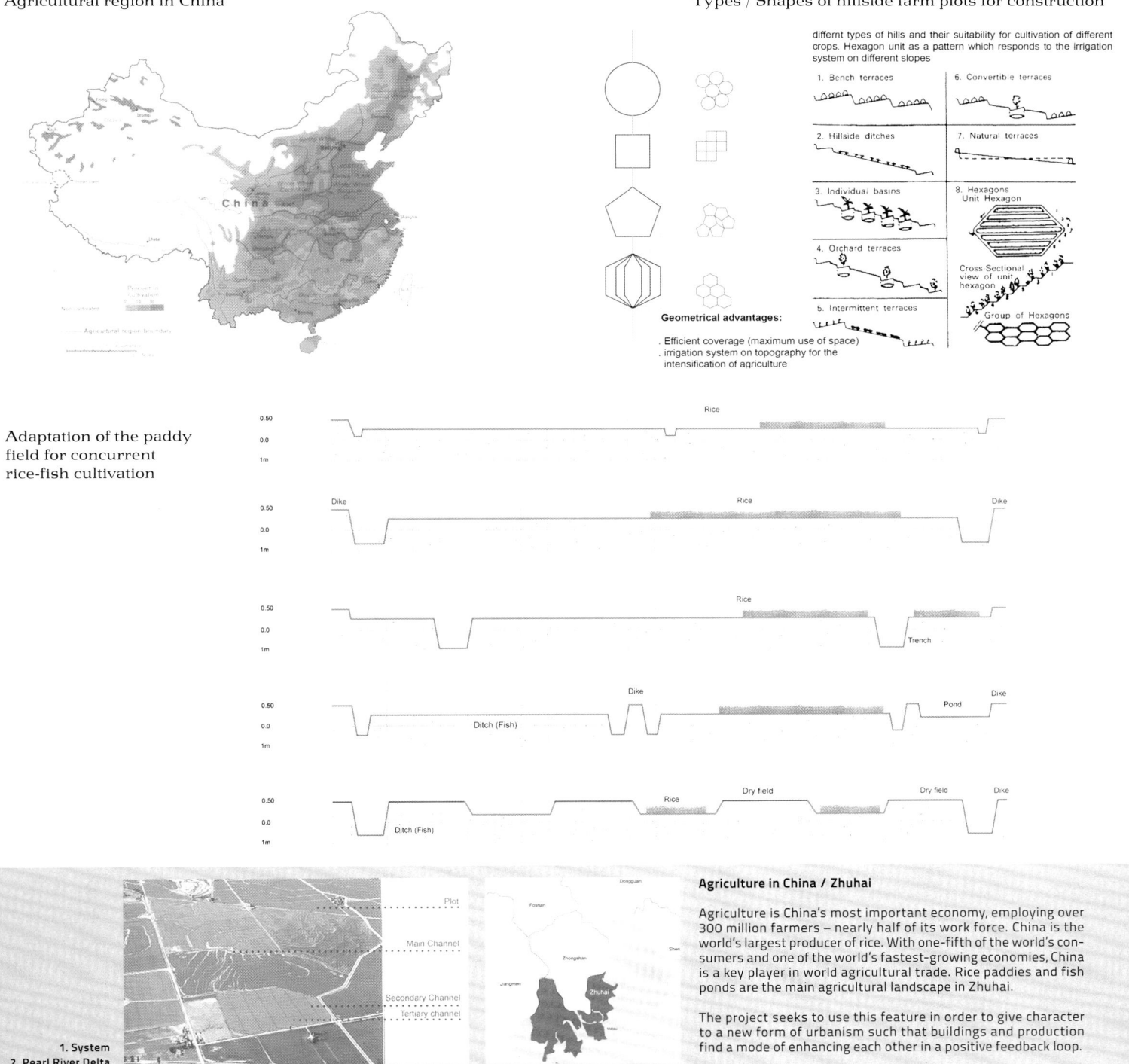

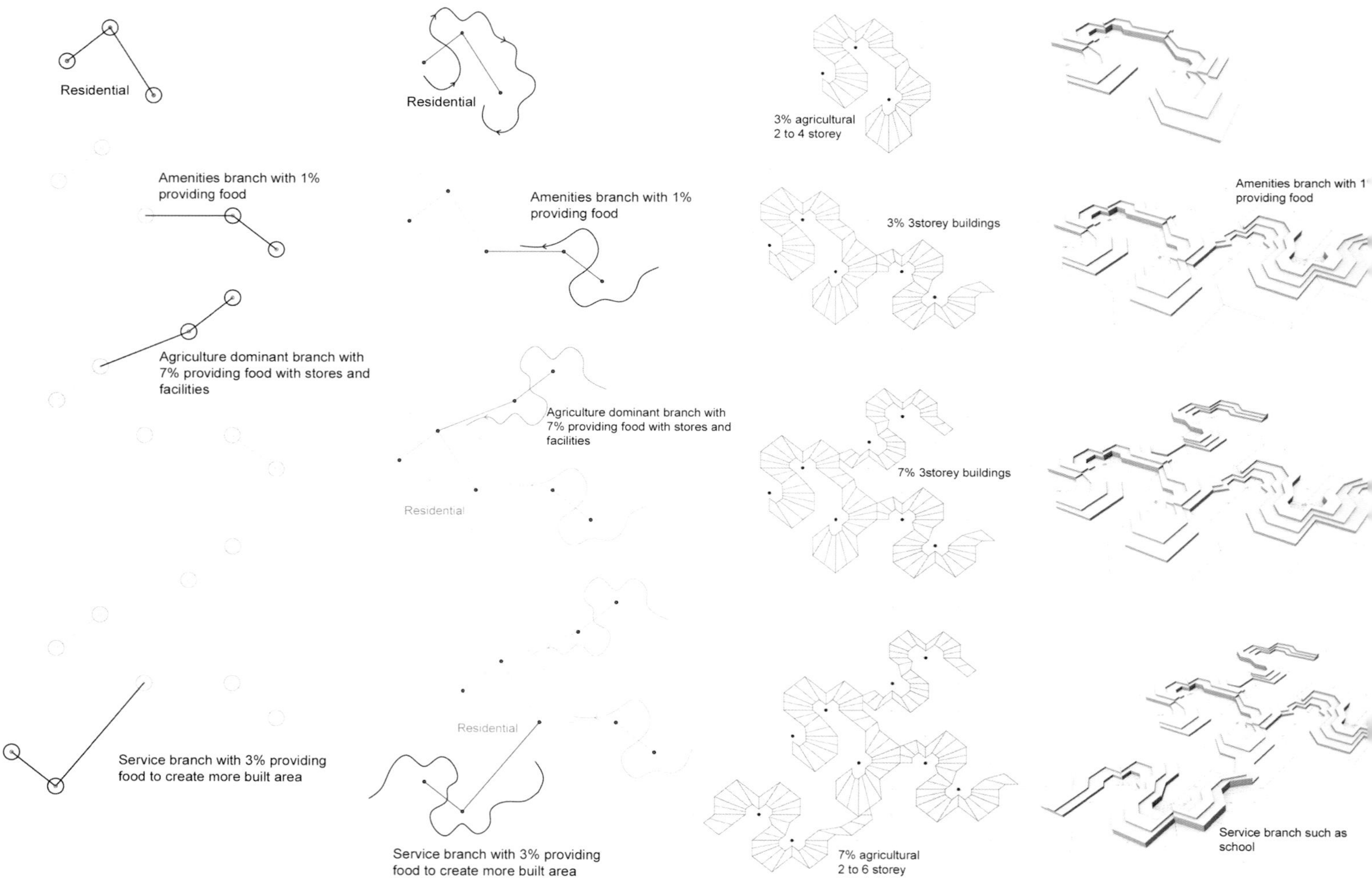

Prototype development

Residential

Amenities branch with 1% providing food

Agriculture dominant branch with 7% providing food with stores and facilities

Service branch with 3% providing food to create more built area

Residential

Amenities branch with 1% providing food

Agriculture dominant branch with 7% providing food with stores and facilities

Residential

Service branch with 3% providing food to create more built area

3% agricultural 2 to 4 storey

3% 3storey buildings

7% 3storey buildings

7% agricultural 2 to 6 storey

Amenities branch with 1 providing food

Service branch such as school

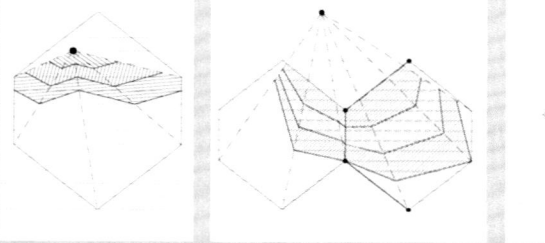

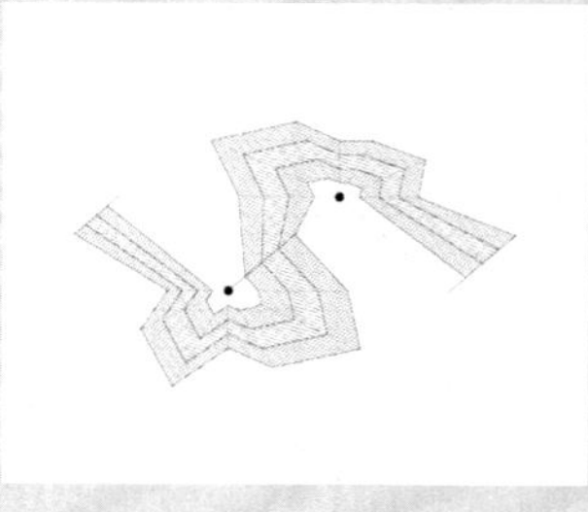

1/2. Convergent point variations
3. Cluster organisation

Convergent points

A convergent point system is used in order to generate the geometry of the terraced buildings. The position of this convergent point will affect organisation of buildings with different functions, width of the terraces and will increase the area for various agricultural uses such as rice paddies (depending on the characters of the urban nodes from predominantly agriculture to predominantly built).

urban pockets where the most intensity of tertiary roads arearea with the least concentration of road network remain agricultural

Urban pockets

Existing rice paddies

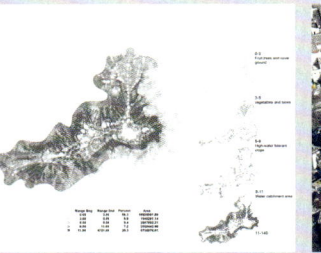

1. Slope analysis
2. Terraced buildings

Convergent points

Nodes are positioned at the intersection of the secondary roads. Convergent points create the central clusters at the end of the nodes and they begin to grow by following the pattern of the tertiary road network. Tertiary roads were defined by following the pattern of the city blocks and agricultural plots. Seven urban nodes are chosen as the starting points, while lines are traced finding the shortest distances to connect them. This network is integrated with the already defined secondary road network.
Buildings are integrated with the landscape creating a second ground. Terraces are used for cultivation of certain types of crops to intensify agricultural productivity. Terraces are also used to provide a means of navigation through the city as these ramps are varied in width and connect different levels together, becoming bridges over the roads.

Urban pocket morphology

urban pockets where the most intensity of tertiary roads arearea with the least concentration of road network remain agricultural

Tertiary road network

Existing rice paddies

1. Etoiles
2. Escalators

Urban pocket morphology

Convergent points create central clusters which are located in strategic parts of the site (water-catchment areas or transport nodes) while other branches with different functions are gradually added as the urban pocket grows.

The site strategy offers different forms of articulating the urban rural binomial. A series of nodes at the top have an agricultural character, becoming more 'urban' as one moves towards the sloped areas. Other nodes have the urban character at the centre, becoming more agriculturally dominated in the proximity of the existing rice paddies.

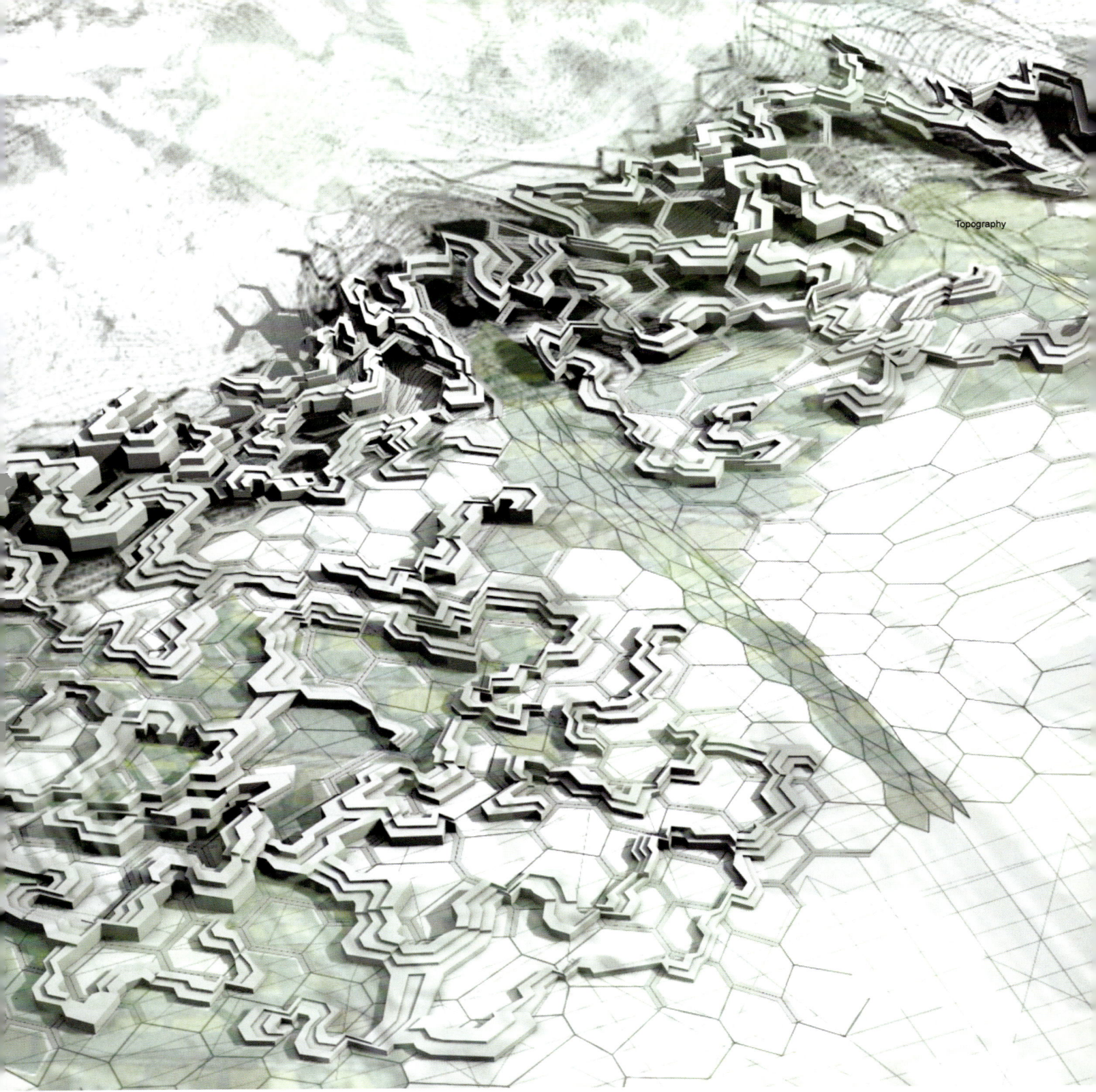

Topography

Prototype proliferation

AALANDSCAPEURBANISM

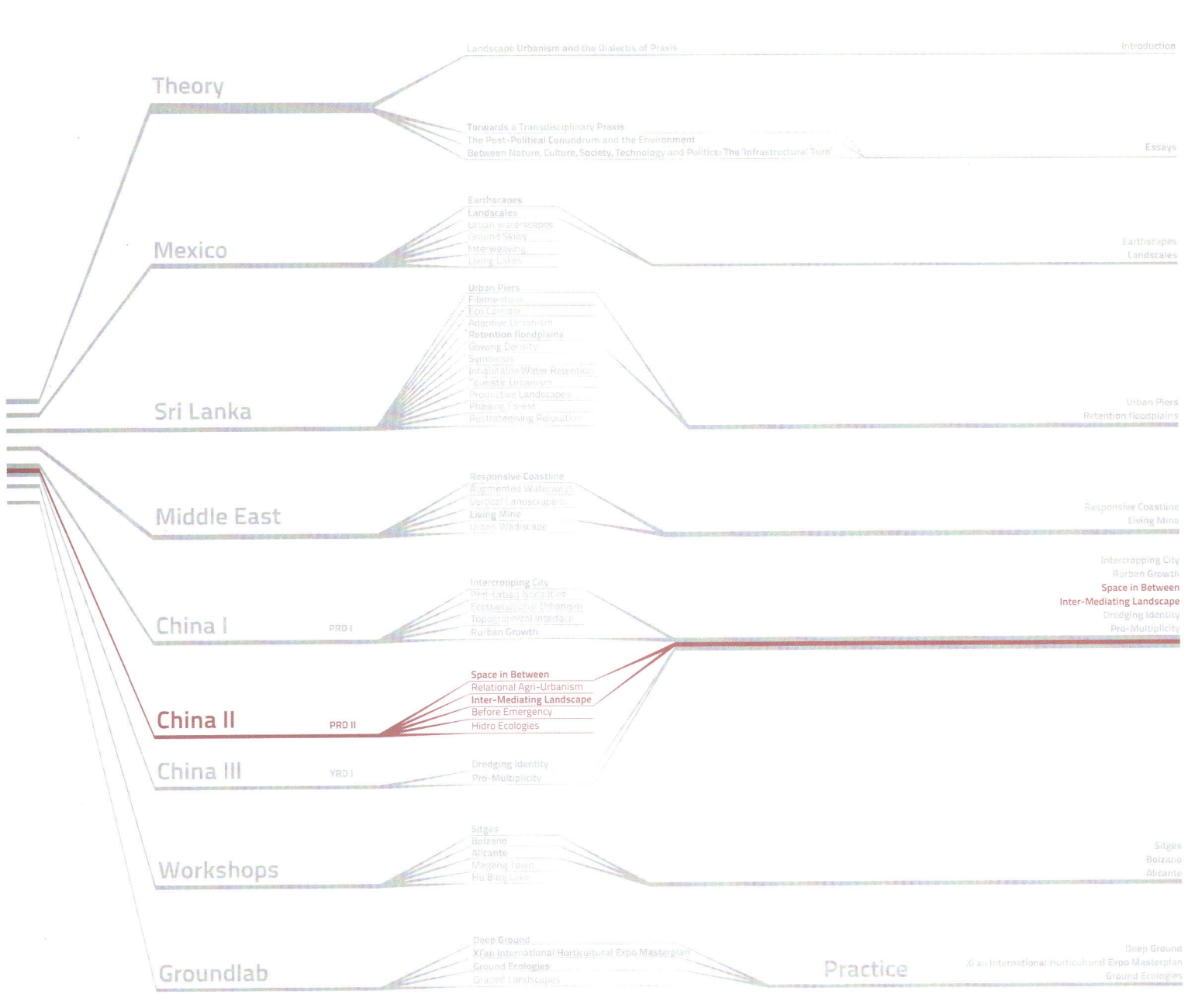

AA Landscape Urbanism 08/09
Prototypical Urbanities - PRD China

AGENDA Building on last year's body of research, LU again took China's ambition to build 400 new cities by 2020 as the basis for its brief. According to this plan, 20 new cities are to be built each year to contain the huge numbers of people – around 12 million annually – who are leaving the countryside for urban areas. Far from resisting this development, we opportunistically generated 'proto-strategies' for new large-scale agglomerations as a means of critically addressing the phenomenon of mass-produced urban sprawl. Our test bed was the Pearl River Delta, where students focused on the emergence of four benchmark conditions identified by our previous research: the underlying dysfunction and creative potential of industrial ecologies in the rapidly urbanising rural hinterland; the rapid deindustrialisation and disintegration of second-cycle city cores; the emerging resistance of traditional and informally grown urban cores to top-down planning procedures; and the terms by which a new sprawling state engages with existing agricultural land. We operated critically, seeking to produce alternative templates of urbanisation based on strategies that stemmed from embryonic processes seeking the integration of cultural tradition, regional ecological systems and economic globalisation.

AALU China 08/09

Space in between

Date **2008/09**
Location **China**
Author **Wenwen Wang**

Project description

Following an examination of National Planning Regulations and informal growth process, the project proposes a critique of national planning regulation on the provision of large-scale transport infrastructure and its relationship with urban fabric. A current oversupply of highway network based on for a car centred approach, combined with the use of mega blocks, is generating the perfect mix for a disjointed urban fabric and the erasure of the existing local fabric of urban villages. The result is a combination of gated communities separated from the rest of the city by fences or motorways, fuelling a growing inequality in Chinese society.

The project proposes, as an alternative, an extended network of transport corridors around which emergent informal growth processes, diversity and complexity of public activities and strong linkages and responses to the surroundings can develop. Departing from the 'super-block' model – regarding mixed land-use and density accumulations – as an urban condenser, the projects seeks to push infrastructure to be the neutral ground to be appropriated in unexpected ways.

Based on the primary structure, it proposes a public transportation system in order to enhance public circulation between urbanised areas and rural villages. Public spaces and semi-public spaces are provided along the public transportation system. Instead of only focusing on the internal organisation block, the proposal seeks to 'thicken' the infrastructural lines, turning them into an actual spatial proposal linked to public works and shared urban spaces.

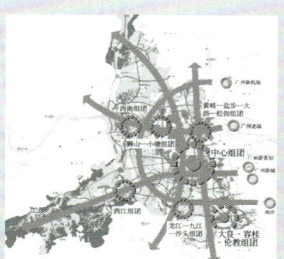

1. Fo Shan city plan
2. Fo Shan housing

The strategy of locating a series of public facilities is based on accessibility and the hierarchy of relations to the proposed street network. It starts from storage and parking spaces, following the typological changes of public spaces between urbanised areas and rural villages, opening the ground level for informal growth. According to programme adjacency and density speculations, super blocks start to grow vertically based on the street network. It tests different formations of the super block, in order to regenerate the city fabric with new urban patterns mediating top-down planning with informal growth.

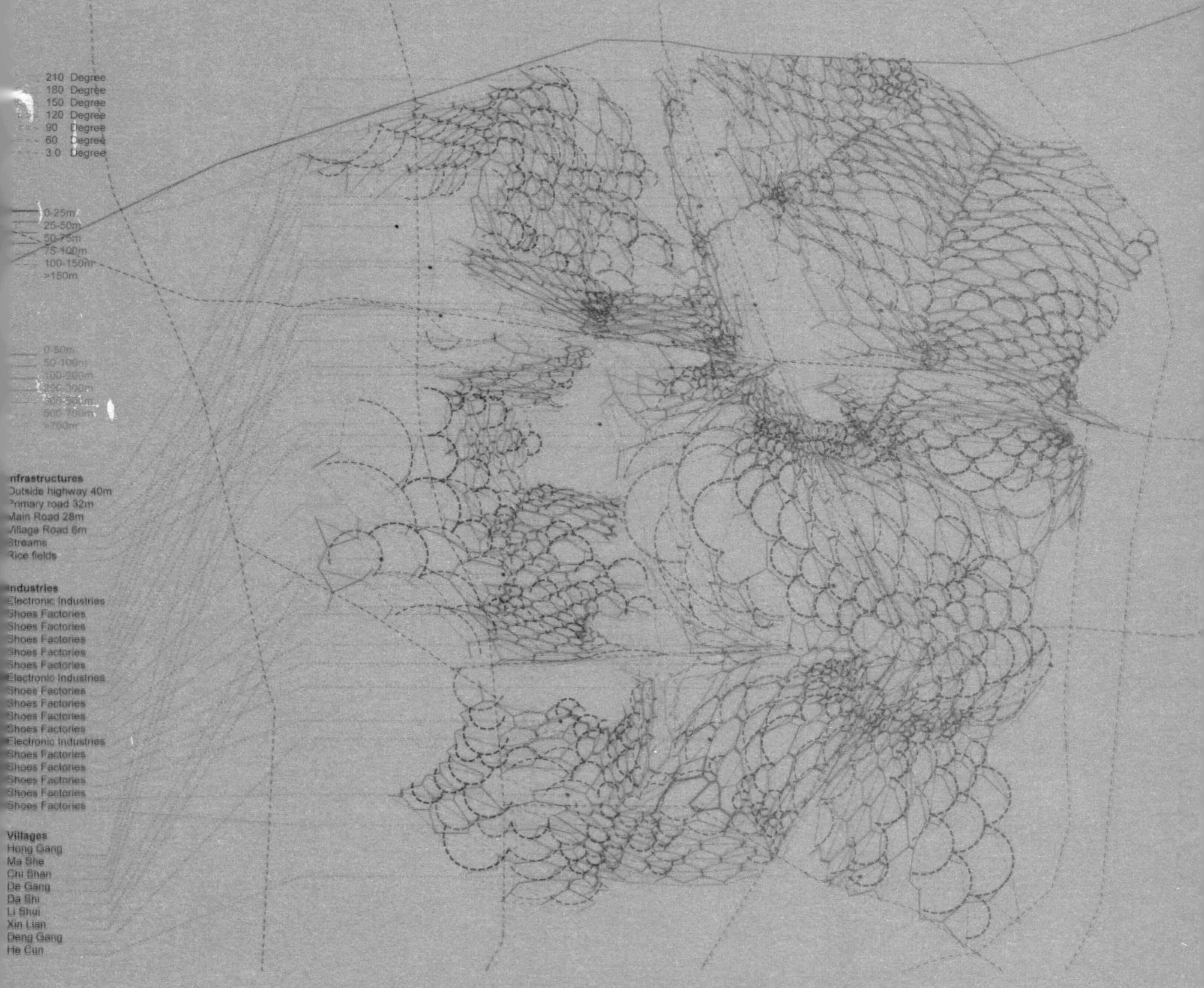

210 Degree
180 Degree
150 Degree
120 Degree
90 Degree
60 Degree
30 Degree

0-25m
25-50m
50-75m
75-100m
100-150m
>150m

0-50m
50-100m
100-200m
200-300m
300-500m
500-700m
>700m

Infrastructures
Outside highway 40m
Primary road 32m
Main Road 28m
Village Road 6m
Streams
Rice fields

Industries
Electronic Industries
Shoes Factories
Shoes Factories
Shoes Factories
Shoes Factories
Electronic Industries
Shoes Factories
Shoes Factories
Shoes Factories
Shoes Factories
Electronic Industries
Shoes Factories
Shoes Factories
Shoes Factories
Shoes Factories

Villages
Hong Gang
Ma She
Chi Shan
De Gang
Da Shi
Li Shui
Xin Lian
Deng Gang
He Cun

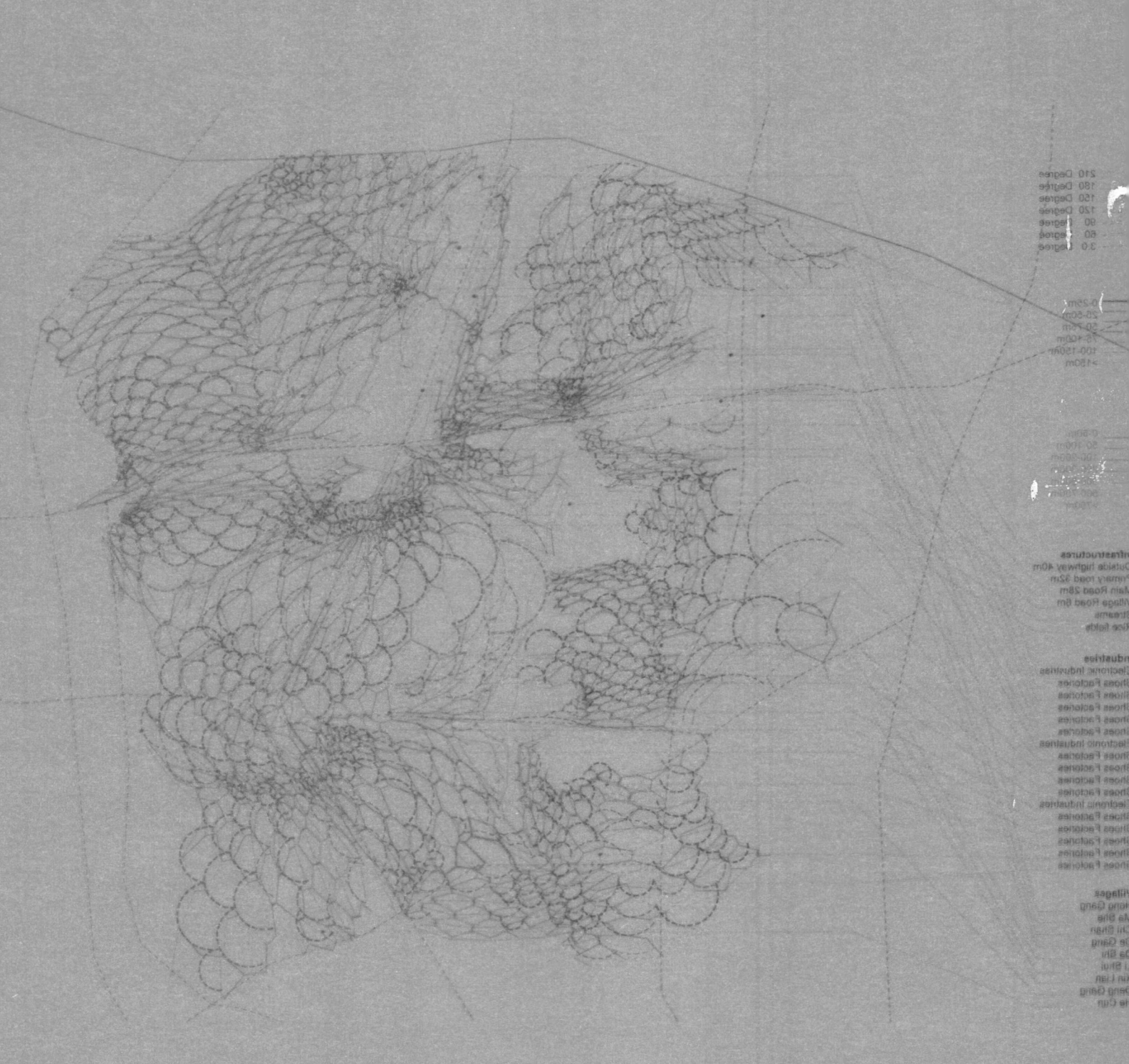

Site mapping

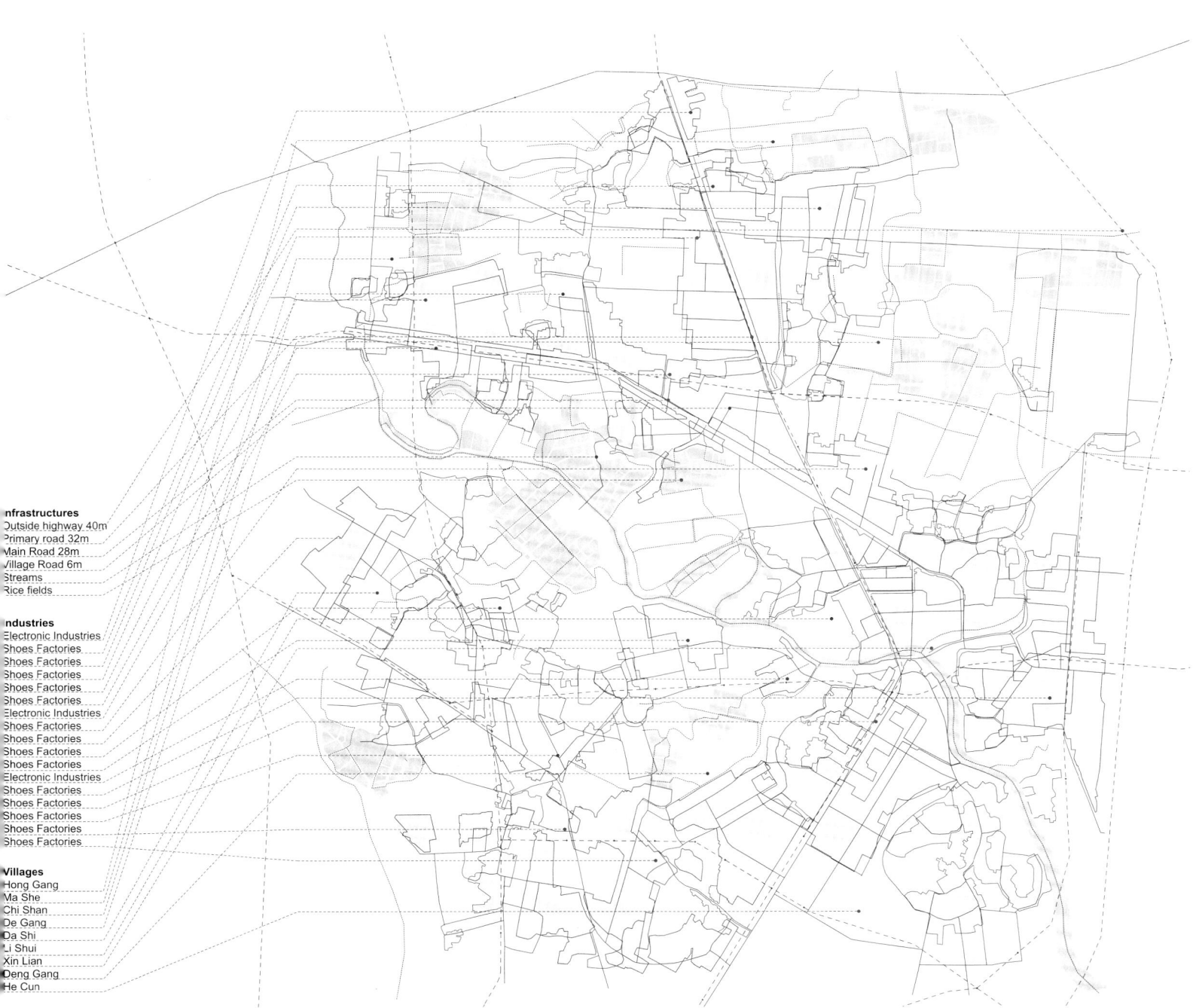

Infrastructures
Outside highway 40m
Primary road 32m
Main Road 28m
Village Road 6m
Streams
Rice fields

Industries
Electronic Industries
Shoes Factories
Shoes Factories
Shoes Factories
Shoes Factories
Electronic Industries
Shoes Factories
Shoes Factories
Electronic Industries
Shoes Factories
Shoes Factories
Shoes Factories
Shoes Factories

Villages
Hong Gang
Ma She
Chi Shan
De Gang
Da Shi
Li Shui
Xin Lian
Deng Gang
He Cun

Transportation system proposal

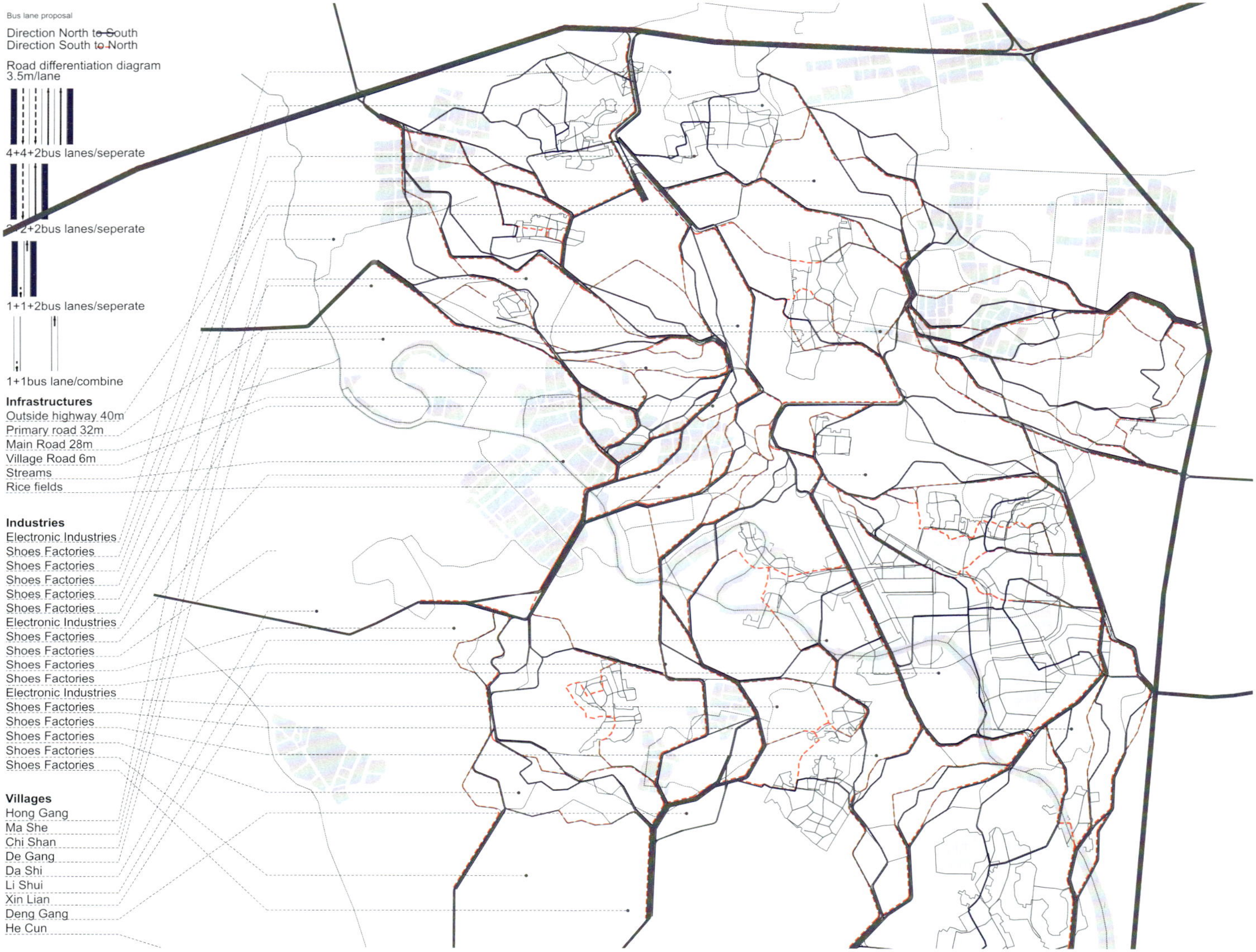

Bus lane proposal
Direction North to South
Direction South to North

Road differentiation diagram
3.5m/lane

4+4+2bus lanes/seperate

2+2+2bus lanes/seperate

1+1+2bus lanes/seperate

1+1bus lane/combine

Infrastructures
Outside highway 40m
Primary road 32m
Main Road 28m
Village Road 6m
Streams
Rice fields

Industries
Electronic Industries
Shoes Factories
Shoes Factories
Shoes Factories
Shoes Factories
Electronic Industries
Shoes Factories
Shoes Factories
Shoes Factories
Electronic Industries
Shoes Factories
Shoes Factories
Shoes Factories
Shoes Factories
Shoes Factories

Villages
Hong Gang
Ma She
Chi Shan
De Gang
Da Shi
Li Shui
Xin Lian
Deng Gang
He Cun

Case study: Highways in Shanghai

The structure

An initial site structure is generated by adapting a prototypical mesh to the spaces between the existing urban villages. Main existing roads and existing entrances into these villages form the anchors to trace the network.

This primary structure is to be transformed into a networked version of an urban condenser, forming points of encounter for citizens as well as providing basic services to local communities.

Street branching system diagrams

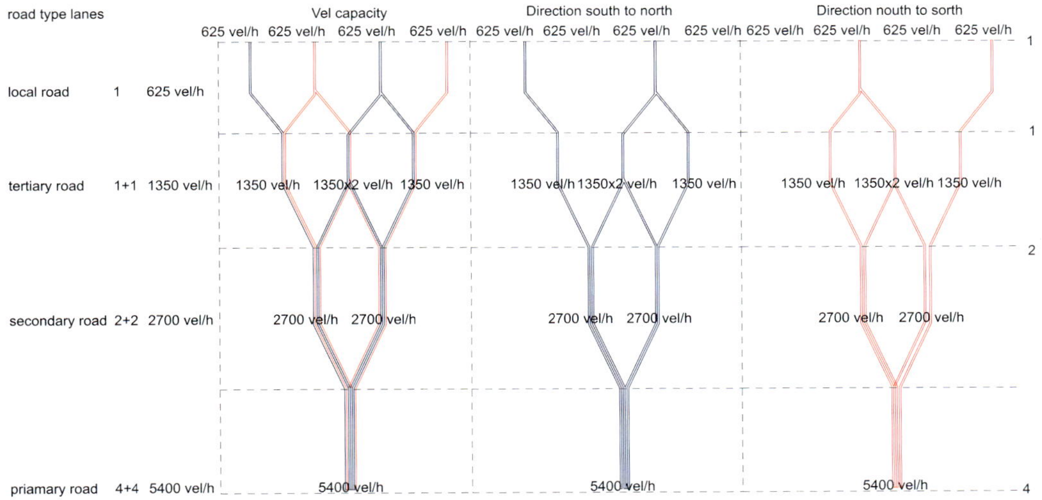

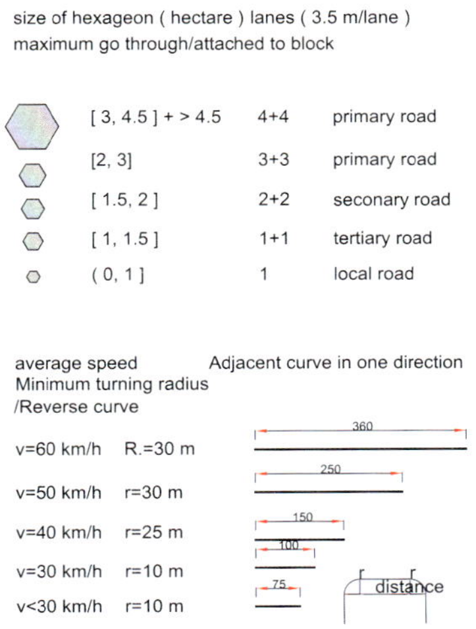

road type	lanes	Vel capacity				Direction south to north				Direction north to south				size of hexagon (hectare)	lanes (3.5 m/lane) maximum go through/attached to block
local road	1	625 vel/h	625 vel/h	625 vel/h	625 vel/h	625 vel/h	625 vel/h	625 vel/h	625 vel/h	625 vel/h	625 vel/h	625 vel/h	625 vel/h	[3, 4.5] + > 4.5	4+4 primary road
														[2, 3]	3+3 primary road
tertiary road	1+1	1350 vel/h	1350 vel/h	1350x2 vel/h	1350 vel/h	1350 vel/h	1350x2 vel/h	1350 vel/h		1350 vel/h	1350x2 vel/h	1350 vel/h		[1.5, 2]	2+2 secondary road
														[1, 1.5]	1+1 tertiary road
														(0, 1]	1 local road
secondary road	2+2	2700 vel/h		2700 vel/h	2700 vel/h		2700 vel/h	2700 vel/h			2700 vel/h	2700 vel/h			
primary road	4+4	5400 vel/h			5400 vel/h			5400 vel/h				5400 vel/h			

average speed / Minimum turning radius / Reverse curve — Adjacent curve in one direction

v=60 km/h R.=30 m — 360
v=50 km/h r=30 m — 250
v=40 km/h r=25 m — 150
v=30 km/h r=10 m — 100
v<30 km/h r=10 m — 75 r r distance

Dtail

Zoom in road network on site
Size 1km x 1km

Road network proposal
100 M
50 M
— Direction South to North
— Direction North to South

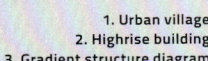

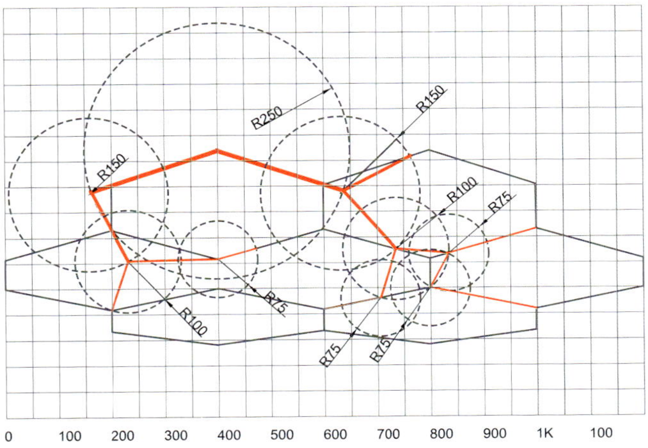

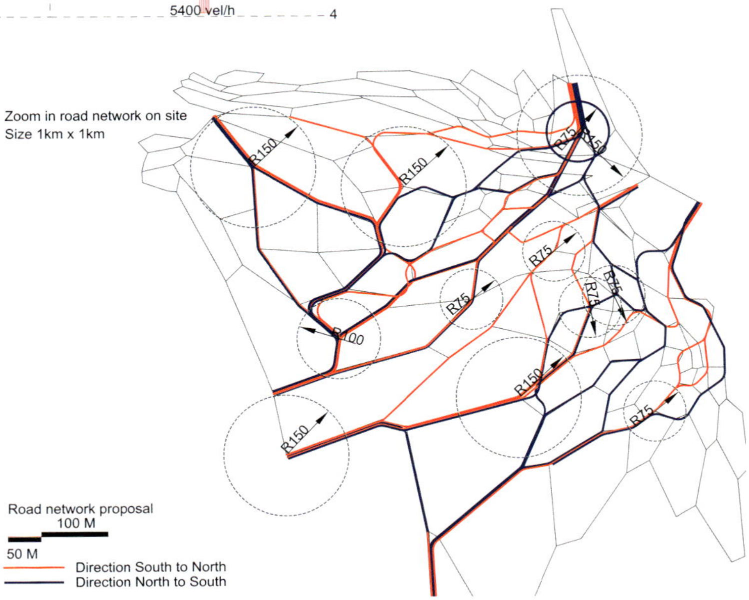

1. Urban villages
2. Highrise buildings
3. Gradient structure diagrams

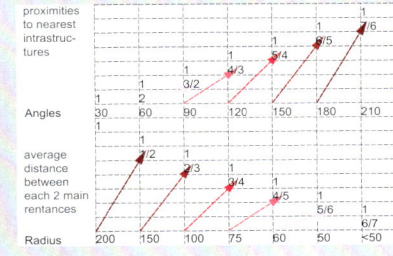

proximities to nearest infrastructures
Angles
average distance between each 2 main rentrances
Radius

The location of super blocks is defined according to width and speed along the primary roads. While 2nd blocks are located along the secondary road, the 3rd blocks are located along tertiary roads and the smallest blocks are located along the local roads. Super blocks are planned to be fully developed with high built ratio with the purpose of generating a critical mass to attract and accommodate the majority of the population in the future.

Urban block classification / super block traffic junction

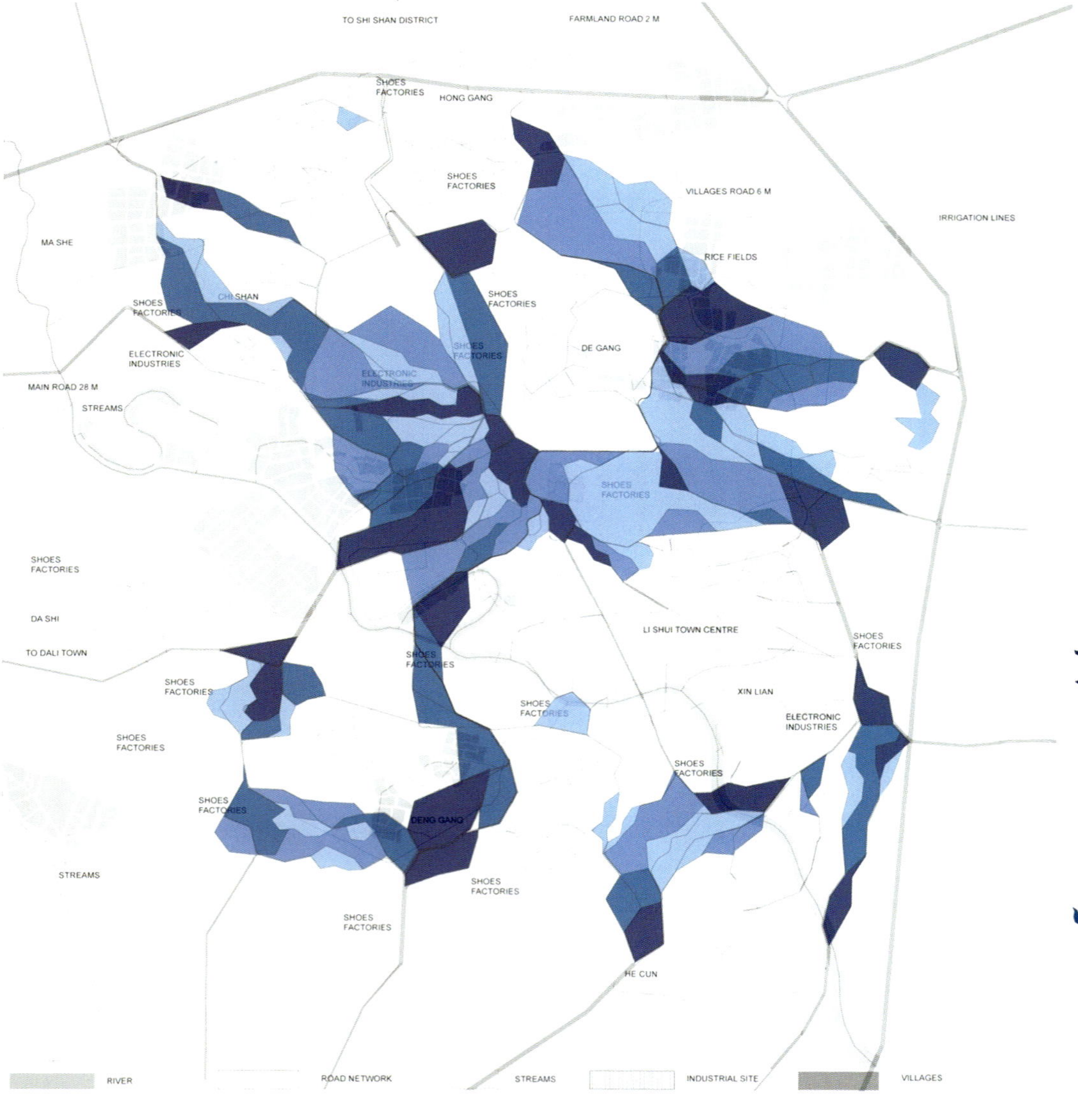

POPULATION DISTRABUTION
TOTAL=160,000 PPL

Super block
132.6811 hectares
fully built, BR=1.2,
20 m2/persopn average
132.6811 X 10,000X1.2 /20 = 79,608 people

2nd block
139.9763 hectares
0.8 built,
25 m2/persopn average
140 X 10,000 /25 = 44,800 people

3rd block
138 hectares
0.6 built,
33 m2/persopn average
138X 10,000 /33 = 25,090 people

4rd block
138 hectares
0.4 built,
50 m2/persopn average
138X 10,000 /50 = 11,040 people

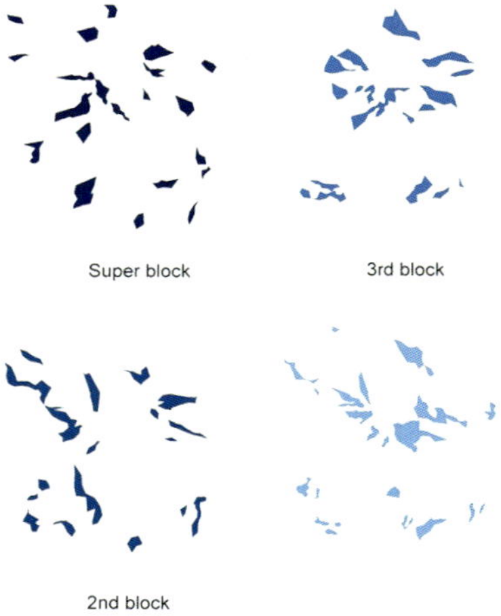

Super block   3rd block

2nd block

Programme diagrams

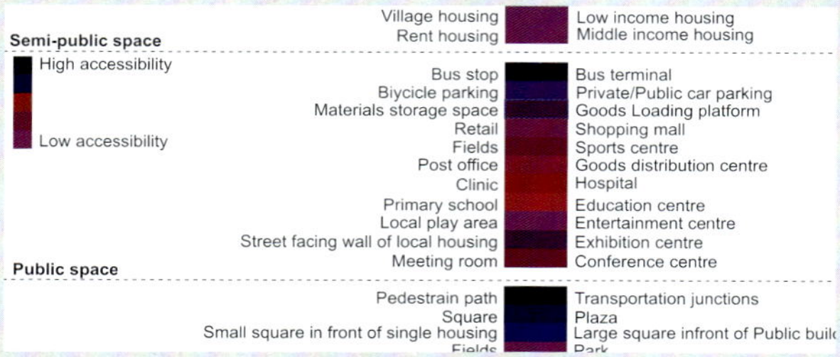

Semi-public space — High accessibility / Low accessibility — Public space

Village housing / Low income housing
Rent housing / Middle income housing
Bus stop / Bus terminal
Bicycle parking / Private/Public car parking
Materials storage space / Goods Loading platform
Retail / Shopping mall
Fields / Sports centre
Post office / Goods distribution centre
Clinic / Hospital
Primary school / Education centre
Local play area / Entertainment centre
Street facing wall of local housing / Exhibition centre
Meeting room / Conference centre
Pedestrain path / Transportation junctions
Square / Plaza
Small square in front of single housing / Large square infront of Public build
Fields / Park

Super block strategy

A whole variety of urban mega blocks is left in the spaces between primary infrastructural lines. These new plots are analysed both in term of their size but also proximity to existing urban nodes and potential for growth and expansion.

Urban block classification / super block traffic junction

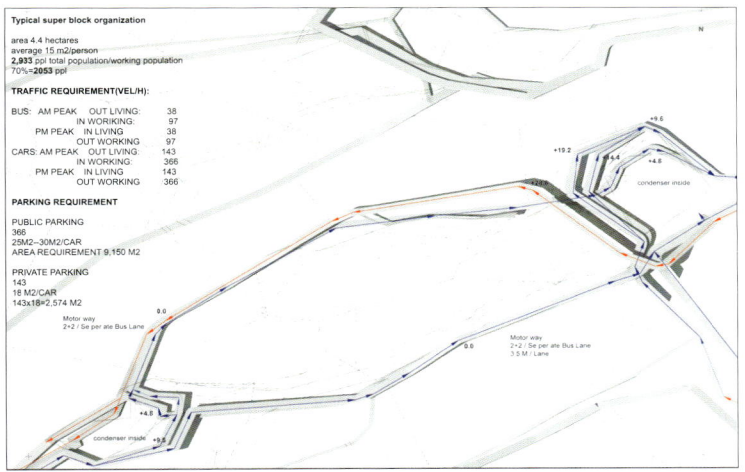

Elevations and platforms

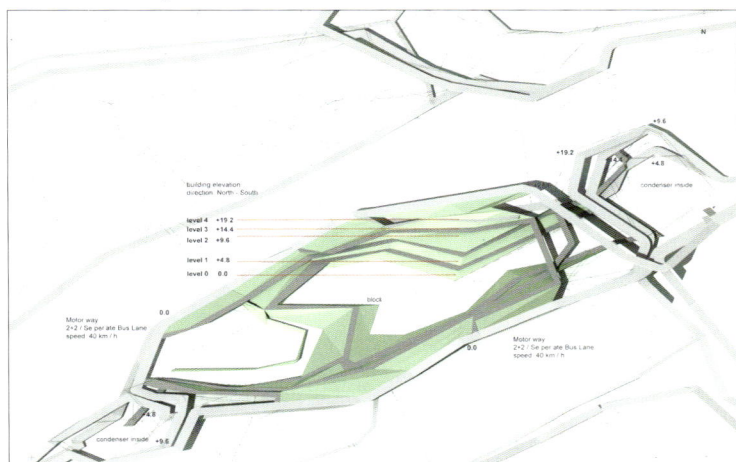

Tower accumulation

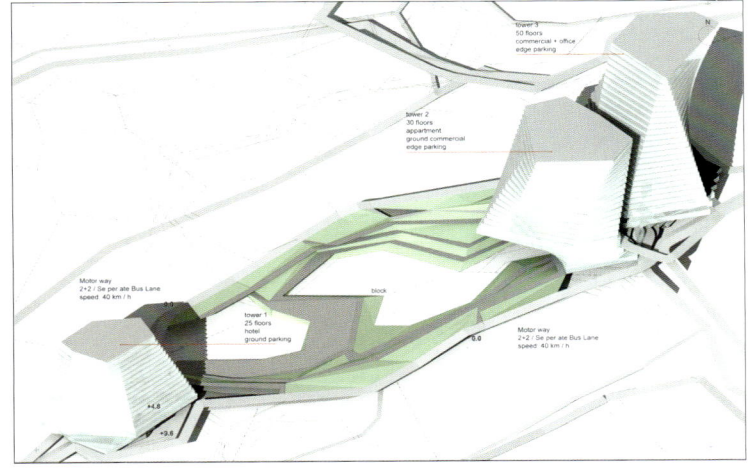

Overall plan

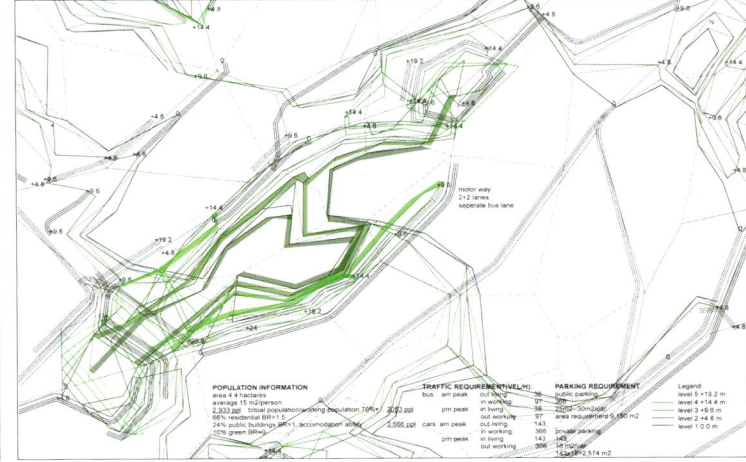

Massing 3D view

Circulations

Depending on traffic speed, bus lanes are combined with motorway when the speed is lower than 40km/h while bus lanes are separated from motorway when the speed is higher than 40km/h. While the number of lanes increases, so do the spaces in between those lanes, generating potential uses underneath and in the adjacent areas of low speed lanes. The ramping and growth of the interstitial volumes is also accompanied by the location of towers and nodes of higher urban intensity.

Massing location guidance

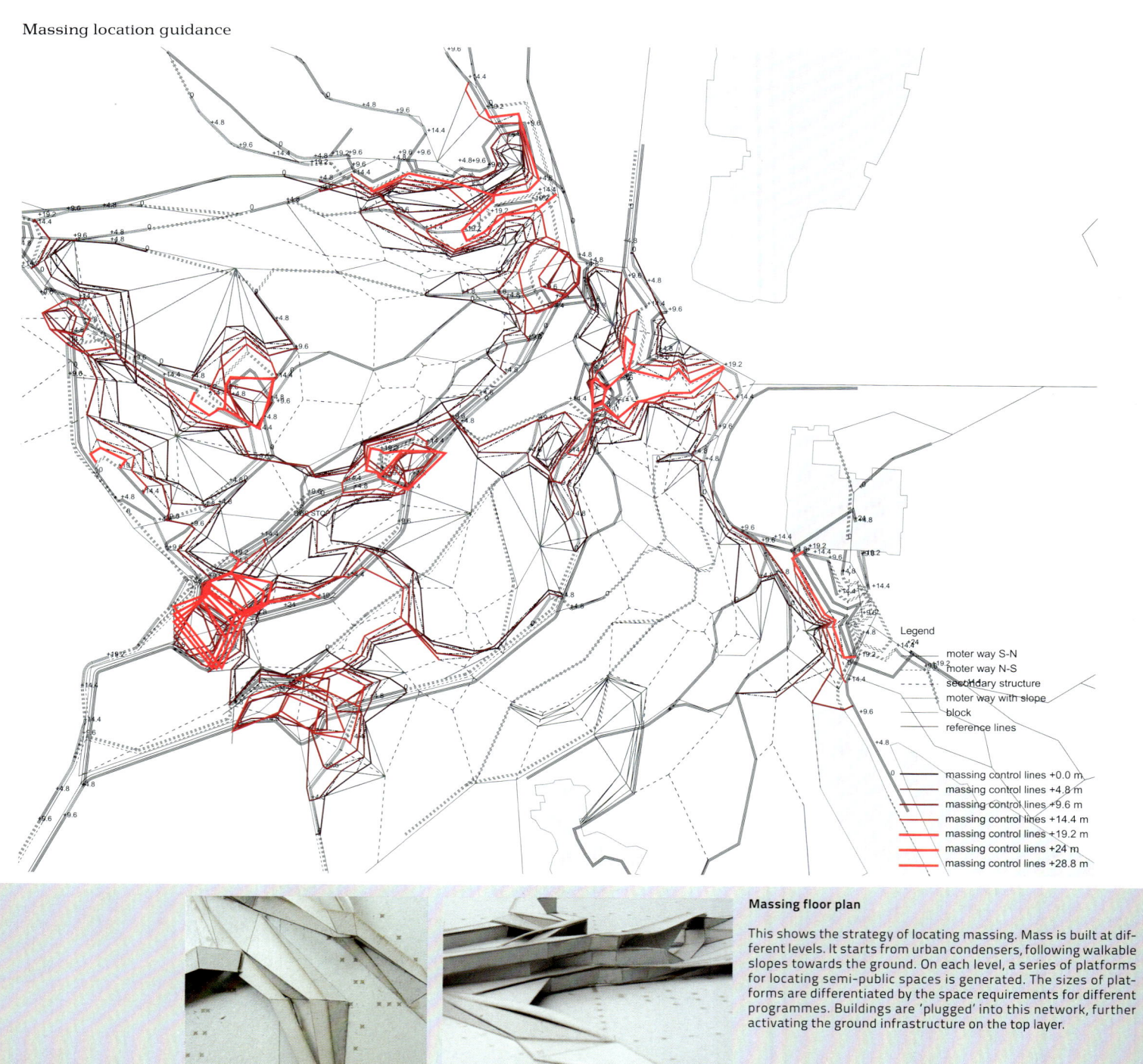

Legend
- moter way S-N
- moter way N-S
- secondary structure
- moter way with slope
- block
- reference lines

- massing control lines +0.0 m
- massing control lines +4.8 m
- massing control lines +9.6 m
- massing control lines +14.4 m
- massing control lines +19.2 m
- massing control liens +24 m
- massing control lines +28.8 m

1/2. Experimental models

Massing floor plan

This shows the strategy of locating massing. Mass is built at different levels. It starts from urban condensers, following walkable slopes towards the ground. On each level, a series of platforms for locating semi-public spaces is generated. The sizes of platforms are differentiated by the space requirements for different programmes. Buildings are 'plugged' into this network, further activating the ground infrastructure on the top layer.

Perspective view

Perspective view, under the condenser

AALU China 08/09

Intermittent landscapes

Date **2008/09**
Location **China**
Author **Cristina Barrios**

Project description

'The difference between city, country, and suburb is fast disappearing... what is left is marked by points of intensity and exchange' James Corner, Stan Allen 2005.

New urban centres

Rapid industrialisation in the Pearl River Delta in China has progressively developed most of its agricultural land into fragmented islands of self-organised industries and generic housing. The scattered urbanisation in peri-urban areas has led to the creation of degraded urban environments, industrial pollution, labour mobility and infrastructural redundancy, leaving the remaining agricultural land as voids for future urbanisation to fill. It is a model of urbanization that starts from the rural village itself, so as one village grows, the remaining ones depend on the new small-scale urban services, access to markets, information and social benefits which are brought by the new industries. The reoccurrence and complexity of these processes throughout the delta demand strategies that can adapt to their specific requirements.

Networking

By networking these scattered urbanisations, the project aims to devise a series of continuously adapting urban condensers whose primary function is to intensify, incentivise or compensate the programmatic orientation of the new fabrics. The condensers would work as templates; they are either informed by or create their own context, thus becoming a medium for social and material exchange.

Assembling the condenser

The condensers plug into existing fabrics and are assembled through programme units which are able to support different spatial and programmatic configurations over time. Through the integration of collective spaces, infrastructure, industry and agriculture production, they become new public cores for adjacent territories. The agriculture 'intent' is strongly retained.

Testing It, Qishi - Pearl River Delta

As a test-bed, the project examines Qishi, in the Pearl River Delta. Primarily agricultural, Qishi has developed into a series of dispersed 'factory towns' and isolated rural villages. Through the analysis of existing and proposed industrial-agricultural ecologies and development patterns of the site, processes of programmatic accumulation and association are underlined so as to articulate and speculate the development of the site.

1. Growth adjacency to Qishi
2. Pearl River Delta

Site condition

Over the last 30 years the Pearl River Delta has experienced a massive industrialisation of unprecedented speed and scale. Most of this process has happened at the expense of agricultural land, converting it into scattered urban formations of industries and low-end housing. The scattered and uncontrolled allocation of industries has also resulted in severe problems of water and waste pollution, which create degraded urban environments that are difficult to solve by further urbanisation.
To feed 1.3 billion people, China is already facing a lack of arable land. While agriculture is 'occupied' in developing areas, it is abandoned on rural sites. The rural villages of the Pearl River Delta are relatively culturally homogeneous and community farming is still the basis of organisation in peri-urban areas. However, industries provide better jobs and opportunities to farmers, encouraging them to leave the fields. Agriculture and industry operate on a big scale which overlaps with small-scale residential living.

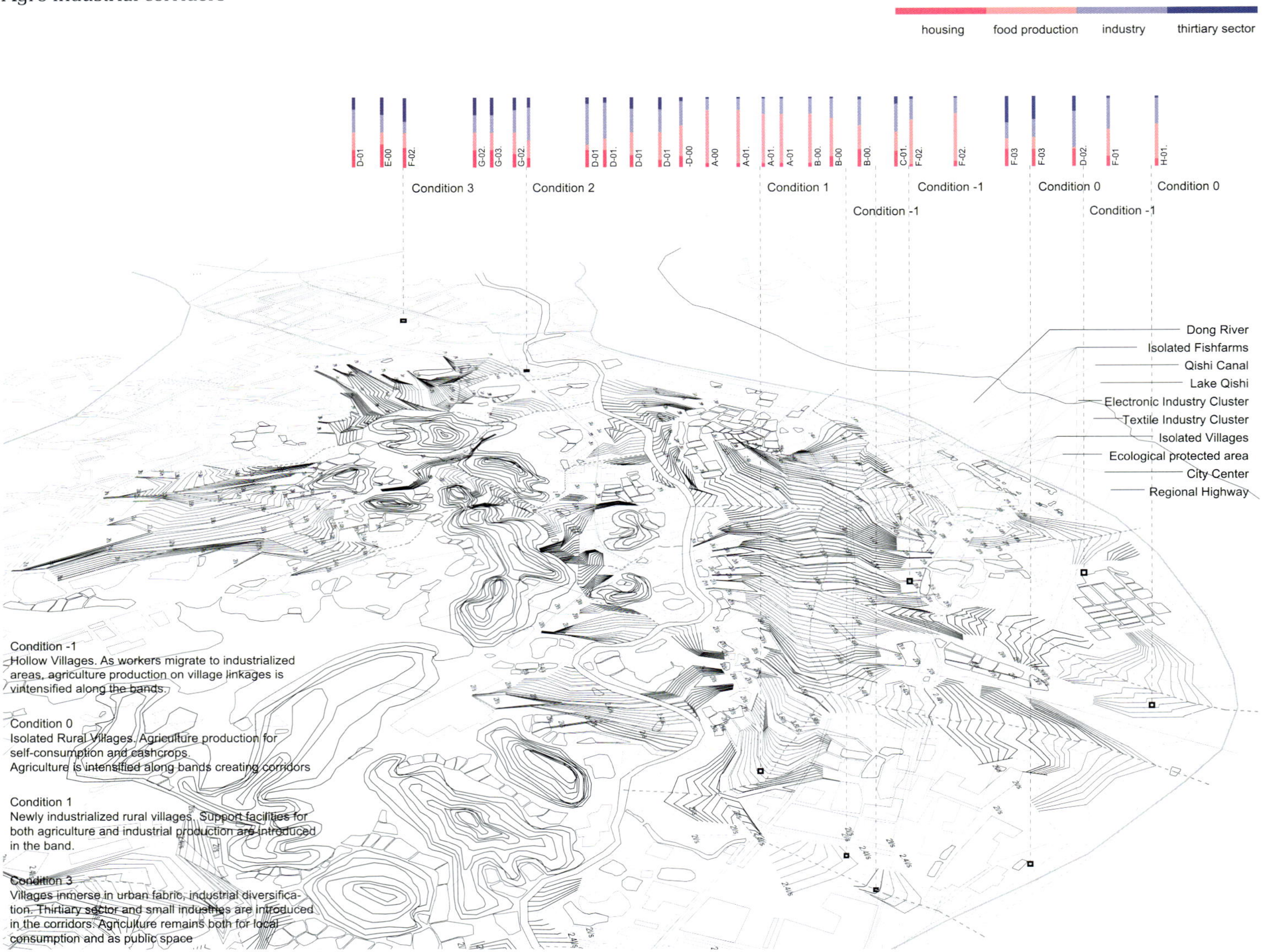

Agro industrial corridors

housing　food production　industry　thirtiary sector

Condition 3　Condition 2　Condition 1　Condition -1　Condition 0　Condition 0
　　　　　　　　　　　　　　　　　　Condition -1　Condition -1

Dong River
Isolated Fishfarms
Qishi Canal
Lake Qishi
Electronic Industry Cluster
Textile Industry Cluster
Isolated Villages
Ecological protected area
City Center
Regional Highway

Condition -1
Hollow Villages. As workers migrate to industrialized areas, agriculture production on village linkages is intensified along the bands.

Condition 0
Isolated Rural Villages. Agriculture production for self-consumption and cashcrops.
Agriculture is intensified along bands creating corridors.

Condition 1
Newly industrialized rural villages. Support facilities for both agriculture and industrial production are introduced in the band.

Condition 3
Villages inmerse in urban fabric, industrial diversification. Thirtiary sector and small industries are introduced in the corridors. Agriculture remains both for local consumption and as public space.

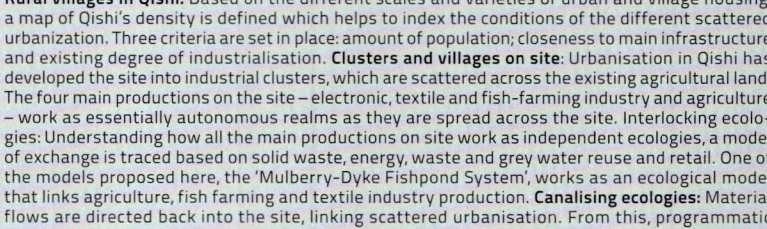

1/2/3/4. Site conditions

Rural villages in Qishi: Based on the different scales and varieties of urban and village housing, a map of Qishi's density is defined which helps to index the conditions of the different scattered urbanization. Three criteria are set in place: amount of population; closeness to main infrastructure and existing degree of industrialisation. **Clusters and villages on site**: Urbanisation in Qishi has developed the site into industrial clusters, which are scattered across the existing agricultural land. The four main productions on the site – electronic, textile and fish-farming industry and agriculture – work as essentially autonomous realms as they are spread across the site. **Interlocking ecologies:** Understanding how all the main productions on site work as independent ecologies, a model of exchange is traced based on solid waste, energy, waste and grey water reuse and retail. One of the models proposed here, the 'Mulberry-Dyke Fishpond System', works as an ecological model that links agriculture, fish farming and textile industry production. **Canalising ecologies:** Material flows are directed back into the site, linking scattered urbanisation. From this, programmatic linkages are traced between the different industries on site, both 'productive' and 'unproductive'.

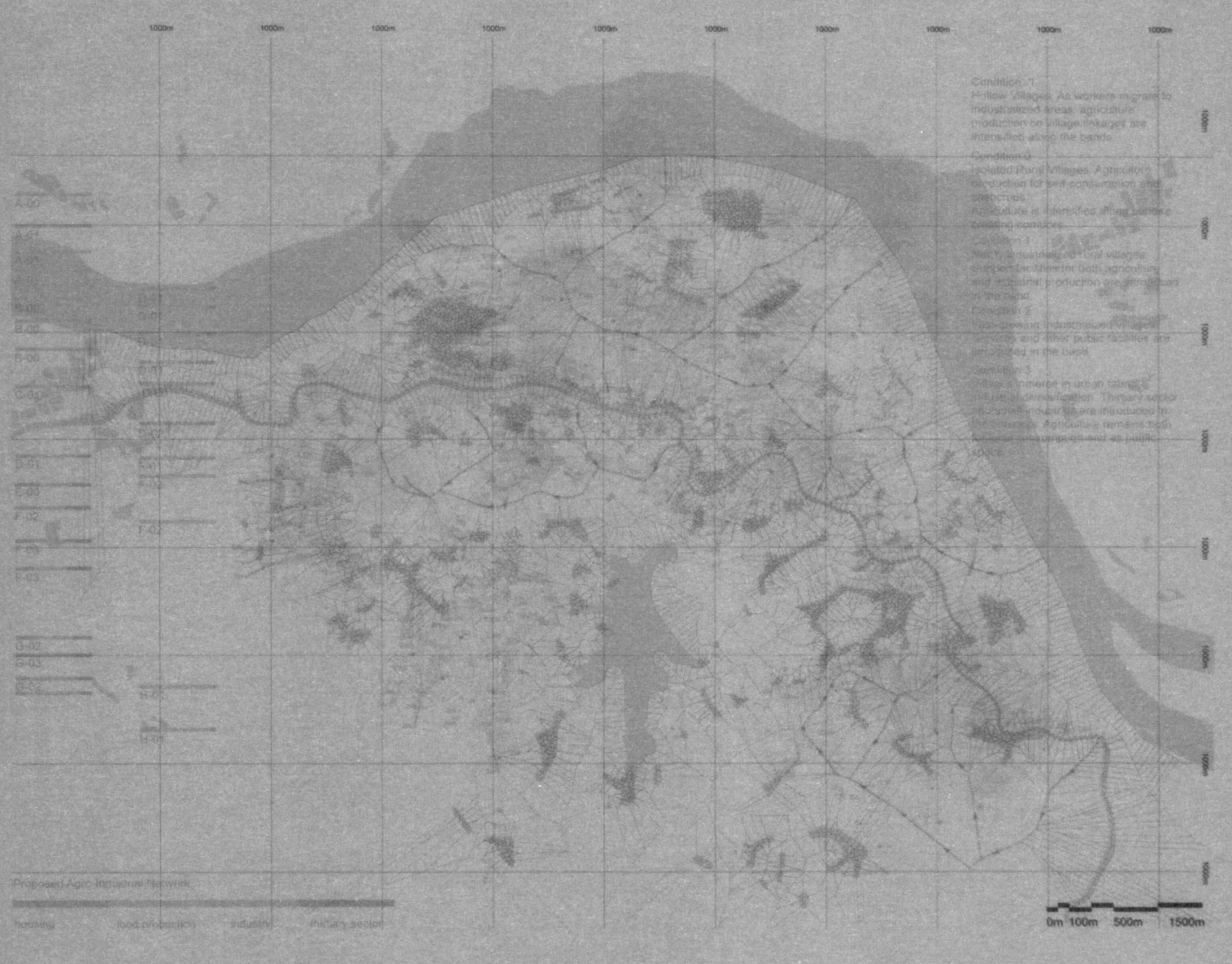

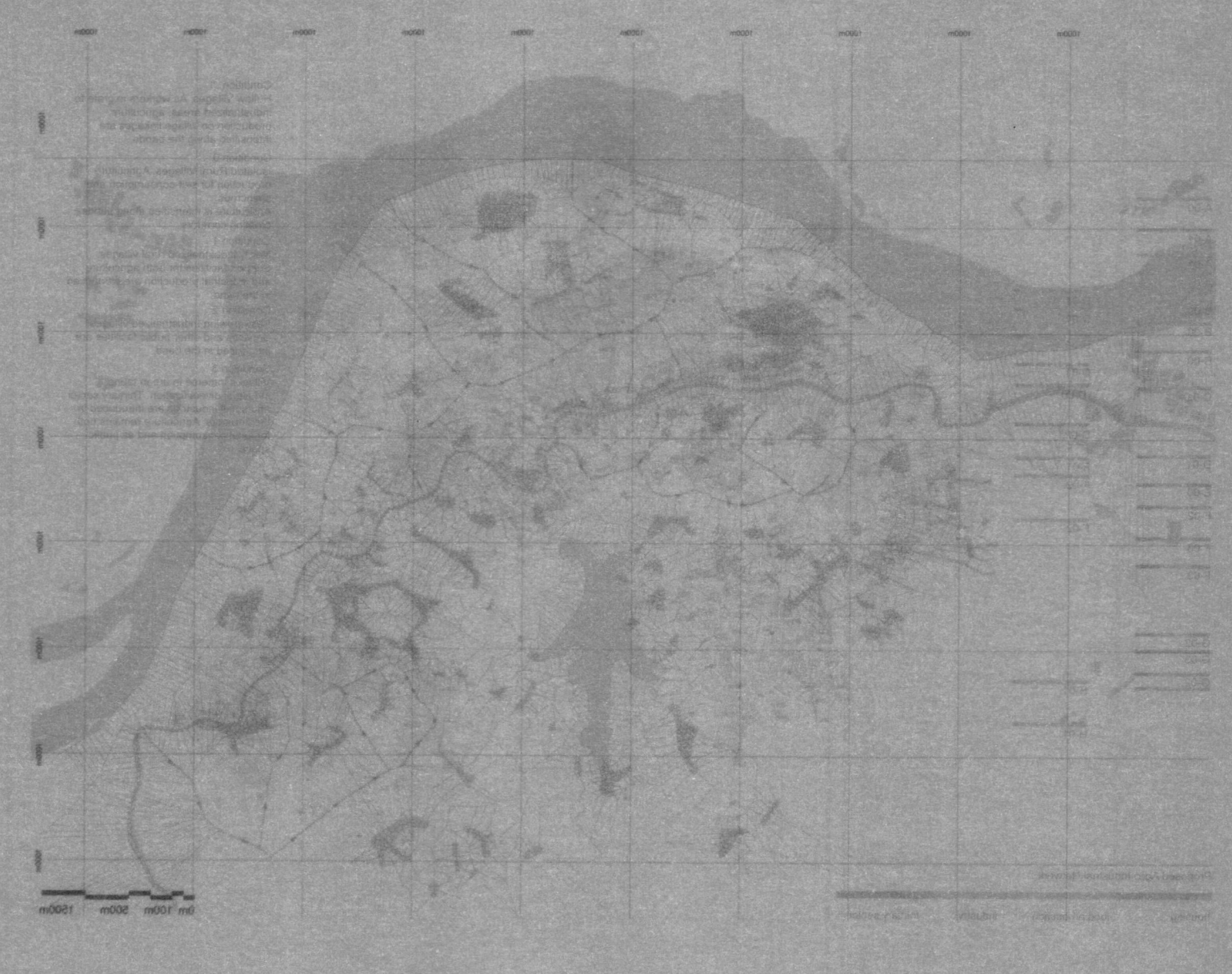

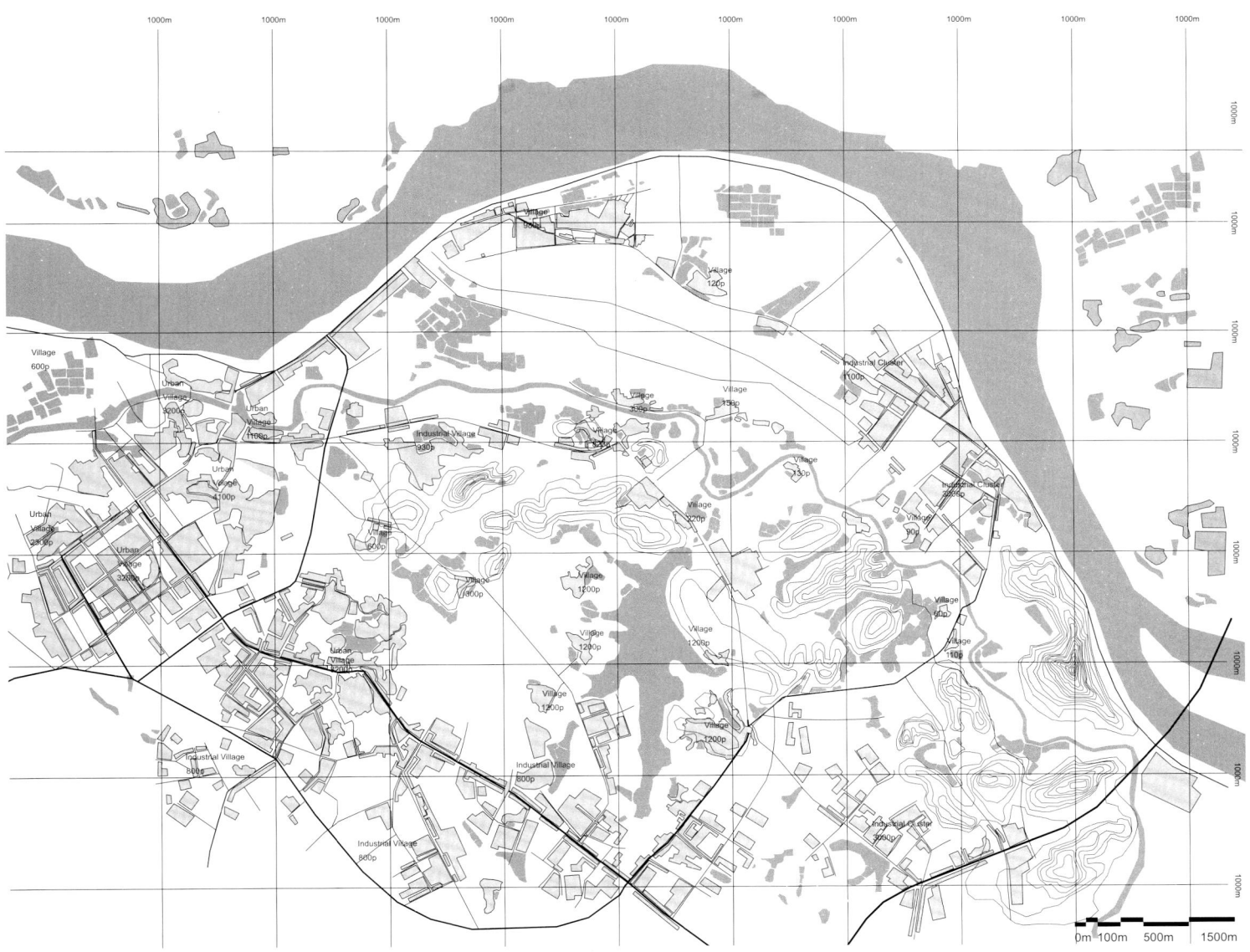

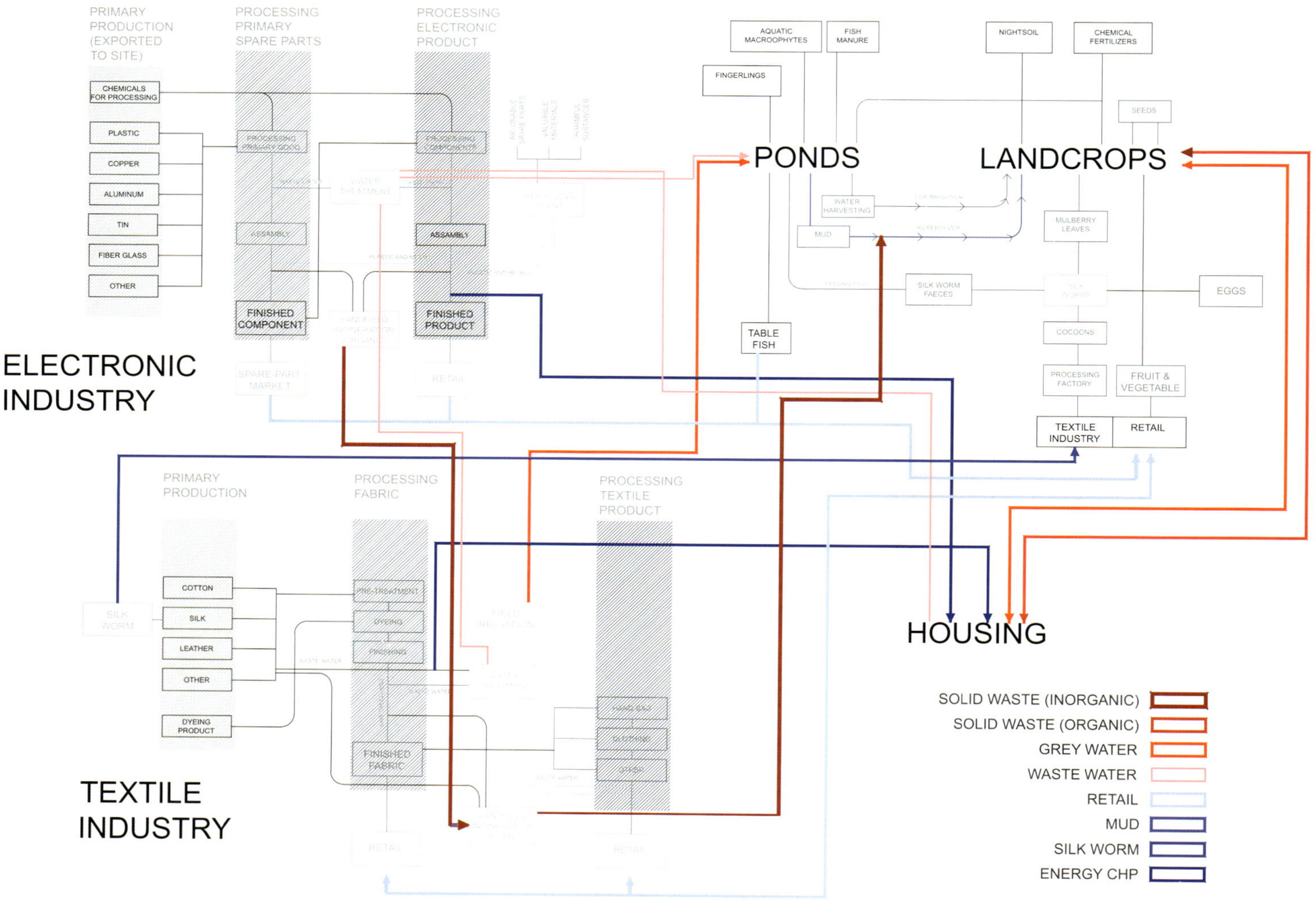

Overall site structure - development conditions

PRIMARY PRODUCTION (EXPORTED TO SITE)
- CHEMICALS FOR PROCESSING
- PLASTIC
- COPPER
- ALUMINUM
- TIN
- FIBER GLASS
- OTHER

PROCESSING PRIMARY SPARE PARTS
- PROCESSING PRIMARY GOOD
- ASSEMBLY
- FINISHED COMPONENT
- SPARE PART MARKET

PROCESSING ELECTRONIC PRODUCT
- PROCESSING COMPONENTS
- ASSEMBLY
- FINISHED PRODUCT
- RETAIL

ELECTRONIC INDUSTRY

- AQUATIC MACROPHYTES
- FISH MANURE
- NIGHTSOIL
- CHEMICAL FERTILIZERS
- FINGERLINGS
- SEEDS

PONDS **LANDCROPS**

- WATER HARVESTING
- MUD
- MULBERRY LEAVES
- SILK WORM FAECES
- EGGS
- TABLE FISH
- COCOONS
- PROCESSING FACTORY
- FRUIT & VEGETABLE
- TEXTILE INDUSTRY
- RETAIL

PRIMARY PRODUCTION
- SILK WORM
- COTTON
- SILK
- LEATHER
- OTHER
- DYEING PRODUCT

PROCESSING FABRIC
- PRE-TREATMENT
- DYEING
- FINISHING
- FINISHED FABRIC

PROCESSING TEXTILE PRODUCT
- HAND BAG
- CLOTHING
- OTHER
- RETAIL

TEXTILE INDUSTRY

HOUSING

Legend:
- SOLID WASTE (INORGANIC)
- SOLID WASTE (ORGANIC)
- GREY WATER
- WASTE WATER
- RETAIL
- MUD
- SILK WORM
- ENERGY CHP

1. Agriculture parcelation
2. Work 10m modules

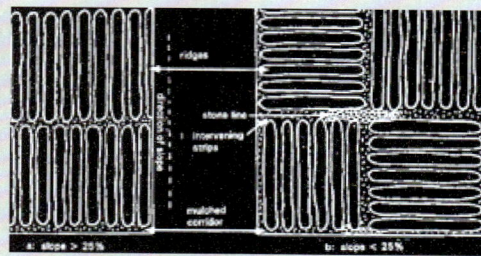

Intensive farming in China: 'Melon on the vine' irrigation system
The system is used as a way of agriculture modernisation in China. It allows economic and operative independence in the irrigation of villages and agricultural fields. It provides flexibility, since it is not affected by the interruption of any of its segments, and also adaptability, since when an irrigation line is no longer required, the corresponding branches can be removed without affecting the rest. The remaining dry canals are either planted again, or used informally as public pathways.

Appropriating the system
The system is used for multicropped cultivation of different products Soybean, Maize, Vegetable, Lettuce. Each of these crops is rotated within the parcels throughout the year so that each can benefit from the nutrients in the soil left by the previous crop, achieving higher yields. The system works in modulated strips of 10m width in which sets of cultivated parcels sit.

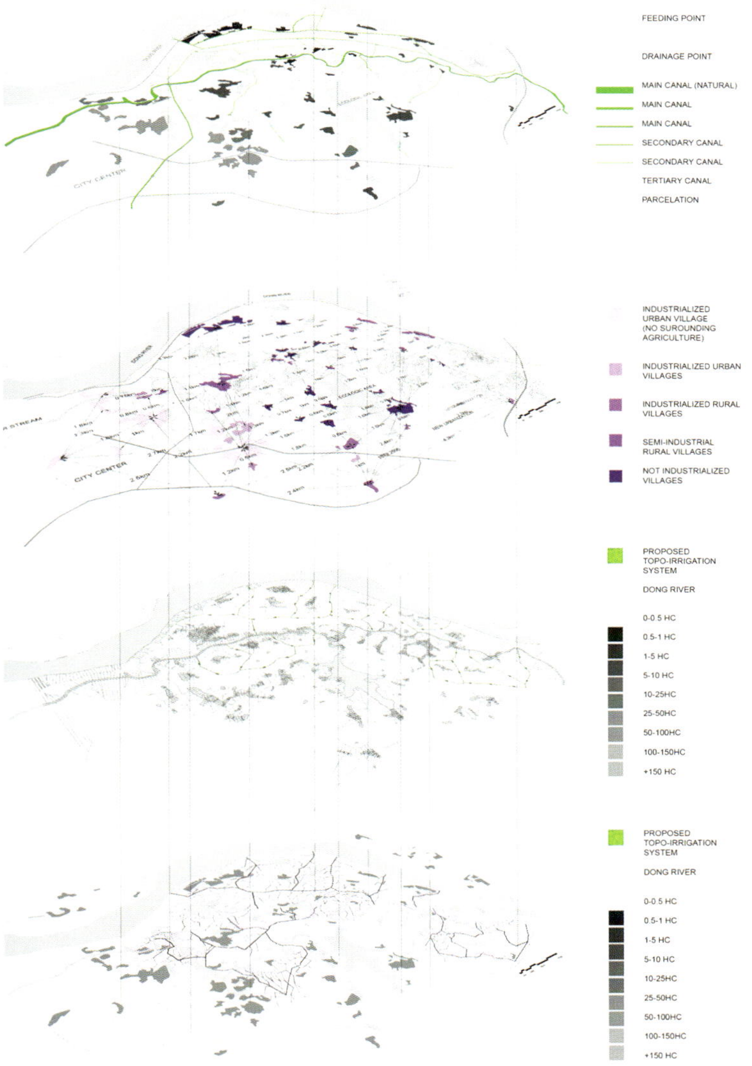

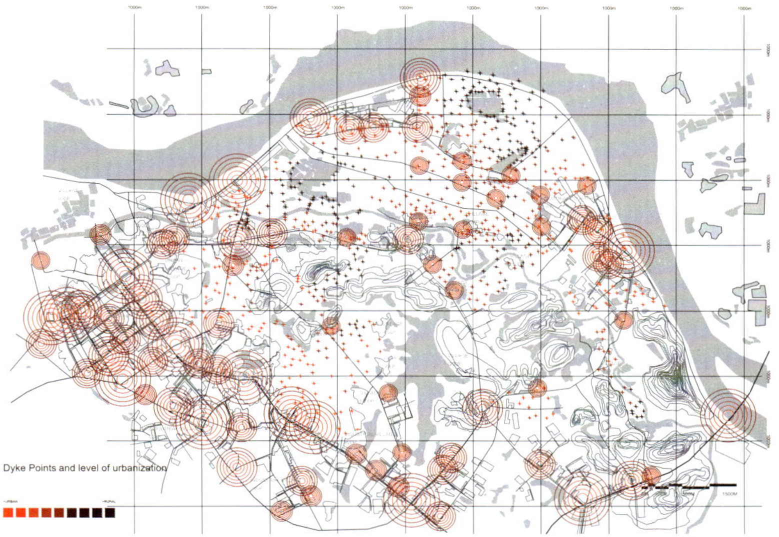

FEEDING POINT
DRAINAGE POINT
MAIN CANAL (NATURAL)
MAIN CANAL
MAIN CANAL
SECONDARY CANAL
SECONDARY CANAL
TERTIARY CANAL
PARCELATION
CITY CENTER
INDUSTRIALIZED URBAN VILLAGE (NO SUROUNDING AGRICULTURE)
INDUSTRIALIZED URBAN VILLAGES
INDUSTRIALIZED RURAL VILLAGES
SEMI-INDUSTRIAL RURAL VILLAGES
NOT INDUSTRIALIZED VILLAGES
PROPOSED TOPO-IRRIGATION SYSTEM
DONG RIVER
0-0.5 HC
0.5-1 HC
1-5 HC
5-10 HC
10-25HC
25-50HC
50-100HC
100-150HC
+150 HC
PROPOSED TOPO-IRRIGATION SYSTEM
DONG RIVER
0-0.5 HC
0.5-1 HC
1-5 HC
5-10 HC
10-25HC
25-50HC
50-100HC
100-150HC
+150 HC

Dyke Points and level of urbanization

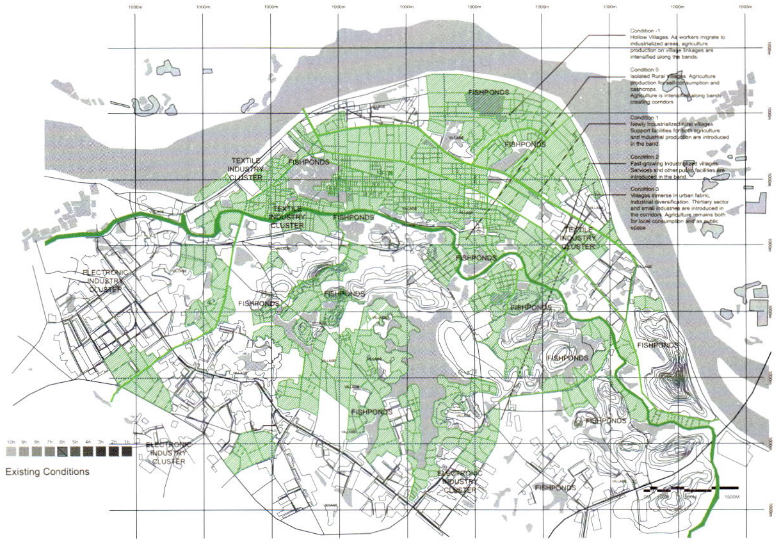

FISHPONDS
TEXTILE INDUSTRY CLUSTER
ELECTRONIC INDUSTRY CLUSTER
Existing Conditions

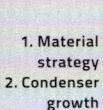

1. Material strategy
2. Condenser growth

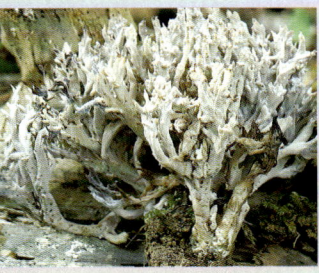

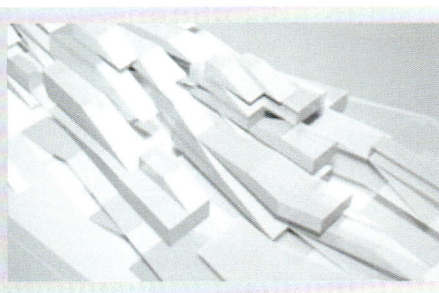

Water influence on site: The use of a voronoi geometry around existing water bodies allows us to assume a highest-dryest line in the territory. The line is then connected to the drainage points of the fabrics in order to structure the site.
Generating site structure: A branching system is proposed by analysing the maximum and minimun angles that the Irrigation system allows, varying the number of dykes as the branches get closer to the urban fabric. From there, the site is structured linking scattered urbanisation.
Site strategy: By indexing the existing and proposed nodes on the site structure according to their distance from the different urban built fabrics, a matrix is created which helps to speculate and propose programmatic distributions in the proposed network. The four main programmes that are first distributed are housing, food production, industry and third sector which vary across the site.

Industrialization model	Nodal growth	Infrastructure layering	Agriculture occupation
Condition 1 Unindustrialized, isolated Villages. Agriculture is Intensified along Bands Connects to fabric. The village is connected to Urbanized settlements	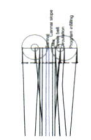	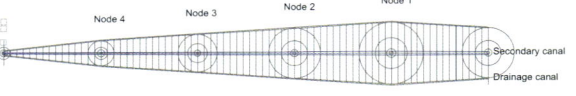	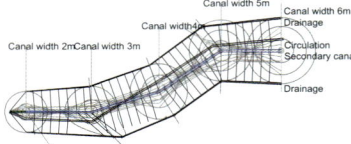
Condition 2 Single isolated industrialized Villages. Public space and support Facilities for industry and Residence are introduced on The band	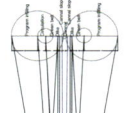	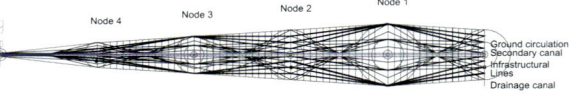	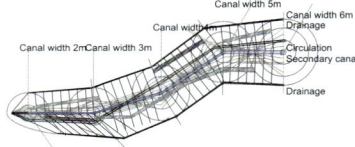
Condition 3 Isolated and fast growing Industrialized village Agrupation. Housing units are introduced, More support facilities and Public space to meet growth Requirements	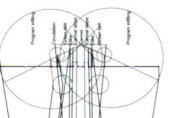	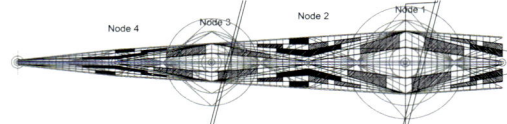	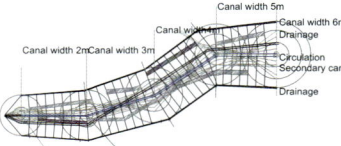
Condition 4 Villages in urban fabric, Industrial diversification. Commerce and small industry are Introduced Agriculture remains both for Local consumption and as public Space	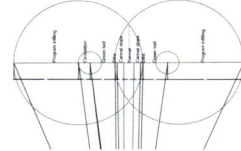	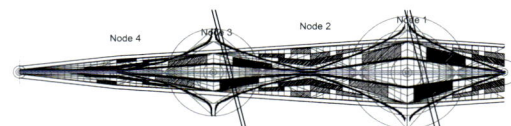	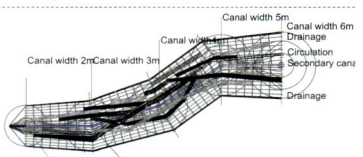

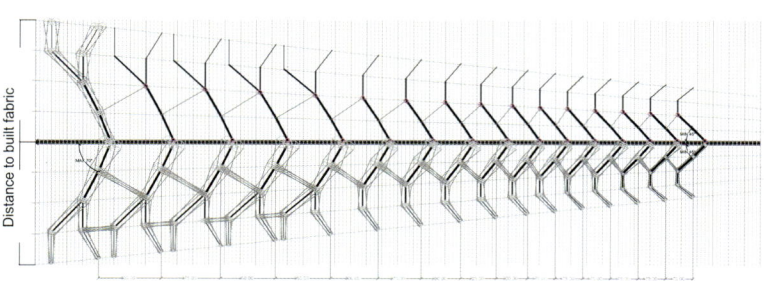

Maximun distance between Branches   Minimun distance between Branches

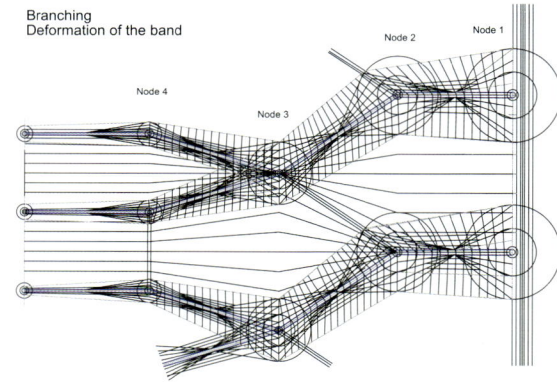

Branching
Deformation of the band

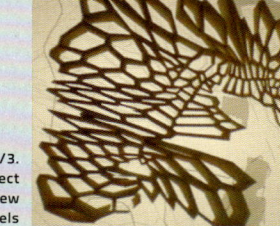

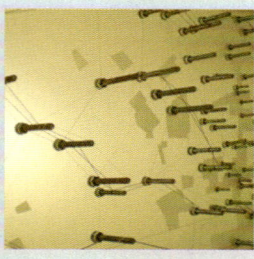

1/2/3. Project review models

Growing condenser
A network of adaptive urban condensers whose primary function is to mediate processes of rural industrialisation, by intensifying, incentivising or compensating the programmatic orientation of the new fabrics.

Programme units
Based on the modulation of intensive agriculture (10m), a set of programme units is derived. The general idea of the unit concept is that as other programmes start to be intensified (i.e. industrial production, tertiary sector, etc), agricultural parcels are taken while others remain active in their optimal dimensions, thus maintaing the 'intensive' intent throughout the condenser's growth
A generic-neutral geometry is chosen to allow continuous circulation and public spaces throughout different programme associations.

Tree logic programme association

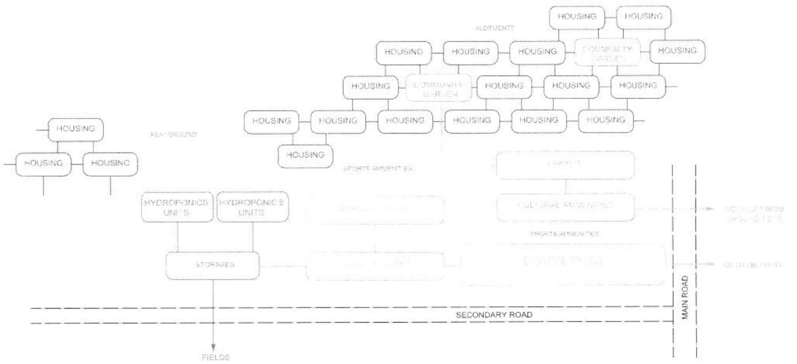

COMERCIAL/
INDUSTRIAL
NODE
TREE LOGIC
PROGRAM ASSOCIATION

- LIVE - HOUSING
- WORK - AGRICULTURE
- WORK - INDUSTRY AND COMMERCE
- PLAY - CULTURAL AMMENITIES
- SUPPORT - SOCIAL SERVICES

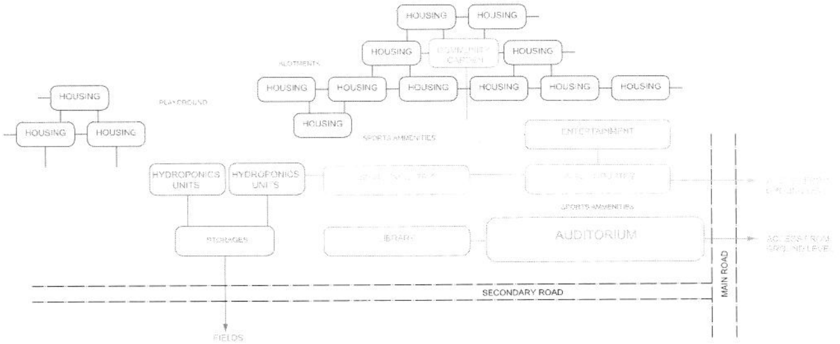

LEISURE
NODE
TREE LOGIC
PROGRAM ASSOCIATION

- LIVE - HOUSING
- WORK - AGRICULTURE
- WORK - INDUSTRY AND COMMERCE
- PLAY - CULTURAL AMMENITIES
- SUPPORT - SOCIAL SERVICES

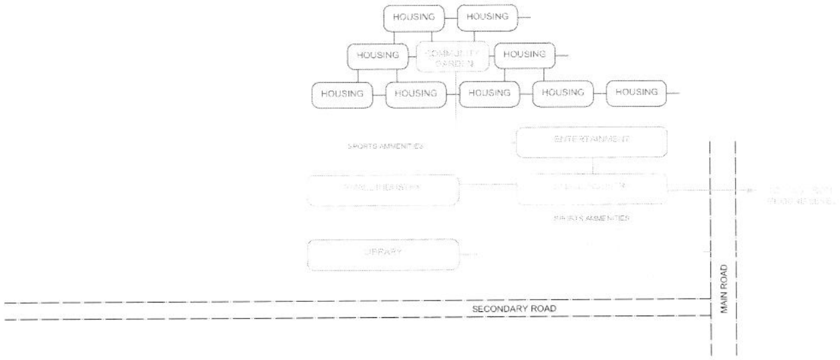

SERVICE
NODE
TREE LOGIC
PROGRAM ASSOCIATION

- LIVE - HOUSING
- WORK - AGRICULTURE
- WORK - INDUSTRY AND COMMERCE
- PLAY - CULTURAL AMMENITIES
- SUPPORT - SOCIAL SERVICES

1. Perspective

Multiplied public space
As the villages grow, new characters and scales of public space and agriculture production are created: intensive multicropping, hydroponic units, community farms, gardens and allotments.
As more housing is required to accommodate a growing population of migrant workers, agriculture production is brought 'up', while lower levels become a new public realm that would connect to the new fabric.

Infrastructural trees
As more units come along, sets of infrastructural 'trees' will work as two ecological systems, inbound and outbound. The general idea is that each programme requires infrastructure but the association of units through infrastructural trees can help create ecological cycles between industry, housing and agriculture, both inside and outside of the condenser.

Condenser development on site

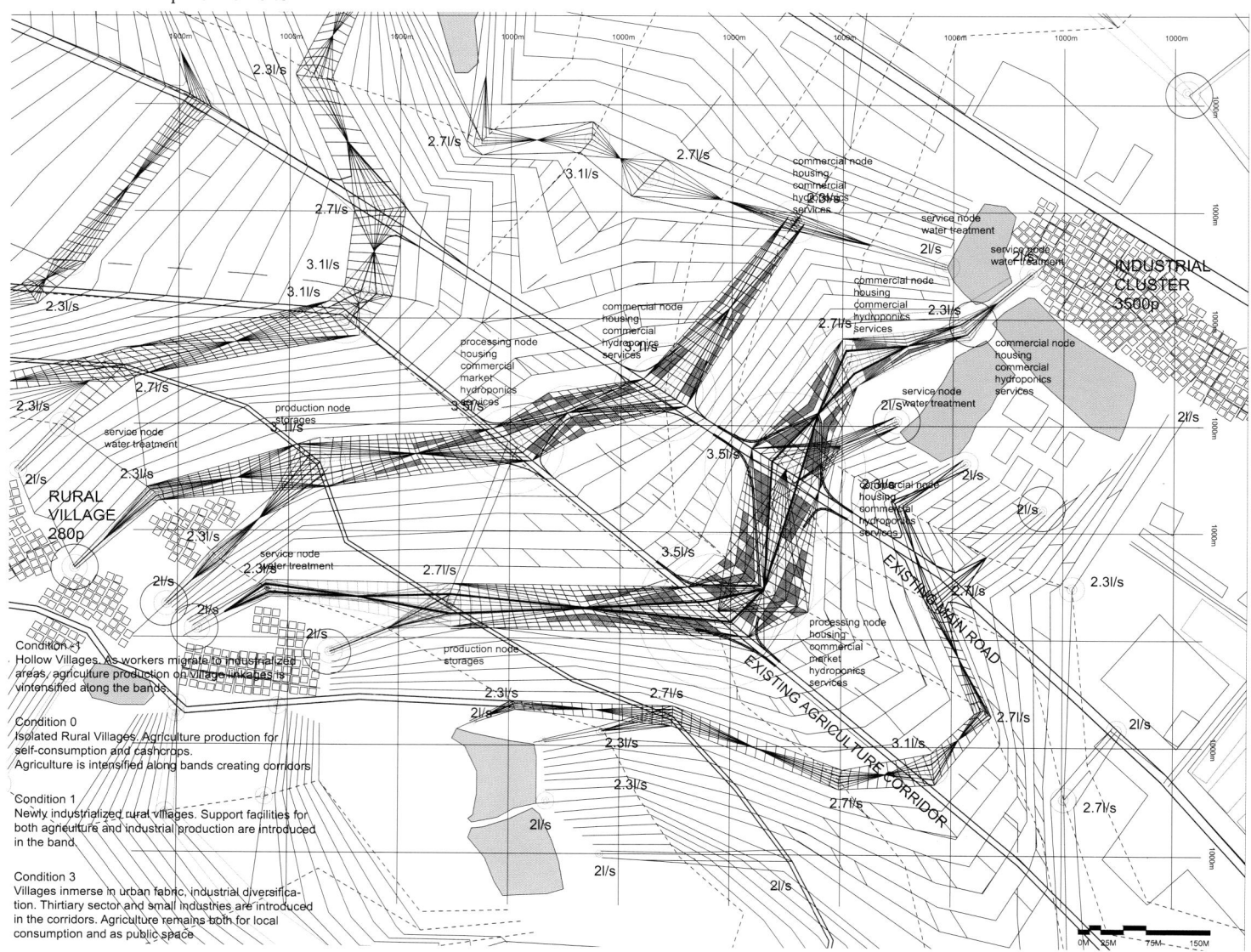

Condition -1
Hollow Villages. As workers migrate to industrialized areas, agriculture production on village linkages is intensified along the bands.

Condition 0
Isolated Rural Villages. Agriculture production for self-consumption and cashcrops.
Agriculture is intensified along bands creating corridors

Condition 1
Newly industrialized rural villages. Support facilities for both agriculture and industrial production are introduced in the band.

Condition 3
Villages inmerse in urban fabric, industrial diversification. Thirtiary sector and small industries are introduced in the corridors. Agriculture remains both for local consumption and as public space.

1. Band programme

Megastructure
The project takes as reference radical urbanism of the 1960s and 70s, and the concept of continuously redefining cities based on their infrastructure, on flexible and growing megastructures in which the association of their constantly changing parts is thought to provide social interaction.

The notion of a megastructure usually implies self-contained entities whose scale becomes a barrier to their surroundings. In order to allow a megastructure to contextualise and 'mediate', here they become informed by the city development, in terms of programmes, scale and connectivity.

Perspective view, condenser development

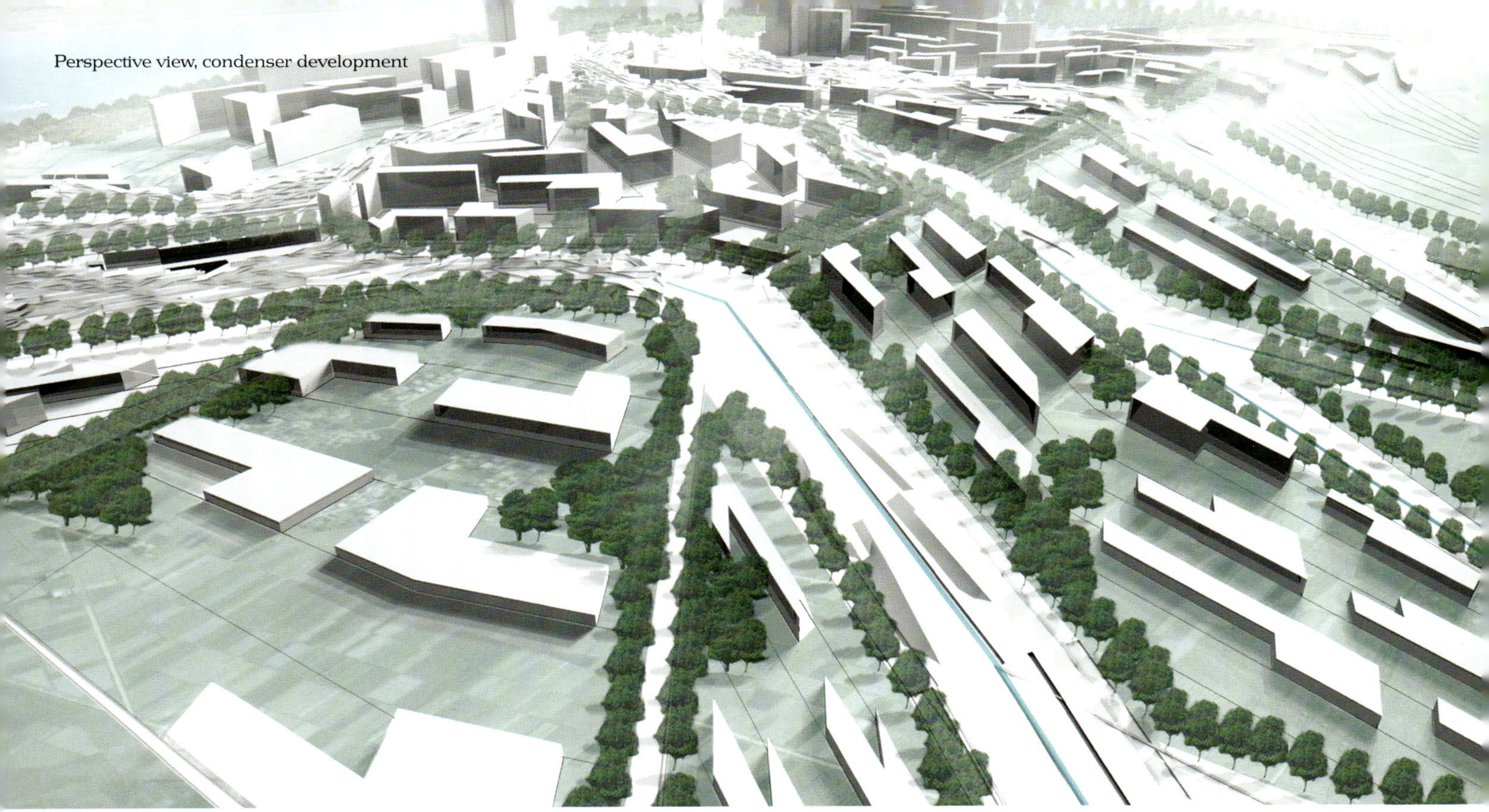

Condenser growth rendering

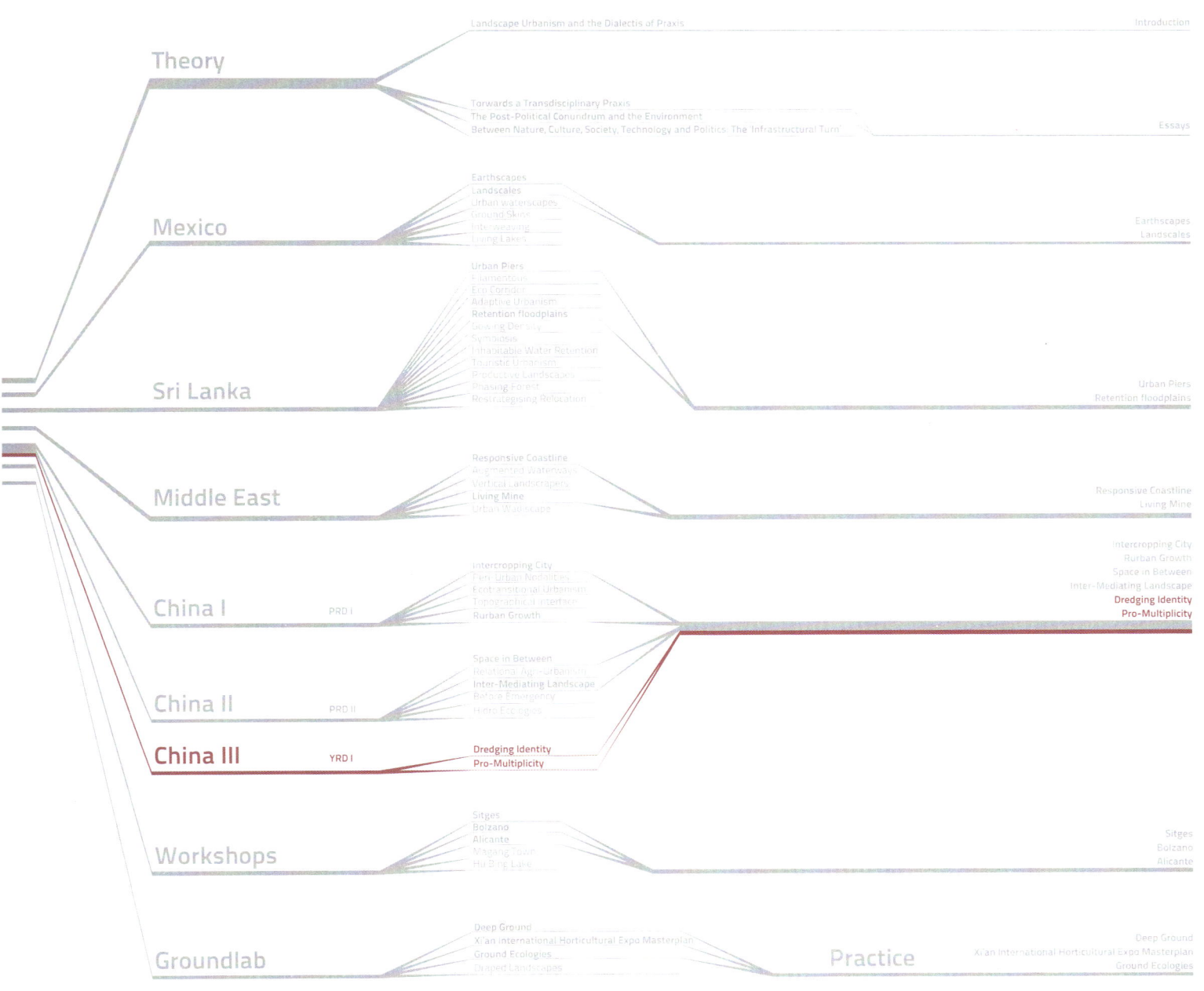

AA Landscape Urbanism 08/09
Prototypical Urbanities - PRD China

AGENDA Building Building upon a body of research established over the previous two years of work in this field, AALU maintained its focus on China's ambitions to build four hundred new cities by the year 2020 — with 12 million people expected to move from rural to urban locations — as the basis for its brief. Far from resisting this development, AALU engaged opportunistically with the generation of 'proto-strategies' for new large-scale agglomerations as a means of critically addressing the phenomena of mass-produced urban sprawl. Our test-bed was the urban agglomerations of the Yangtze River Delta — including Shanghai, Nanjing, Hangzhou, Suzhou, and Ningbo — with students focusing on the emergence of three benchmark issues in this area:

- Metabolic Rurbanism: the emergence of 'desakota' (urban villages) in which urban and rural processes of land use are combined, and the potentials it presents for the origin of industrial ecologies.
- Tactical Resistance: where generic, top-down masterplanning collides with informally developed urban cores, the potential to locate the fault lines of this dynamic as a space from which a tactical urbanism that is qualitatively informed and territorially specific, might be produced.
- Material Identities: the inadequacy of attempts to provide new urban settlements with an instant 'identity', through the application of either vernacular or western styles of building, in the context of 'post-traditional' urbanization.

AALU China 09/10

Dredging identity

Date **2009/10**
Location **China**
Author **Nicola Saladino**

Project description

Lingang is a new city at the mouth of the Yangtze River Delta, designed as part of the 1966 plan for the development of the metropolitan area of Shanghai.

The creation of the new Yangshan deep-water port, connected to the mainland through the Donghai bridge, gave the government the opportunity to develop a new industrial zone which is planned to house up to 800,000 inhabitants by 2020 and will have a crucial role in the economic growth of the coastal region.
The new city will occupy an area of almost 300 km2. Approximately half of this surface (on the east side) is constituted by newly reclaimed land, while the inner part is characterised by the presence of an agricultural pattern of canals and linear villages. Here, the waterbodies provide irrigation, transportation and public space, generating a strong local identity.

In the original design, the presence of these villages was completely neglected and big industrial estates substitute all the pre-existing fabric. The creation of huge mono-functional blocks quite distant from each other forces the immediate construction of all the infrastructures and a very low density makes the project functionally and economically inefficient. Furthermore, the rigid geometric scheme of the masterplan does not allow any flexible phasing strategy and the structure of the city could hardly make sense before all the phases are completed.

On the environmental level, the process of land reclamation produced an important alteration to the original water system: the construction of a dyke eliminated the natural daily fluctuation of the sea level and forced the construction of an underground drainage for all the existing canals. As a result, the valuable ecosystem of salt marshes and fish ponds has been lost and the poor drainage capacity of the terrain generates a high risk of flooding during the wet season.

This project aims to create a more dynamic system of multifunctional clusters that can better adjust the future changes in the growth of the city. A higher density respects the original goals of the masterplan placing all the functional clusters in the reclaimed area, thus preserving the linear villages. At the same time, the solution to the drainage problems gives the opportunity to create a new network of canals and water bodies that organise and structure the new urban fabric, becoming a crucial element for the public space. The new design maximises the coastline, generating a higher land value that compensates the costs of the dredging and earthwork needed, making the development economically attractive.

1. 1966 Plan
2/3. Existing linear villages

1966 Plan Shanghai's population has reached 20 million people. The concentric growth of the city and the strong dependence of the peripheries on the centre constantly expose the metropolis to great problems of congestion. According to the 1966 plan, Lingang is one of the 9 new cities that were created in the metropolitan area in order to shift the future growth of Shanghai from a monocentric model to a polycentric decentralised urban network.

Linear Villages The site is partially occupied by linear villages which are strongly connected to the canal system. Canals are key elements of the urban space: in fact, they provide irrigation, transportation and public space. The linear villages are very valuable not only for their architectural and environmental beauty, but also for their strong social identity. The plan of the local government to relocate all the rural population to the new city centre would destroy not only hundreds of houses, but a very characteristic life style.

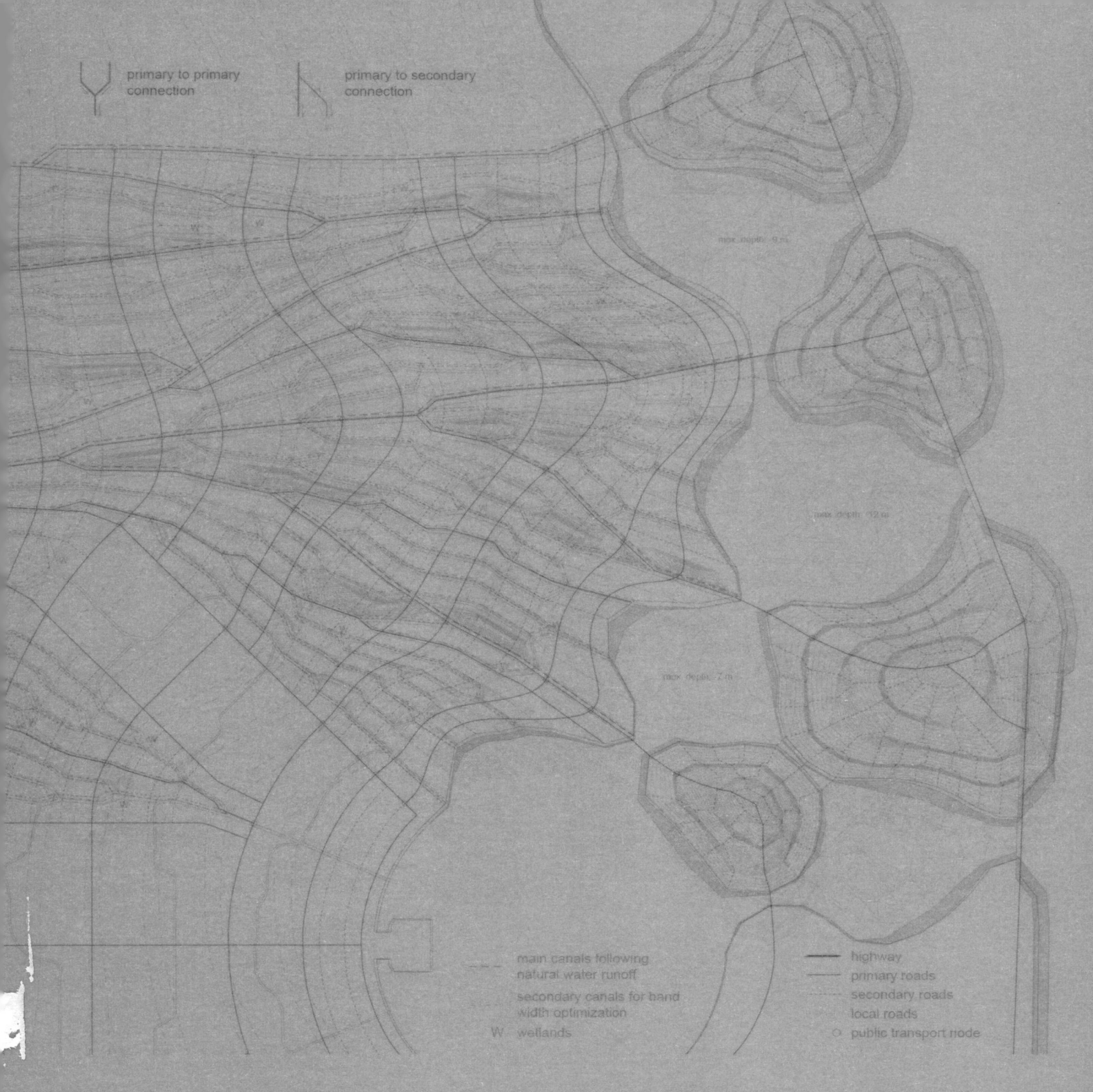

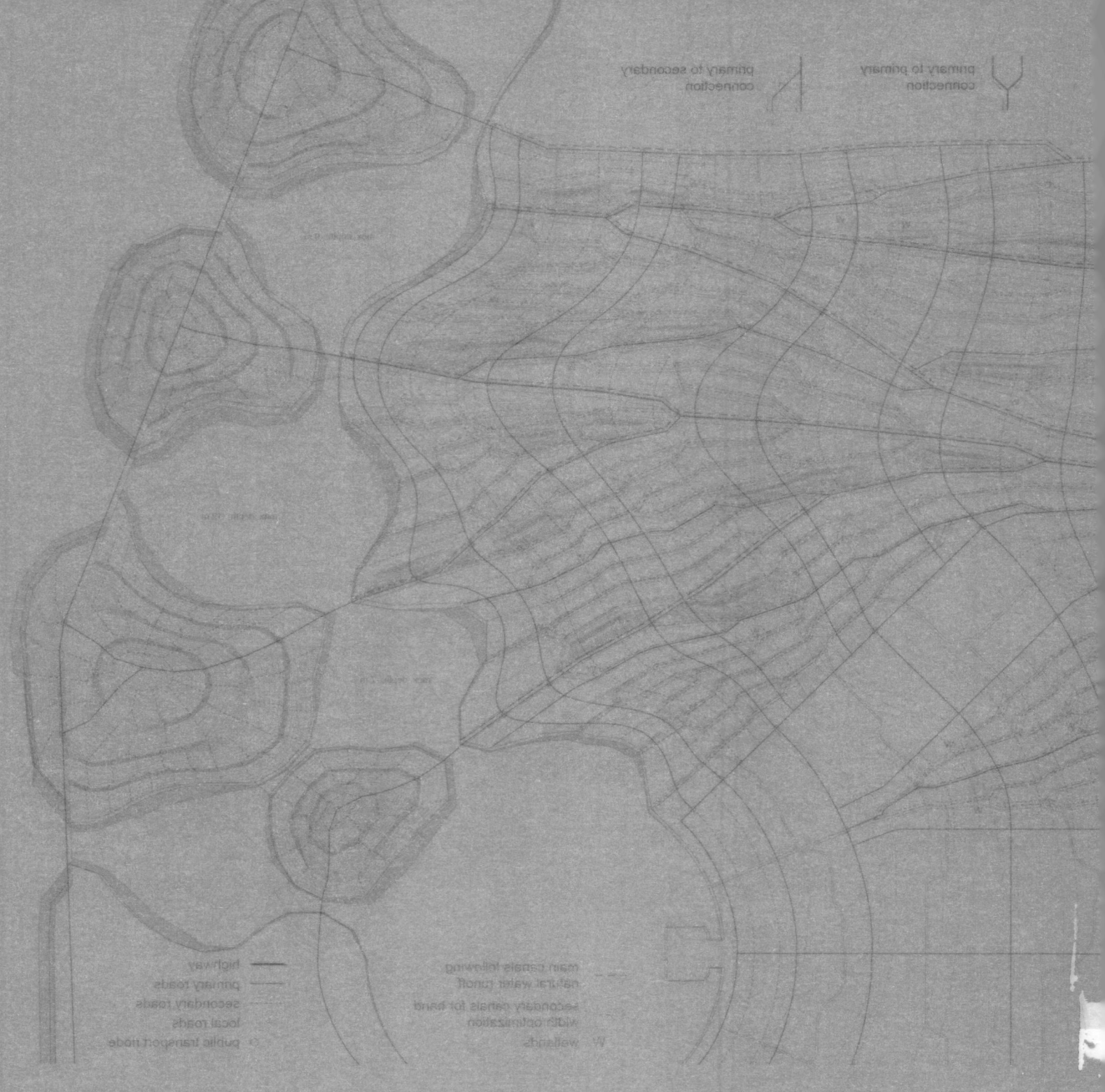

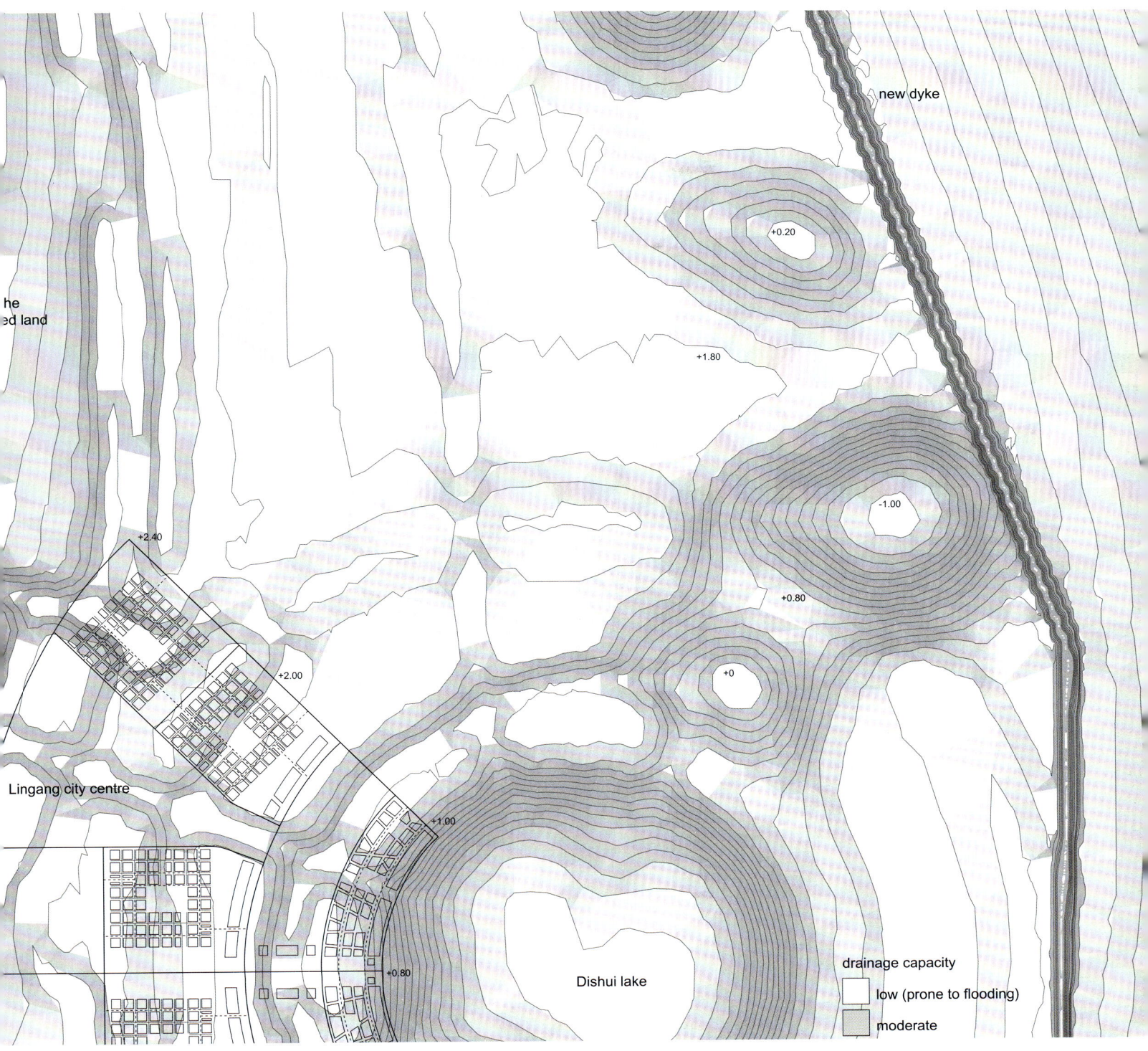

Original masterplan and flood risk

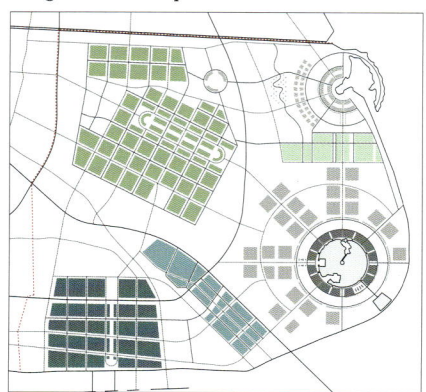

Distribution of uses
The economy of Lingang is strongly associated with the Yangshan port so most of its industrial sites depend on the new logistic centre.
While the residential areas and offices are concentrated on the east coast, specially around the lake, huge blocks of industry are spread around the site, leaving big green buffer areas in between.
Such centripetal distribution of uses augments considerably the distance between different functional areas. The commuting of the workers from the city centre and the movement of the goods from and to the new logistic area can easily create major problems of traffic congestion.

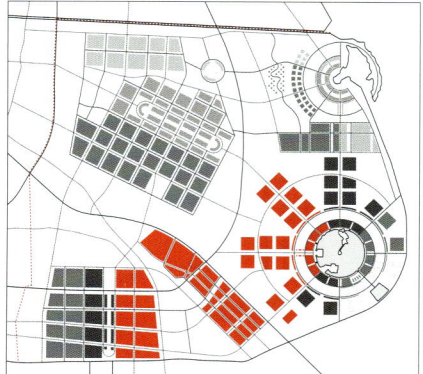

Phasing strategy
Currently in its first phase of development, Lingang already hosts around 100,000 inhabitants. The geometrical scheme of the masterplan does not allow any flexible phasing strategy and the structure of the city could hardly make sense before all the phases are completed. Furthermore, the location of monofunctional packages quite distant from each other forces the immediate construction of all the infrastructures, generating a difficult financial situation for the promoters: the initial investments can only be recovered at the final stages of the development and the commercial success of the operation becomes an unpredictable long term bet. This proposal takes the fully developed first phase as the starting point for an alternative growth strategy.

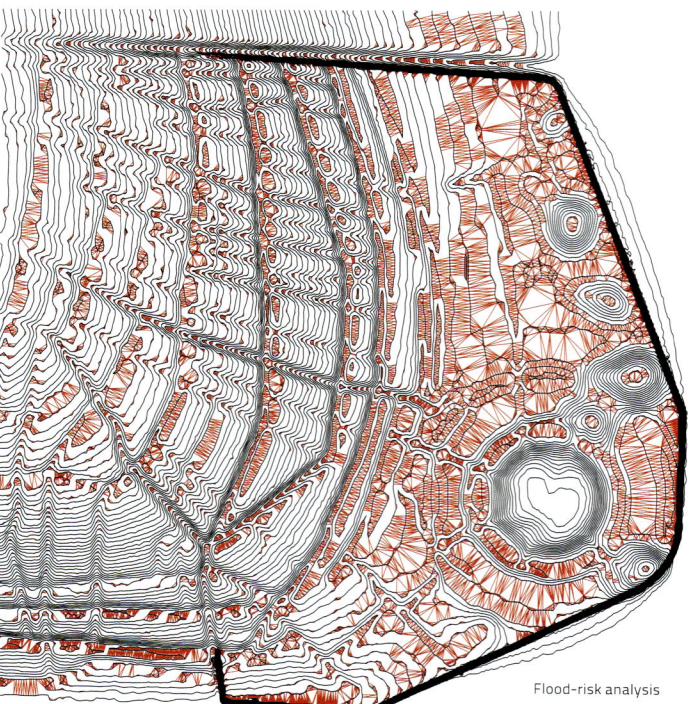

Flood-risk analysis

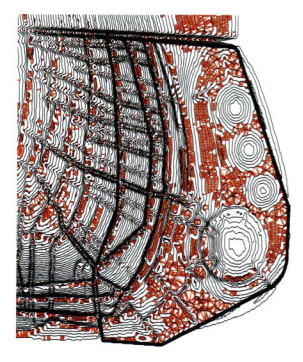

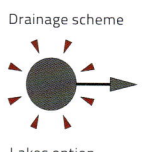

Drainage scheme

Lakes option

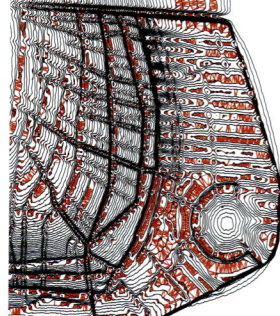

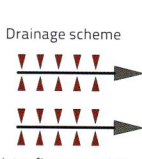

Drainage scheme

Water fingers option

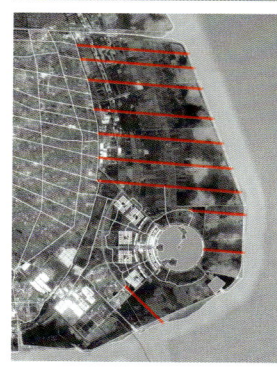

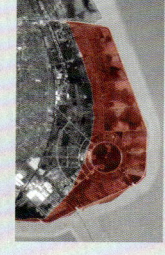
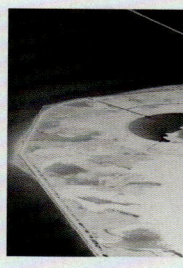

1. New reclaimed area
2. Problems of water stagnation along the coast
3. Current water system

Flood risk
The land reclamation produced a topography with very low drainage capacity, leading to serious risks of flooding during the wet season.
Various possible solutions to the problem were tested, involving different processes of dredging and earthwork that modify the coastline and connect the existing canal network to the sea.
The Yangtze River Delta has a very humid climate, characterised by strong precipitations during summer.
Even considering the optimistic hypothesis that the new underground drainage conduits could deal with all the water coming from the canals, no superficial system has been developed to take care of the rainfall. The new topographic conditions make the drainage even more difficult and generate serious risks of flooding during the wet season.
The solution to this drainage problem is the starting point for this alternative masterplan proposal.

Topography and water system

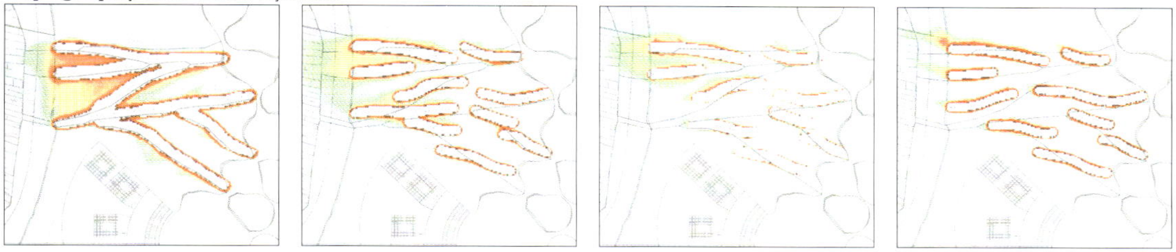

Wind analysis
The new topographic system helps structure the urban fabric and provides green spaces and public facilities throughout the whole site.
Furthermore, the new hills channel the wind coming from the sea and make it penetrate as much as possible inland, providing ventilation to the residential areas and cleaning the industrial pollution.

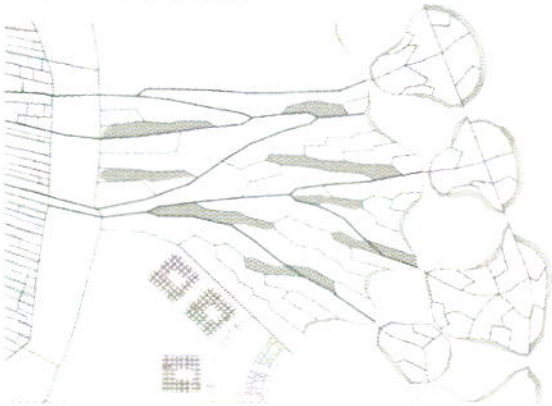

Module: 300m

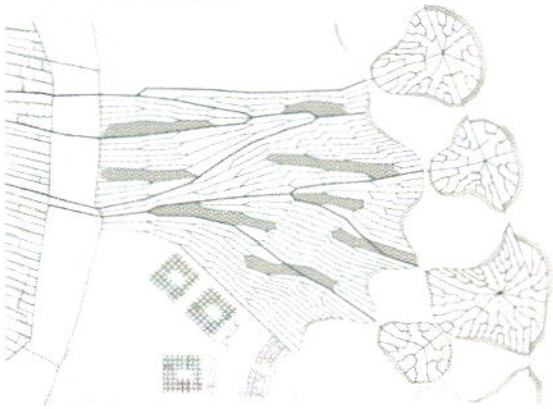

Module: 200m

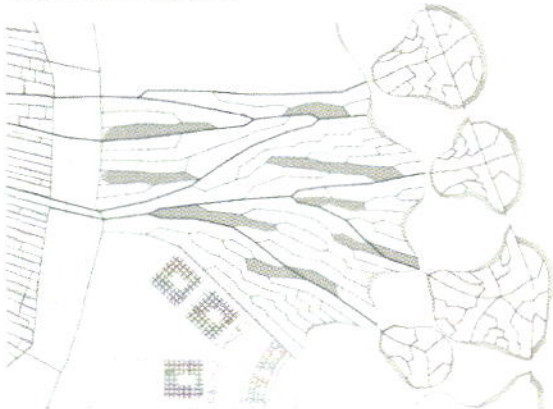

Module: 100m

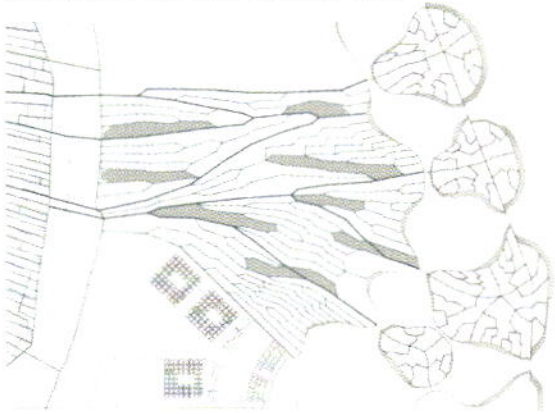

Module: Varied distances

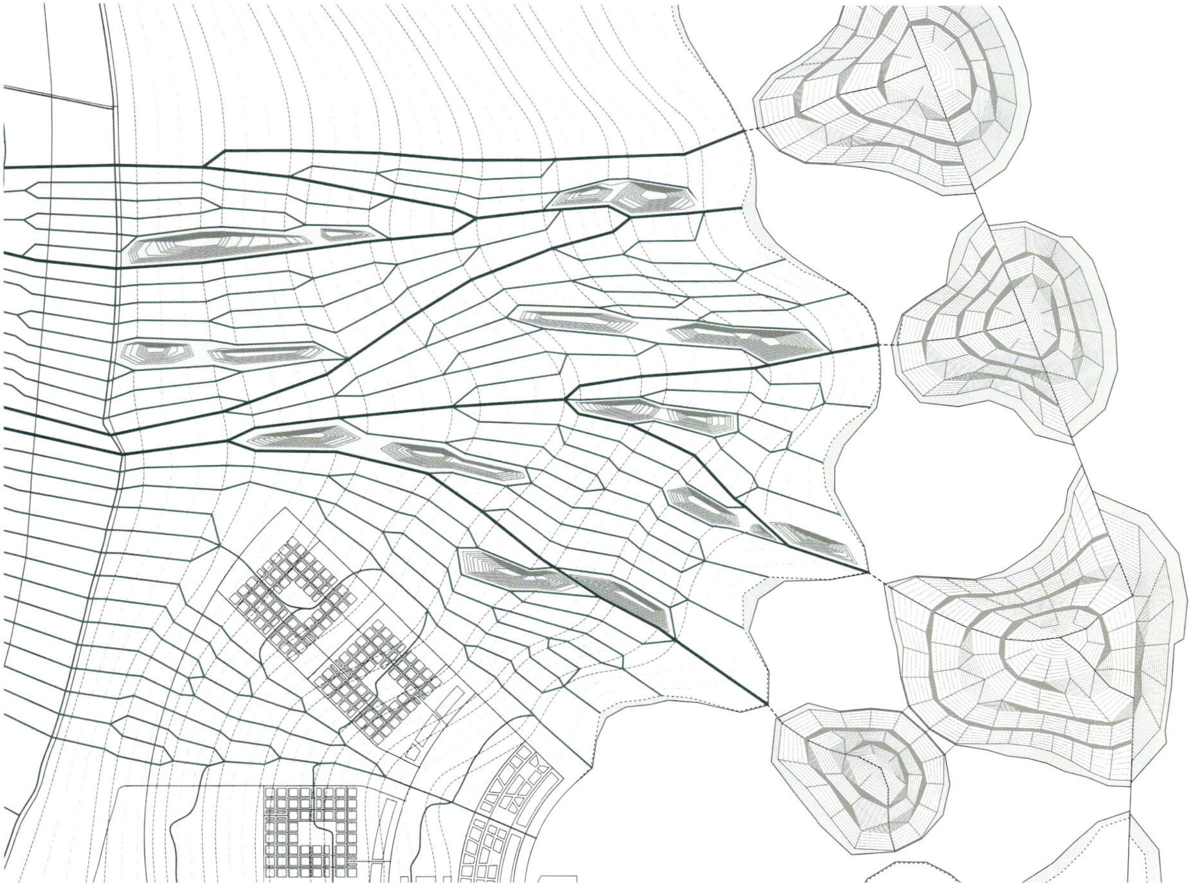

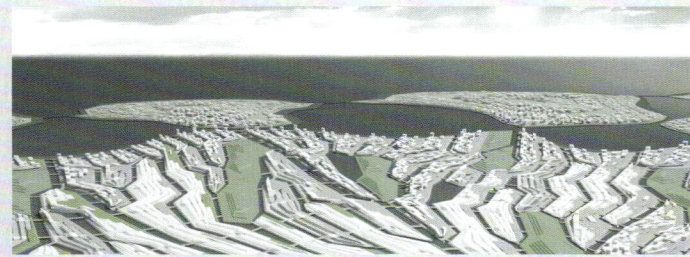

1. View of the new coast line

Branching system parameters
After the excavation of the new lakes, the final step of the earthwork operations is the creation of a new network of secondary canals. While the main canals were directly responding to the new topography and the original water system, the secondary canals have a different logic: they are related to the final plot sizes and the functional requirements of each area. A parametric approach to the problem allows testing different configurations. The distance between canals can be fixed for the whole system - thus generating a homogeneous distribution of water across the territory - or can vary according to specific necessities: either a stronger drainage deficiency or a higher water requirement in a specific zone can originate more or less subdivisions.
Since the secondary canals are responsible for the final geometric organisation of the urban fabric, a similar branching system is also used on the islands, where the water system is substituted by the new road network, 'irrigating' the complete surface from the top.

General masterplan

Road system sections

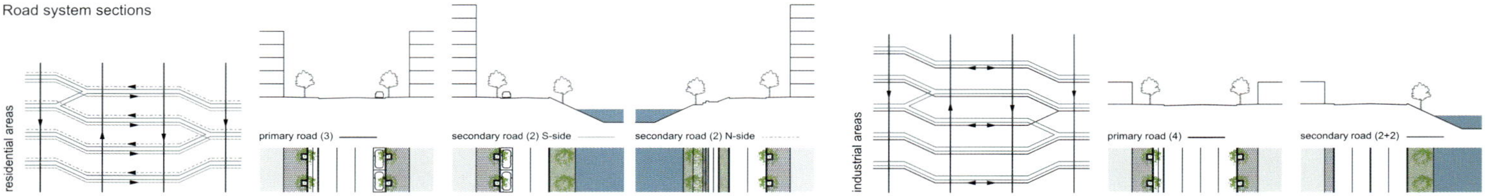

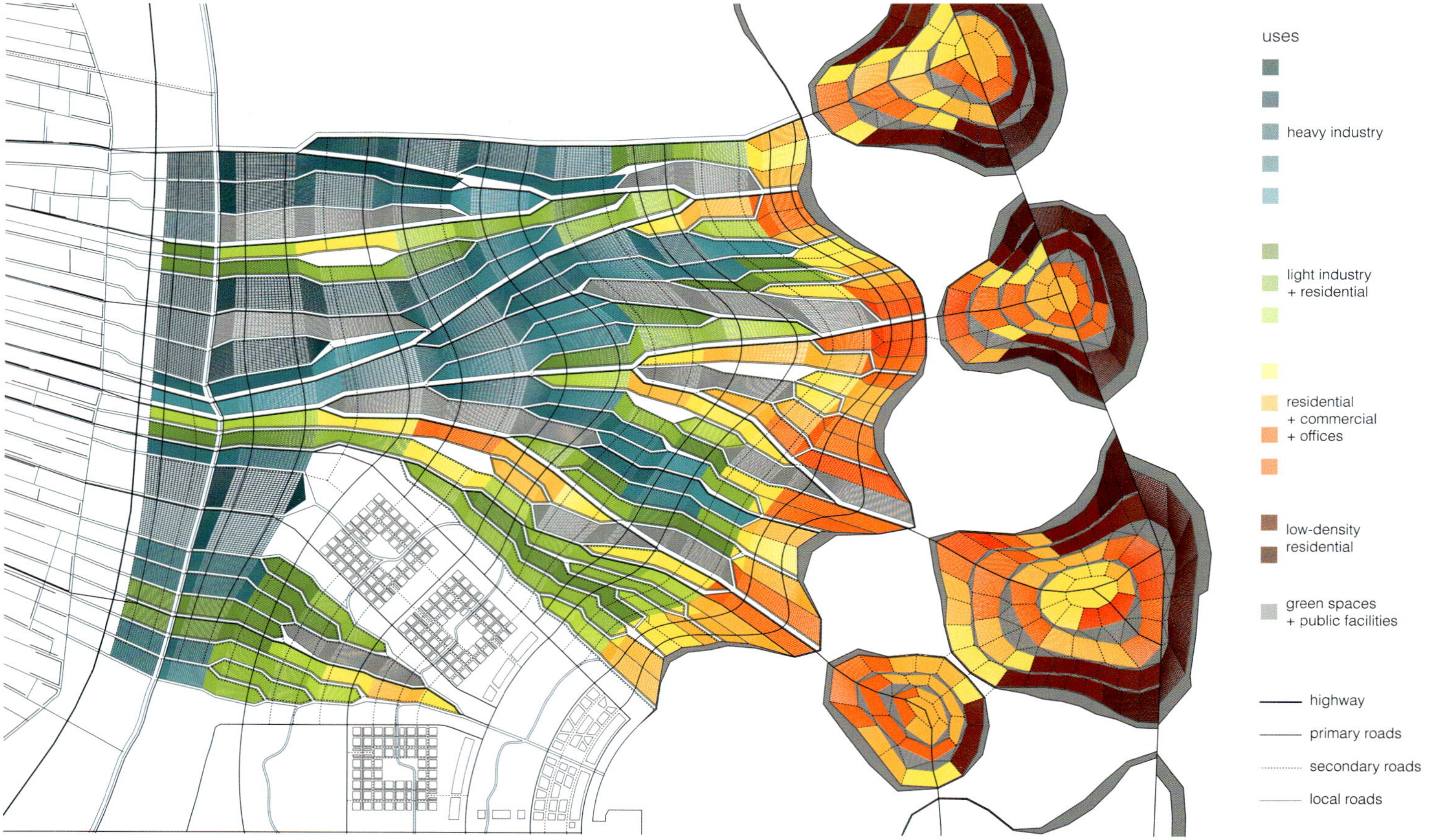

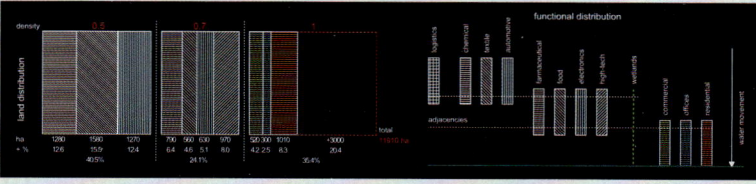

1. Densities and functional adjacencies

Functional clusters

The proposal aims to eliminate the programmatic segregation of the original masterplan, thus reducing the commuting distances and avoiding functional disequilibriums that often evolve in deserted areas at certain times of the day. The heavy industry is placed inland in direct relationship with the existing primary roads, favouring its connection to the logistic centre and the Yangshan port. To make the industrial area more 'permeable', some corridors of light industry and housing are generated along the main canals, taking advantage of the green hills to separate themselves from the most polluting industrial sites.
Separated from the polluting factories by a buffer area of clean industry, the denser multifunctional blocks, hosting most of the residential, commercial and office surfaces, are located along the lake shore.
Finally, some low-density, low-rise residential developments take place on the oceanic coast, allowing clear views to the sea from the inner high-rise buildings.

Proliferation components

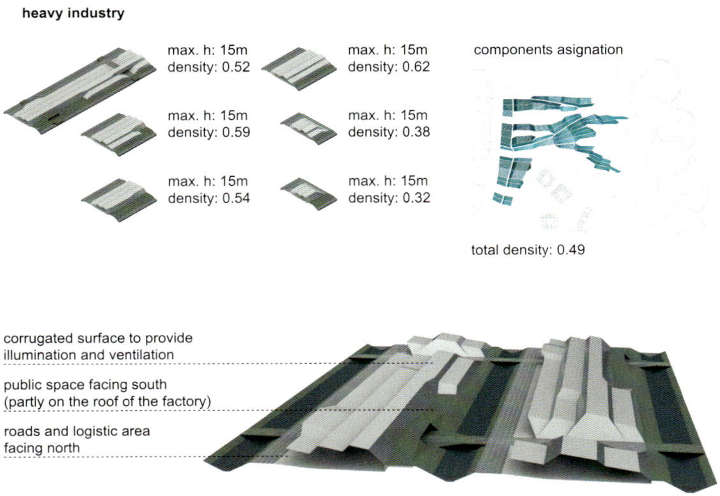

heavy industry

max. h: 15m density: 0.52
max. h: 15m density: 0.62
max. h: 15m density: 0.59
max. h: 15m density: 0.38
max. h: 15m density: 0.54
max. h: 15m density: 0.32

components asignation

total density: 0.49

light industry

max. h: 6 floors density: 0.61 — 61 13 26 %
max. h: 6 floors density: 1.10 — 39 19 42 %
max. h: 15m density: 0.55 — 100 %
max. h: 15m density: 0.35 — 100 %
max. h: 15m density: 0.52 — 100 %
max. h: 15m density: 0.64 — 45 11 44 %
max. h: 6 floors density: 0.62 — 68 19 13 %

components asignation

total density: 0.61

- corrugated surface to provide illumination and ventilation
- public space facing south (partly on the roof of the factory)
- roads and logistic area facing north

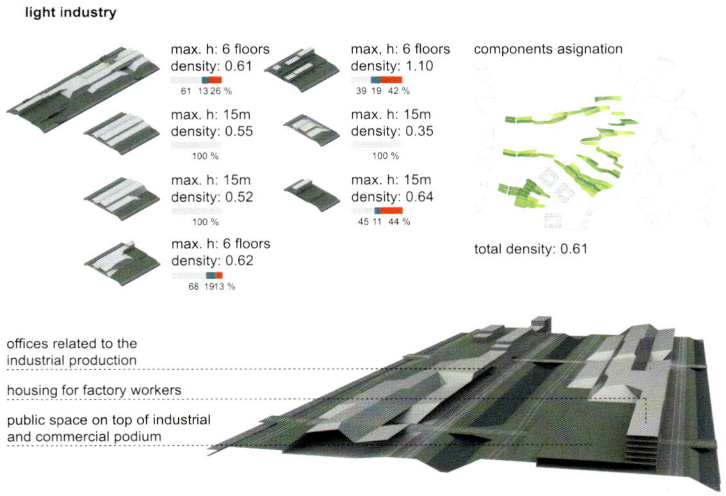

- offices related to the industrial production
- housing for factory workers
- public space on top of industrial and commercial podium

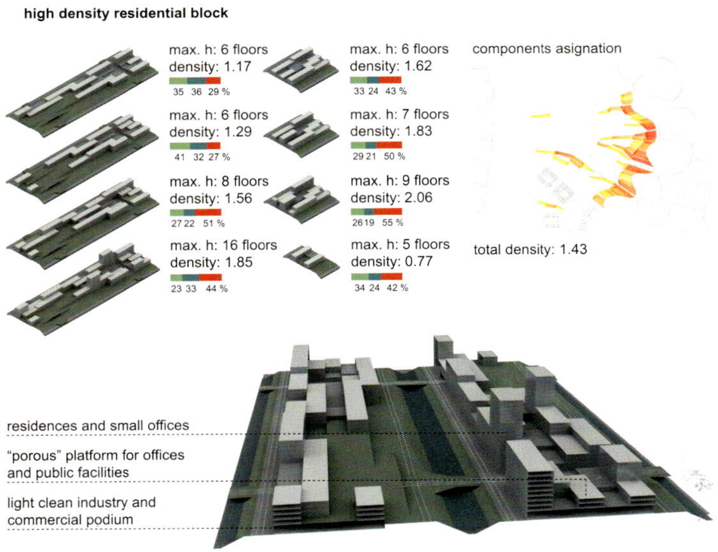

high density residential block

max. h: 6 floors density: 1.17 — 35 36 29 %
max. h: 6 floors density: 1.62 — 33 24 43 %
max. h: 6 floors density: 1.29 — 41 32 27 %
max. h: 7 floors density: 1.83 — 29 21 50 %
max. h: 8 floors density: 1.56 — 27 22 51 %
max. h: 9 floors density: 2.06 — 26 19 55 %
max. h: 16 floors density: 1.85 — 23 33 44 %
max. h: 5 floors density: 0.77 — 34 24 42 %

components asignation

total density: 1.43

medium - low density residential block

max. h: 6 floors density: 0.40 — 100 %
max. h: 6 floors density: 2.08 — 26 24 50 %
max. h: 8 floors density: 0.79 — 16 84 %
max. h: 9 floors density: 2.52 — 22 20 58 %
max. h: 16 floors density: 1.12 — 23 17 60 %

components asignation

total density: 1.13

- residences and small offices
- "porous" platform for offices and public facilities
- light clean industry and commercial podium

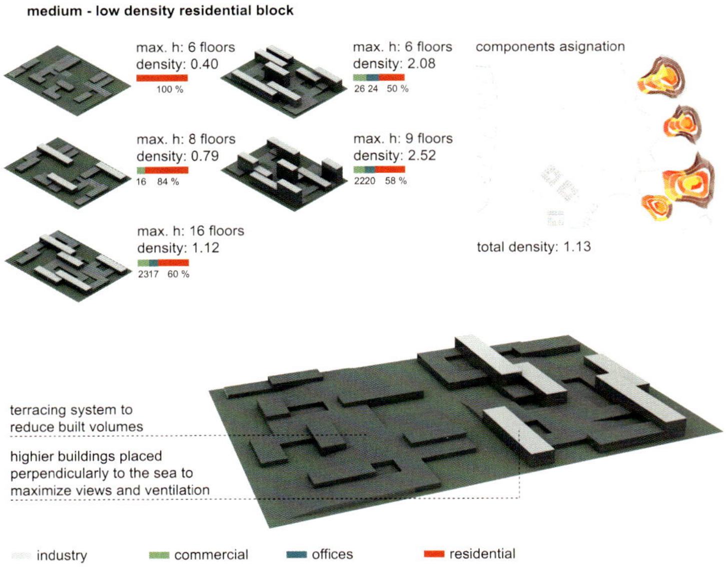

- terracing system to reduce built volumes
- highier buildings placed perpendicularly to the sea to maximize views and ventilation

■ industry   ■ commercial   ■ offices   ■ residential

1. Existing residential block
2. Proposed high-density urban block

High-density urban blocks
Close to the lake shore, the density becomes considerably higher and the blocks present all the functional spectrum of a city centre: clean industrial production, commercial activities, public facilities and parking areas are placed on the ground floor in direct relationship with the street, while the offices and residential spaces are located in linear volumes on the higher floors. A 'porous' platform guarantees good conditions of natural ventilation and illumination to the offices and public facilities in the lower levels and generates a series of courtyards that give a special character to the neighbourhoods. With the same purpose, the limits between the public and the private space is blurred, with the creation of semi-public terraces on the first floor.
While the low density of the existing residential quarters strongly reduces the presence of commercial activities on the street level, the denser block of the proposal could provide all sorts of public activities on the street, thus favouring social interaction.

Satellite view

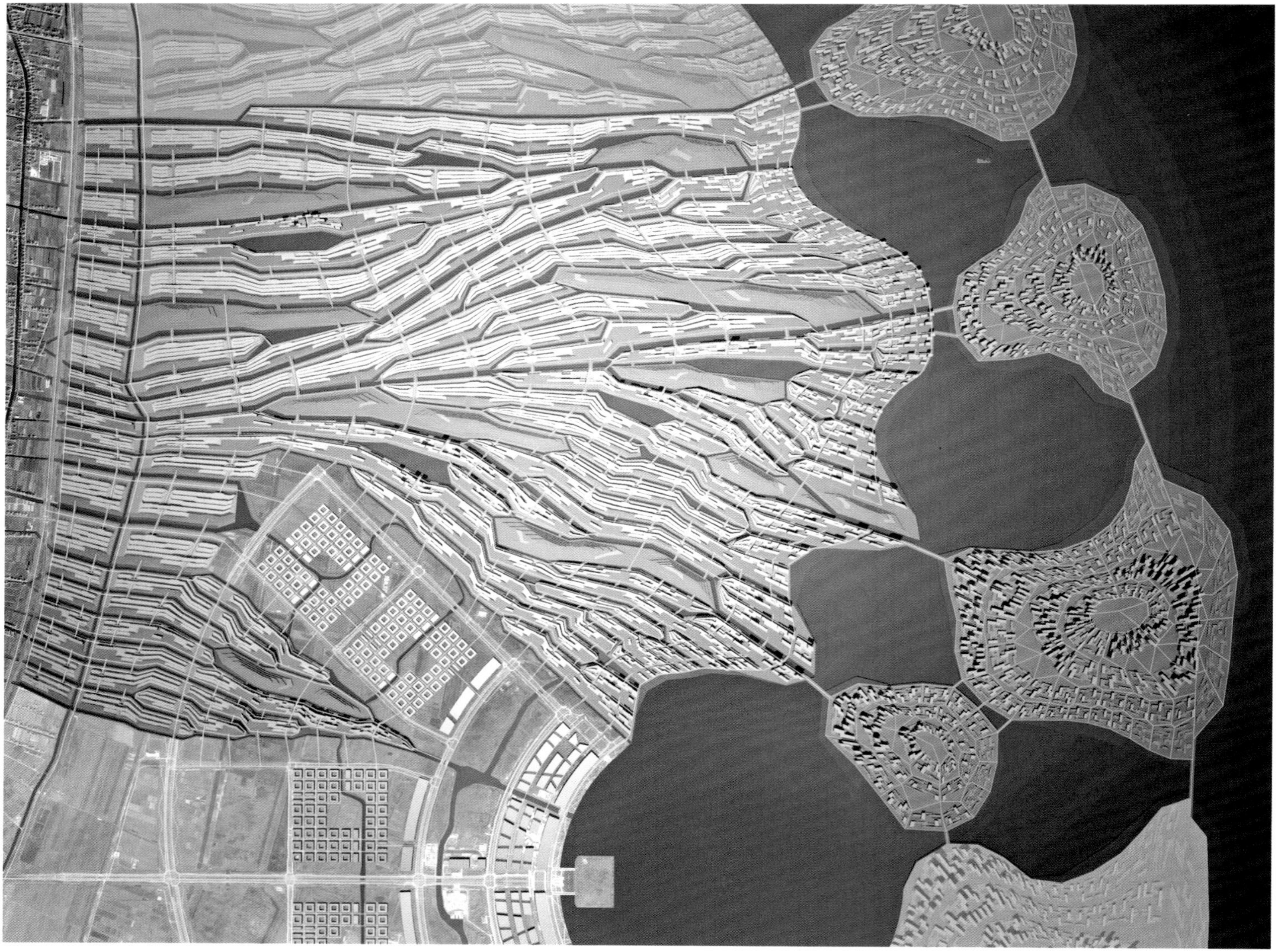

1/2/3. Possible growth scenario

Phasing strategy

The aim of the project is to create a dynamic system, able to adapt itself to the needs that the future growth of the city generates. Unlike from the original masterplan where most of the infrastructure is developed at once, this scheme allows the separation of the different phases of growth, thus spreading the initial economic investment in time. Each phase is fully meaningful in itself and the final site configuration can be adapted to the real evolution of the city. In other words, the economic success of one phase provides the funds for the following one and the process can be stopped at any given time without compromising the quality of the output.

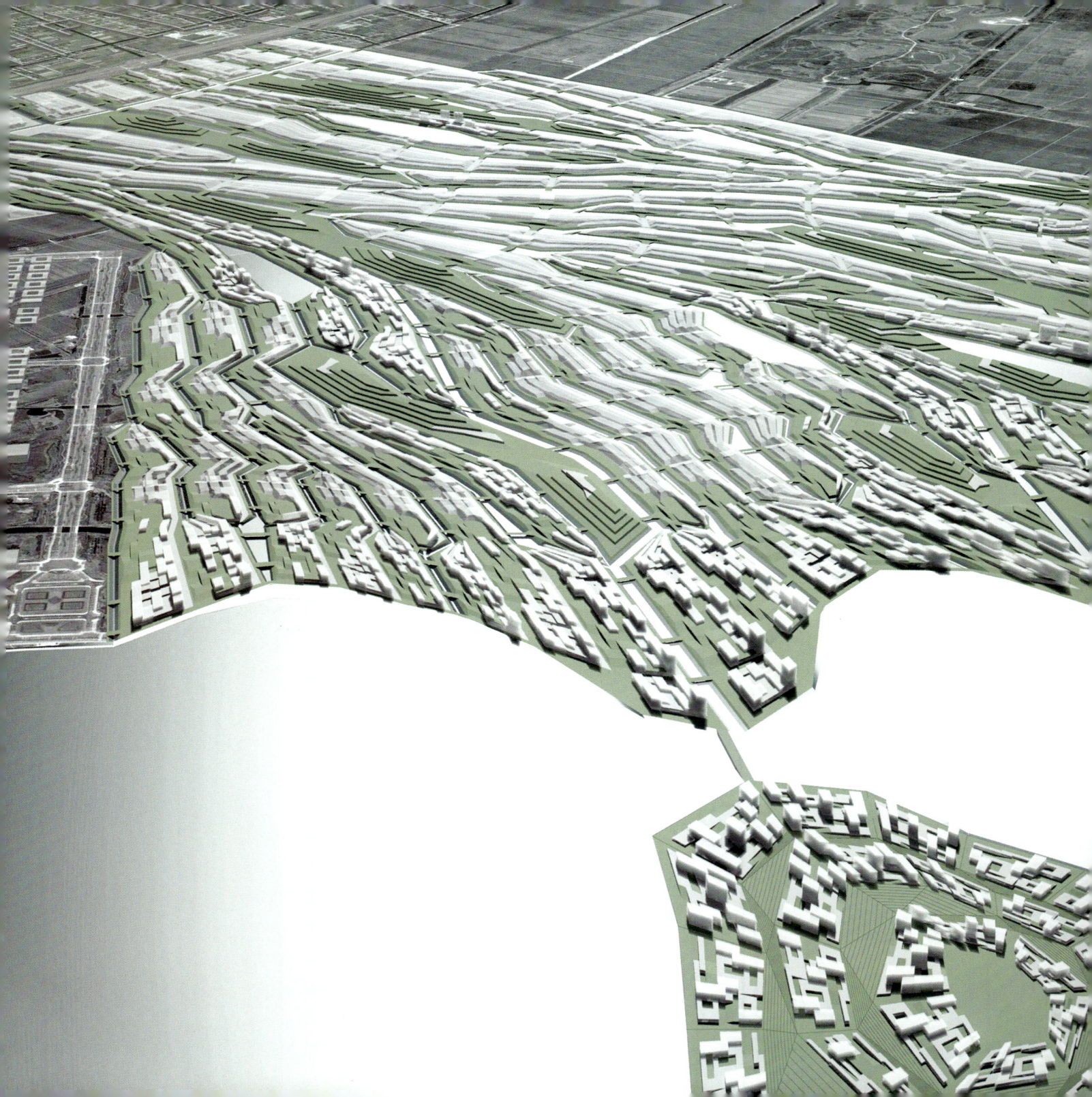

AALU China 09/10

Pro-Multiplicity

Date **2009/10**
Location **China**
Author **Karishma Desai**

Project description

'PRO - MULTIPLICITY' is a belief that contemporary urbanism can be made more interactive by inducing spatial multiplicity between the Landscape and Urbanism. The proposal exemplifies how local intelligence has the potential to create co-existent communities as an alternative model of future urbanism.

Under the theme of 'Prototypical Urbanities' and expanding on the research of past few years, the studio intends to address the issues revolving around China's ambition to build 400 new cities by the year 2020, with a target to move around 12 million people from rural to urban areas. Taking this as a broad scenario, the AALU Studio 2009-10 has focused on the Yangtze River Delta in East China including the region around Shanghai, Nanjing, Hangzhou, Suzhou and Ningbo, which are the epicentres of large-scale infrastructure development and thereby rapid industrialisation.

The Yangtze River Delta in China is one of the most rapidly developing regions of the world today; exhibiting massive urbanisation trends, huge infrastructure development and a stupendous building boom, invoking issues of large-scale migration, pollution and loss of arable land. These rapid processes constantly create new generators of urbanism, as a result of which the area is in a perpetual state of flux, in turn threatening the material conditions of the existing ecologies. Port of Ningbo and the decision for its expansion is acting as one such attractor, creating a wave of transformations and rapid urbanisation along the Hangzhou Bay area, home to a very interesting mix of agro-based and industrial systems, located within a very sensitive and productive ecological zone.

Taking this as an opportunity to explore the complexities of these systems in relation to each other, the idea is to propose adaptive spatial strategies, addressing these normative processes on one hand, while harnessing the material conditions of the site by amalgamating 'self-production modules' and recovery systems, as a means to generate new forms of social, infrastructural and industrial programming to bridge these otherwise fragmented entities.

1. Existing masterplan
2. Cixi city
3. Industrial zone

Cixi is a city within the sub-provincial city of Ningbo located in the Zhejiang province of China, along the Hangzhou Bay Area; becoming a vital part of the 2-hour-traffic ring within Shanghai, Hangzhou and Ningbo, and therefore playing a role as another transportation hub in Yangtze Delta area. 60% of the area remains rural with heavy dependence on agriculture and agro-based industries. Cixi has experienced a growth of 14.5% in 2008-09 as a light manufacturing base. The East Cixi Industrial Zone is one such development plan. The top-down scheme completely disregards the local ecology as well as existing villages and proposes to build over the tidal flats, further aggravating conditions of flooding and storm surge. The proposal aims to provide an alternative strategy to these existing patterns of urbanisation, while fulfilling the demand for industries and infrastructure. Introducing Artificial Topography, based on actual calculations on the dredging of canals and wetlands, along with an analysis of the slope criteria required for the efficiency of different programmes. The topography helps mitigate flooding and thus create performative landscapes responding to the tidal variations in the East China Sea, while giving an opportunity to integrate landscape and the built form.

Final programmatic distribution on site

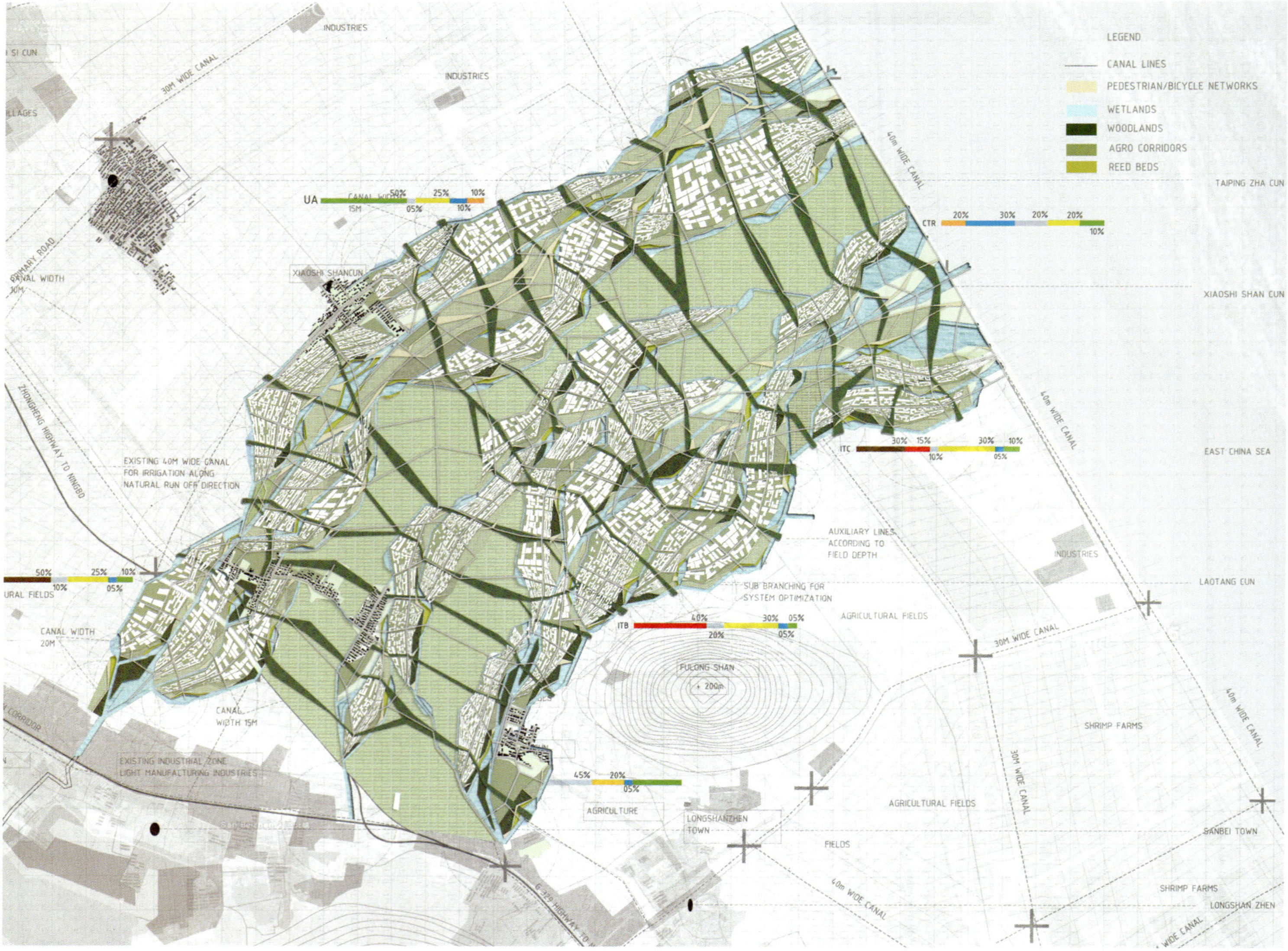

1. 3D explorations
2. Understanding material identities

Material identities

Identity is commonly understood as 'the distinguishing character or personality of an individual'. The idea of identity has always been dialectical no matter where one starts from, be it philosophy and psychology, physics and chemistry or the very field of architecture and urbanism: this occurs predominantly because the world has the ability to take positions by either taking us back into history and therefore a belief in the preservation of identities, when various civilisations started shaping up; each associating itself with particular materialisations in terms of their culture, technology or architecture, or by prompting us to cast off all labels and look into a new future for human civilization as a whole. In fact, it is in these times of globalism where one seems to have become conscious of striving for certain kinds of identity– either by defending one's inherent (historical) identity or by introducing a pastiche identity that one aspires to, or at the other end of the spectrum, just dismissing the past and injecting new beginnings of materialising domains.

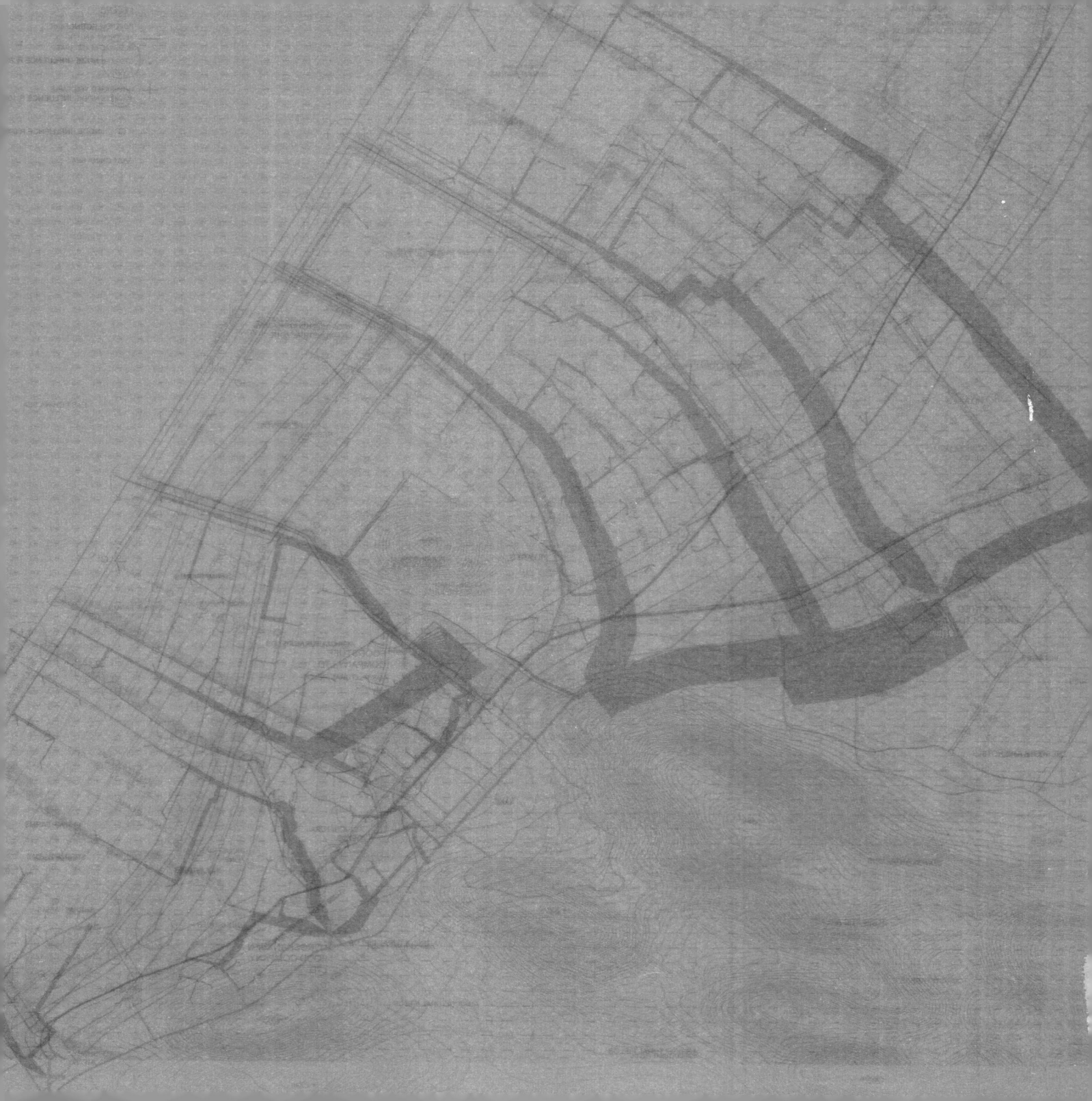

Catalogue: parametric control of branching and its spatial implications

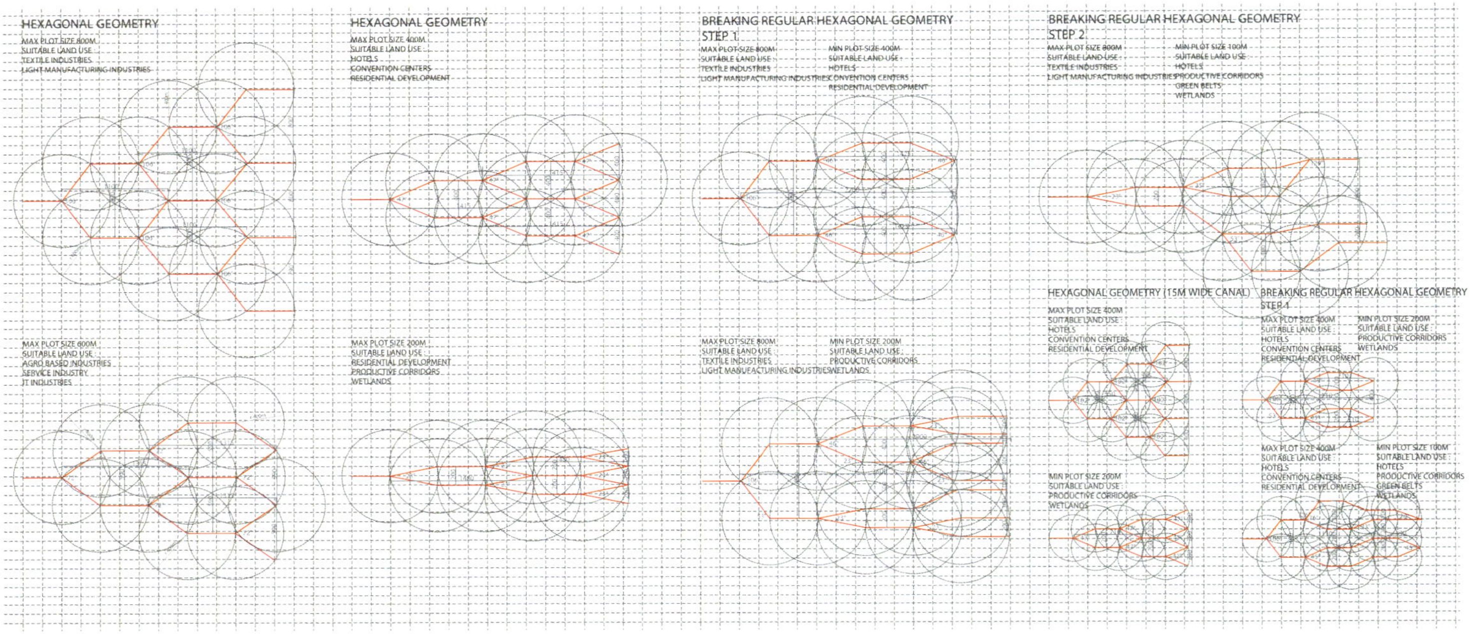

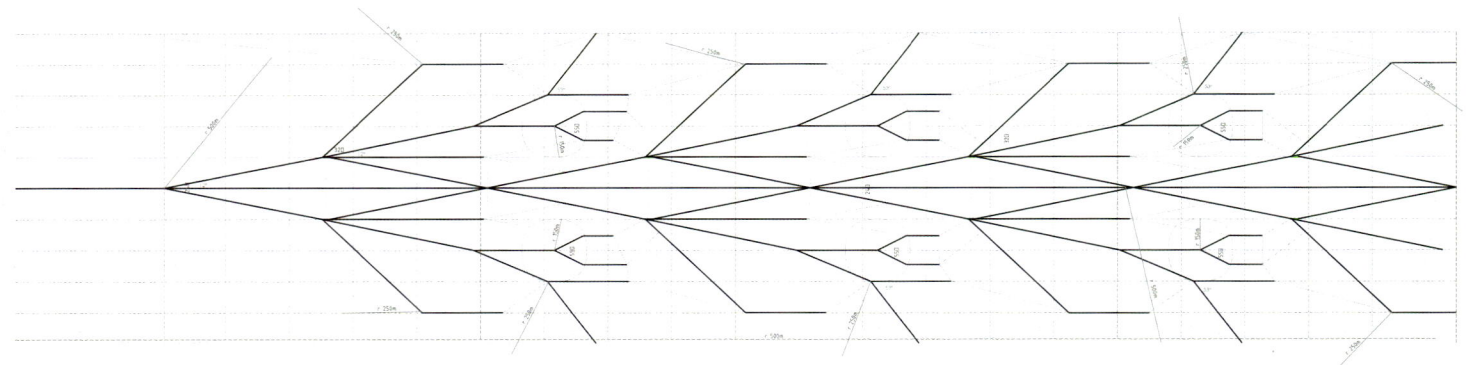

Prototype development: component with the most efficient branching system

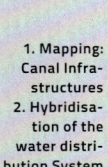

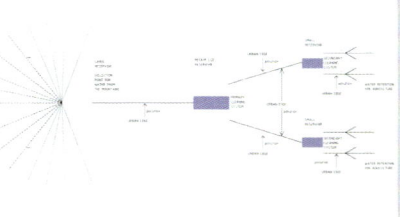

1. Mapping: Canal Infrastructures
2. Hybridisation of the water distribution System

Component development
The design of a canal infrastructure was based on the development of a component able to control the material restriction posed by its design. Applying the defined rules of this component helps to generate a potential catalogue of spatial conditions within the hierarchy of canals. First, a basic geometry is achieved, in the form of hexagonal cells allowing for different plot sizes and thereby programmatic translations, ranging from 800m deep plot which can be used for industrial purpose to 100m deep plot, which can be used as a green corridor or wetland. However, the system still has the danger of being monofunctional and inflexible. Attempts to induce flexibility in the component begin with the breaking away from stiff hexagonal geometry and instead opening up the system to generate varying sizes of plots, which can take up different uses and thereby have the ability to create a richer mix of programmes. Geometric explorations on this are carried out in order to explore and test different configurations.

Component development

Component Sections

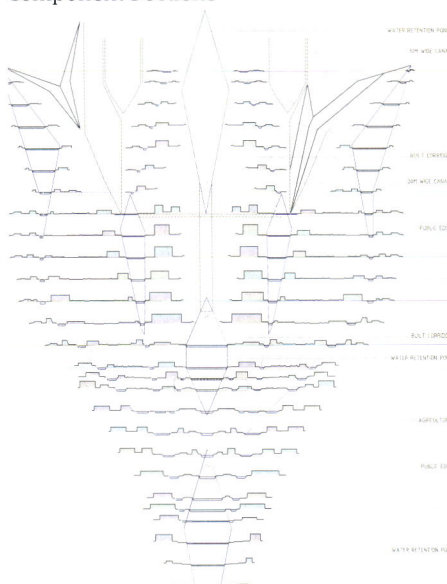

3d tests

Sectional Modifications

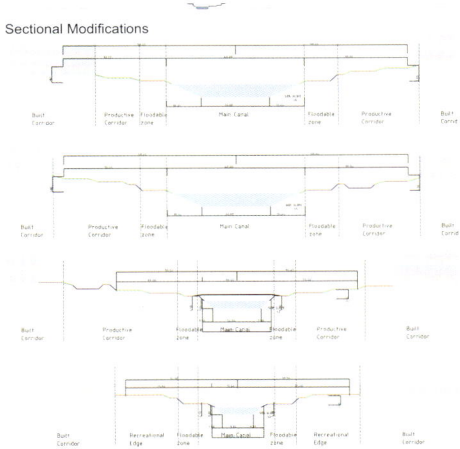

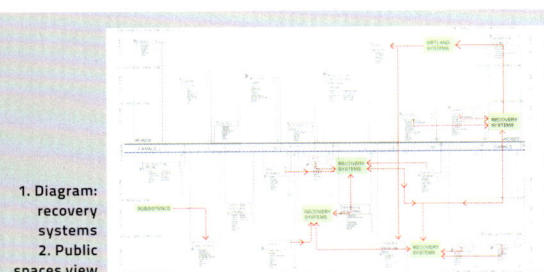

1. Diagram: recovery systems
2. Public spaces view

Instrumentalisation of the strategy

The proposed programme adjacencies are bridged together by water infrastructures and recovery systems like wetlands to induce spatial relations between the landscape and the built form, for instance the introduction of productive corridors allows for healthy social interactions and a unique dependence of the urbanism on the native landscape. The proposal thus attempts to understand Infrastructures to create spatial identities as a response to the embedded territorial value already in place, thereby creating unique material identities. The built component has been understood as being generic in aesthetics, with a strong concept of allowing permeability in terms of its usability. The project thus demonstrates that local intelligence can be considered and be improved upon to appropriate to contemporary urban conditions.

Introduction of cleaning nodes

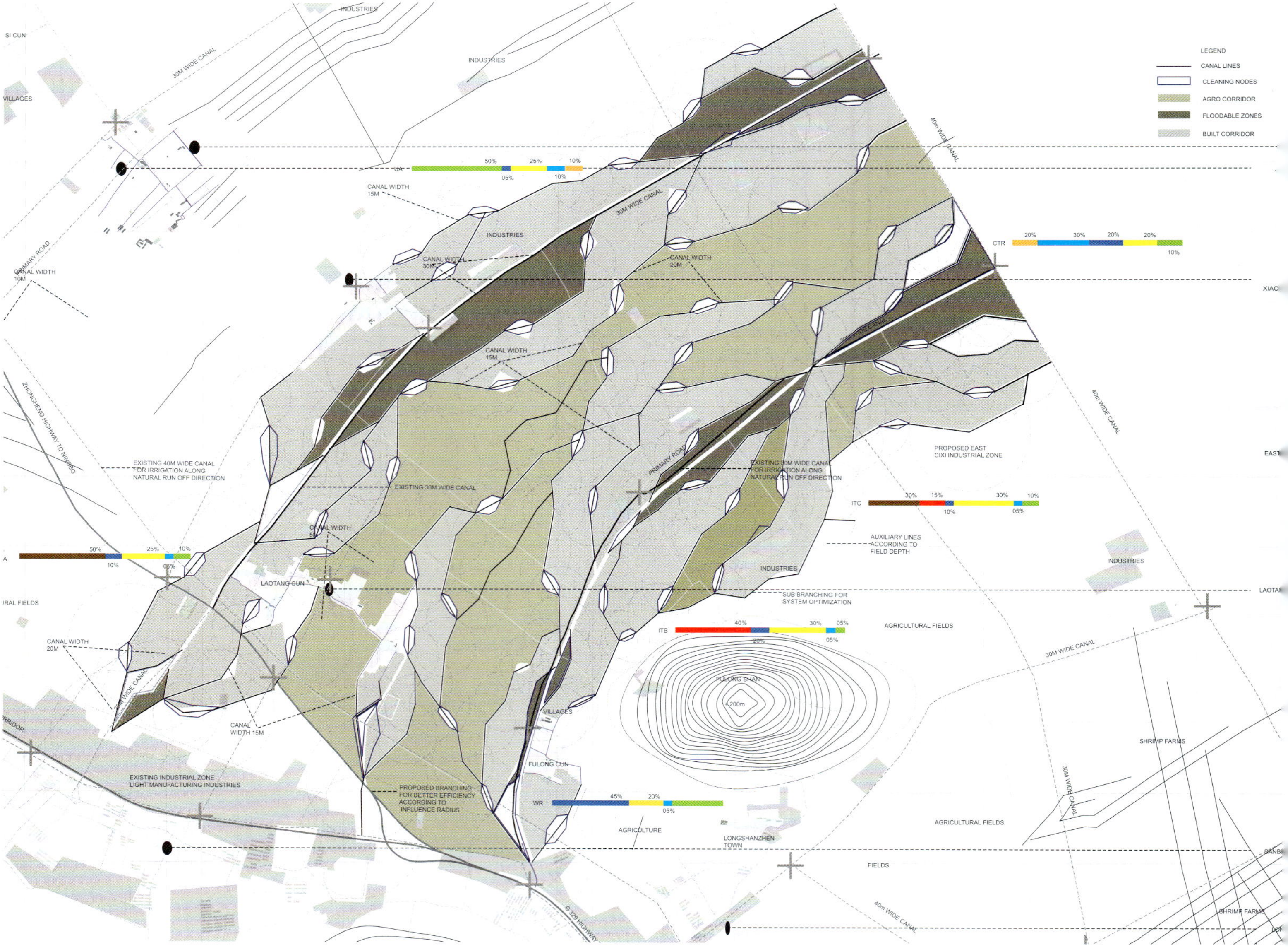

LEGEND
— CANAL LINES
▢ CLEANING NODES
▨ AGRO CORRIDOR
▨ FLOODABLE ZONES
▨ BUILT CORRIDOR

1. Study cases: Shanghai Chemical Industrial Park, AECOM
2. Typical water distribution system
3. Traditional melon-on-the vine water distribution system

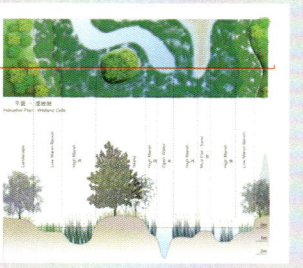
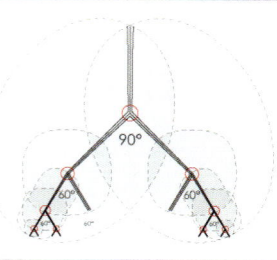
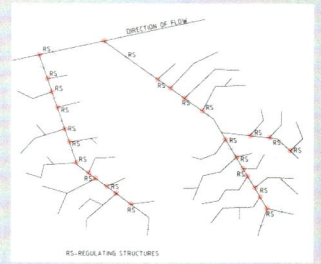

Actualisation on site

The 3D explorations are tested by introducing modifications to the existing canal sections. This brings out the potential of the component to create multiple edge morphologies. Just by varying the angles of response of the canal section, it is possible to introduce wetlands and floodable zones. The section extends to create productive corridors and recreational spaces to have innovative relationships with the surrounding built fabric.

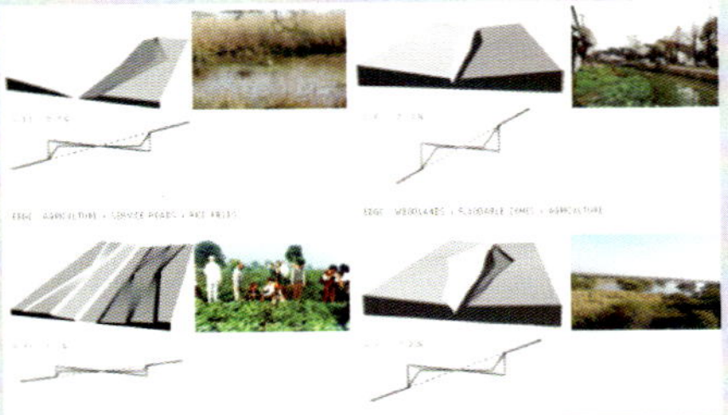

Design development

Programmatic explorations in 3D

The 3D catalogue is also tested by a catalogue of sections translated into physical models, to further understand the possibilities of spatial organisations and built-in relationships. Tests of programmatic permutations and combinations on the 3D catalogue are performed, based on adopting conventional landscape standards. A catalogue of green programmes is thereby generated and detailed out with working dimensions.
The catalogue of green programmes is also tested in the third dimension further generating a catalogue that demonstrates its spatial connotations and cut-fill criteria and slopes. References for possible materialisation of the edge is also demonstrated in the catalogue on the right.
Further explorations on the aggregation of these programmes in plan and perspective were carried out in relation to the integration built into the system.

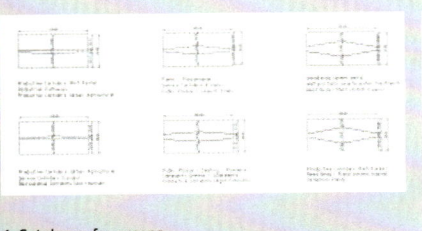

1. Catalogue for greens
2. Catalogue of green programmes

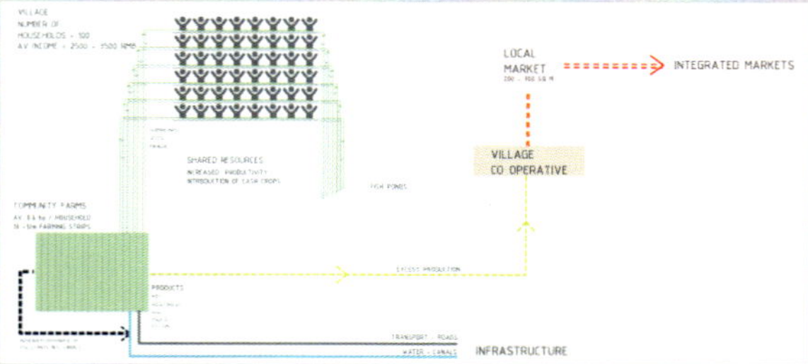

1. Canal edge view
2. New scales of production

The introduction of the programme in the green corridors must respect calculations of the population, wetland requirement, etc. To make the proposal more sustainable, public transport along the arterial roads will be introduced as a means to reduce dependence on automobiles within the development.
Green corridors between the islands will be infiltrated to act as pedestrian networks, bicycle paths and public transport routes. Different densities are assigned to the public transport nodes, based on their proximity to green corridors or coast and existing settlements.
Urban blocks are defined for development on the basis of their proximity to canals, green corridors, arterial roads or the coast. The definition of land use must respect the nature of urban blocks.

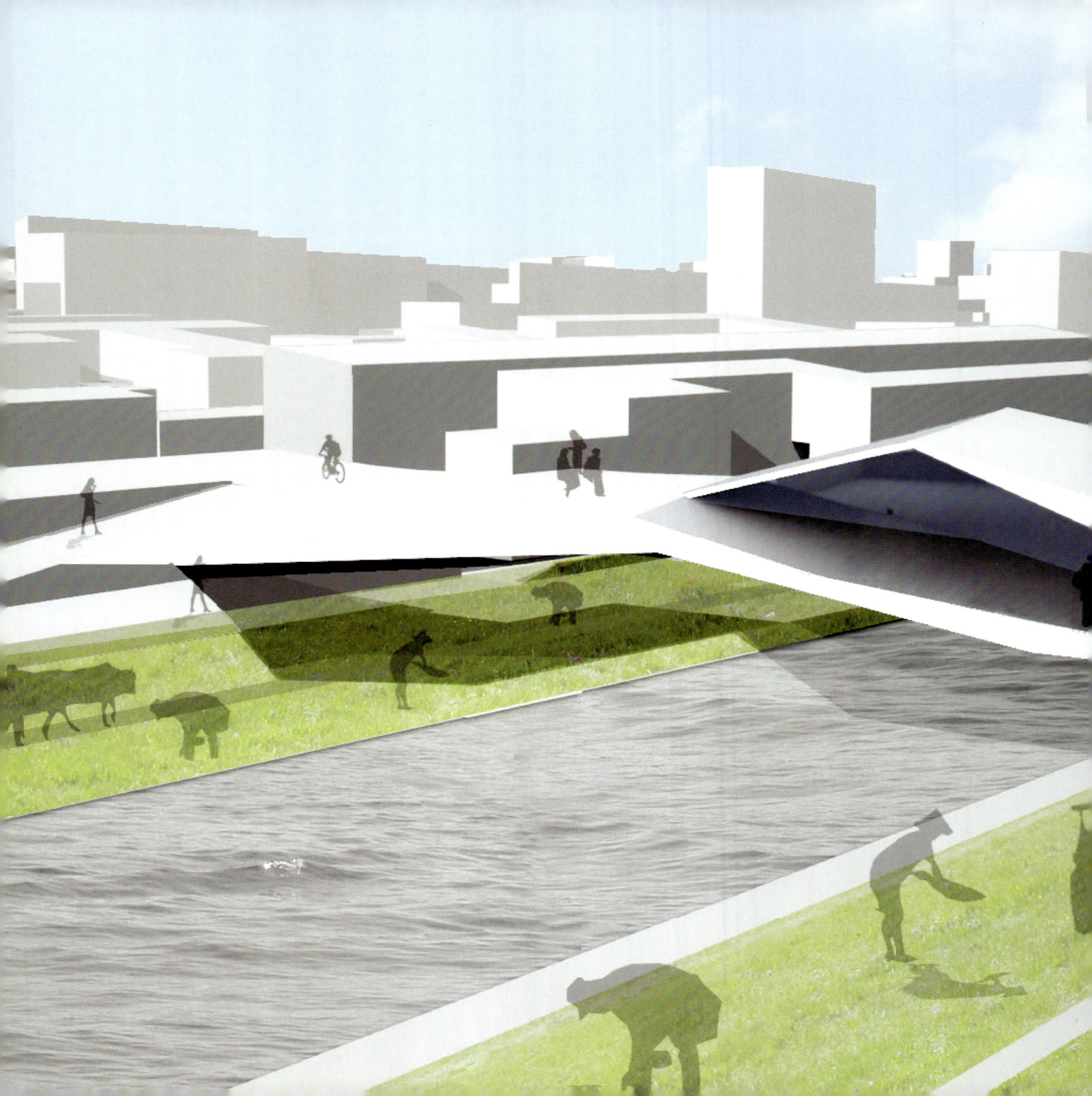

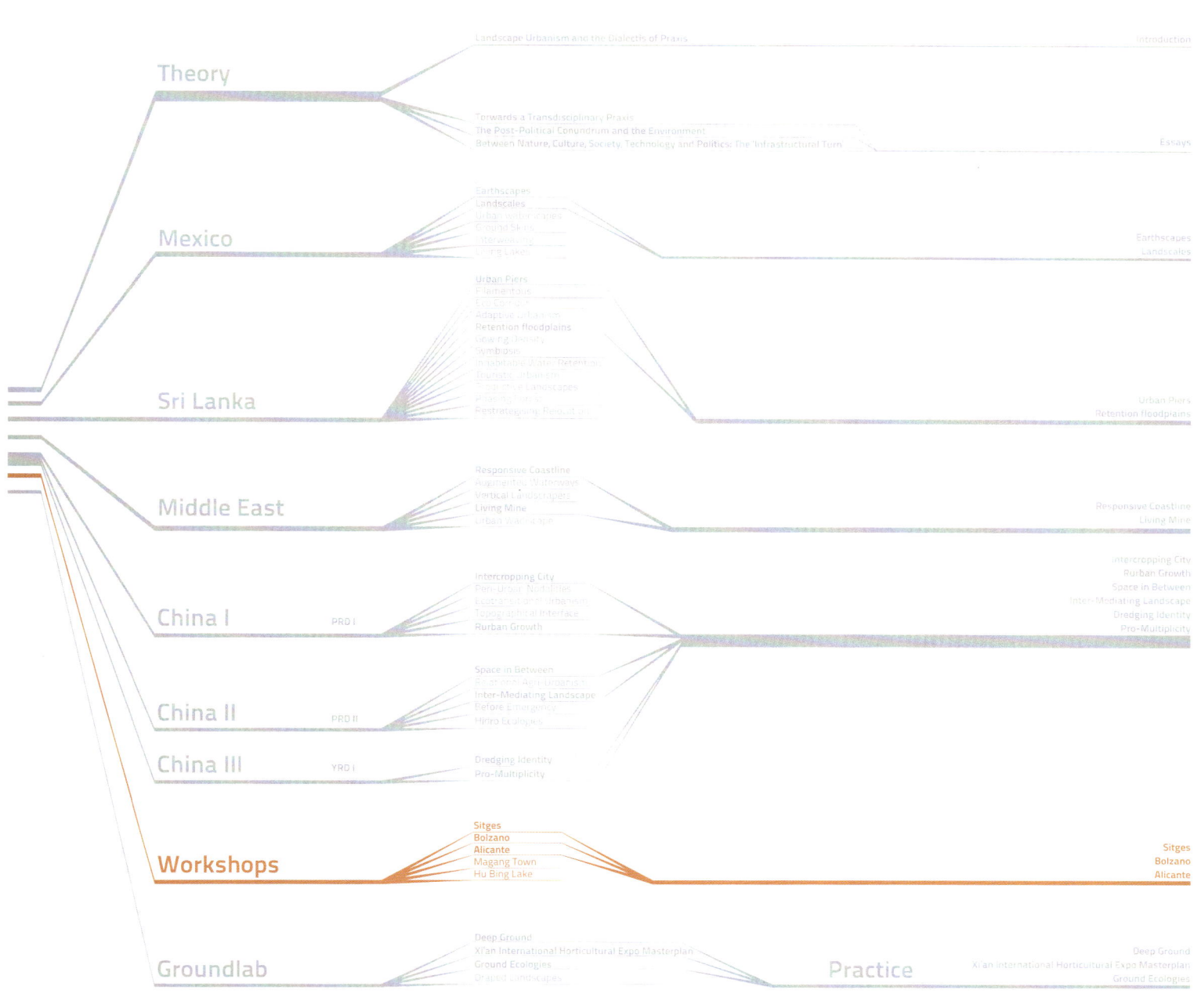

AA Landscape Urbanism 09/10
Workshops

AGENDA The AA Landscape Urbanism MA (AALU) organises a series of workshops to be held each year during the spring break in collaboration with different AA Landscape Urbanism partners. During the past three years the workshops have taken place in European cities: Sitges, Alicante, and Bolzano. AALU has been invited to provide alternative proposals to existing projects and explore new ideas at a territorial scale in order to promote and develop possible urban scenarios in specific contexts. The objective of these exercises is to serve as a quick and intense test bed for the application of the AALU methodology and the techniques developed within the master's programme. Ideas on Indexing, Meshing and Prototyping are actualised within specific conditions and clients' requirements. The work is usually developed with a multidisciplinary team, formed primarily by Landscape Urbanism staff in addition to local experts and experienced consultants. Finally, the workshops end with public presentations to authorities and stakeholders where the students have the opportunity to practise real-life scenarios and are exposed to questions about the work produced.

AALU Workshop

Paisatges de Catalunya Workshop
Circuito de innovacion del garraf

Date **2007/2008**
Location **Sitges, Catalonia, Spain**
Author **Landscape Urbanism Students and Teaching Staff**

Project description

Sitges is a town located in the municipality of Barcelona, part of the community of Catalonia. The town is placed between the Garraf Massif and the sea and is conveniently located 45 minutes by car from Barcelona. Sitges is well known for its beaches, nightspots and historical sites and therefore relies heavily on its tourism industry.

The AALU programme was invited to Sitges in April 2008 in order to participate in a five-day intensive workshop to come up with ideas and a proposal that reflect the strategic opportunities of the town. A group made of students and staff applied the methodology of Landscape Urbanism to read, understand, collect and analyse the existing conditions in order to deploy a coherent and integrated proposal.

Between Sitges and Sant Pere de Ribes village lies a piece of land with the potential to house a development capable to expand the singular economy of Sitges. The project is surrounded by major infrastructural highways and railway lines. This high connectivity feature allows the site to be strategically close to Barcelona and the City airport and therefore attractive for investment. In this available land, the Sitges municipality proposed the development of a technology park where new high-tech companies could settle and benefit from the advantages of the land: its connectivity as well as competitive land prices.

The AALU team developed a proposal that intends to choreograph the various interests and land uses, existing and proposed, in order to integrate the technology park with the city of Sitges. The main objective was the use of this major investment opportunity to expand the economy of Sitges while integrating the design within the city fabric for the benefit of Sitges as a whole.

This event is part of a long-term engagement of AALU + Groundlab with the Fundacion Metropoli, which fosters innovative research and cutting-edge practice in urban design and planning. The work was presented and discussed with the Mayor of Sitges and other key decision-makers during a final presentation in April 2008.

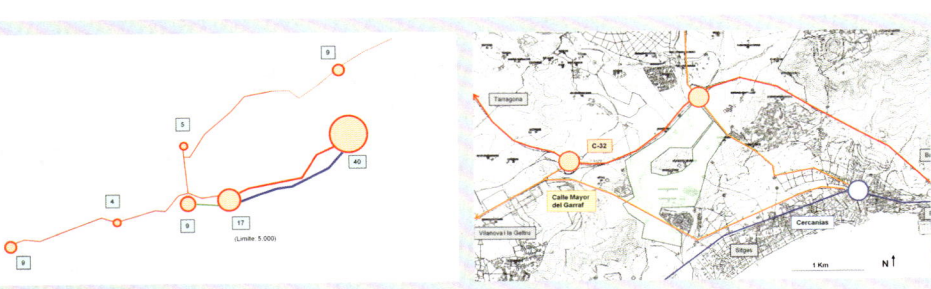

1. Connectivity
2. Project location

The project is located between the municipalities of Sant Pere de Ribes and Sitges Town and it is surrounded by major infrastructural highways and railway lines. This high connectivity feature allows the site to be strategically close to Barcelona and the City airport and therefore attractive for investment.

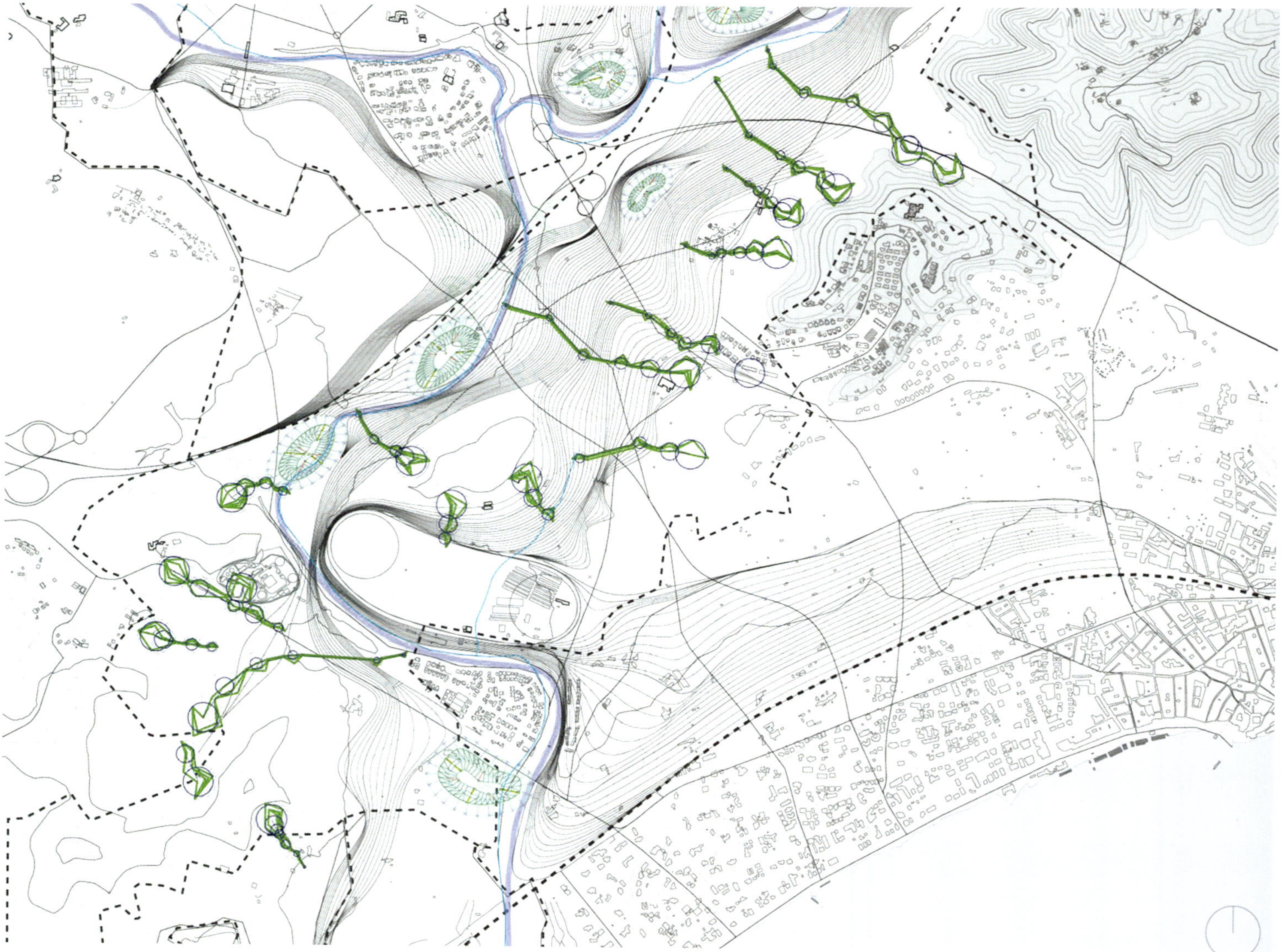

Paisatges de Catalunya Workshop

1/2. Landscape generated by natural waterflows

The AALU team began by reading and understanding the local conditions on site. One of the first main issues that arose was the dry weather conditions and consequently the lack of water in the area. A water strategy was developed, including different sources of water to ensure the continuous supply throughout the year. A series of centralised and networked wetland systems was introduced as a cleansing device and as the spine of the future development. These green fingers become the basis for the public and green system of the proposal. Along with this, a basic structure was developed in the territory based on the existing block sizes in Sitges and the interlacing of the wetland system deployed on site.

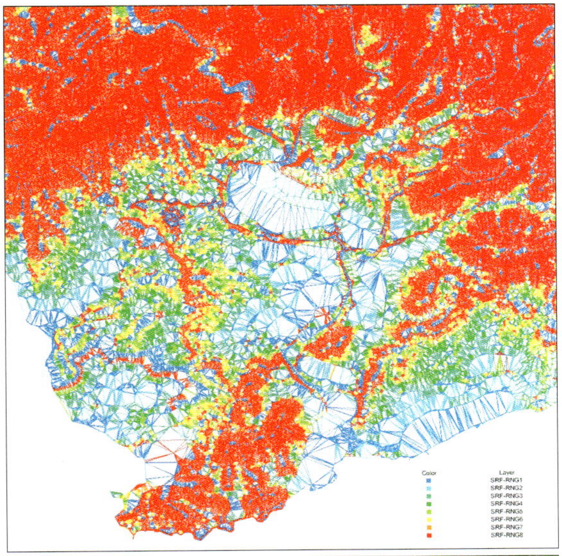
Color
Layer
SRF-RNG1
SRF-RNG2
SRF-RNG3
SRF-RNG4
SRF-RNG5
SRF-RNG6
SRF-RNG7
SRF-RNG8

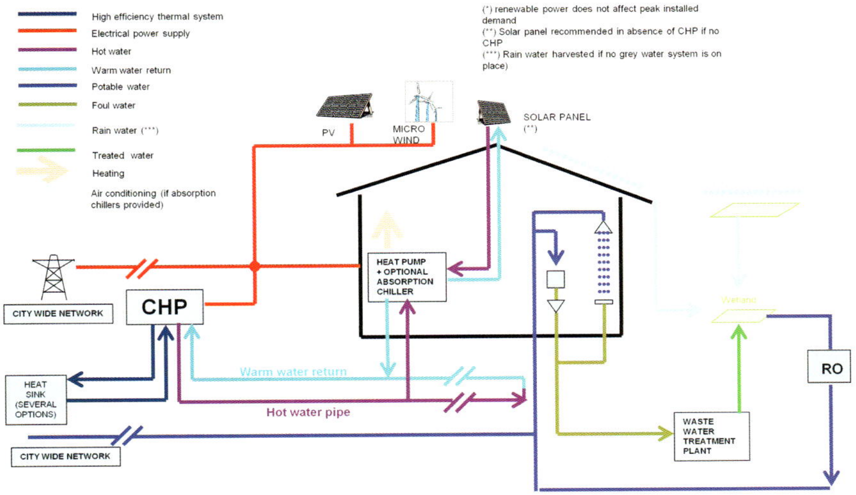
High efficiency thermal system
Electrical power supply
Hot water
Warm water return
Potable water
Foul water
Rain water (***)
Treated water
Heating
Air conditioning (if absorption chillers provided)
(*) renewable power does not affect peak installed demand
(**) Solar panel recommended in absence of CHP if no CHP
(***) Rain water harvested if no grey water system is on place)
PV
MICRO WIND
SOLAR PANEL (**)
HEAT PUMP + OPTIONAL ABSORPTION CHILLER
CITY WIDE NETWORK
CHP
HEAT SINK (SEVERAL OPTIONS)
Warm water return
Hot water pipe
CITY WIDE NETWORK
RO
WASTE WATER TREATMENT PLANT

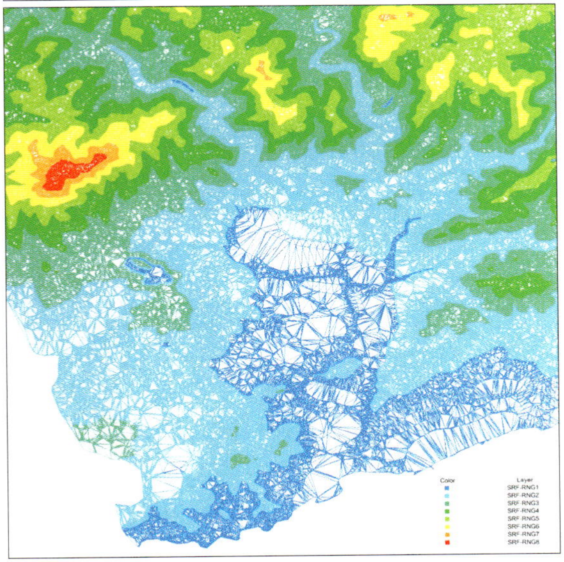
Color
Layer
SRF-RNG1
SRF-RNG2
SRF-RNG3
SRF-RNG4
SRF-RNG5
SRF-RNG6
SRF-RNG7
SRF-RNG8

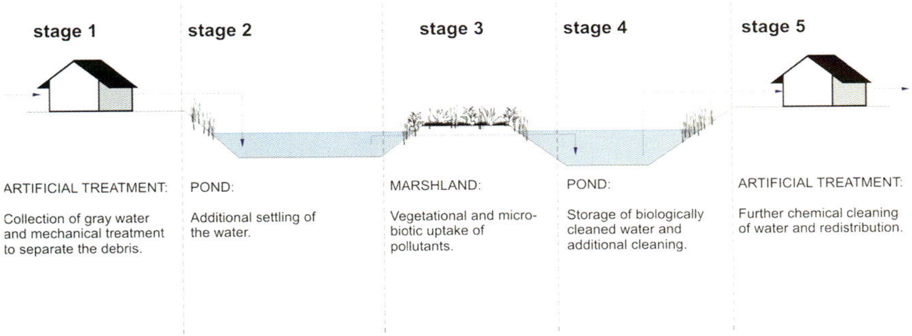
stage 1
stage 2
stage 3
stage 4
stage 5
ARTIFICIAL TREATMENT:
Collection of gray water and mechanical treatment to separate the debris.
POND:
Additional settling of the water.
MARSHLAND:
Vegetational and micro-biotic uptake of pollutants.
POND:
Storage of biologically cleaned water and additional cleaning.
ARTIFICIAL TREATMENT:
Further chemical cleaning of water and redistribution.

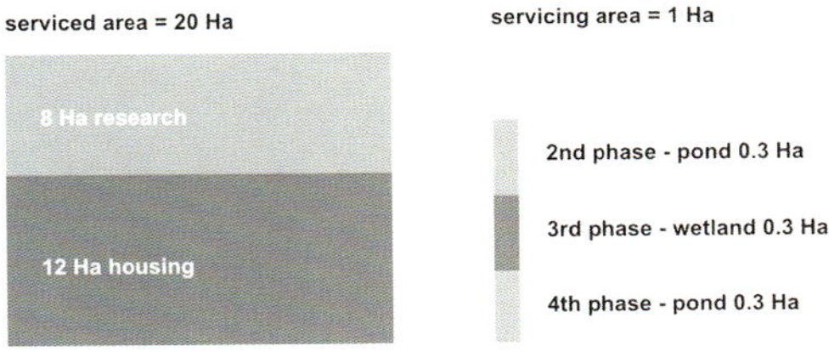
serviced area = 20 Ha
8 Ha research
12 Ha housing
servicing area = 1 Ha
2nd phase - pond 0.3 Ha
3rd phase - wetland 0.3 Ha
4th phase - pond 0.3 Ha

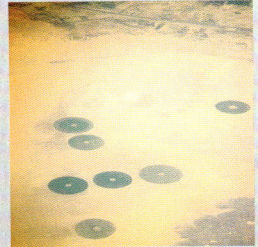

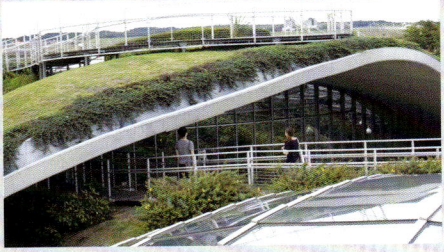

1. Center pivot irrigation system
2. GrinGrin Building, Fukuoka, Japan, by Toyo Ito

The reading of topographical conditions and the understanding of cleansing technology were fundamental to the proposal. In terms of cleansing strategies, a selection of natural devices, such as wetlands and similar systems, (SUDS sustainable drainage systems) were arranged. These strategies were seen as the basis for the proposal's framework and as part of the public space allocation.

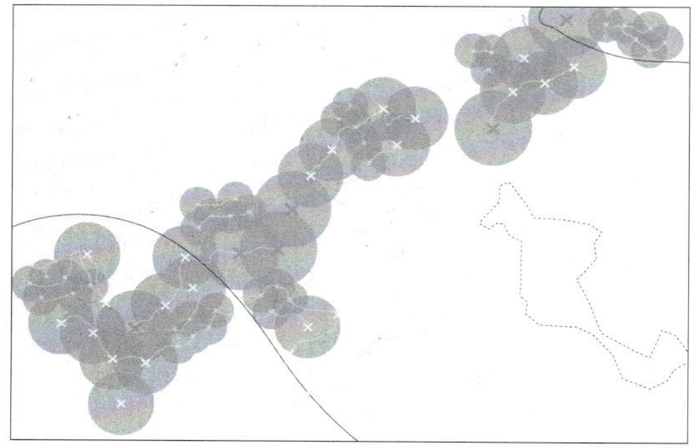

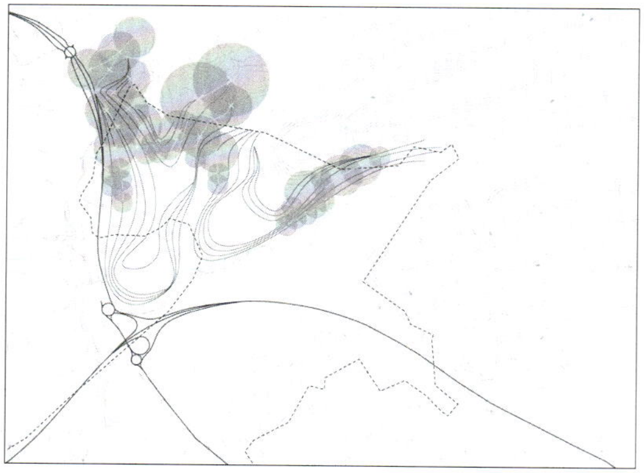

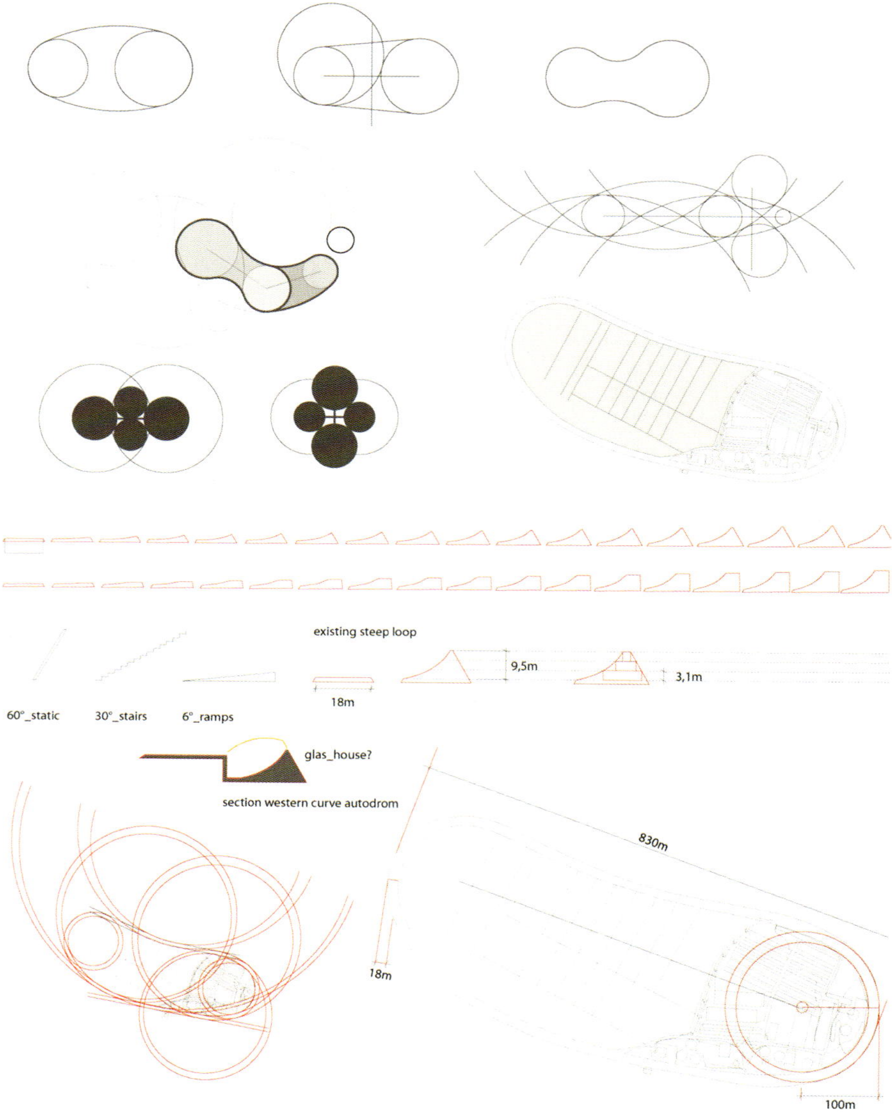

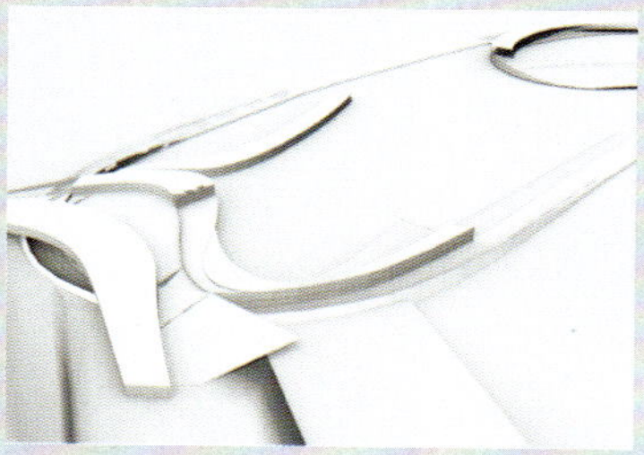

1/2. Views of public facilities

An existing race track within the site's boundary was used as the hinge-point between the existing city of Sitges and the new development. Inside the track, a number of public facilities serve both Sitges and the new development. The particular geometry allows a multifunctional use and its strategic location connects the past and future of the city.

The masterplan intent was to accommodate the programme for a technology park within an urban pattern that was not only able to house corporate offices and necessary facilities but also allowed the introduction of residential and commercial uses. This urban pattern was informed by several parameters including the use of the wetland system as a framework, the use of existing Sitges block modules and the introduction of mixed-use and interactive programmes to encourage spatial integration and the generation of a vibrant urban environment.

AALU Workshop

Metropoli Workshop
Alicante, a City in Flux

Date **2008/2009**
Location **Alicante, Spain**
Author **Landscape Urbanism Students and Staff**

Project description

The city of Alicante is the capital of Alicante province located south of Valencia community. Alicante is home to more than 300,000 inhabitants and hosts a historic Mediterranean port. The geographic conditions of the city have fostered a vital maritime life and the development of an important port and related facilities.

In recent years, the decline of the port infrastructures caused by the global shift of maritime activities and the impossibility to compete amongst the high volumes of the logistic markets has prompted the rethinking of its future role in the region.

In 2009 the AALU was invited by the local authorities to propose and develop ideas for the future of the port and the overall relation between Alicante and its coastline. Historically, Alicante has lived detached from its coastline. The existing topographical configuration defined by the Serra Grossa and the port activities has been crucial to the separation of the city from the sea. The inhabitants live less than 100 metres away from the sea but a continuous physical barrier, consisting of a port and a hill, has kept them unaware of the potential and advantages of a post-industrial coastal city.

The AALU team proposed the development of a wider masterplan that enhanced the redevelopment of the port and the integration of the hill within a continuous but differentiated coastline. Both conditions were seen as crucial elements for the viability of Alicante and its role in the region.

As part of a wider research, Fundacion Metropoli has been studying the area as well as the potential interventions in the coastline. Using these studies as a background, the AALU team defined three areas of intervention: the redevelopment of the port infrastructure, the landscape design of the the Serra Grossa hill and the expansion of the existing public beach.

These three projects and their masterplan framework were presented to a series of experts and professors of Architecture and Urbanism as well as to the Port Authorities, local politicians and media in Alicante.

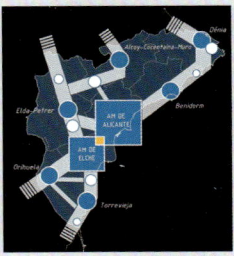

1. Regional corridors
2. Main aerial connections
3. Marityme connections

Alicante is understood as a major node due to its strategic location in Spain, the Mediterranean Sea and Europe. In Spain, Alicante is the key part of a series of regional corridors with a crucial logistic weight in the region of Valencia. Its location on the Mediterranean coast allows the development of various economies such as the tourist industry that could take advantage of the existing port infrastructure. Within Europe, Alicante airport has extended its destinations and therefore, managed to position Alicante within a network of medium-size cities in the European spectrum.

 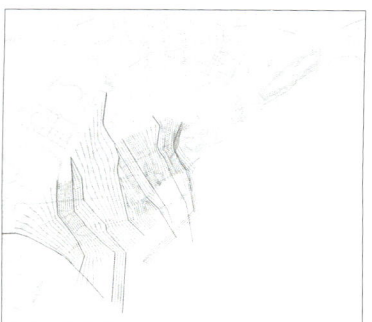 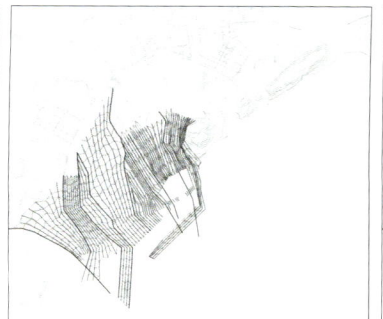 

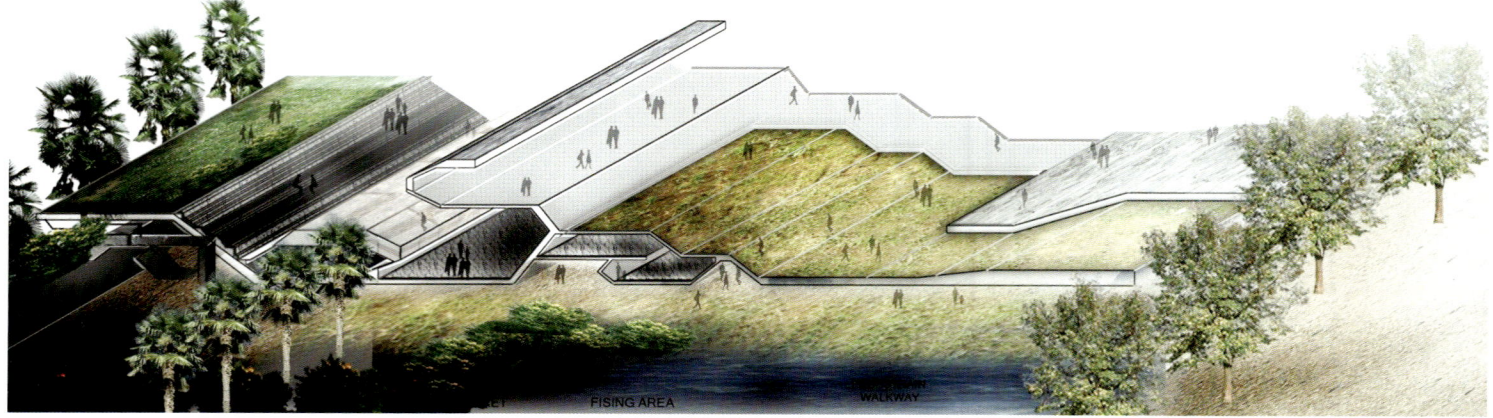

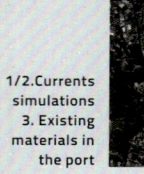
1/2. Currents simulations
3. Existing materials in the port

The AALU team took these conditions as the starting point and developed a series of indexing drawings to read the local specificities of the site. Indexes such as the maritime currents and other simulations to understand the impact of the port on the coast were incorporated in the design process.
At the same time, the team developed several material organisations to redesign the abandoned port structures in order to accommodate new uses such as commercial and leisure, among others. Fundamental to this was the understanding of port activities as a gradual process of transformation where several contradictory programmes overlapped over time.

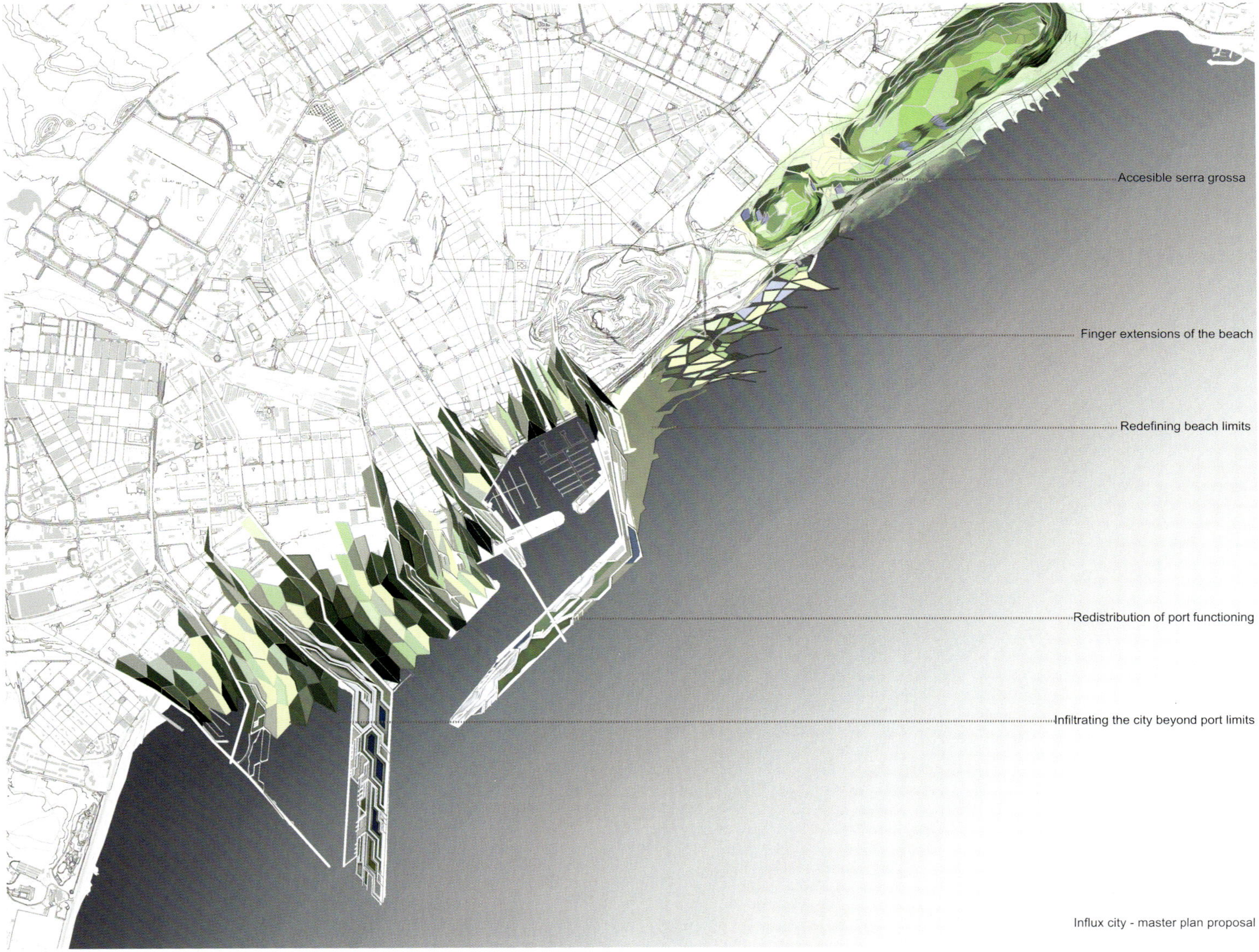

Accesible serra grossa

Finger extensions of the beach

Redefining beach limits

Redistribution of port functioning

Infiltrating the city beyond port limits

Influx city - master plan proposal

1. Views within the piers
2. Aerial view of the piers

The wider masterplan describes the entire coastline of Alicante as a differentiated landscape where existing structures and uses as well as the proposed design reconnect the city of Alicante with the sea. The port is understood as an extension of the city fabric and the design utilises the existing piers to develop linear buildings and structures to bridge physical barriers such as existing railway lines.

The Serra Grossa hill is analysed in terms of slopes and vegetation to determine a network of accessibility and programmes which makes use of the privileging and unique location of the hill.

Connecting the port and the hill, the team also proposed a floating structure next to the existing beach. This artificial structure will expand the existing offer of leisure activities along the coast.

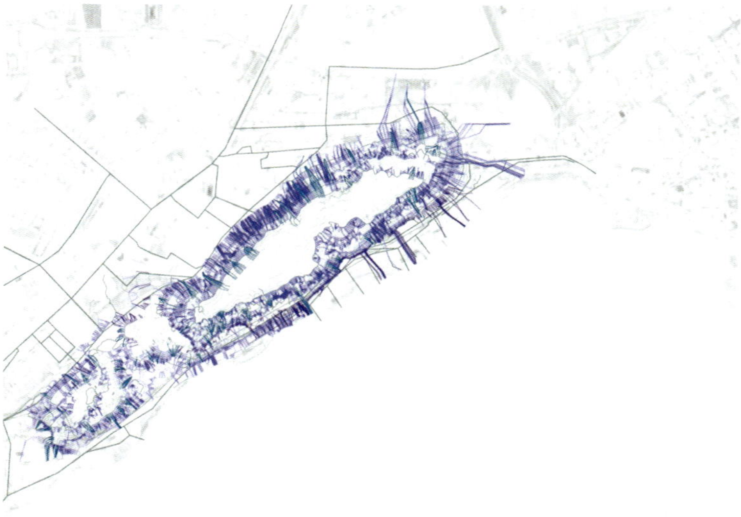

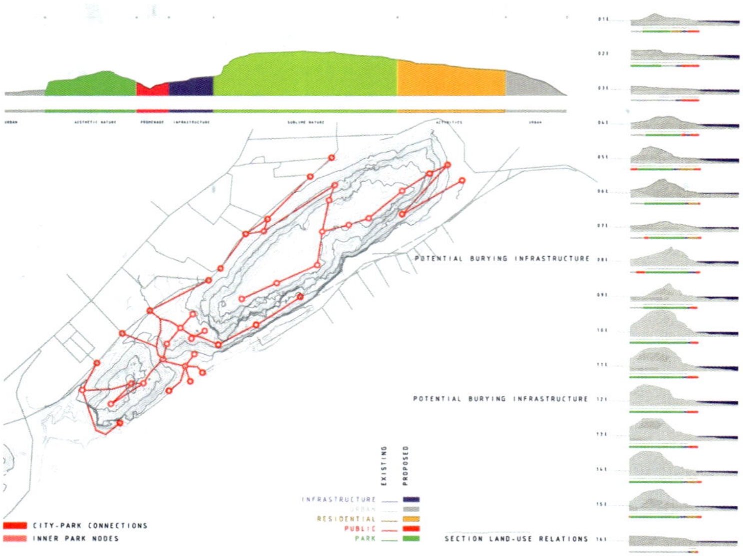

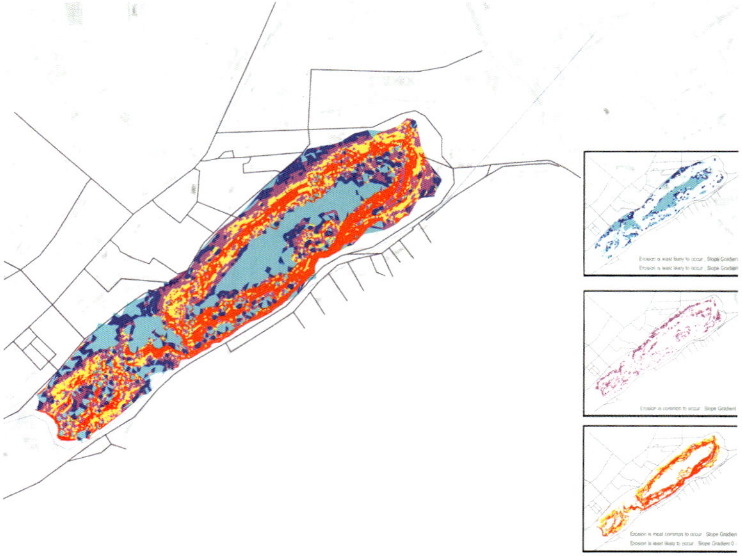

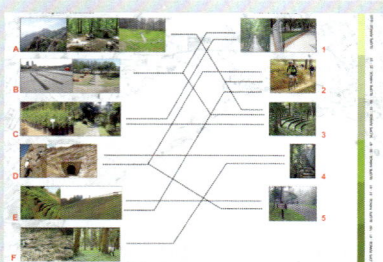

1. Relationship between programme and landscape typology

Serra Grossa is an existing hill between the Mediterranean Sea and Alicante city. An important geographic landmark 161 m above sea level, it is an abrupt topographical feature that defines the geography of Alicante. Serra Grossa is rarely used by local inhabitants, despite being a prominent and privileged feature in the city.

The project aims to read its physical conditions in terms of accessibility, existing vegetation, etc, to design an infrastructure to enable local inhabitants to appropriate its territory. A network of pedestrian paths was proposed through a careful study of the slopes. A number of water collection ponds were identified in order to introduce specific facilities to cater for a number of potential leisure activities.

	Water collection
	Facilities
	Trees
	Shrubs
	Ground cover

1. View from the hill access
2. View from top of the hill

The overall aim was to recover the Serra Grossa landscape beyond its visual presence into a territory that can be inhabited and used by local people, as well as becoming one of the most attractive areas in the city. The existing flora and location are very appealing so the design used these conditions as the starting point. A series of interventions was selected in order to lay out a pedestrian network. These interventions are thought of strategically along the hill and will generate particular characters such as sports, landscape, viewpoint or water collection.

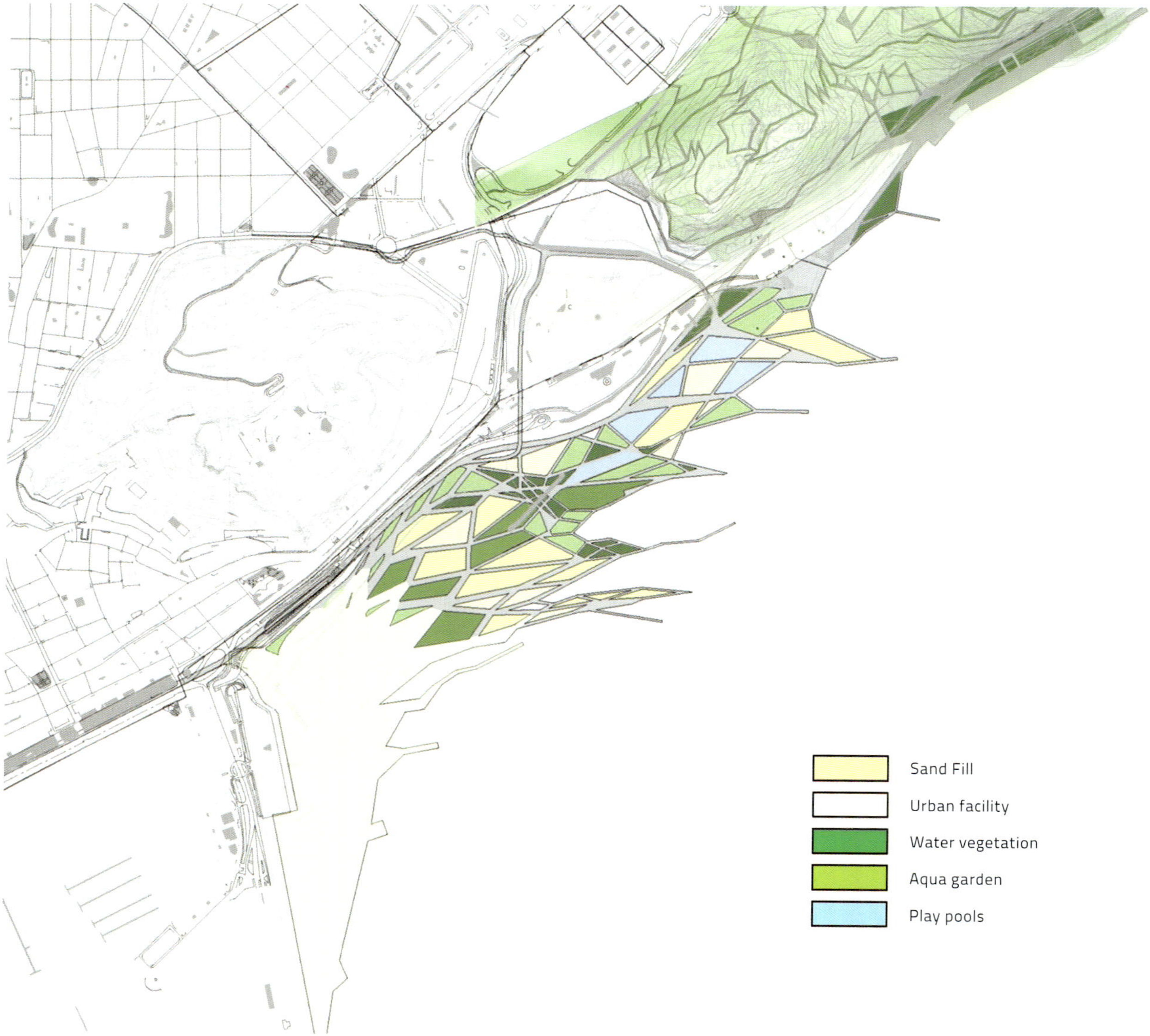

- Sand Fill
- Urban facility
- Water vegetation
- Aqua garden
- Play pools

1. View of intervention proposal

A third intervention was the extension of the existing beach on the coastline of Alicante. This part of the project was designed to expand the spatial capacity of this public beach tapping into the natural sedimentation process occurring along its edge.

The proposal includes a floating structure that organises the sediment areas forming firstly a pedestrian network that further subdivides the water landscape into smaller cells. Each of these cells will have the potential to host different programmes: play pools, aqua gardens, and an artificial beach.

AALU Workshop

Bolzano Workshop

Date **2009/2010**
Location **Bolzano, Italy**
Author **Landscape Urbanism Students and Staff**

Project description

The Easter workshop 2009/10 was framed as a collaboration with Trento University and the municipality of Bolzano in Italy. AALU students worked on the visions for the southern area of Bolzano, confined between the A22 Brenner highway and the Virgolo hill. The existing plans to tunnel the A22 outside the city are transforming the role of this quarter, allowing the potential expansion of the city and ultimately a place for renewed eco-industrial activities. The municipality of Bolzano asked AALU to generate a vision for this emergent part of the city, based on the academic work and professional experience of the staff.

The area is perceived as being isolated from the main area of Bolzano since it is located south of the Isarco river and the A22 elevated highway. Furthermore, Virgolo residential area is east of the industrial estate and the railway. It was clear from the start that for the overall site to succeed, it was necessary to generate links to this residential area and across the river into the town centre. The group started to study the overall site connectivity area and concluded that it was not the A22 but the existing railway line that was the main urban barrier.

The proposal turned around the tunnelling of the railway and the reincorporation of the A22 elevated section into a green infrastructure coming down from the hill. The study of the existing topography and landscape systems was fundamental in order to propose a new kind of thickened fabric knitting together infrastructure and new typologies hosting new economic activities. The group also undertook studies of urban typologies incorporating the vineyard terracing systems on south-facing slopes. The final proposal was meant to serve as the spatial framework for urban ecologies for the emergent research and development economies with eno-tourism profiting from the stunning landscape of the city.

The project was discussed in a roundtable chaired by Technology Innovation Service and was attended by members of the Urbanism council of Bolzano, planning authorities of Trentino Region, members of Trento University, the director of Il Corriere del Alto Adige as well as other architectural professionals, AALU students and members of the general public, various newspapers and local television.

1/2. Views of the city

The project had to deal with the distinct qualities of the landscape of Bolzano, with flat areas around the Isarco river and the steep hills surrounding the city, some of which (south-facing slopes) currently produce wine amongst other crops.

Public Networks

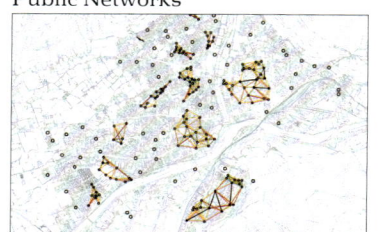 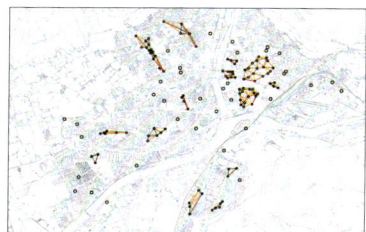 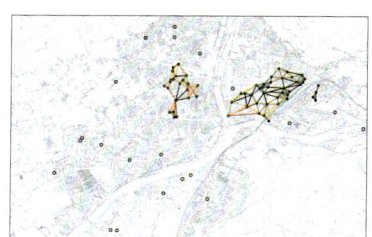 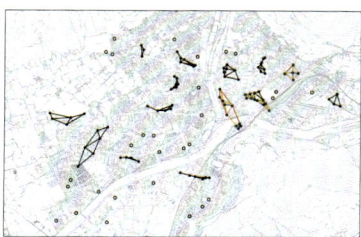

Public Spaces

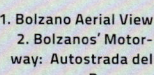

1. Bolzano Aerial View
2. Bolzanos' Motorway: Autostrada del Brennero

The redevelopment of the eastern side of the Isarco rests upon the connection of its various centres of activity (currently Virgolo residential area) with the rest of the city (image above on connectivity) and the area across the railway line. This shall prove to be the most appropriate form of obtaining an integrated new urban fabric that benefits the local people but also maximises future real estate value.

Isarco River Analysis

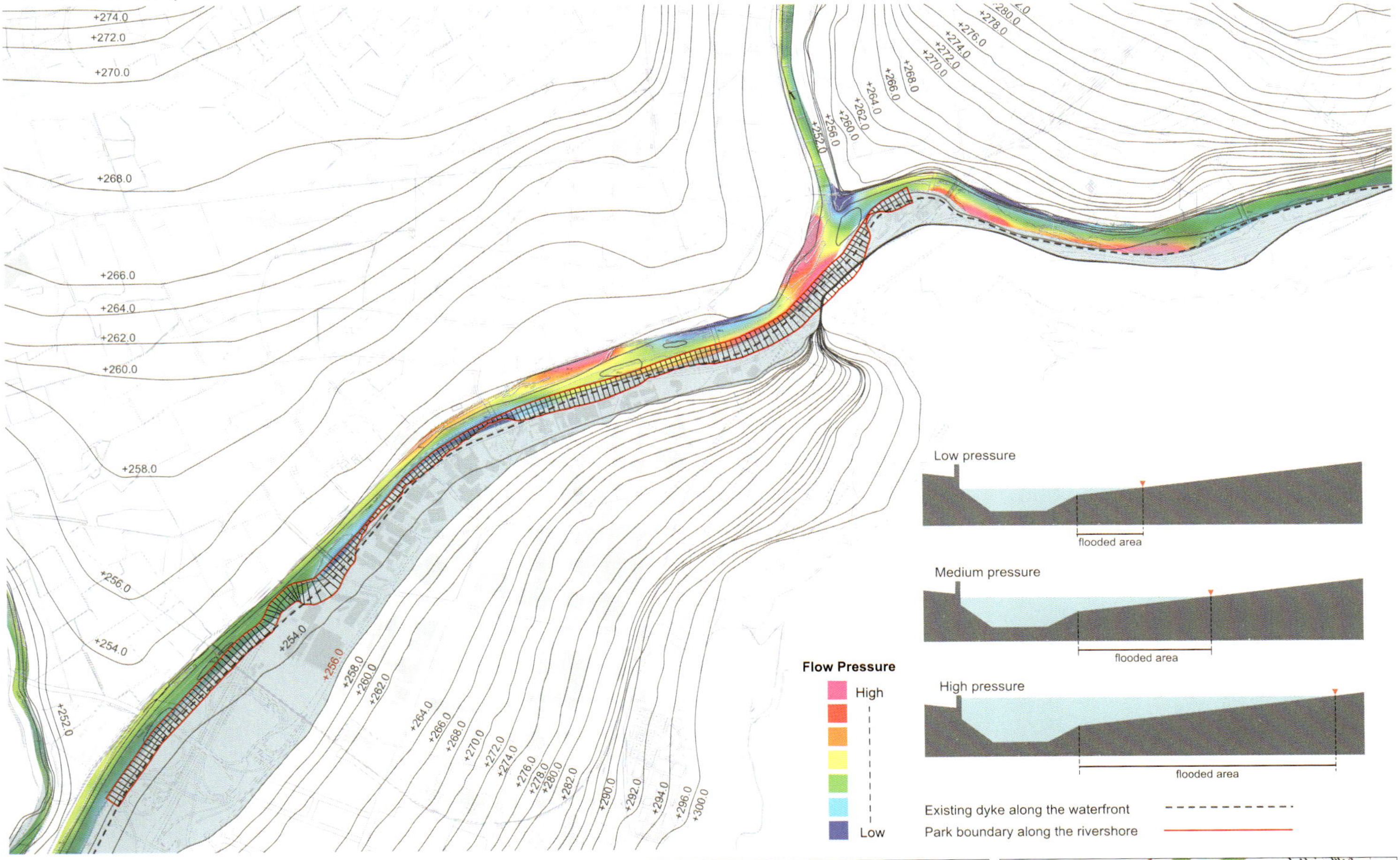

+274.0
+272.0
+270.0
+268.0
+266.0
+264.0
+262.0
+260.0
+258.0
+256.0
+254.0
+252.0
+254.0
+256.0
+258.0
+260.0
+262.0
+264.0
+266.0
+268.0
+270.0
+272.0
+274.0
+276.0
+278.0
+280.0
+282.0
+290.0
+292.0
+294.0
+296.0
+300.0
Low pressure
flooded area
Medium pressure
flooded area
High pressure
flooded area
Flow Pressure
High
Low
Existing dyke along the waterfront
Park boundary along the rivershore

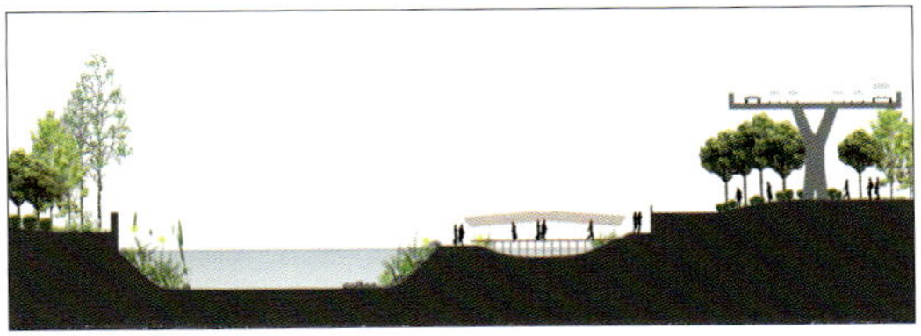

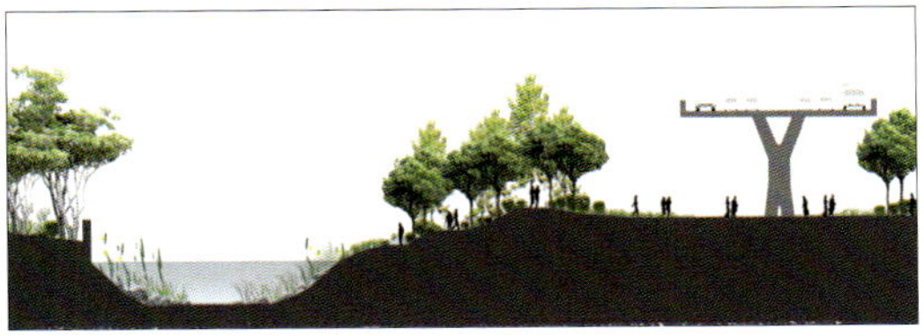

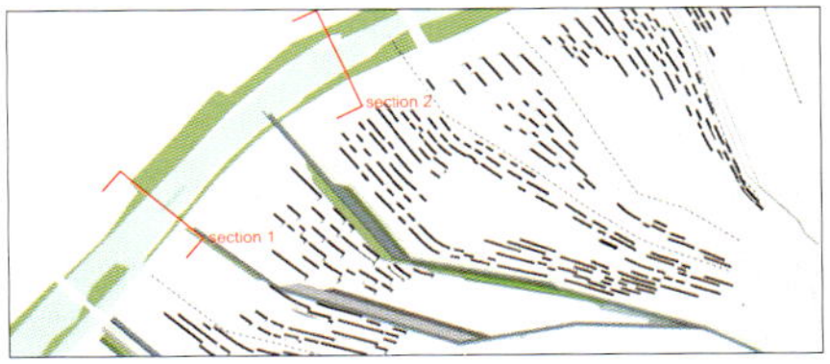

section 2
section 1

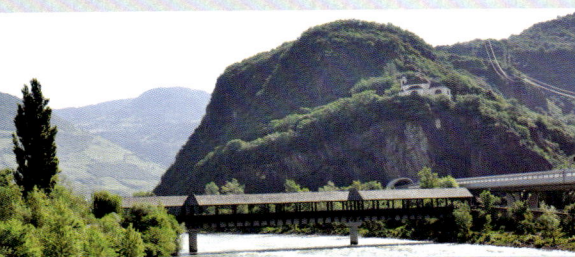

1. The Eisack river

Although the A22 produces a strong visual sense of a barrier with the city (30m wide deck 10m high) there is the potential to connect across to a wide strip of land beside the river, turning this area into a green corridor and making the most of its south exposure. Studies of river depth and currents were carried out in order to locate activities along this potential public space.

Mesh development

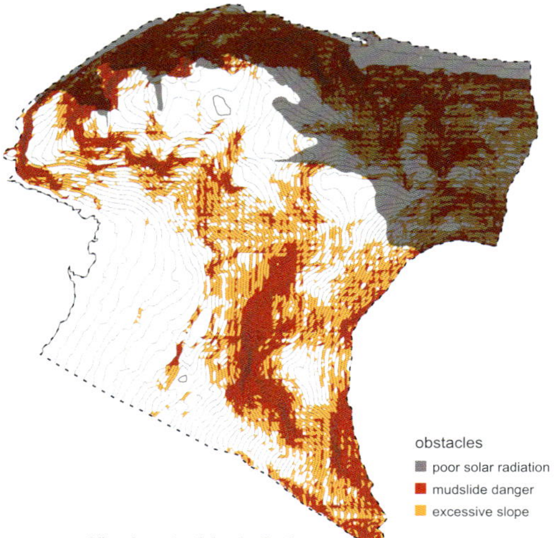

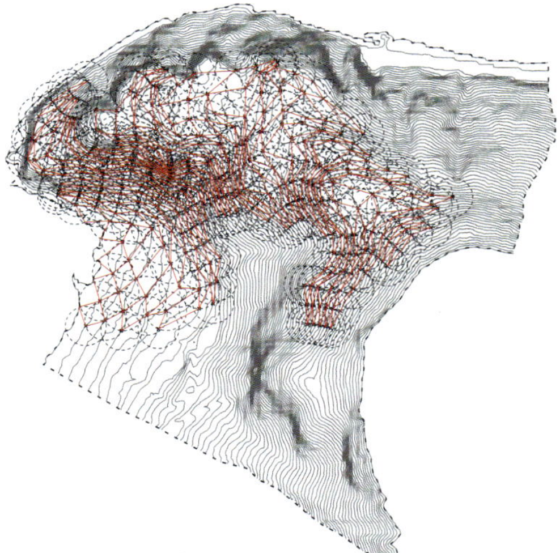

obstacles
poor solar radiation
mudslide danger
excessive slope

Virgolo potential colonization

10%-gradient mesh

solar exposure
(in the equinox)
8:00 am
10:00 am
12:00 pm
14:00 pm
16:00 pm

terracing system

slope
0 - 10 %
10 - 20 %
20 - 30 %
30 - 40 %
40 - 50 %
50 - 60 %
60 - 70 %
70 - 80 %
80 - 100 %
> 100 %

terracing system - slope analysis

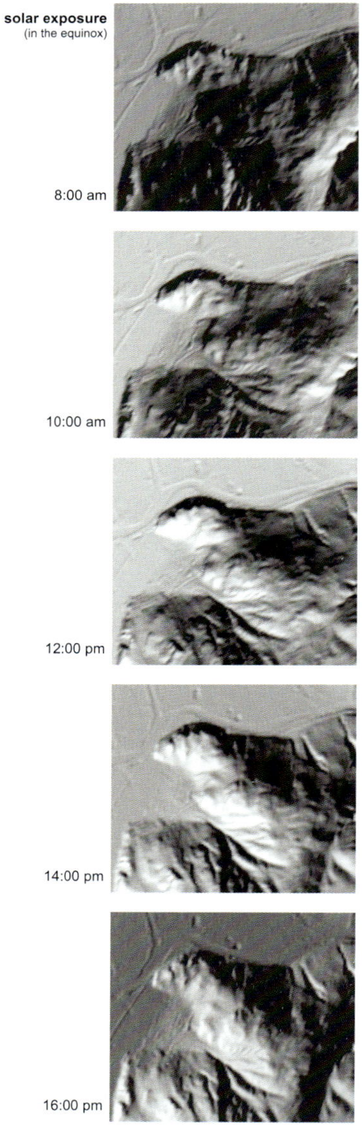

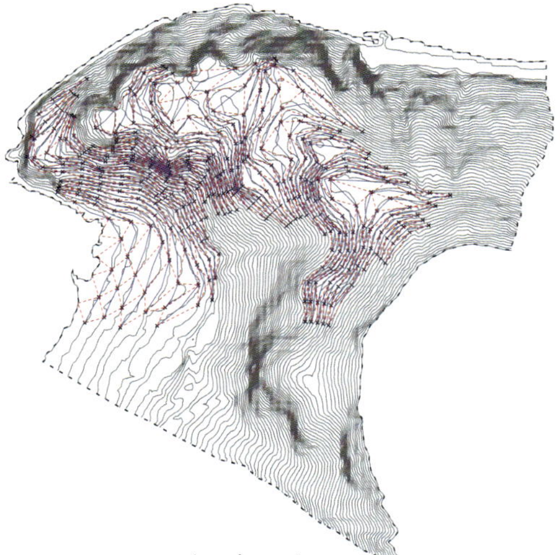

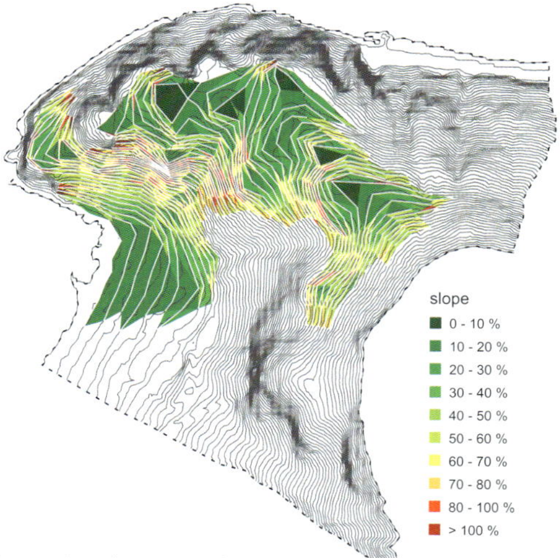

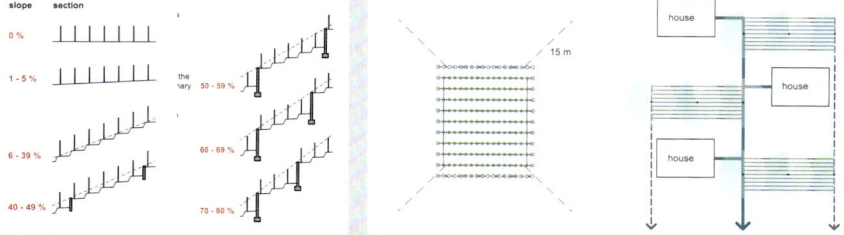

1. Slope distribution and earth containment structures for vineyard production
2. Vineyard organization and water movement.

slope
section
0 %
1 - 5 %
6 - 39 %
40 - 49 %
50 - 59 %
60 - 69 %
70 - 80 %

15 m
house
house
house

Virgolo hill
The slopes of Virgolo bear the potential to host a series of activities that make the most of the wine production character of the area. Since part of these zones are south-facing, the project proposes the generation of architectural typologies that use the character of the existing terracing systems as a generator for the new image for these prominent areas of the city.

Mesh development

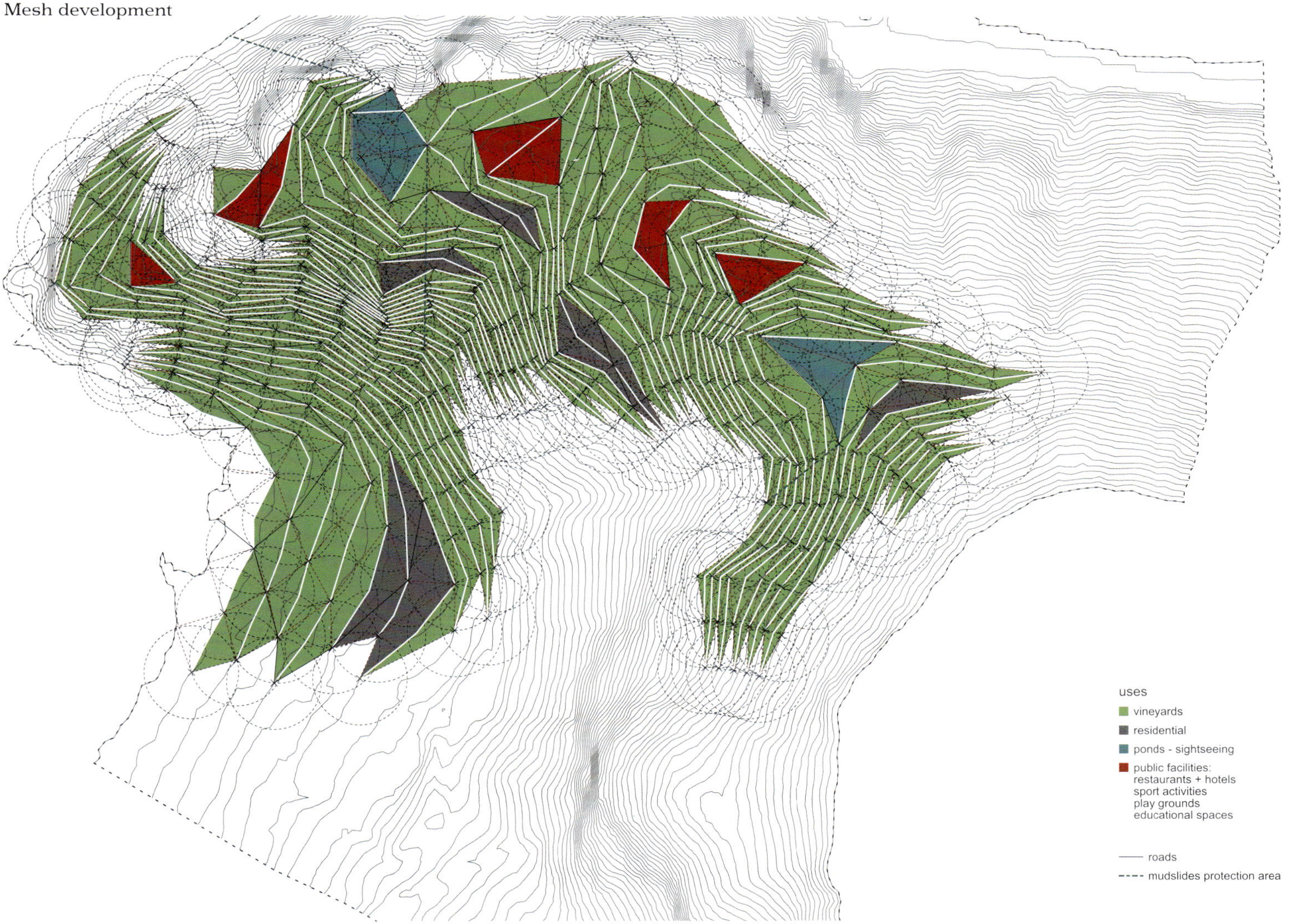

uses
- vineyards
- residential
- ponds – sightseeing
- public facilities:
  restaurants + hotels
  sport activities
  play grounds
  educational spaces

——— roads
- - - - mudslides protection area

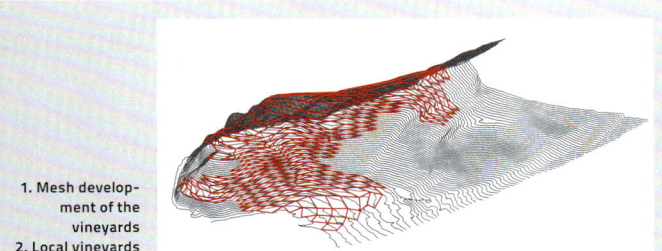

1. Mesh development of the vineyards
2. Local vineyards

Virgolo hill

The masterplan explores the possibility of developing different activities on the Virgolo hill and connecting it to the city centre in order to integrate it with the existing network of green and public spaces. An analysis of the slopes and a study of the solar radiation help establish an efficient functional distribution, while a 10%-gradient mesh structures the site.

Road and drainage Connectivity Strategy

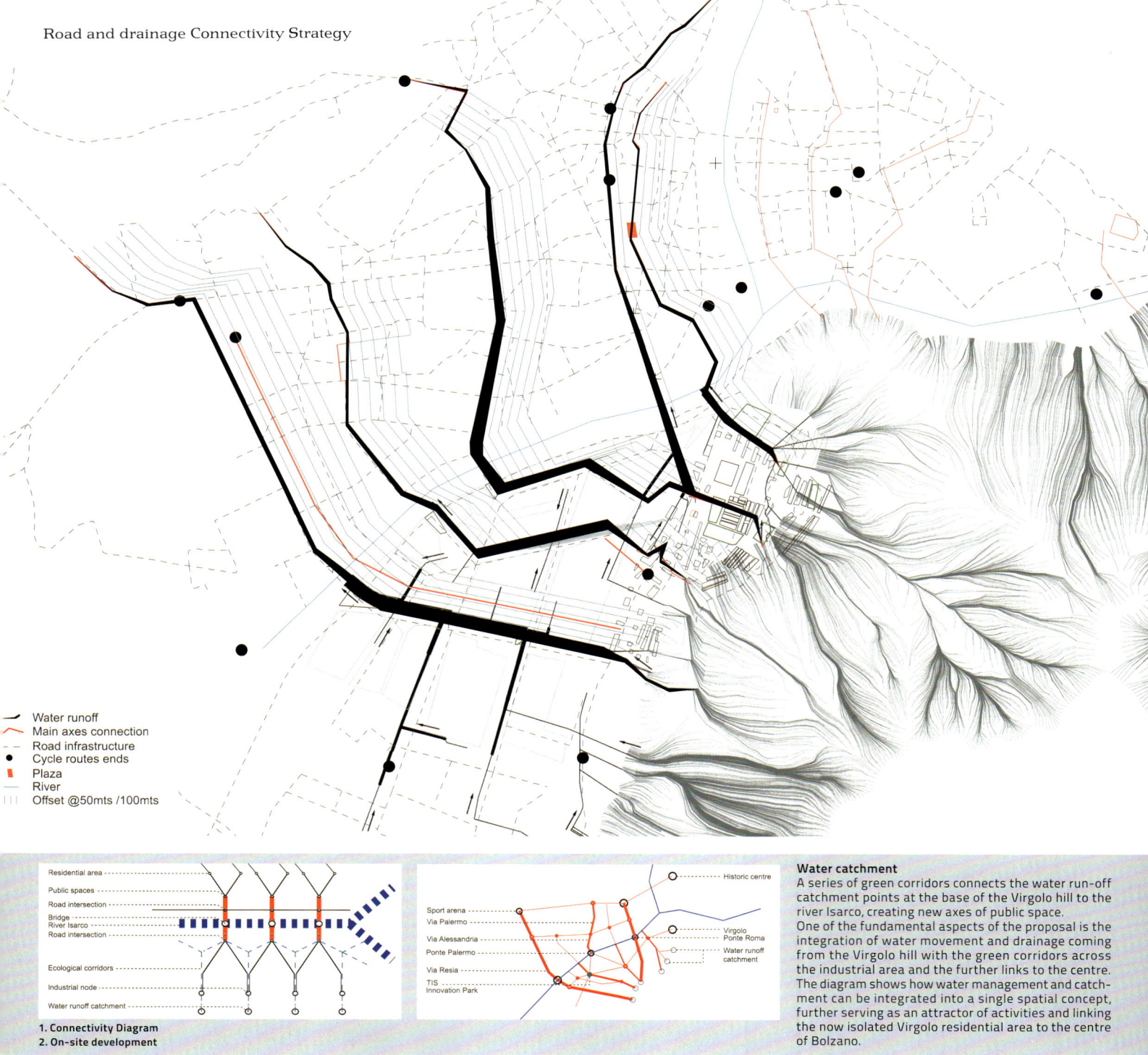

Legend:
- Water runoff
- Main axes connection
- Road infrastructure
- Cycle routes ends
- Plaza
- River
- Offset @50mts /100mts

1. Connectivity Diagram
2. On-site development

Water catchment
A series of green corridors connects the water run-off catchment points at the base of the Virgolo hill to the river Isarco, creating new axes of public space.
One of the fundamental aspects of the proposal is the integration of water movement and drainage coming from the Virgolo hill with the green corridors across the industrial area and the further links to the centre. The diagram shows how water management and catchment can be integrated into a single spatial concept, further serving as an attractor of activities and linking the now isolated Virgolo residential area to the centre of Bolzano.

Existing and proposed transport network

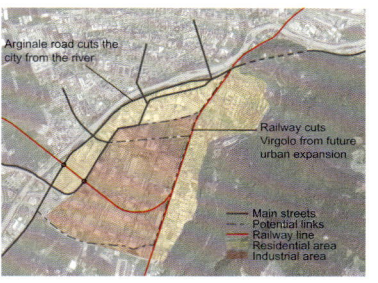
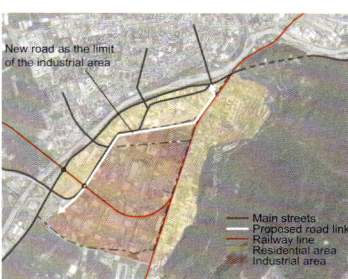
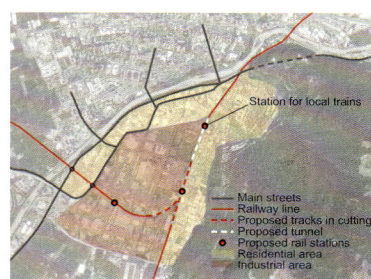
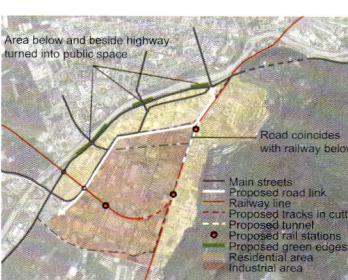

Proposed Road Network

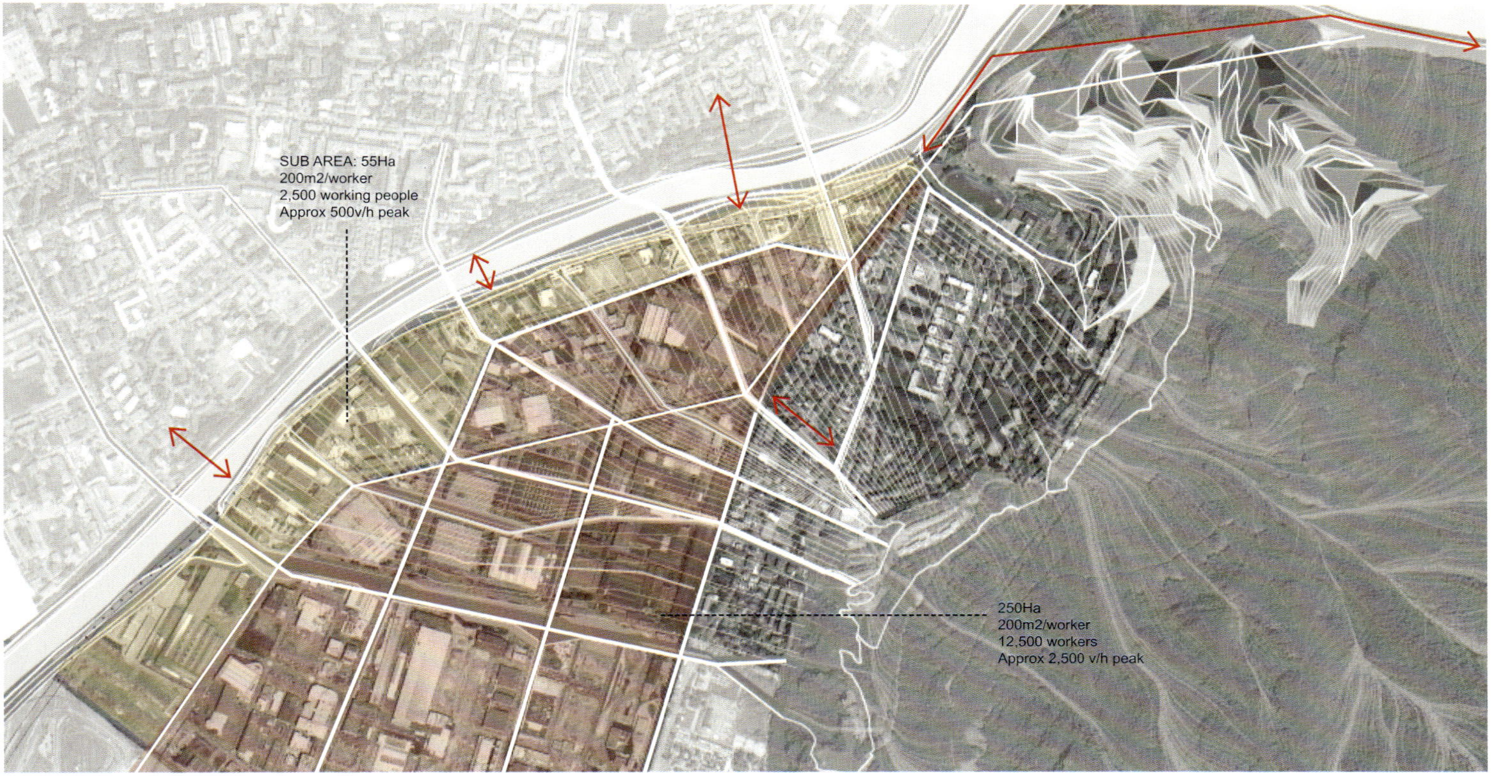

SUB AREA: 55Ha
200m2/worker
2,500 working people
Approx 500v/h peak

250Ha
200m2/worker
12,500 workers
Approx 2,500 v/h peak

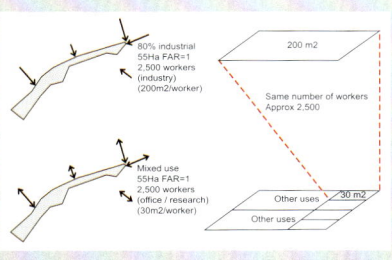

Land Use strategy:
1. Retaining number of workers
2. Balanced mix

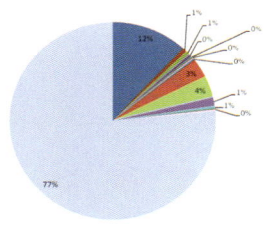

(Above) An initial study of existing flows showed how the main urban barrier is the railway, rather than the A22. Intervention of a railway tunnel and a reconfiguration of internal distributing roads will allow the reconnection of the Virgolo area back into the city and the river with a much lower cost than the proposed A22 tunnel.

(Middle) The road network linking Virgolo to the city is used as spatial structure for the reconfiguration of the industrial area along the river as a new economic driver for the entire city.

(Below) Land use is optimised considering traffic constraints, assuming an increase in office space as opposed to existing industrial uses.

Green corridors

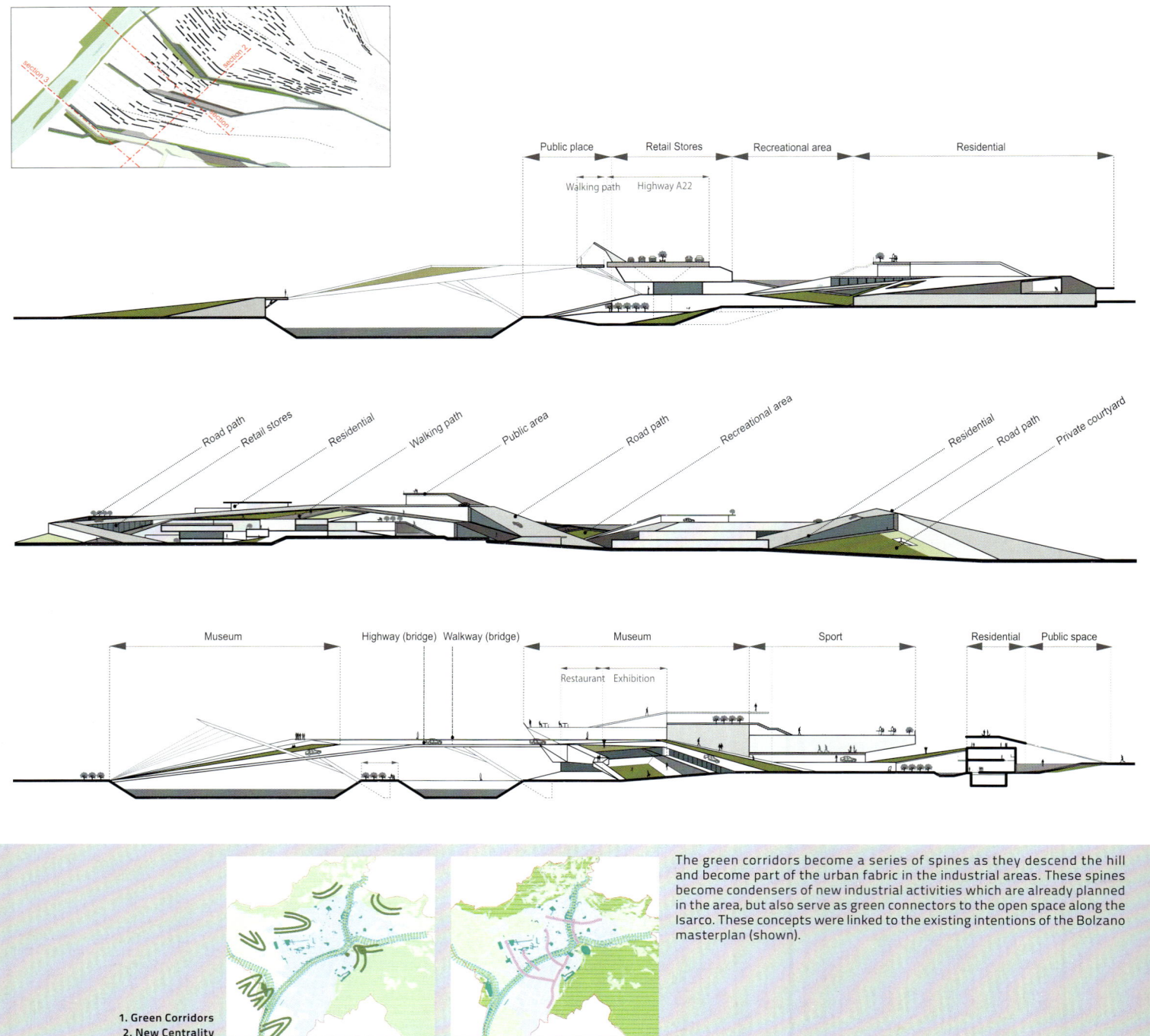

The green corridors become a series of spines as they descend the hill and become part of the urban fabric in the industrial areas. These spines become condensers of new industrial activities which are already planned in the area, but also serve as green connectors to the open space along the Isarco. These concepts were linked to the existing intentions of the Bolzano masterplan (shown).

1. Green Corridors
2. New Centrality

Bolzano and proposed Masterplan Birdview from Virgolo hill

General Masterplan

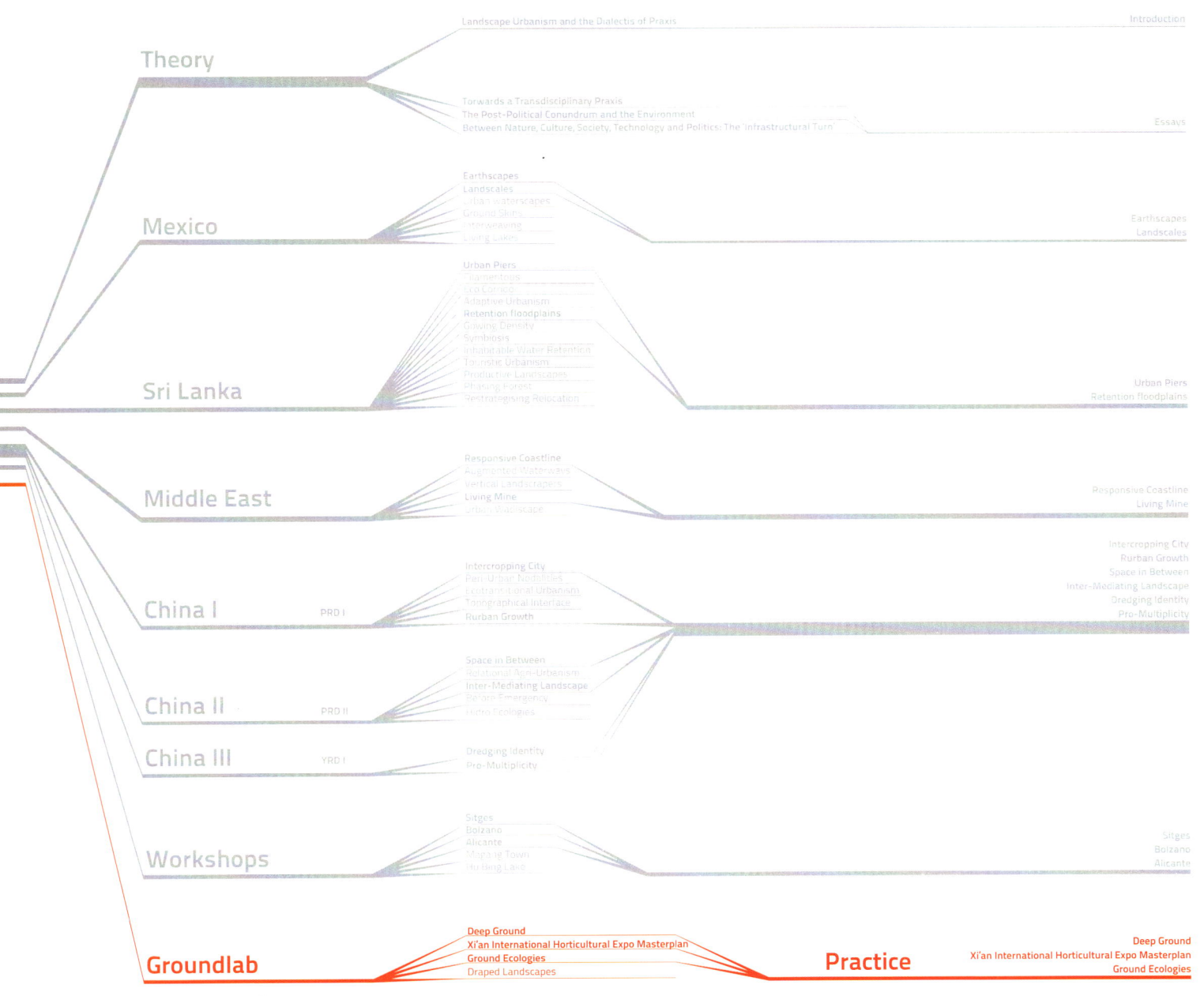

Groundlab
Practice

AGENDA Groundlab ltd. is an emerging international practice of Landscape Urbanism led by five partners - Eva Castro, Holger Kehne, Alfredo Ramirez, Eduardo Rico and Sarah Majid. The practice employs architects, urban designers, engineers and landscape architects, to bring together different expertise into close collaboration, and explores Landscape Urbanism as a new mode of practice as a response to the contemporary social, economical, and environmental conditions.

With an inherently multidisciplinary approach, the studio sees the cities and the landscapes in between as natural processes that constantly change and evolve, therefore requiring flexible and adaptable mechanisms and designs to emerge, to configure and to reconfigure the existing and future urban environments.

Groundlab develops its work out of the close analysis of existing and potential conditions on site and utilises the temporal and dynamical forces that are currently shaping the cities: from the social and economical realm to the current environmental and infrastructural conditions. Groundlab practises a constant research and development initiative, creating urban models and new techniques to provide a direct and immediate response to contemporary urban conditions.

The practice has recently won first prize in an international competition to develop a new masterplan for Longgang City, Shenzhen, China and led the design for the International Horticultural Fair in Xi'an, China, a 37ha landscape design with a wide range of buildings which opened in 2011.

AALU China 08/09

Longgang City masterplan
Deep Ground

Location **Shenzhen, China**
Client **Shenzhen Municipal Planning Bureau Longgang Branch, China**
Size **9 Km²**
Date **2009**

Project description

Deep Ground is Groundlab's winning entry for the international design competition for Longgang Centre and Longcheng Square. The project radically expands the scope of urbanism in order to deal with the contemporary challenges of modern China: through the concept of 'thickened ground' multiple ground datums are fused to foster intuitive orientation and connectivity. The polluted and neglected river will become an ecological corridor, whilst the existing urban villages are retained to form nuclei to lend identity, vitality and human scale to the new development.

Design concept

The project includes the regeneration of 11.8km² of the city centre of Longgang, northeast of Shenzhen in the Pearl River Delta, with an estimated population of 350,000 and 9,000,000m² of developable area. The proposal for this project is a practical deployment of the methodology currently used in the Landscape Urbanism Master Programme in the Architectural Association. Elements of this methodology are multi-scalar strategies, bottom-up design, mapping of information and indexing territories, as well as relational urban models.

Thickened ground

The concept of thickened ground describes the spatial strategy Groundlab has used for the implementation of the underground development in conjunction with public space design and the river crossing. The ground thickening, through a system of open programmes and pathways, develops spatial complexity and a non-hierarchical division of pedestrians and traffic. In contrast to the traditional urban design elements in western society that tend toward compartmentalisation, this strategy introduces high density and integration of functions as a mode of weaving an overall fabric. The strategy of the thickened ground also challenges the traditional opposition of building vs. landscape, and generates a higher density in areas which are currently under-used, increasing the overall value, open space usage and intensity of life at street level.

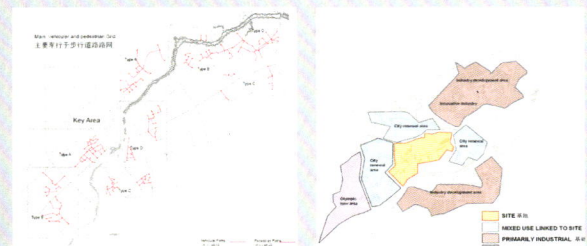

1. Branding strategy: Type and circulation
2. Transportation Strategy

Landscape strategy

Longgang River is located at the heart of Longgang City but is radically separated from it with no interaction or relation apart from being used as a backyard and wastewater sewer. The infrastructural landscape project used this contradictory condition to propose the recovery of the river triggering the revitalisation not just of banks and surrounding areas but of the whole city, driving the landscape strategy, greenery and river as one interactive and interconnected system. The infrastructure designed along the river will serve as an anchor point to deploy cleansing strategies, rainwater collection and flooding defence while creating green areas, ecological corridors, public open spaces, sports fields and leisure areas.

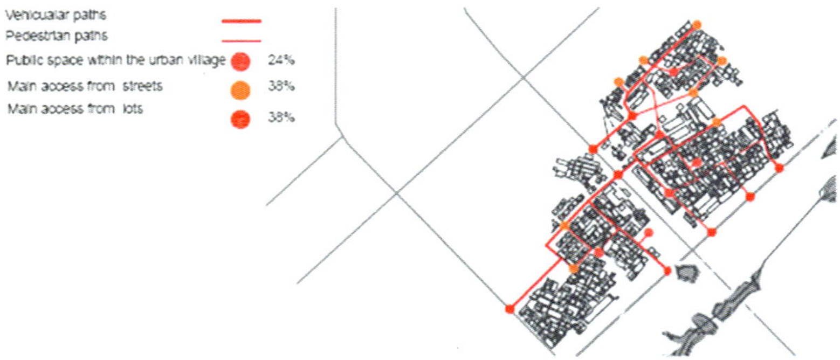

Branding strategy intervention

Vehicular paths
Pedestrian paths
Public space within the urban village — 24%
Main access from streets — 38%
Main access from lots — 38%

Porosity and connectivity between CBD area and main rail way _ the creation of commercial corridors within the urban village

Vehicular paths
Pedestrian paths
Public space within the urban village — 45%
Main access from streets — 17%
Main access from lots — 38%

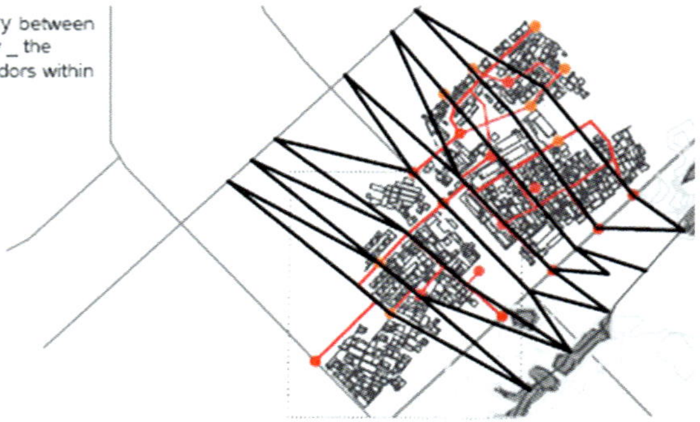

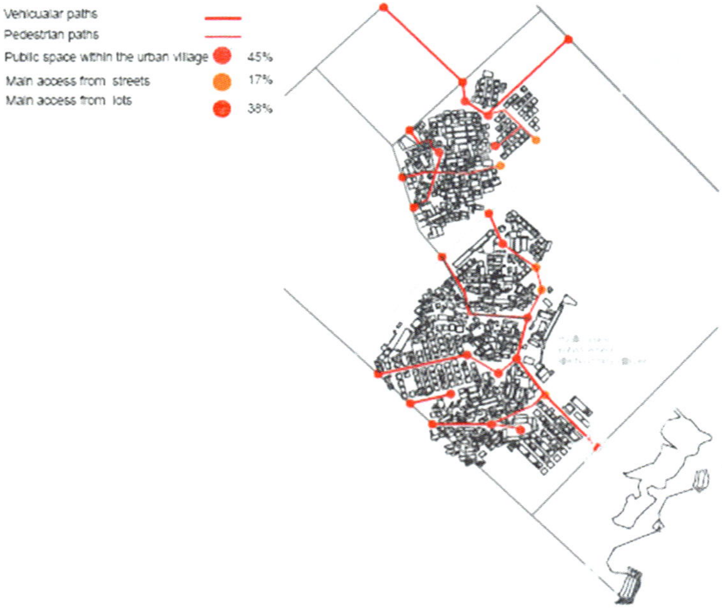

Intensifying and nesting the urban spaces within the village _ site boundary condition

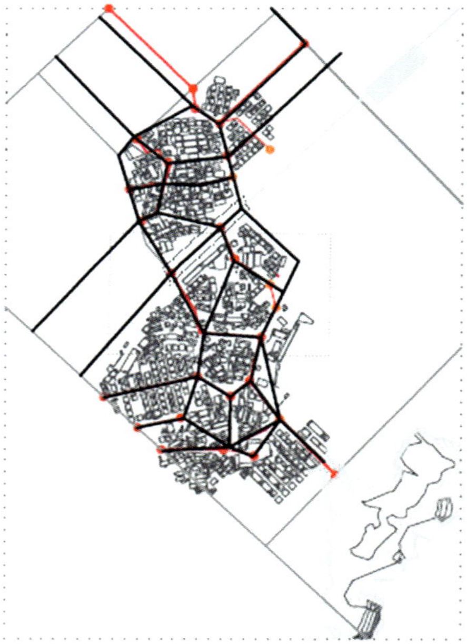

1/2/3. Site conditions

The landscape network creates a major framework to articulate the urban fabric, the public areas and the infrastructural equipment of the city and will be able to generate a great variety of programmes which do not exist or are in poor condition, linking the river to the neighbourhoods and with the city. This in fact will generate ecology inside the city, highlighting the presence of the river in the city not just as an aesthetic element but as a strategic element, active and vital for the present and future viability of the city.

The design for the infrastructural landscape incorporates a number of principal elements: river and waterscapes, ecological corridors, river valleys, as well as others in relation with them: biodiversity, connectivity, use and activity and character. These elements are combined to produce an inspiring, hardworking, accessible, safe, sustainable and contemporary landscape.

Landscape strategy

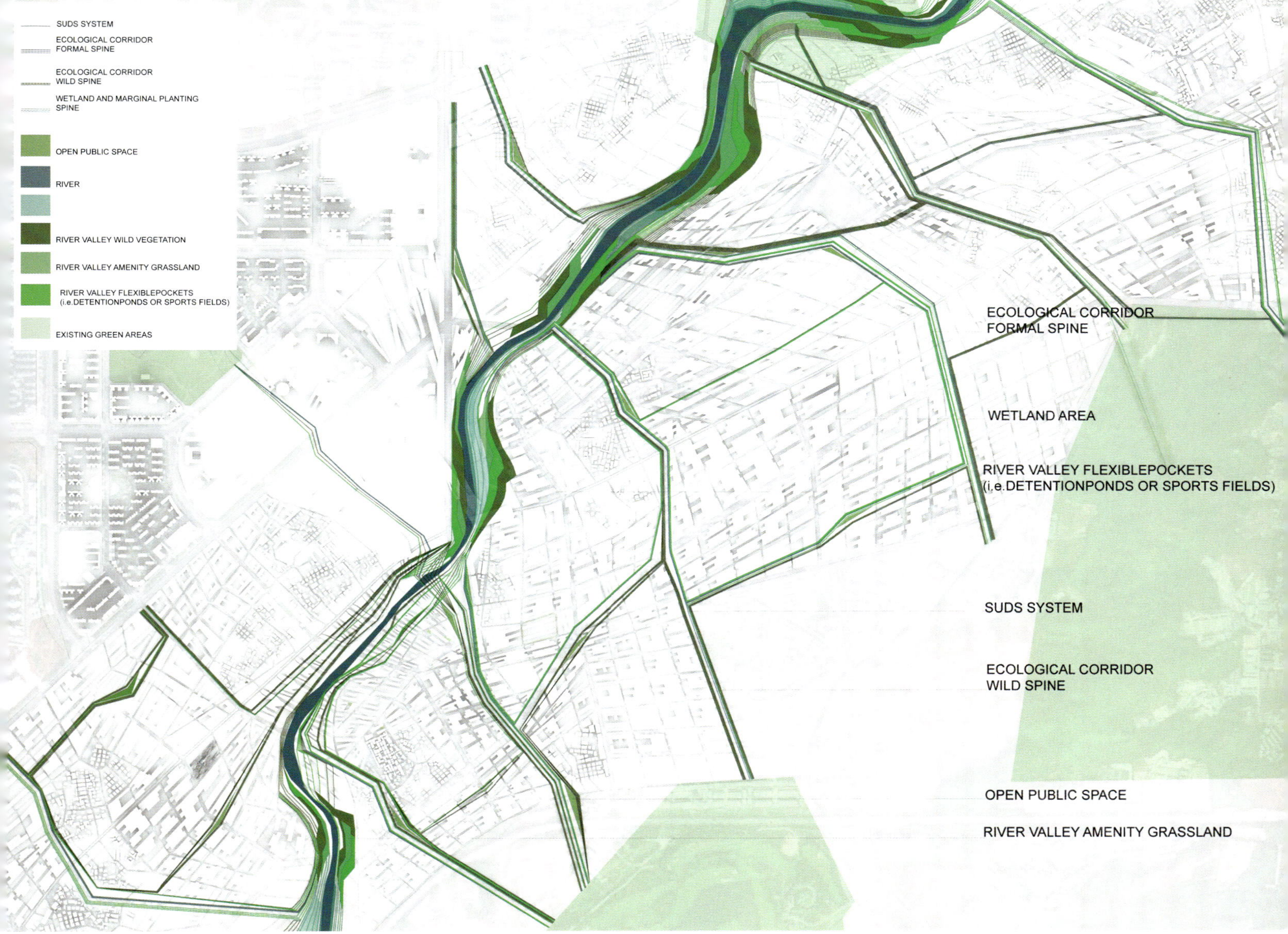

SUDS SYSTEM
ECOLOGICAL CORRIDOR FORMAL SPINE
ECOLOGICAL CORRIDOR WILD SPINE
WETLAND AND MARGINAL PLANTING SPINE
OPEN PUBLIC SPACE
RIVER
RIVER VALLEY WILD VEGETATION
RIVER VALLEY AMENITY GRASSLAND
RIVER VALLEY FLEXIBLEPOCKETS (i.e.DETENTIONPONDS OR SPORTS FIELDS)
EXISTING GREEN AREAS
ECOLOGICAL CORRIDOR FORMAL SPINE
WETLAND AREA
RIVER VALLEY FLEXIBLEPOCKETS (i.e.DETENTIONPONDS OR SPORTS FIELDS)
SUDS SYSTEM
ECOLOGICAL CORRIDOR WILD SPINE
OPEN PUBLIC SPACE
RIVER VALLEY AMENITY GRASSLAND

playground
woodland
sunbathing
towpath
reebed
river
towpath
reebed
informal theatre seating
open air theatre
theatre seating
woodland
amenity grassland

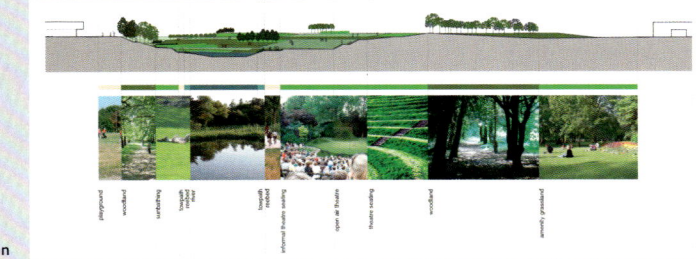

1. River section

The urban villages

The concept of the urban villages is key in the project, as is an urban typology which clearly defines the character and history of many cities in China and Longgang in particular. There is a set of urban villages which have been identified as potentially interesting to be preserved. The project proposes the use of these areas as part of a strategy for the generation of various brands across the site, providing certain characteristics and differentiation which will be the key for the success of the city as a whole.

Definition of attractors

Waste water treatment infrastructure

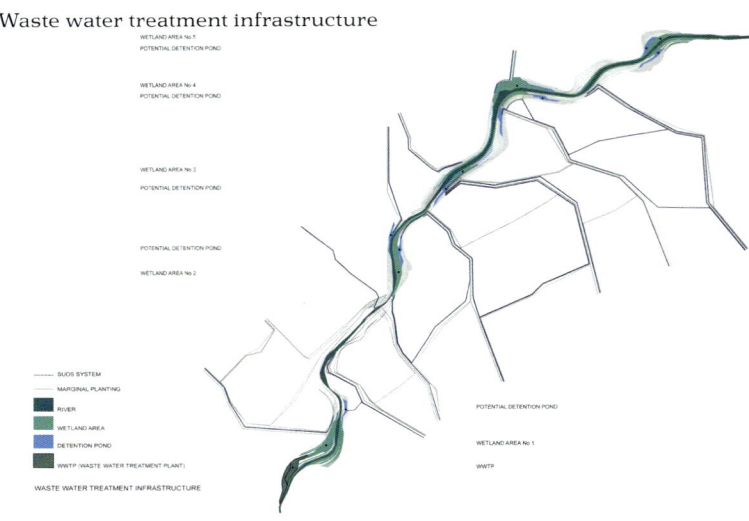

Main access points and public spaces

Urban villages tend to show an extraordinary character which in many cases attracts visitors due to its distinctiveness. This is the case of the so-called Dafan Oil Painting Village, also in Shenzhen, where an industry of production of painting replicas has generated an unprecedented interest from tourists, which in turn has sparked the arrival of different kinds of artists and creative professionals.

In the case of this project, the villages show different characteristics which make them unique, like the presence of a market or prominent historical building. This fact is key in the management strategy of the urban villages as it can be an important point around which to anchor urban life.

1. Physical model

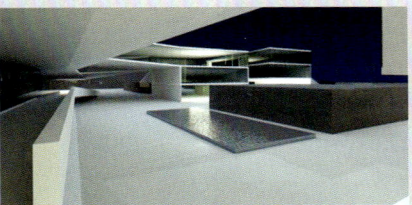

1/2. Buildings detail

Parametrical Model

For the purposes of this project, a relational urban model has been created which can control simultaneously built mass quantities as well as a 3D model of the built fabric. The model is based on sets of urban relationships which connect one another, hence the name of relational. One of the advantages of this working methodology is that it enables the generation of different options with a relatively minor effort, as most of the drawing gets automatically produced, while there is potentially the chance to evaluate the overall built volume before the volume is even generated. It also enables the combination of variables related to density with variables related to typology. This can be used to produce varied and diverse urban patterns with simple controls. The volume of the proposed built fabric shown in the final drawing and renderings has been modelled to suit the quantity of land-use calculated in the Transport Chapter (around 9,000,000m^2).

Landscape network strategy

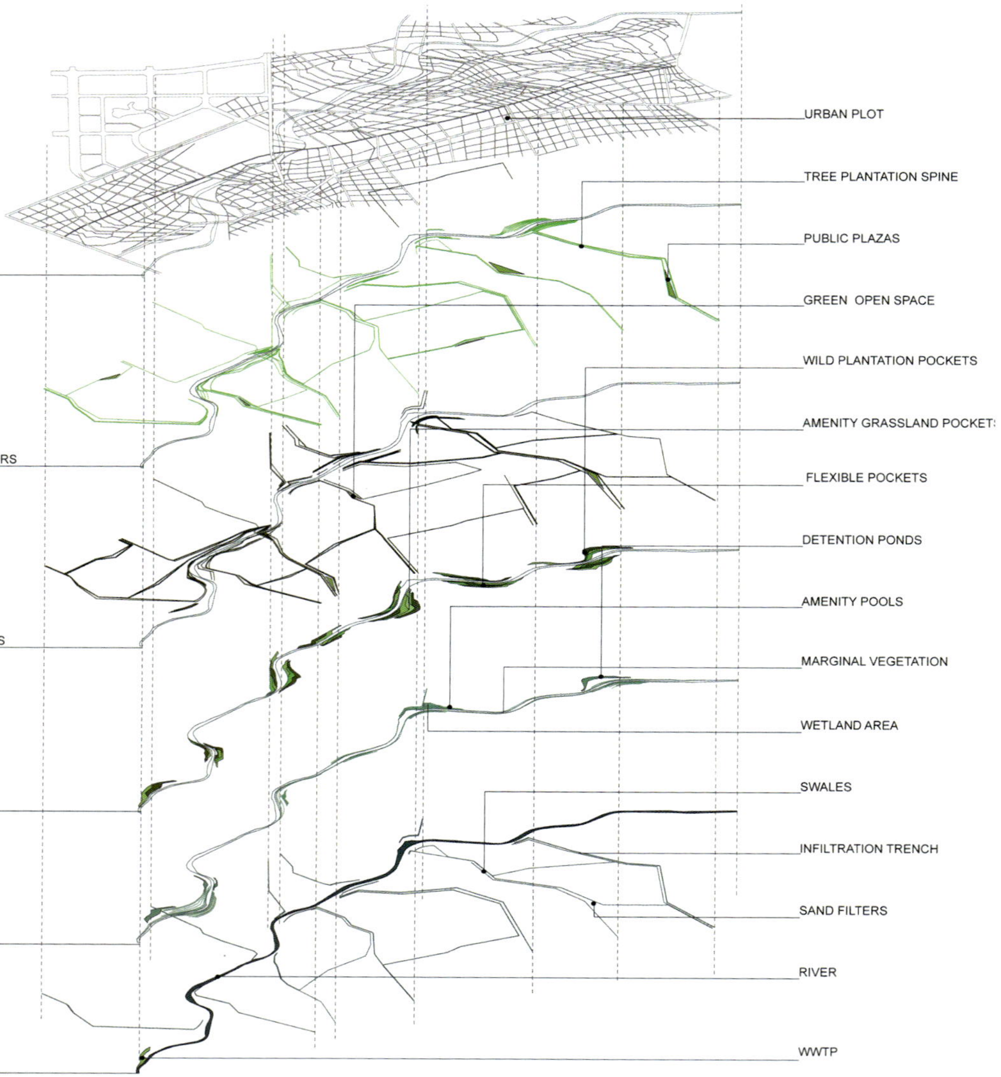

URBAN PLOT
TREE PLANTATION SPINE
PUBLIC PLAZAS
GREEN OPEN SPACE
WILD PLANTATION POCKETS
AMENITY GRASSLAND POCKETS
FLEXIBLE POCKETS
DETENTION PONDS
AMENITY POOLS
MARGINAL VEGETATION
WETLAND AREA
SWALES
INFILTRATION TRENCH
SAND FILTERS
RIVER
WWTP
URBAN FABRIC
GREEN URBAN CORRIDORS
FORMAL SPINE
ECOLOGICAL CORRIDORS
WILD SPINE
RIVER VALLEYS
WETLAND SYSTEM
SUDS SYSTEM

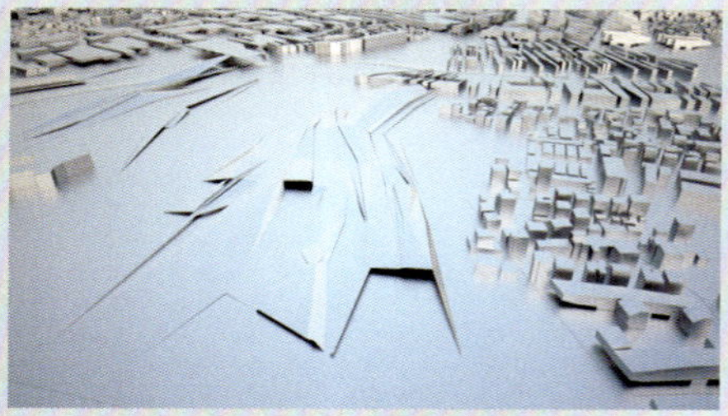

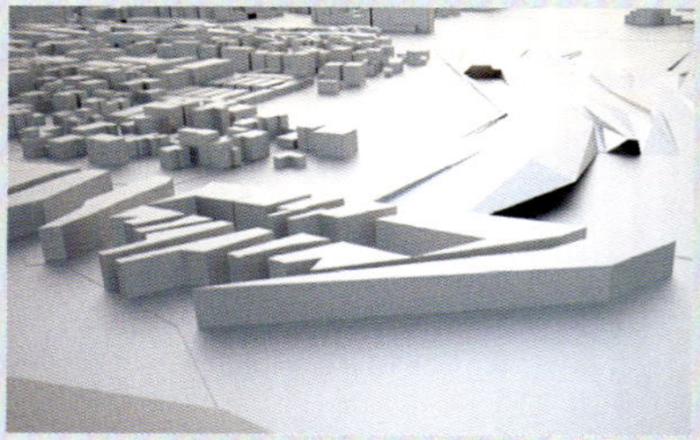

1/2. Parametrical model

The result of this work is a series of options which allow us to study simultaneously the effects of different massing options in terms of GFA (m^2) and spatial arrangement as well. The image shows the type of iterations that the model allows, evaluating options where the centre of intensity of the model as well as the overall quantity of buildings are modified in order to get a totally different, yet related, urban configuration. This leads to the concept of Adaptable Design applied for the Longgang masterplan, where changes on different variables (location and number of density nodes, particularities in building catalogue, etc) can be added into the design almost in real time so that further discussion on the urban fabric and architectural qualities can be put forward during the decision-making process.

Thickened ground view

AALU China 09/11

Xian International Horticultural Expo Masterplan

Location **Xian, China**
Type **Masterplan**
Client **Xian City Government, China**
Size **37ha**
Date **2009 / 2011**

Project description

Xian International Horticultural Expo 2011
The International Horticultural Expo becomes the instigator and core for the redevelopment of a large area between the airport and the ancient city centre of Xian, known as the home of the Terracotta Army and business centre of the vast Chinese interior. Plasma Studio with collaborators GroundLab won this invited international competition with a radical self-sustainable vision for the future: Flowing Gardens creates a consonant functionality of water, planting, circulation and architecture into one seamless system.

The proposal comprises of a 5000 sqm Exhibition Hall, a 4000 sqm Greenhouse and a 3500 sqm Gate Building sitting in a 37 ha landscape that will house the International Horticultural Expo and a park for Xian City as legacy. The Expo will open in 2011, receiving approximately 200,000 visitors a day.

Flowing Gardens unfolds many sinuous paths, creating a network of intermingling circulation, landscape and water. The given topography and its existing slopes were used to draw out the paths in a way similar to how roads ribbon around a mountain, negotiating steepness with gradients. These paths vary in width ranging from main walkways and arteries to towpaths. The patches between these paths become the zones for various planting types and wetland areas. The three projected buildings, located at the intersections of the major pathways are developed as the nodal articulation and intensification of the landscape.

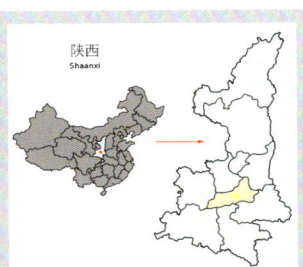 

1. Site location - Xian City
2. Xian landscape

Xian is a city based on thousands of years of ancient culture. As the home of the Terracotta Army and the beginning of the Silk Road, Xian has claimed its place in China's eternal history. In this tradition, Flowing Gardens is a harmonic relationship between Xian's wondrous past and its exciting future; horticulture and technology; landscape and architecture. Flowing Gardens enhances the inherent beauty of Xian by intensifying the characteristics of the existing fabric while creating a self-sustainable landscape for the future.
Flowing Gardens begins from a single line – an axis extends from the Gate to the Greenhouse, travelling through the East and West Hills and over the lake while extending into many sinuous paths, creating a network of intermingling circulation, landscape and water. Much like the legendary Silk Road, Flowing Gardens is connectivity, circulation, rejuvenation and elegance.

Overall masterplan

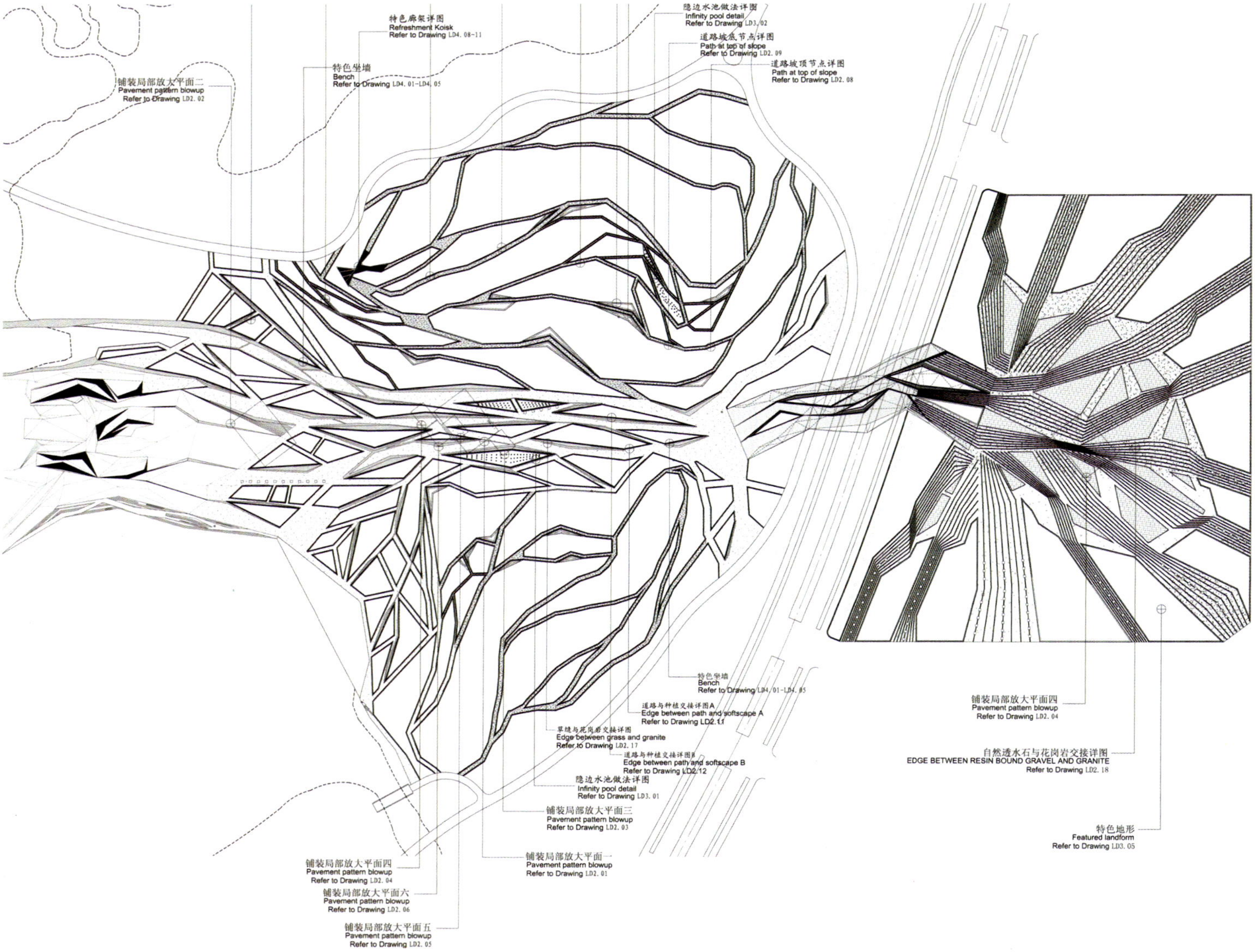

1/2/3. Xian

The project proposes a hybrid of both natural and artificial systems. These two opposing systems are brought together in a synergy of waterscapes. Considering the amount of water needed for irrigation, the project seeks to introduce various technologies and designs found in nature, yet customised by man to suit his specific needs. Rainwater is collected and channelled into wetland areas; there, natural plants and reed beds are used to clean and store the water to be dispersed and used as irrigation water. These natural systems are integrated into the landscape as wetlands and ponds, which can also be enjoyed by the visitors as points of tranquillity and oases. The water cycle becomes more complex with the introduction of grey and black water treatment. We propose to make use of the initial investment and organisation during the exhibition to set up a system which becomes autonomous in function and character. The gardens transform the two conditions of artificial and natural into a sustainable system that becomes more and more maintenance-free once the exhibition is over, allowing the park to become a new model, or paradigm, within the horticultural industry.

Overall view

1. Section of programmes

The park creates a variety of scales in association with very specific planting, surfacing and lighting, thus providing a gradient of experiences that range from the very intimate with semi-enclosed, shaded, self contained, one-to-one spaces, to the very public with communal plazas formed by wider pedestrian paths with full sun exposure and a direct visual link to the main hiatus on the site. The given topography and its existing slopes were used to draw out the paths in a way similar to how roads ribbon around a mountain, negotiating steepness with gradients. These paths vary in width ranging from main walkways and arteries to towpaths. The patches between these paths become the zones for various planting types and wetland areas, which retain a quality of ease of maintenance.

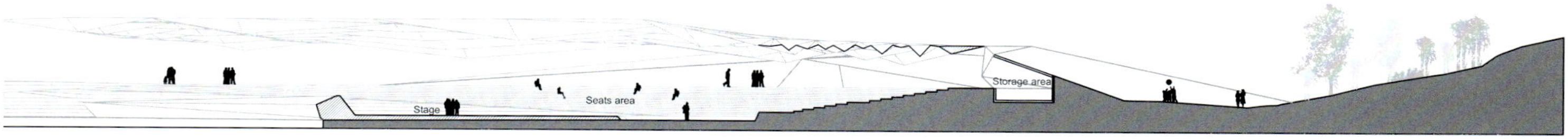

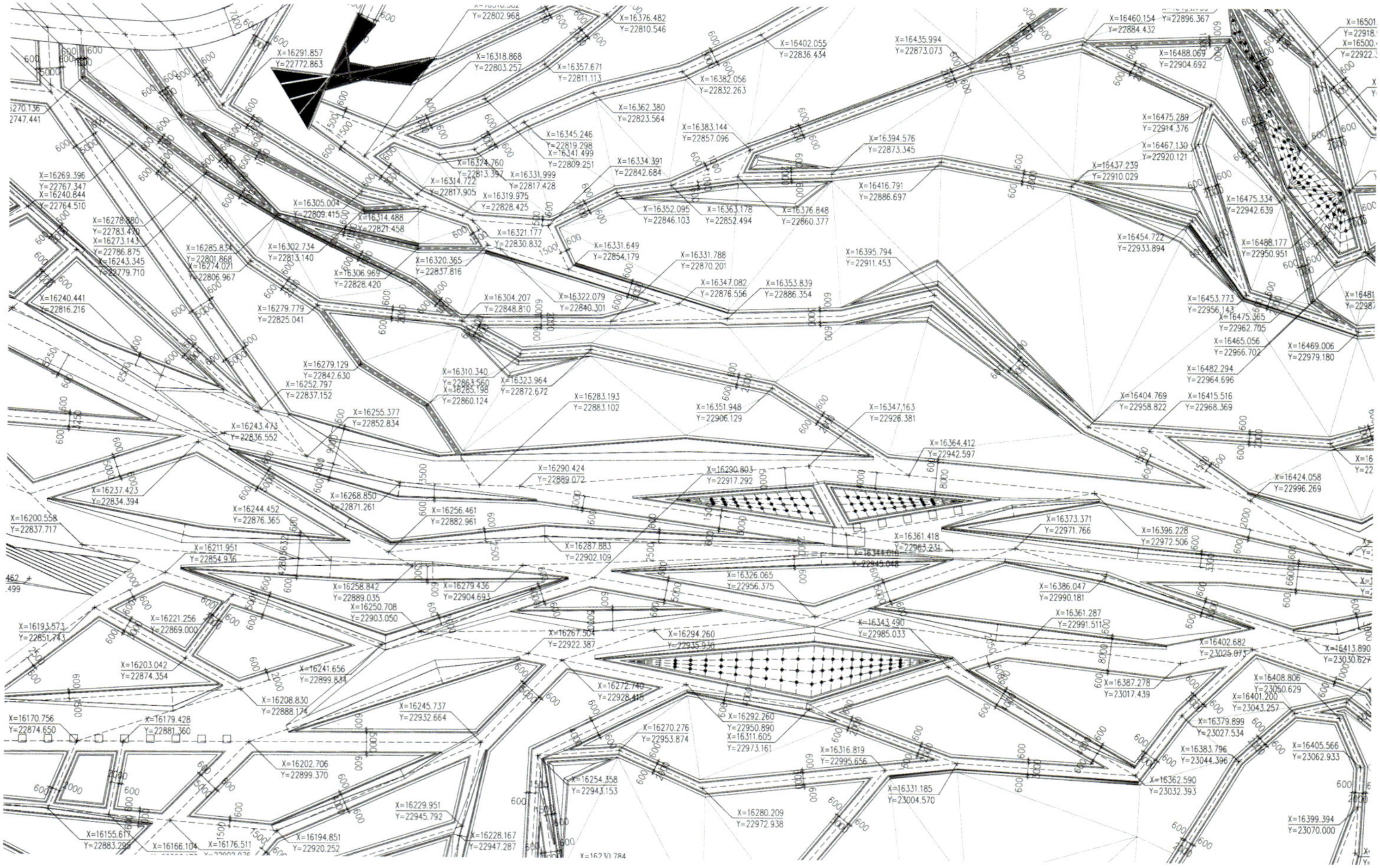

Landscape

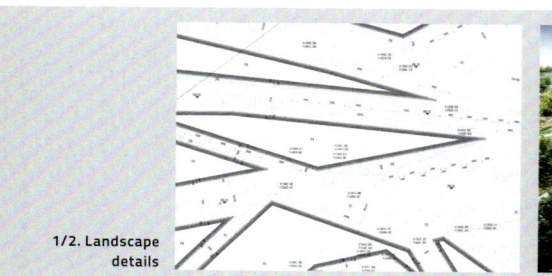

1/2. Landscape details

Flowing Gardens creates a consonant functionality of water, planting, circulation, and architecture into one seamless system. At the major intersections of these pathways lie three buildings; the architecture is an intensification of the ground condition, where each building stands alone as an object yet speaks of the interconnectivity of the landscape.

The Gate is created at the junction of public meeting space, landscape, and circulation; one enters the site through the Gate along the major axis of Flowing Gardens, creating framed views of the gardens. The Exhibition Centre is formed at the seam of landscape, circulation and water; one experiences the Exhibition Centre's fluid lines as an extension of the landscape with vistas of the lake and the South Hill. The Greenhouse sits at the top of the South Hill, at the connection of various landscape features. The Greenhouse allows one to experience the beauty of Flowing Gardens from across the lake while appreciating plants and flowers from four different climatic zones.

The flowing gardens

1/2/3. Landscape details

Landscape

The project proposes a hybrid of both natural and artificial systems, brought together as a synergy of waterscapes. With consideration to the amount of water required for irrigation, the project seeks to introduce various technologies and designs found in nature, but it is enhanced to meet the specific needs of the new population. Rainwater is collected and channelled into the wetland areas, where natural plants and reed beds clean and store the water, which is later dispersed and used for irrigation. These integrated wetlands and ponds are also to be enjoyed by the visitors as oases and points of personal tranquillity. More complex water cycle issues are sensitively controlled with the introduction of grey and black water treatment systems.

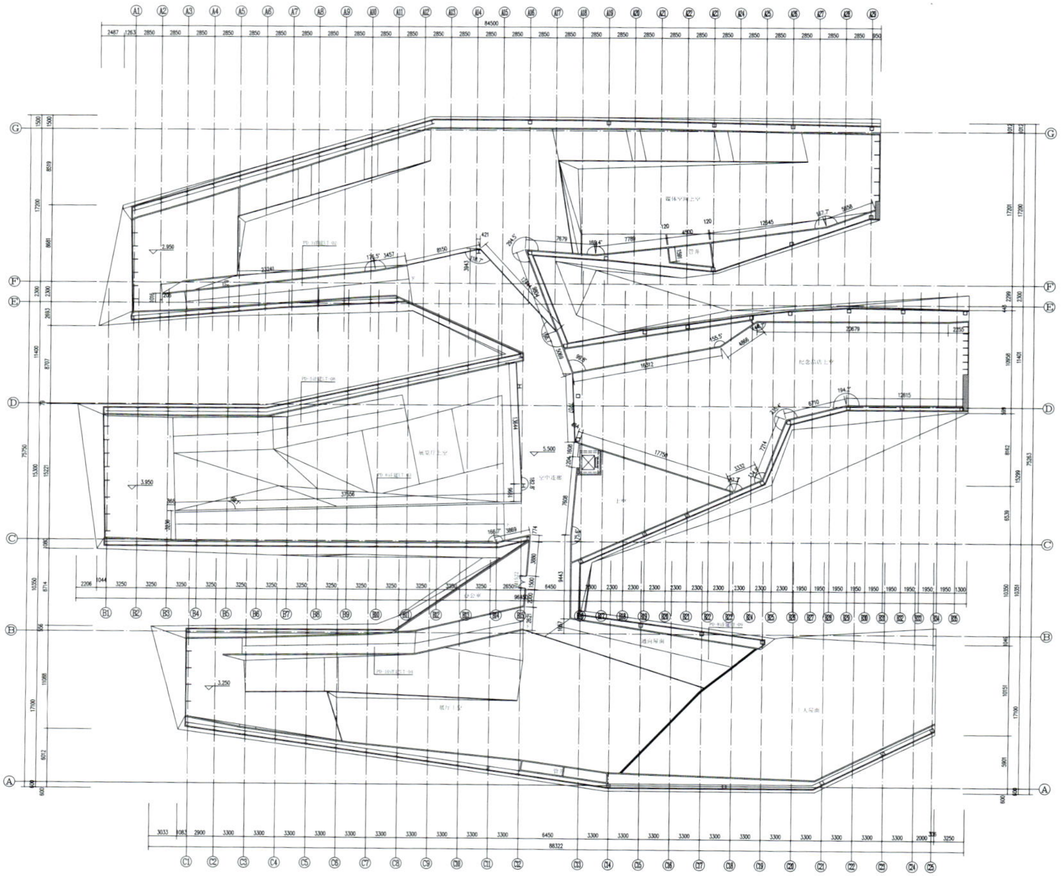

The Creative Pavilion

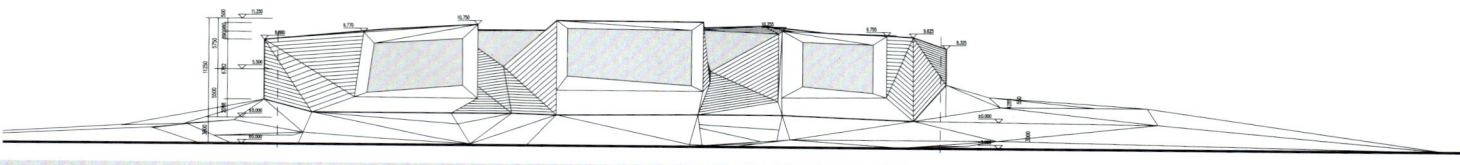

Floorplan

1/2. Creative Pavilion under construction

The proposal aims to make use of the initial investment and organisation during the exhibition, to set up an environment, which becomes autonomous in function and character. The gardens transform the artificial and natural conditions of the site into a sustainable system that becomes increasingly more maintenance-free once the exhibition is over, allowing the park to develop into a new model, or paradigm, within the horticultural industry. The park area manifests in a variety of scales in association with very specific planting, surfacing and lighting, thus providing a sandbox of experiences that range from the very intimate with semi-enclosed, shaded, self contained, one-to-one spaces, to the very public with communal plazas formed by wider pedestrian paths with full exposure to the sun and a direct, uninterrupted visual link to the main hiatus on the site.
The Creative Pavilion is located on the edge of the lake as the endpoint to the central axis that starts with the Gate Building, and is the starting point for the water crossing by boat.

1/2. Creative pavilion interior views

It ties in with a series of piers that follow the landscape jutting out into the water. The built volume is interwoven with the articulating ground, producing continuities on many levels integrating the landscape and building together.
From this flows the organisation of the building massed as three parallel volumes within the landscape, flowing through and underneath, leading to the piers. The volumes themselves hover as cantilevers over the lake. The fluid experience of passing through the landscape continues inside, where all zones are generous and interconnected.

The Guangyun Entrance

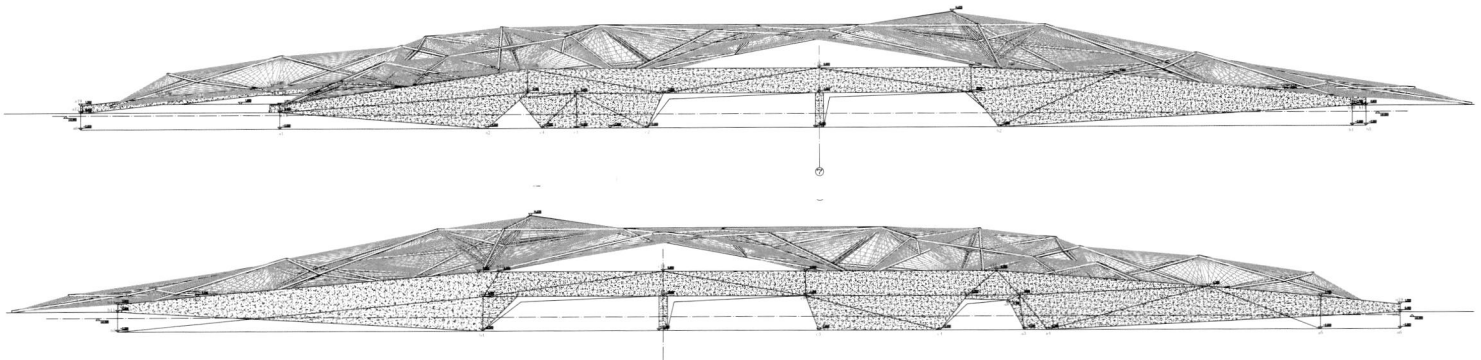

Elevation

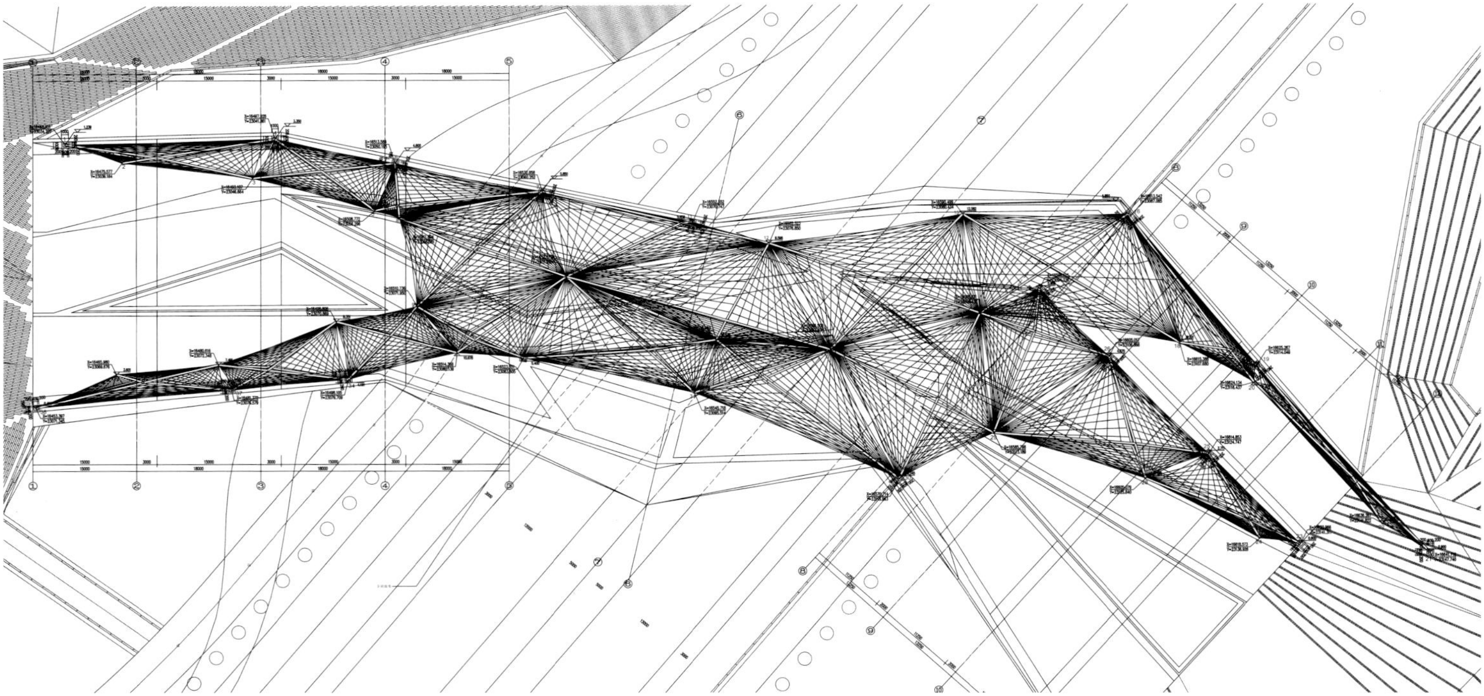

1/2. Guangyun Entrance under construction

Guangyun Entrance

The Guangyun Entrance operates on the level of infrastructure and fulfils the role of bridging over the main road that dissects the site. Thus it channels the visitors from the entry plaza, where they congregate and orient themselves after having entered into the Expo and sets them in a definite direction. By bringing them up to +7.00m the bridge offers vantage points from where to gain an overview of the different zones of the Expo ahead.

Functionally, the bridge needs to have two lanes for incoming and outgoing traffic. Naturally, these flows are very uneven and change greatly between the beginning and end of the day. Taking the idea from the London Underground escalators, we devised the bridge to have three lanes, where the middle lane switches from the incoming direction in the morning to outgoing later in the day.

1. Guangyun Entrance from above

The three bands read as interwoven braids, and together with a trellis roof structure give the appearance of bands of landscape peeling off and turning into structure. Between the three bands are green areas and a water feature for visitors to stop, have a rest and enjoy the view. Above them an open trellis steel structure forms a shading device that becomes overgrown with climbing plants forming a green roof, and suggesting to distant onlookers the theme of the Expo.
For this lightweight roof, we developed together with Arup an innovative tensegrity structure that appears as beams seemingly free-floating in space.

The Greenhouse

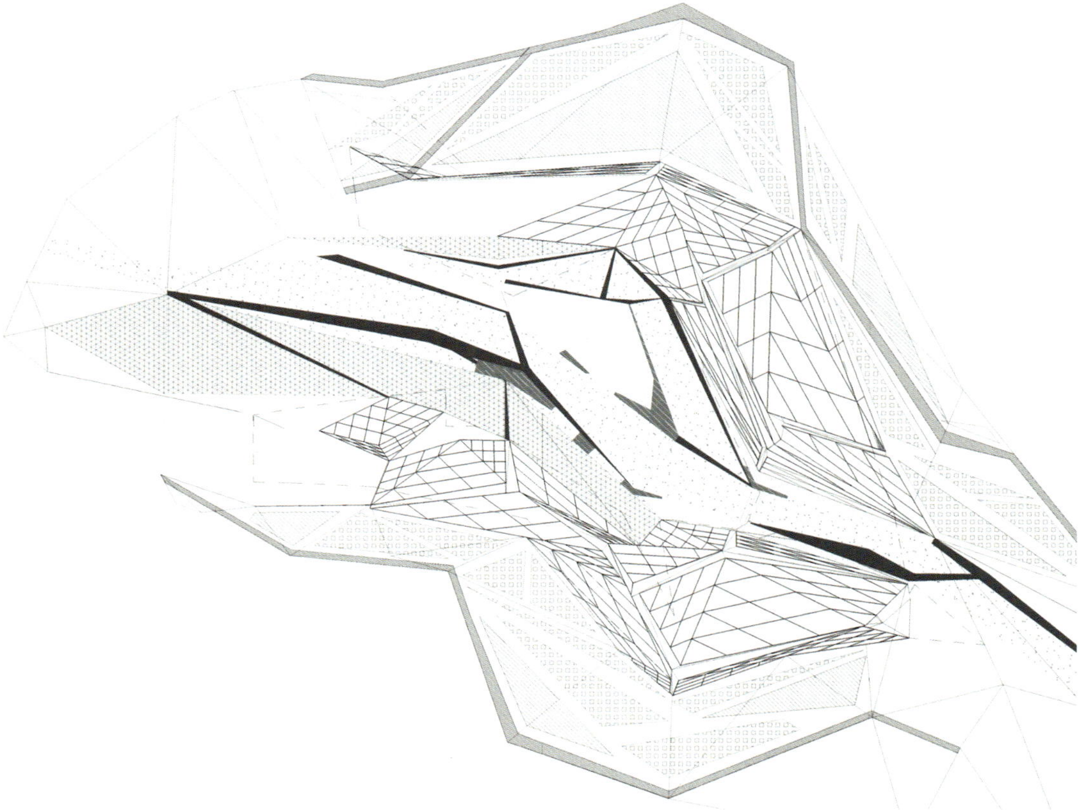

Floorplan

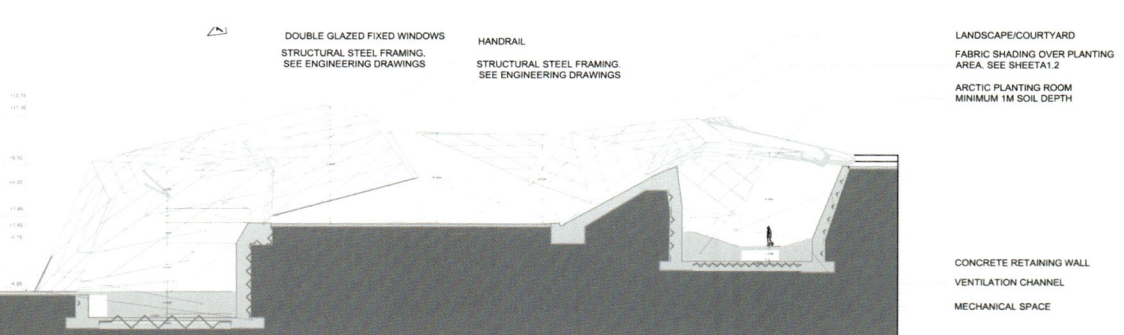

TROPICAL PLANTING ZONE
MIN 3M SOIL DEPTH
STRUCTURAL CONCRETE FOUNDATION
SEE ENGINEERING DRAWINGS

DOUBLE GLAZED FIXED WINDOWS
STRUCTURAL STEEL FRAMING.
SEE ENGINEERING DRAWINGS

HANDRAIL
STRUCTURAL STEEL FRAMING.
SEE ENGINEERING DRAWINGS

LANDSCAPE/COURTYARD
FABRIC SHADING OVER PLANTING
AREA. SEE SHEETA1.2
ARCTIC PLANTING ROOM
MINIMUM 1M SOIL DEPTH

CONCRETE RETAINING WALL
VENTILATION CHANNEL
MECHANICAL SPACE

1/2. Greenhouses

The Greenhouse is formed as a precious crystal, semi-submerged in splendid isolation, reached by boat across the lake followed by a short walk from the shore. The Greenhouse blends into the hillside even more so than the other two structures. The building is entered through a prolonged cut, literally scooped out of the ground, emerging within a light-filled cavernous reception space. From here the visitor passes along a tessellated mesh of paths through three different climatic zones with corresponding plant environments. The Greenhouse has a horseshoe plan creating a loop that changes radically in section to accommodate a sequence of different planting and spatial conditions. With the ground inside and out, gradually changing in relation to each other, the visitor experiences sequences of visual enclosure alternating with long vistas out and across. The horseshoe shape also generates an inner courtyard of outside space, making it the natural centre of the building and creating a three-dimensional interweaving of interior and exterior circulation.

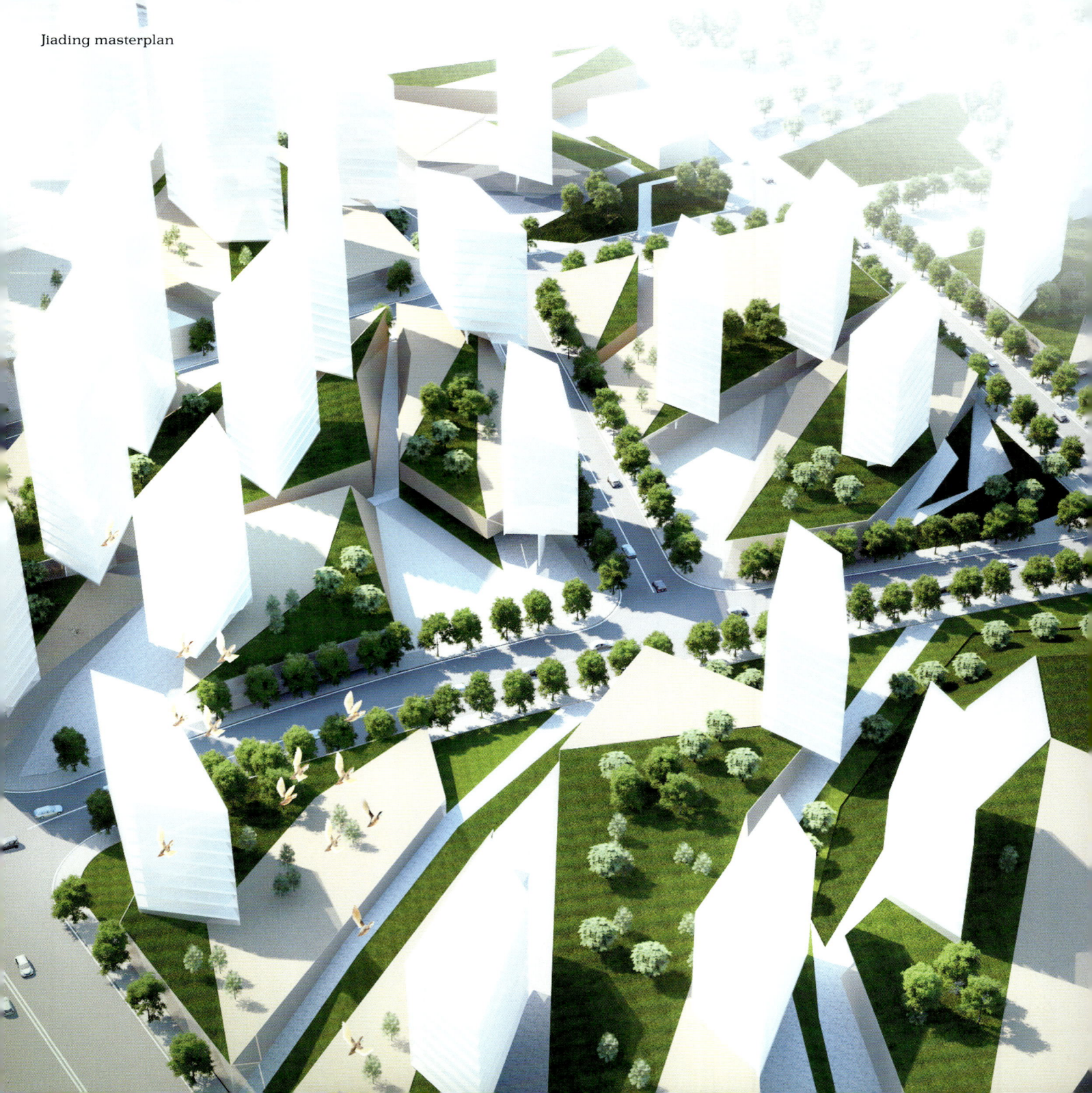
Jiading masterplan

AALU China 2010

Ground ecologies
Jiading District urban design and masterplanning

Location **Shenzhen, China**
Type **Masterplan**
Client **Jiading District Local Government, Shanghai, China**
Size **5 km².**
Date **June 2010**

Project description

Ground Ecologies is a winning competition entry for the redevelopment of the Jiading District. The site is located in the outer area of Shanghai City and is part of the greater masterplan of the city to develop peripheral new districts that can cope with the rapid urban development and the need to provide residential zones with direct access to the centre.

The competition called for the transformation of the industrial site into a high-density residential area boost by the newly open metro line station on the border of the site and a highway that ensure direct and close connections to the centre of Shanghai, allowing Jiading to become an important local centre in the near future.

The project inception is based on the local ground conditions and its transition from being a heavy industrial site into a new high-density residential district which includes business and commercial zones. The challenge was to integrate the necessary techniques and methods to prepare the ground for the future development with the residential, commercial and business programmes.

The structure of the project was layout using three different engineering techniques: soil remediation, water treatment and traffic and street systems.
These three different techniques were intertwined in order to create a basic framework from which the new programme can be introduced. The potentials and possibilities from a new a clean canal system, a new ground configuration, and the reorganisation of the street layout, were used to generate a project with a new ecology that can create a sustainable diverse and inclusive community.

1. People in Jiading
2. Hospital
3. Jiading industrial areas and polluted river

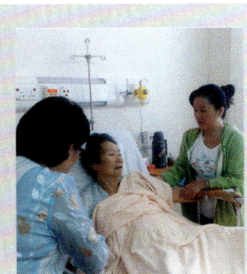

Currently Jiading District, Shanghai is basically a heavy-industrial site. However, the proposed masterplan seeks to allocate most of the new development and residential areas to these existing industrial grounds. The implications of developing heavy-industrial ground vary in terms of higher economic costs due to the difficult structural design, and difficulty to grow and vegetation, thus affecting the general well-being of the new inhabitants.

Old heavy-industrial ground became heavily polluted over the years. New developments built upon these areas have serious problems of structural instability and all future planting has to deal with soil that has been affected by chemicals, heavy metals or oils for extended periods of time, it can also affect the health and the overall well-being of the people that inhabit this area.

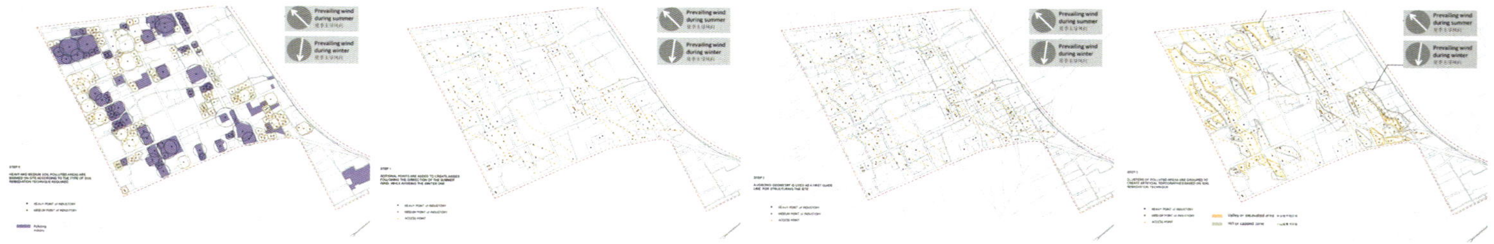

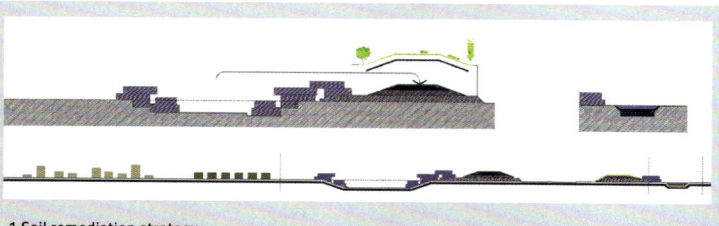

1. Soil remediation strategy

Soil remediation

Most of the site is covered by industries that have been polluting the site for several decades. Ground Ecologies project proposes to excavate the contaminated soil and place it where it can be capped and treated. This operation creates a hill and valley ground configuration which starts to change the conditions on the site.
The creation of this artificial topography allows for a new accessibility of the site at different levels, and the opportunity to use roofs and terraces as part of the public realm, thus multiplying the opportunities and widening its conditions. At the same time it introduces a network of green spaces that links the whole site with a pedestrian paths system.
The artificial topographies are fitted into the road and water network, and remaining buildings. Based on the pollution values of the existing soil condition, an artificial typography is generated.

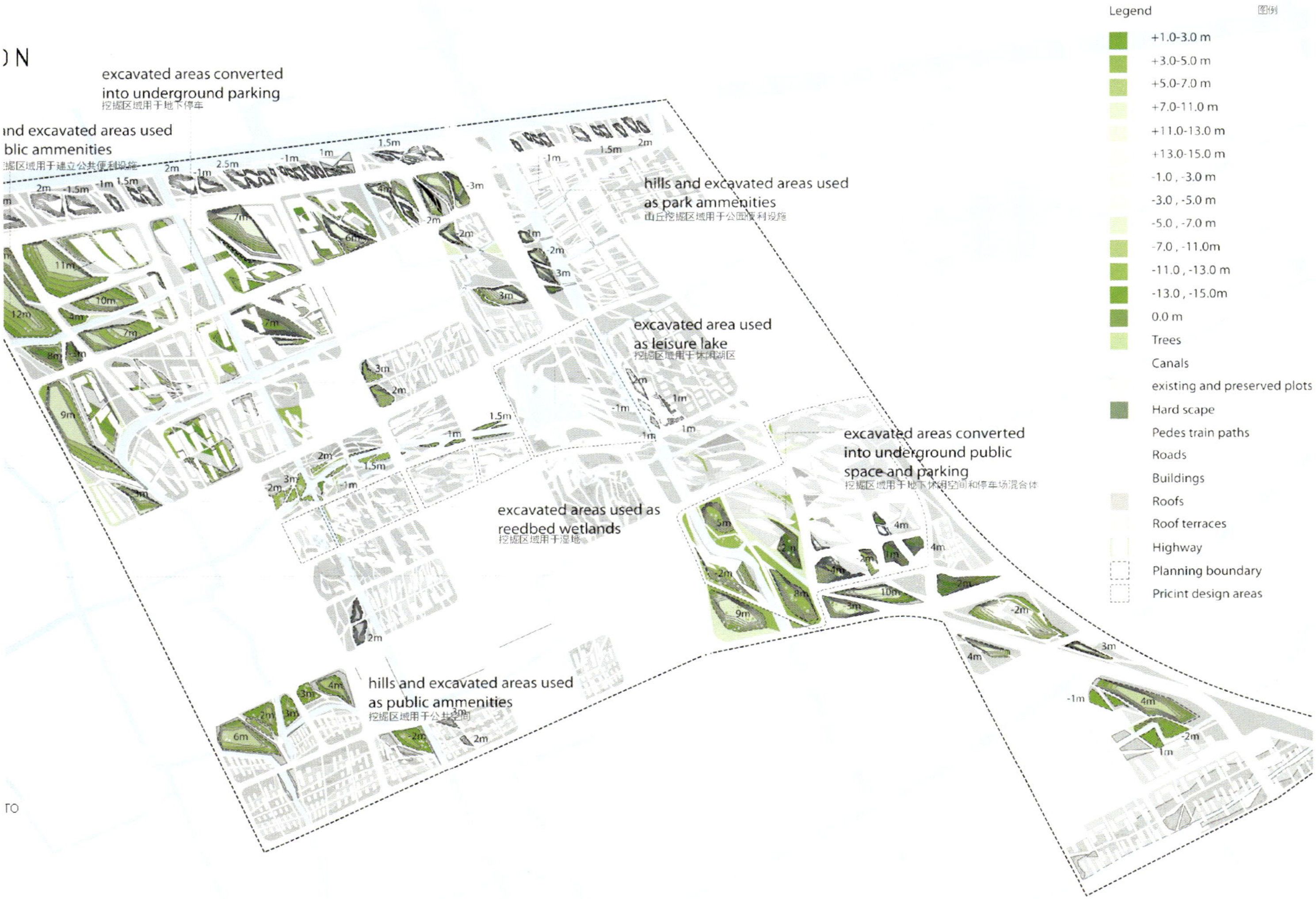

excavated areas converted into underground parking
挖掘区域用于地下停车

and excavated areas used
blic ammenities

hills and excavated areas used as park ammenities
山丘挖掘区域用于公园便利设施

excavated area used as leisure lake
挖掘区域用于休闲湖区

excavated areas converted into underground public space and parking
挖掘区域用于地下休闲空间和停车场混合体

excavated areas used as reedbed wetlands
挖掘区域用于湿地

hills and excavated areas used as public ammenities
挖掘区域用于公共空间

Legend 图例
+1.0-3.0 m
+3.0-5.0 m
+5.0-7.0 m
+7.0-11.0 m
+11.0-13.0 m
+13.0-15.0 m
-1.0, -3.0 m
-3.0, -5.0 m
-5.0, -7.0 m
-7.0, -11.0 m
-11.0, -13.0 m
-13.0, -15.0 m
0.0 m
Trees
Canals
existing and preserved plots
Hard scape
Pedes train paths
Roads
Buildings
Roofs
Roof terraces
Highway
Planning boundary
Pricint design areas

1. Soil remediation strategy
2. Polluted soil

The main logic is use valley a construction base, the hill and mountains are unbuildable since the soil is highly polluted. The main spaces generated by artificial typography are as follows:

1 Excavated areas used as underground parking.
2 Hills and excavated areas used as public amenities.
3 Excavated areas used as wetland roadbed.
4 Excavated areas used as public amenities.
5 Hills and excavated areas used as park amenities.
6 Excavated areas used as recreational lake amenities.
7 Excavated areas used as underground space and parking.

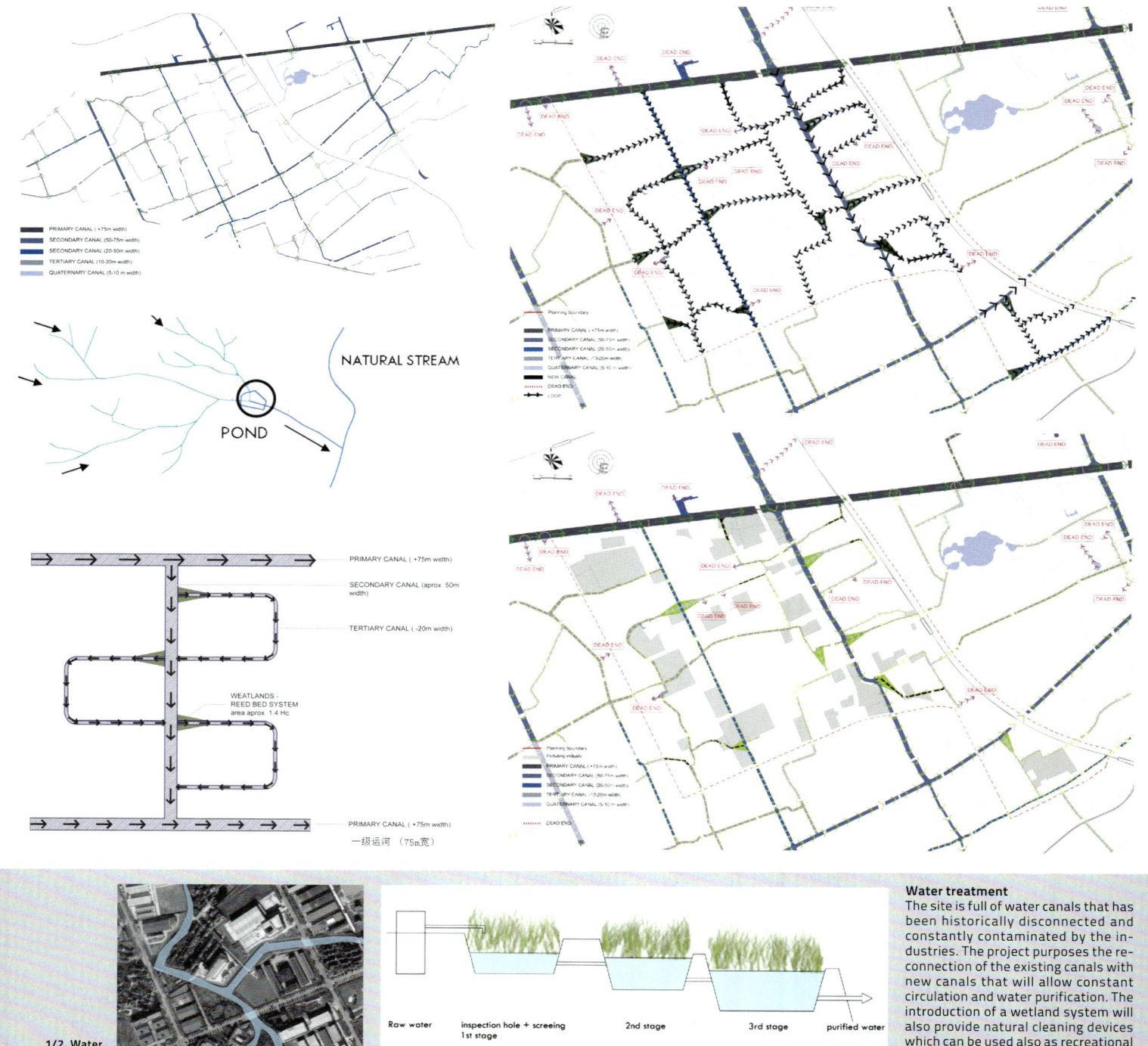

Water treatment
The site is full of water canals that has been historically disconnected and constantly contaminated by the industries. The project purposes the reconnection of the existing canals with new canals that will allow constant circulation and water purification. The introduction of a wetland system will also provide natural cleaning devices which can be used also as recreational and ecological areas.

1/2. Water treatment

legend:
- existing heavy industrial areas
- canals nodes
- new proposed canals
- removed canals
- primary canal (>75m width)
- secondary canal (50-75m width)
- secondary canal (20-50m width)
- tertiary canal (10-20m width)
- quaternary canal (5-10m width)
- underground
- existing empty space
- planning boundary
- preserved areas

No. 11 underground line
global park station
nan xiang station
nan xiang station

01 lake
02 sports center
03 elderly people center
04 mixed housing unit
05 governmental area
06 C.B.D.

1/2. Redirecting water

Canal system

This classifies the existing canal system as four categories based on width: primary canals, secondary canals, tertiary canals and quaternary canals. Based on the analysis of existing heavy industrial areas and important canal nodes, it removes certain canals and places new canals in order to promote the water clearance system. Also based on different local environment, canal landscape areas are classified as river of reflection, river of years, river of rural, river of sparkling and river of life.

Based on water clearance system proposal, it calculates the required areas of wetlands, proposes vegetation. The overall distribution of canals clearly shows the categories of canals both kept and removed. The strategy controls the water flow on-site according to proposed land-uses, avoiding infrastructure redundancy and water pollution.
Different hierarchy levels in the canal system are redirected in order to generate a comprehensive water cleansing strategy, according also to the land-uses each level serves.

Masterplan

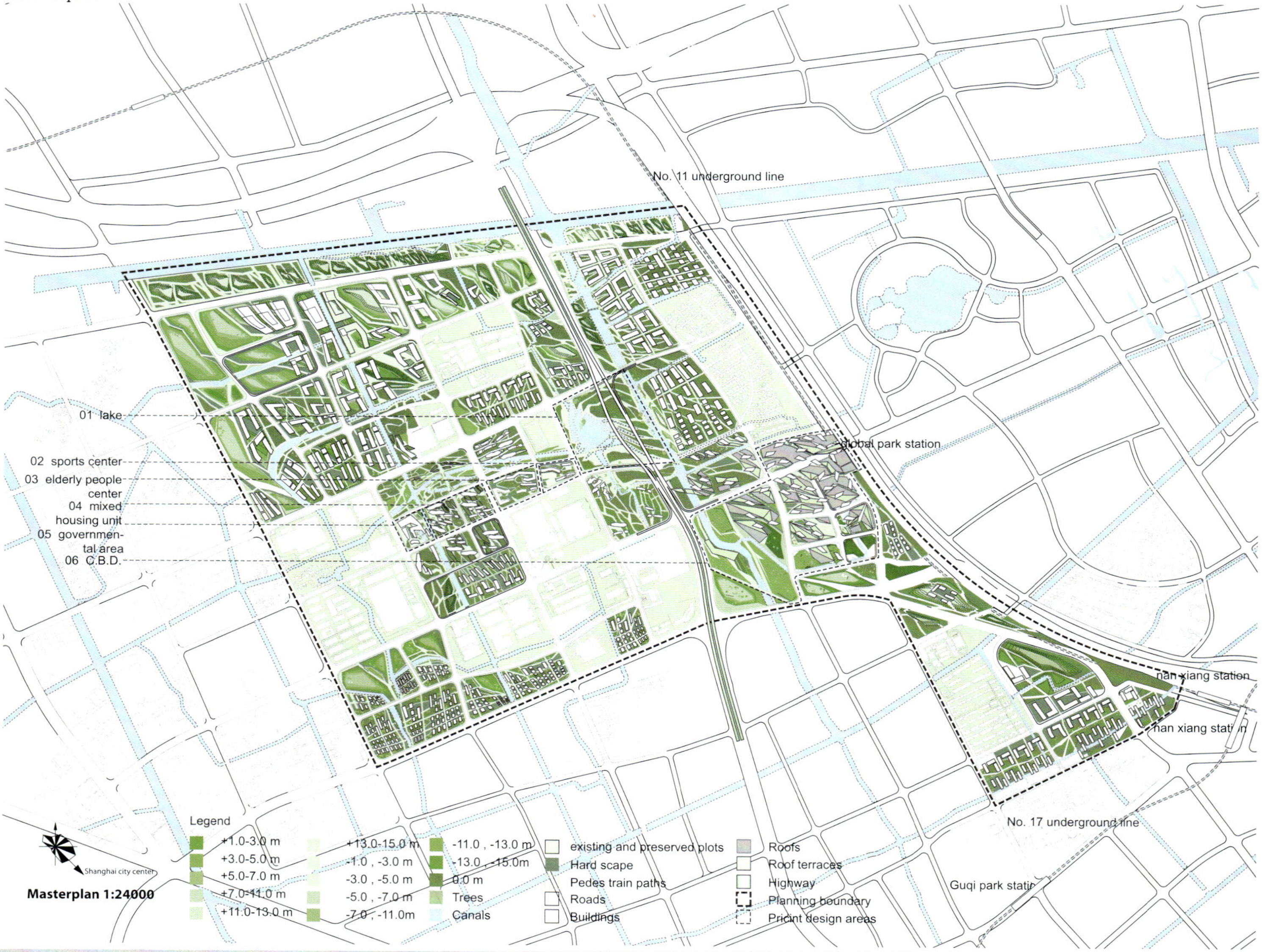

01 lake
02 sports center
03 elderly people center
04 mixed housing unit
05 governmental area
06 C.B.D.

Legend
- +1.0-3.0 m
- +3.0-5.0 m
- +5.0-7.0 m
- +7.0-11.0 m
- +11.0-13.0 m
- +13.0-15.0 m
- -1.0, -3.0 m
- -3.0, -5.0 m
- -5.0, -7.0 m
- -7.0, -11.0 m
- -11.0, -13.0 m
- -13.0, -15.0 m
- 0.0 m
- Trees
- Canals
- existing and preserved plots
- Hard scape
- Pedestrian paths
- Roads
- Buildings
- Roofs
- Roof terraces
- Highway
- Planning boundary
- Pricint design areas

Masterplan 1:24000 — Shanghai city center

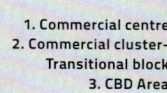

1. Commercial centre
2. Commercial cluster- Transitional block
3. CBD Area

Urban character typology breakdown:

1. Commercial centre: Ground floor mainly live-work and some commercial for city wide supply (destination area) but small-scale business. F&B and entertainment mixed. Second floor mainly live-work or extension of commercial.
2. Commercial cluster- Transitional block. Previous typology is used as a plinth on top of which to plug high-rise purely residential. Ground floor mainly live-work and some commercial mainly for local supply of daily needs, neighbourhood oriented.
3. C.B.D. Area. Commercial and office podiums creating elevated public mid semi-private elevated areas. Tower levels used for residential, hotel and high-end office spaces. Higher-income oriented but allowing low-income residential spaces in lower towers.

Elderly people centre perspective view

1. Bus Stop
2. Buildings with terraces and vegetation

4. Mixed use -infrastructural link: Continuous massing with underground program directly linked to elevated metro line. Towers attached to podium.
5. Residential areas: Parametric typology variating density, height, built area and character strong built mass courtyards closing patios and inner squares detached from external circulation to detached and semi-detached housing blocks patios and interior urbanism strategies linking public program and residential civic-cultural activities shared interior-exterior school, libraries, hospital healthcare.
6. Landmarks and riverside areas leisure lake and green riverside areas create a strong axis that generates an enclosed area with commercial program in the bottom max 60m woe, will work on 30-40
6-9 stores consistent façade.

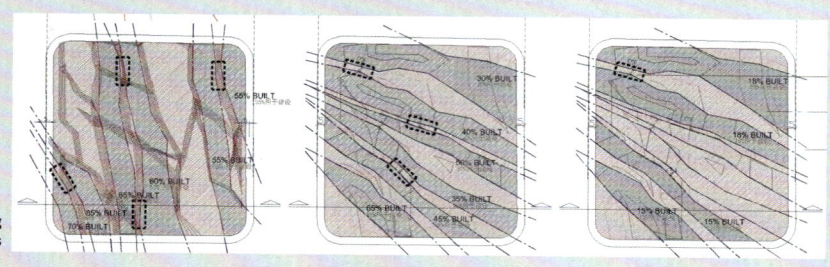

1. Massing guidelines

The different areas of the site were strategised in six different catogories:
1 Zone close to canal and main road can have potential for strong character - boulevard-style urbanism. Franchise, top brand commercial character.
2 Small-scale water areas likely to improve urban quality when remediated. Local commerce, smaller retail recommended. More suitable for live-work.
3 Large complexes not compatible with pedestrian environments due to barrier effect. Programmes can act in a more clustered / isolated fashion around them.
4 Area beside the main highway likely to have heavier noise and particle pollution.
5 Metro station gives high connectivity most appropriate for CBD
6 Zones close to node of more intense environmental stress, more suitable for big box arrangements.

Governmental centre perspective view

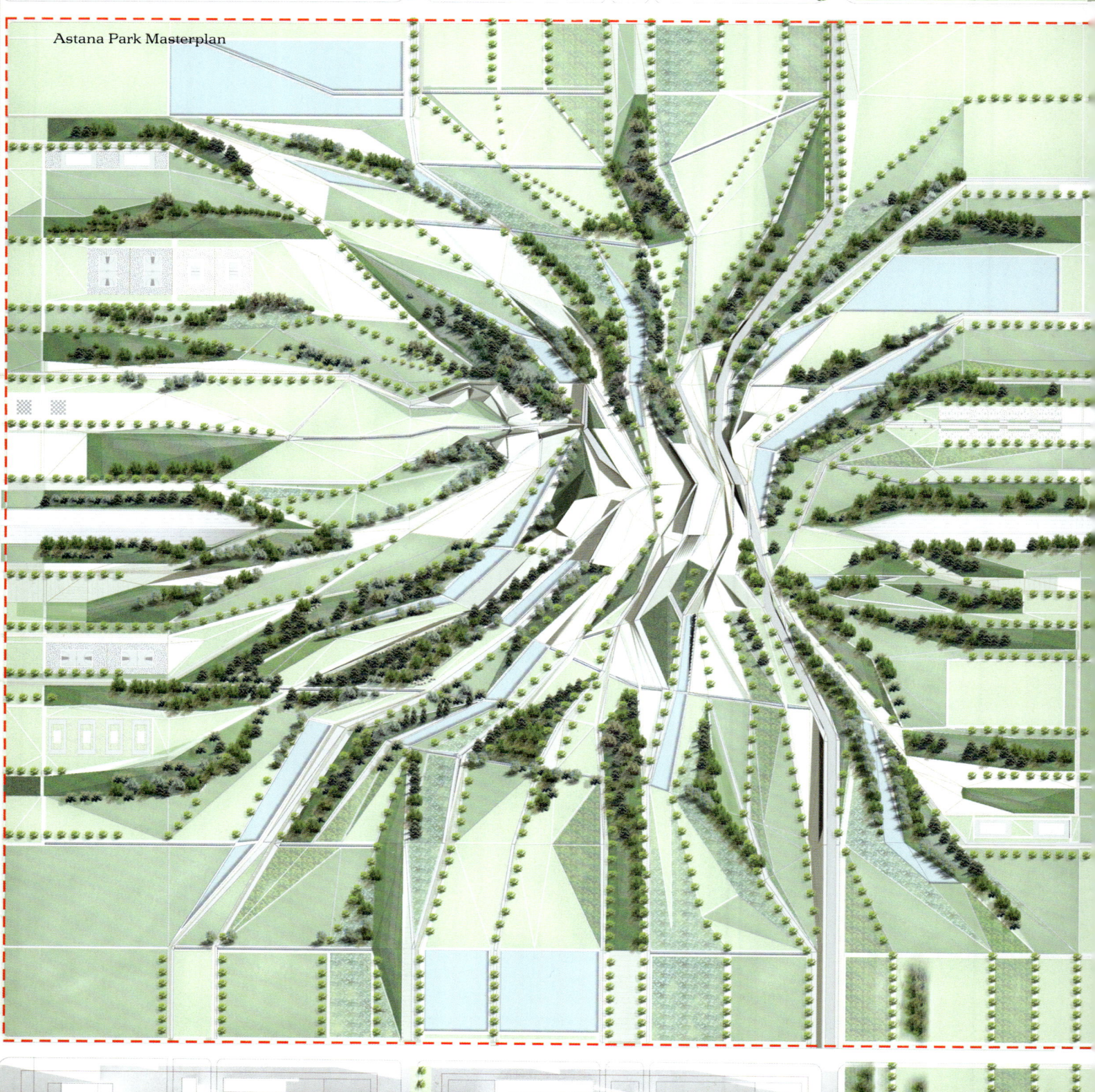

AALU China 2009

Astana Park
Multiplying Grounds

Location **Shenzhen, China**
Type **Masterplan**
Client **Shenzhen Municipal Planning Bureau Longgang Branch, China**
Size **9 km²**
Date **2009**

Project description

Ground

Strategic Location - east meets west
Landscape, ground and nature will become increasingly important to future users and through its location, perfect symmetry and the axial and programmatic relationships to the surrounding urban grain, this new park is destined to become a major place to enjoy an extended range of activities in addition to the usual recreational facilities.
Our project is developed to enhance the given framework, highlight the axis and develop a central meeting place in a contemporary, dynamic and exciting way. Starting from the fact that Astana is located on the intersection of east and west and exponentially develops as a major link between those cultural and economic spheres, our intention is to make the park into a place where this is symbolised and can be experienced too.

Diagram in context

We set up a diagram as a magnetic field with two poles - one in the east and another in the west. This results in a funnel that runs north-south which in turn constitutes the local axis in contrast to the global axis of east and west. This arrangement aligns itself perfectly with the non-directional square geometry of the park and the urban system around it. The western field naturally becomes the extension of the Olympic sports grounds, additional sports facilities will be located here and the atmosphere will be driven by western garden principles and related vegetation.
The eastern field will have an emphasis on Asian sports and activities, arrangements and vegetation will be dominated by eastern influences.

Despite these subtle contrasts, we envisage the primary use of local vegetation in order to create a robust low-maintenance and gradually maturing parkscape. Ultimately this park will be a local expression of the amazing Kazakhstan landscapes.

Park activation

Along the conceptual development of the magnetic field diagram we propose a two-folded strategy that will activate the park regardless of the extreme weather conditions in winter and the time of day.

1. Topographic activation
On the one hand, we integrate all the necessary earthworks to build the park and facilities into a comprehensive rippled topography.
This artificial topography has been guided by the intention to shelter specific zones, in particular sports areas from wind, as well as allowing the introduction of basic facilities such a changing rooms, toilets, etc., inside the hills, thus allowing indoor and outdoor activities in both winter and summer conditions.

2. Programmatic activation
In the centre of the park, a plethora of low buildings are employed to facilitate hospitality, shopping and entertainment. These single-storey volumes read as extensions of the hills. They frame and shelter the main public plaza in the very centre.

1. East meets west
2. Concept

At the western apex of this central area, we located a spa and wellness centre. This is just one example of potential additional functions and programmes that would enhance the park's role and complexity. The design concept allows for careful calibration of the desired density as buildings and topography can be exchanged whilst adhering to the same overall logic and experience.

Park strategies are:
Earthwork strategy, Traffic strategy, Ground strategies, water management strategy, lighting strategy, and Planting strategy.

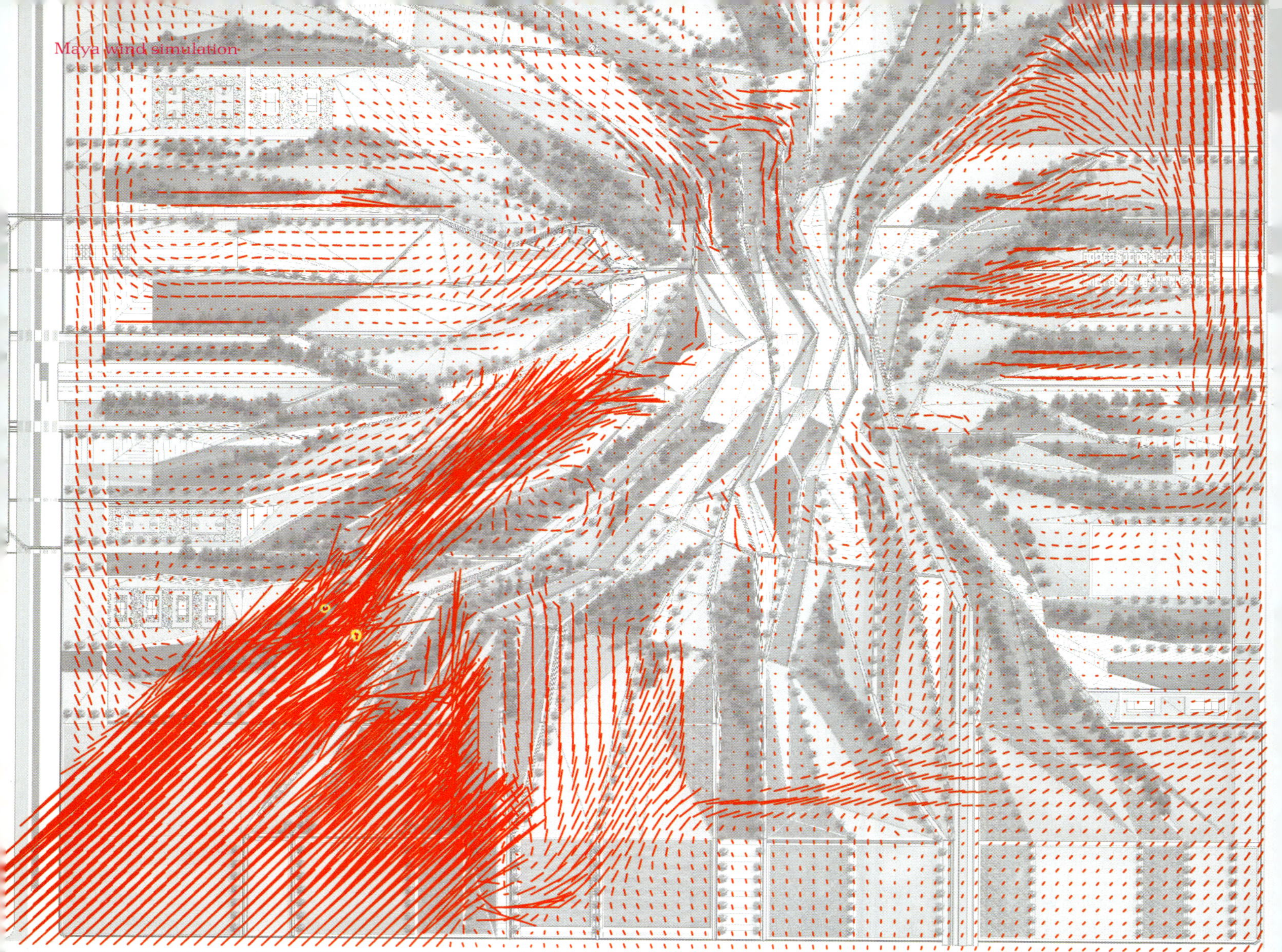

Maya wind simulation

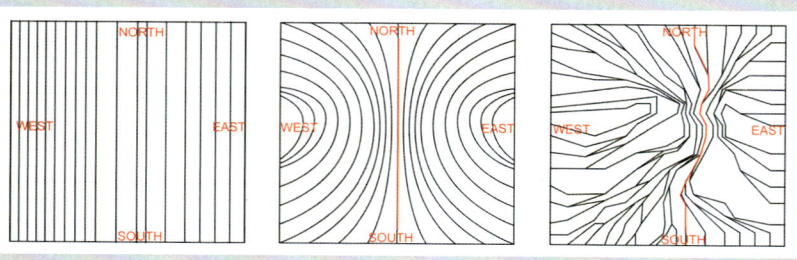

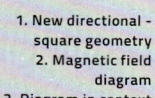
1. New directional - square geometry
2. Magnetic field diagram
3. Diagram in context

Traffic strategy

The road strategy across the park tries to strike a balance between the need to cross the park as well as creating a secluded environment with minimal contact with vehicles and traffic. The east-west connectivity is provided through the direct connection across the park in a tunnel under the main land bridge and centre of activities in the park. The tunnel section is also the access to the parking areas which are meant to serve the park as well as the adjacent districts. The required headroom for the road (6m + 2.5m structure + build up) is achieved through a combination of reduction of the level of the road (-3.5m) and the building up of the terrain adjacent to it (land bridge and central area of the park).

Pedestrian path

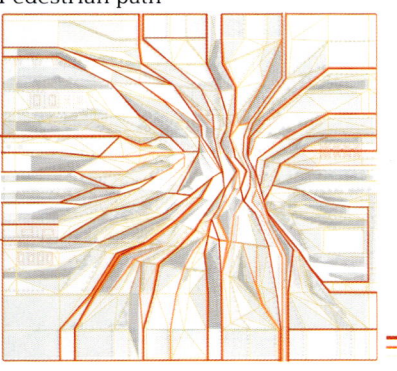

Cycling tracks

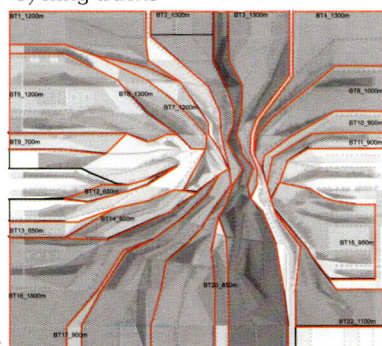

Sports activities

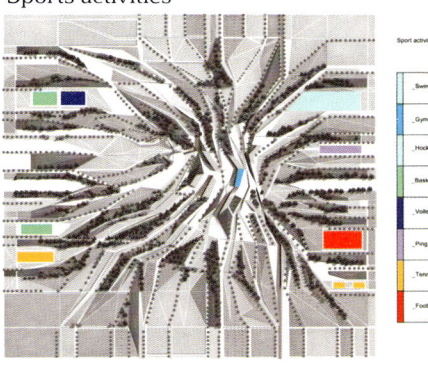
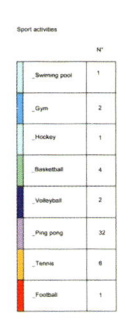

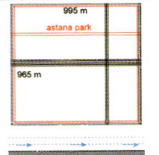
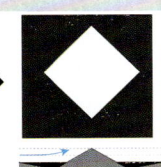

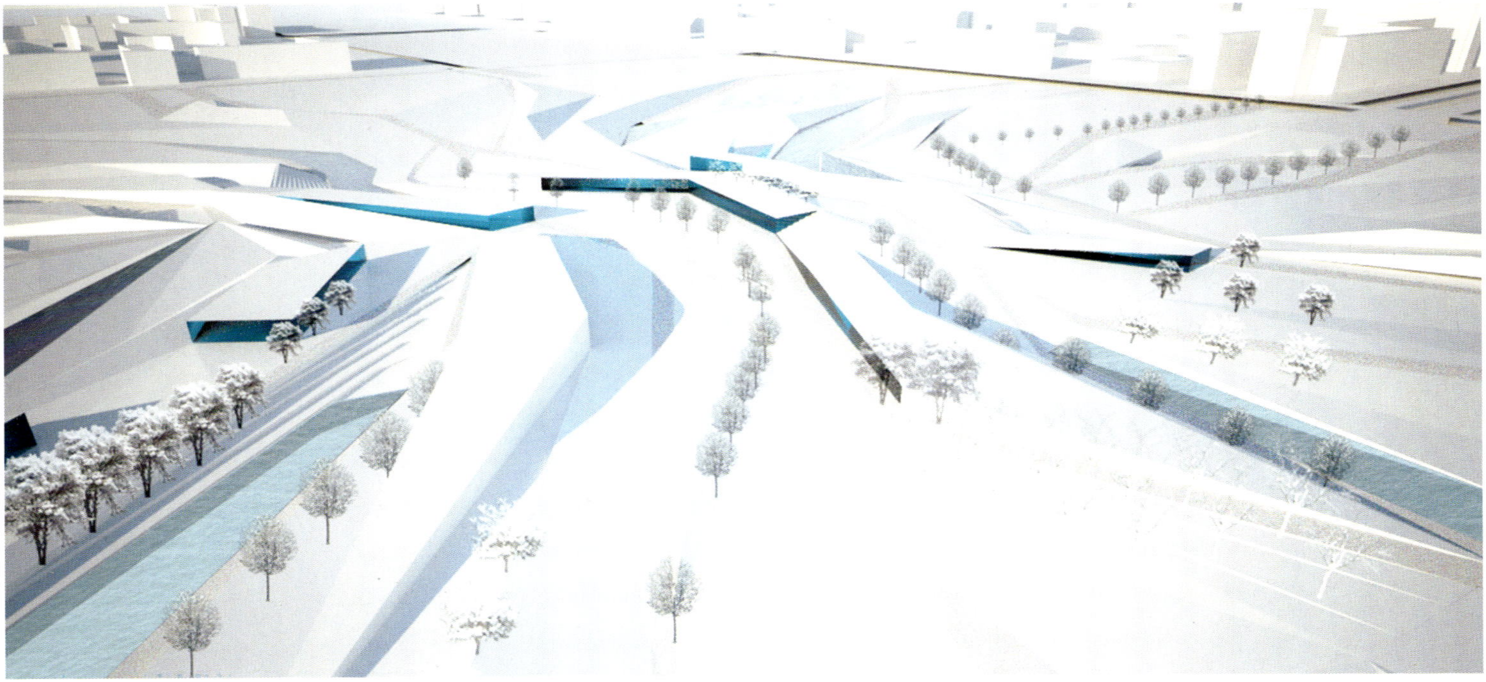

1. Rippled topographies
2. Flat generic square
3. General accumulation of earthworks
4. Earthworks distribution

The north-south connectivity is partially limited to one slow connection across the park, with the other proposal of the masterplan (lesser hierarchy) removed and converted into a right in-right out connection into the peripheral road around the park. The road crossing the park does so under conditions of traffic and speed reduction, serving the purposes of local access, deliveries and maintenance for the park.

Earthwork strategy

The earthworks strategy of the park has been designed in such a way that there is a NET BALANCE between imports and exports of material. There is a series of sources of cut, as well as areas of fill. The design has managed to avoid import/export of any material, except top soil, thus improving sustainability credentials of the project.

Pedestrian path

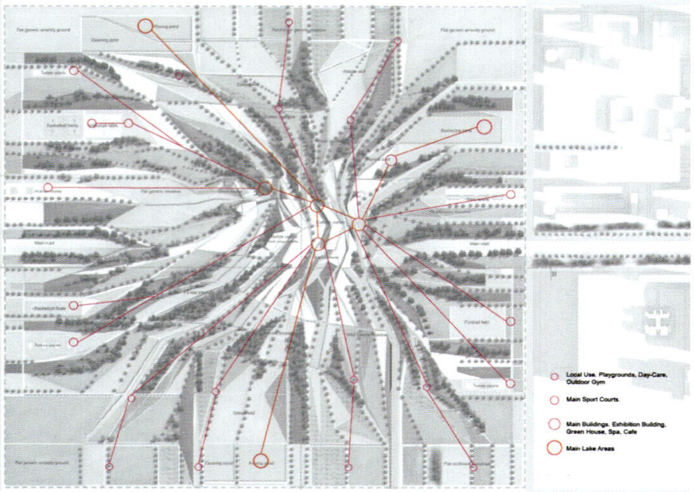

Local Use. Playgrounds, Day-Care, Outdoor Gym
Main Sport Courts.
Main Buildings. Exhibition Building, Green House, Spa, Cafe
Main Lake Areas

Planting strategy 1/3 trees

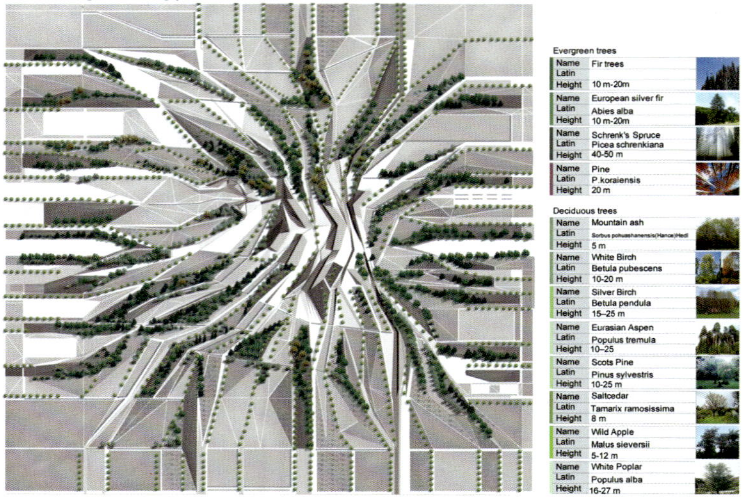

Evergreen trees
Name Fir trees
Latin
Height 10 m-20m
Name European silver fir
Latin Abies alba
Height 10 m-20m
Name Schrenk's Spruce
Latin Picea schrenkiana
Height 40-50 m
Name Pine
Latin P.koraiensis
Height 20 m
Deciduous trees
Name Mountain ash
Latin Sorbus pohuashanensis(Hance)Hedl
Height 5 m
Name White Birch
Latin Betula pubescens
Height 10-20 m
Name Silver Birch
Latin Betula pendula
Height 15–25 m
Name Eurasian Aspen
Latin Populus tremula
Height 10–25
Name Scots Pine
Latin Pinus sylvestris
Height 10-25 m
Name Saltcedar
Latin Tamarix ramosissima
Height 8 m
Name Wild Apple
Latin Malus sieversii
Height 5-12 m
Name White Poplar
Latin Populus alba
Height 16-27 m

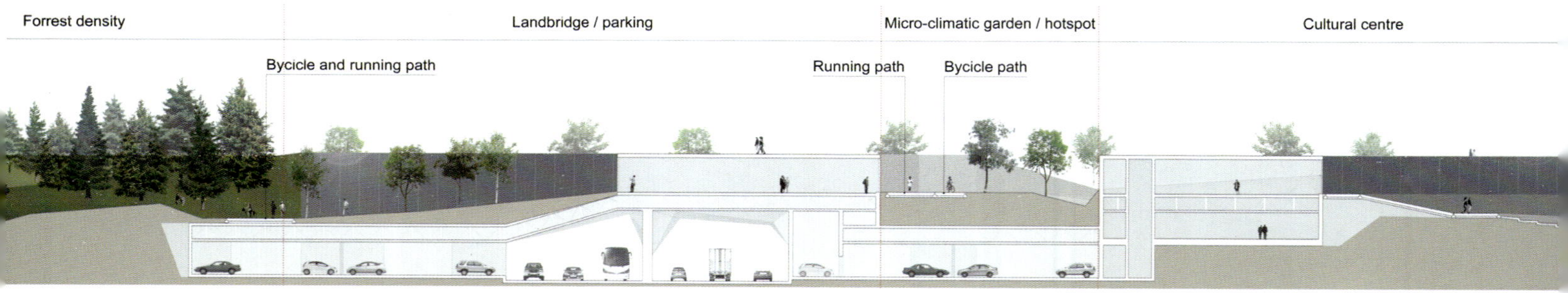

Forrest density
Landbridge / parking
Micro-climatic garden / hotspot
Cultural centre
Bycicle and running path
Running path
Bycicle path

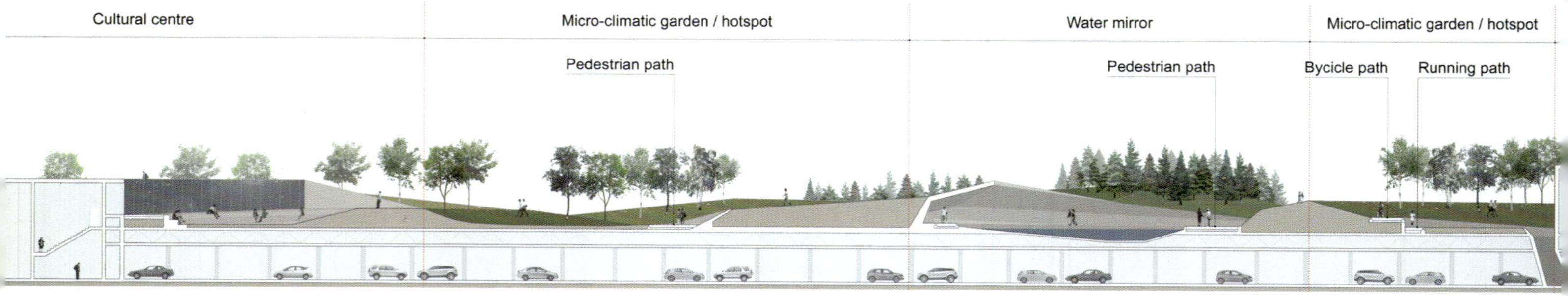

Cultural centre
Micro-climatic garden / hotspot
Water mirror
Micro-climatic garden / hotspot
Pedestrian path
Pedestrian path
Bycicle path
Running path

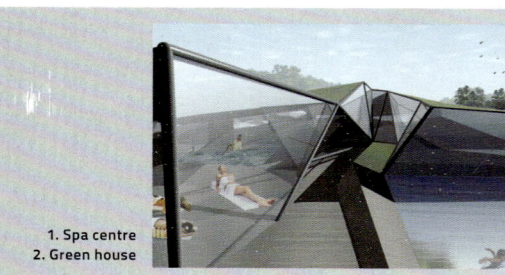

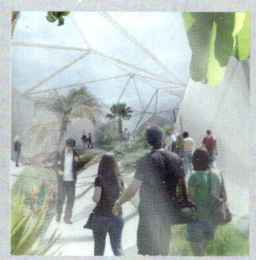

1. Spa centre
2. Green house

Planting strategy

A planting strategy has been devised to generate a number of different conditions throughout the park. From flat amenity grassland to forest and lake environments, the project attempts to bring together the amazing natural landscape of Kazakhstan and Astana, while blending the best of west and east landscape and parkland traditions into a contemporary park, a melting pot of cultural landscapes and social encounters for the inhabitants of Astana.

We proposed two sets of plants that will evolve in parallel to achieve a blended landscape.

1. Native vegetation will be used as the natural framework for the park to evolve in the long term. Different species, especially trees, will be used to ensure that the basic structure of the park remains throughout the year with evergreen plantation and vegetation that can endure the weather conditions whilst allowing native wildlife to colonise the park.

Planting strategy 2/3 Ground-

Couch grass		
Name	Zoysia tenuifolia	
Height	0.2- 0.4m	
Name	Elytrigia repens	
Height	0.4- 1.50m	
Name	Rheum altaicum	
Height	0.4- 1.50m	
Name	Stipa capillata	
Height	0.4- 1.50m	
Name	Stipa Lessingiana	
Height	0.4- 1.50m	
Name	Stipa pennata	
Height	0.4- 1.50m	
Flowers		
Name	Tulip	
Latin	Tulipa schrenkii	
Height	0.2- 0.6m	
Name	Dusty Miller	
Latin	Centaurea gymnocarpa	
Height	0.4- 1m	
Name	Siberian Fawn Lily	
Latin	Erythronium sibiricum	
Height	0.2- 0.6m	
Name	Moss Campion	
Latin	Silene acaulis	
Height	0.4- 1m	
Name	Dwarf Russian Almond	
Latin	Prunus tenella	
Height	0.4- 1m	
Name	Curry Plant	
Latin	Helichrysum italicum	
Height	0.4- 1m	
Name	Cytisus nigricans	
Height	0.2- 0.6m	
Name	Limonium gmelinii	
Height	0.4- 1m	

Planting strategy 3/3 Shrubs

Evergreen		
Name	Juniperus	
Latin	Juniperus formosana Hayata	
Height	6-8 m	
Name	Savin	
Latin	Juniperus sabinea	
Height	3-4 m	
Name	Salicornia Strobilacea	
Latin	Halocnemum strobilaceum	
Height	2-4 m	
Name	Artemisia	
Latin	Artemisia shrenkiana	
Height	1m-2m	
Deciduous		
Name	Lonicera/honeysuckle	
Latin	Lonicera ruprechtiana	
Height	3m-5m	
Name	Artemisia pauciflora	
Latin	Artemisia pauciflora	
Height	1m-2m	

Amphitheatre — Bycicle and running path — Skating ring — Water mirror — Forrest density

Commercial centre — Roof terrace — Forrest density — Winter sport slope — Flat generic meadow — Bycicle

1. Paths and water ponds
2. Green fields and water ponds

2. Seasonal vegetation has been integrated into the design to produce different character areas that the concept 'east meets west' suggests. This will enhance the local landscape by creating different scenarios whilst also attending to the different necessities of the park's programme. The seasonal planting will focus mainly on ground cover such as flowers and grasses. Flowers will be introduced in gardens and the pockets of climatic comfort zones, high resistance grasses will be used in areas of full access for amenity areas, and wild flower meadows and plants with cleaning capacities will be integrated within the water treatment lagoons. Water management strategy is one of the main drivers in the design of the park. Creating a water ecology is organised around three main water bodies and a variety of smaller ones that serve and complement different functions and roles. These water bodies are interconnected by a series of canals running east-west allowing the circulation and distribution of water throughout the whole park.

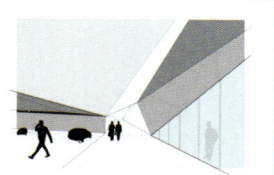
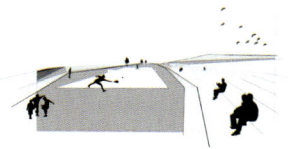

1/2/3. Programmatic activation

Water management on site

From an infrastructural point of view the park collects water from different sources, ensuring its provision for different uses, and for the maintenance of the park and complementary buildings.
Boreholes, greywater coming from existing and future developments, water city network, collection of surface water, rain and snow collection when possible, are among the main sources. Water coming from all the main sources is concentrated in two water treatment lagoons. Clean water is then redistributed through the other canals to be used for different purposes before it is collected again to be recycled in the water treatment lagoons.

AALU China 2011

Taichung Park
Woven Grounds

Location **Taiwan, China**
Type **Park Masterplan**
Client **Taichung Gateway City Government**
Size **67.5 Ha.**
Date **2011**

Project description

Woven Grounds

The reason for a park is to provide a chance to weave the cityscape of our urban environments with ecologies and places with an entirely different character. A park becomes a melting pot of different territories, where citizens can experience in a positive way, the distance between their urban lives and that of a distant countryside. To design a park is to work with these relationships and experiences, playing with them in order to generate a space where citizens can relate to their environment in new and provocative ways, making them more aware of each other and their relationship with nature.

In this sense, the park weaves distant and local territories into the ultimate form of metropolitan experience, helping to forge character and a long-term vision of the entire city. The design of this park in Taichung becomes the key to produce a resolutely cosmopolitan and distinct experience for Gateway Development and, to a certain extent, the entire city. In a nutshell, weaving will become the main concept to turn the landscape of Gateway Park into the strongest form of urbanism.

It is this idea of weaving experiences, territories and ecologies that drives the design of our proposal. The whole aspiration of the design becomes encapsulated in the space of the landscape, with the very materials of the park, water, earth and plants, being woven into a new ground from which to build the Gateway Community. Woven Grounds presents a story made of three different weaving patterns: weaving of the infrastructure of Taichung, weaving the scales of the park and finally weaving the ecologies around the Gateway Development.

Concept

We understand that its development as an ecological BRAIDED RIVER that will radiate and consolidate the lifestyle, innovation, culture and biodiversity of the Taichung Gateway City project through the intertwining and interweaving of landscape, infrastructure, architecture and urbanism in a seamless design.

Thus, the proposed network braids the flows of infrastructure, inhabitants and urban fabric creating - following from the analogy with a braided river - a set of islands or bars that contain and define the proposed ecologies and programmes within the park.

Therefore, at the core of the park design is the water management system, a strategic element of the project and its development. Local climate, average precipitation, natural disasters mitigation, maintenance and energy generation are some of the issues to which the water management strategy responds in order to become the framework for the park and the overall masterplan.

1. Taiwanese braided river

Masterplan

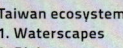

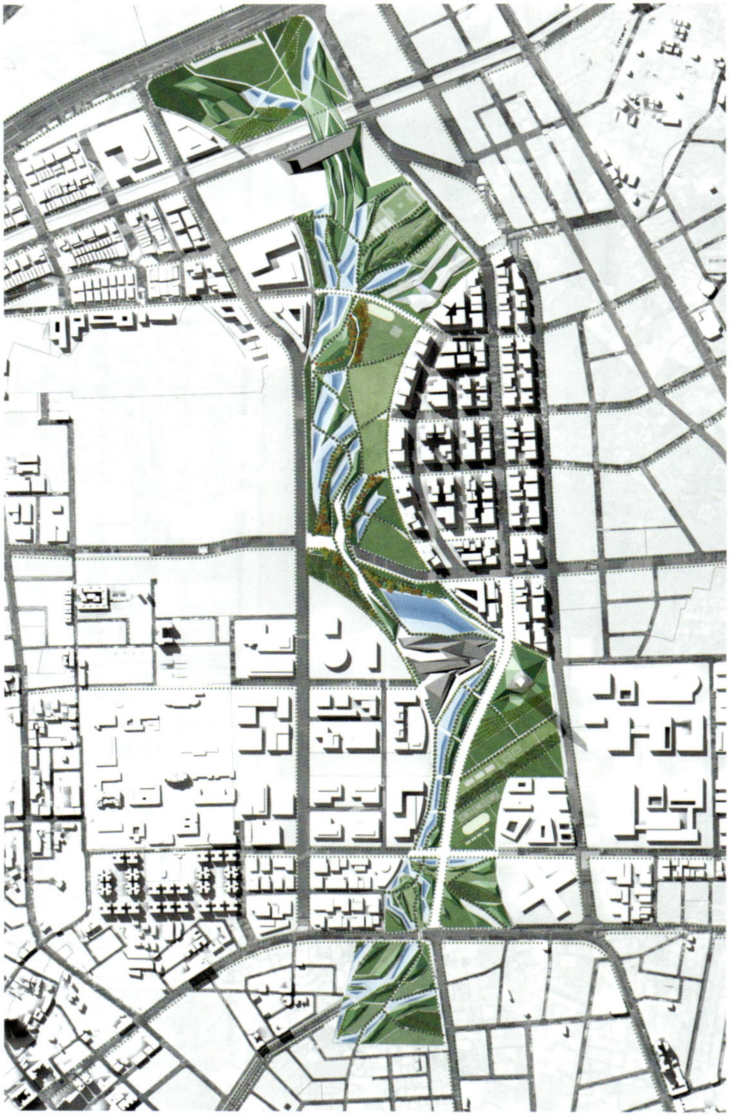

Taiwan ecosystems:
1. Waterscapes
2. Plains
3. Mountains

Taiwan ecosystems
The project aims to use indigenous ecosystems from Taichung and Taiwan as the basis for the park design and development, combining nature's performance with innovative technologies to provide the city of Taichung with a strong and vigorous infrastructural landscape whilst allowing the inhabitants to enjoy vibrant recreational programmes in a great diversity of spaces and environments.
In order to utilise the local intelligence inherent to natural systems within Taiwan we look at its most representative ecosystems. The island is characterised by the contrast between the eastern two-thirds, consisting mostly of rugged mountains running in five ranges from the northern to the southern tip of the island, the flat to gently rolling Chianan Plains and the coastline and wetlands that surround them.

Components axonometric view

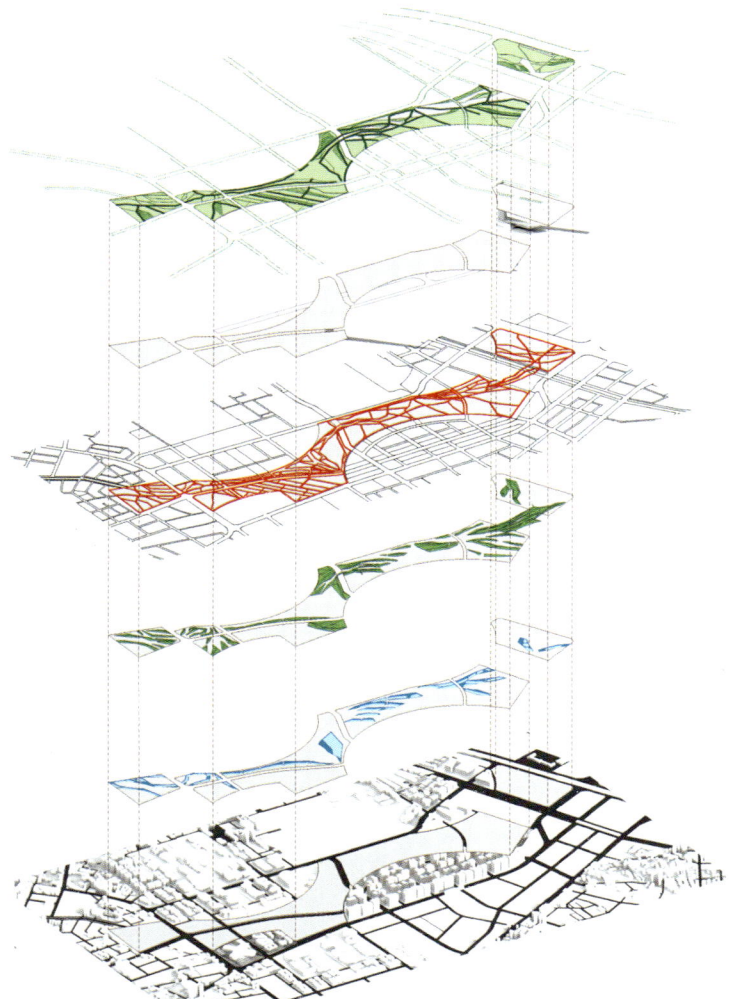

Components axonometric view

The enclosed gardens

1. Water ponds perspective view
2. Physical model

We bring together these three ecosystems from Taiwan and intertwine them along the water infrastructure to create a park that combines and provides tranquillity, ecology, landscaping, sustainability, disaster mitigation, biodiversity and recreation to Taichung Gateway City project.

Woven Grounds understands water, its performance and processes, as the main feature that guides the design. The index of natural movement and dynamics of water in the existing site provide the basic layout for the park to ensure its functioning as a recreational facility and infrastructural landscape.

The structure that water creates in the park is also the layout for the creation of different habitats and environments that provide a variety of experiences for visitors.

Woven Grounds aims at connecting and linking the urban issue of the surrounding fabric. A set of entry points is located in direct relation to the streets to ensure the continuity of the proposed layout. The diagram shows studies of potential connections and their materialisation in the proposal.

Connections strategy

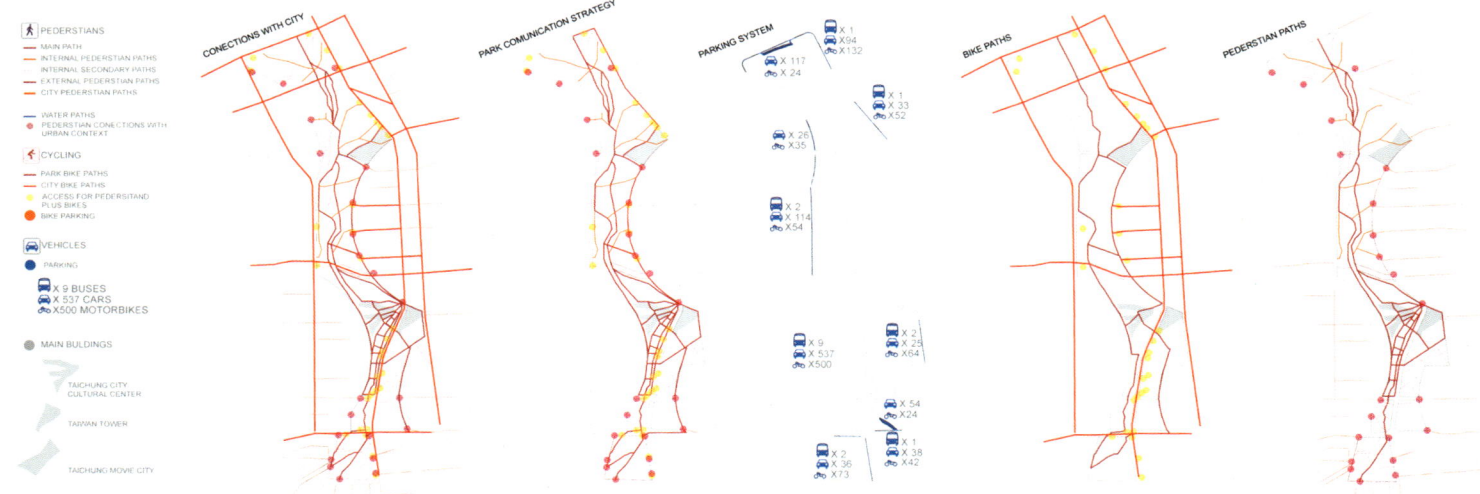

1. The landbridge
2. Bike lanes

The creation of small topographies and hills is a natural by-product of the previous three diagrams. The storage and recycling of water generates a certain amount of earthworks to enhance and create different environments. The excavation of different types of lagoons and the remediation of possibly contaminated areas also provide an opportunity to shape and mould the landscape into a series of high and low points. On the one hand the earthworks are a necessary engineering solution to store and clean water and soil and on the other they expand and multiply the experiences and spaces that Taichung Gateway park will offer to the community.

Zoning: Weaving the scales of the park

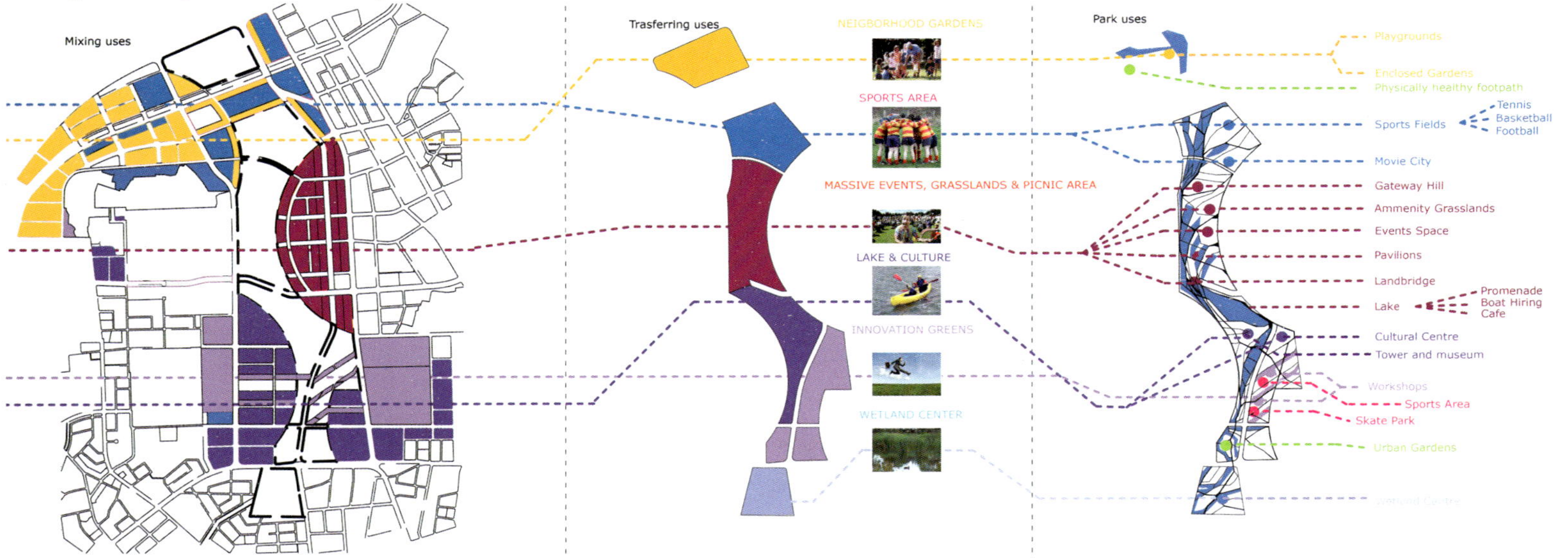

Mixing uses — Transferring uses — NEIGHBORHOOD GARDENS — Park uses — Playgrounds / Enclosed Gardens / Physically healthy footpath / Sports Fields → Tennis, Basketball, Football / Movie City / Gateway Hill / Amenity Grasslands / Events Space / Pavilions / Landbridge / Lake → Promenade, Boat Hiring, Cafe / Cultural Centre / Tower and museum / Workshops / Sports Area / Skate Park / Urban Gardens

SPORTS AREA
MASSIVE EVENTS, GRASSLANDS & PICNIC AREA
LAKE & CULTURE
INNOVATION GREENS
WETLAND CENTER

1. Sports fields
2. Cultural centre, tower and museum

Woven Grounds takes into account the surrounding land-uses to input directly the activities and environments that the park will create. While doing so the project calls for a more intimate relation between the development and the park.

In order to avoid security problems, we propose giving the park surroundings a use that will continue at night, so we reorganise the residential area to allow that role.

This necessary feedback between the park and the whole development will offer a potentially strong mix of land-uses which in turn will provide the park with a bigger variety of uses, residents, office workers, sportsmen, children, etc.

Woven Grounds creates a multiplicity of experiences deriving from specific character areas created to relate intimately with its immediate surroundings and the land-uses of the masterplan.

Planting strategy

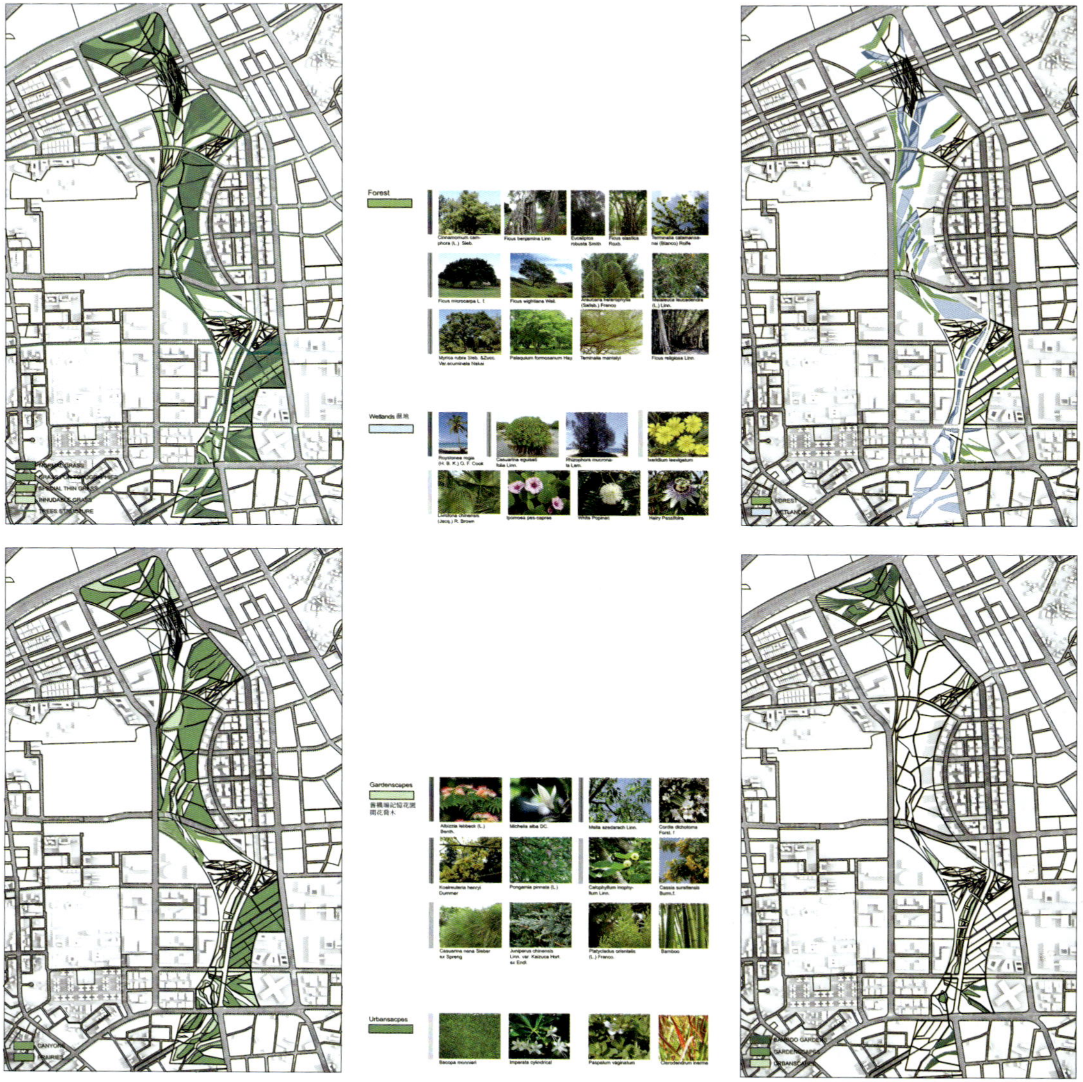

1. Hills ecology - canyon landscape
2. Linear and structural trees
3. Urban scapes

Planting strategy

The planting strategy follows the creation of three main ecosystems (water-scapes, hill-scapes, plain-scapes) linked and fuelled by the flowing of a meandering spine of water-infrastructure throughout the park.

Existing trees and proposed species are placed according to these ecosystems which in turn produce naturally symbiotic webs of plants allowing different species to enhance their performance, therefore aiding the development of a robust park, from an ecological point of view, with an inherent reduction of maintenance and energy waste. At the same time the close interaction and gradual transitions in between the proposed ecosystems will create a variety of conditions and environments throughout the park from undisturbed wetland areas to fully equipped sports fields.

To this end, time, performance and interaction were extracted as key concepts for the deployment of the overall planting strategy, thus triggering an ecological park in its widest sense.

Water strategy

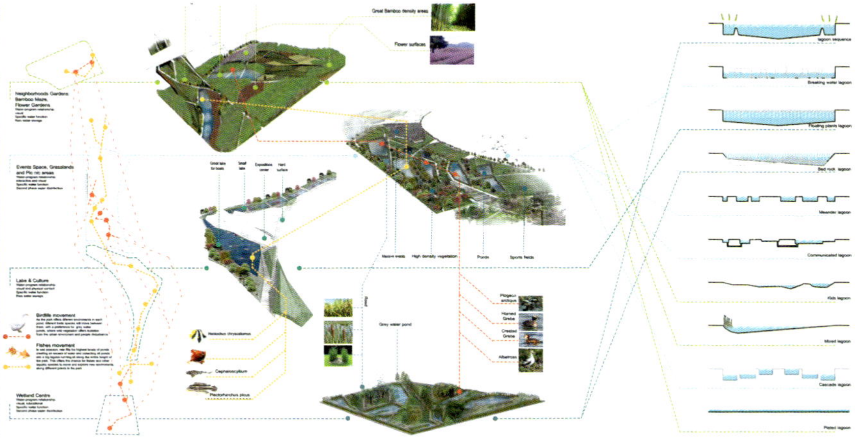

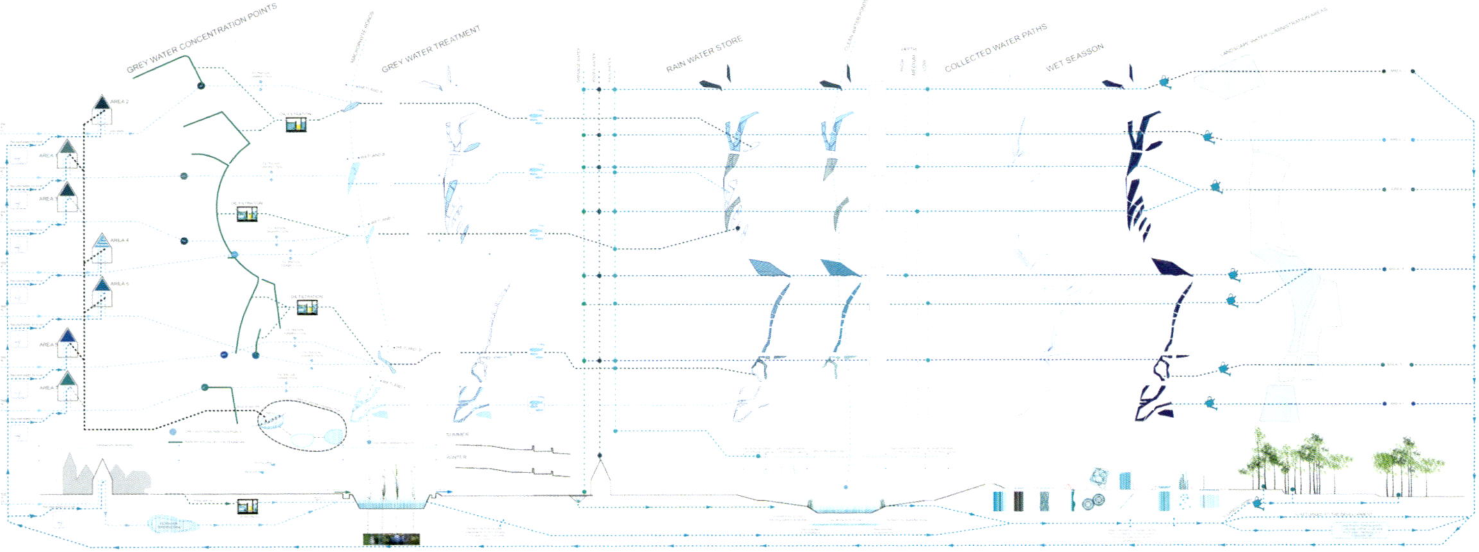

1. Continuos waterscape
2. Lagoon strategy

The system proposes a two-tier system of ponds in order to provide attenuation capacity, harvest stormwater for future reuse within the Gateway City development and store and give final treatment to greywater harvested in the Gateway City development. The purpose of these lagoons is collecting stormwater both for reuse in the Gateway City development as well as providing the attenuation volume required in the competition brief. These lagoons will tend to be located on relatively lower ground, so that the amount of water harvested is maximised. The level strategy for these ponds is: - Low fixed level, enough to maintain active flora and aquatic fauna. - Wet season level: water is allowed to flood areas adjacent to the low level ponds for prolonged periods of time during the rainy season. Depth of these areas will be shallow offering an aspect similar to that of a rice field. - Harvesting fluctuation: approximately 0.5m level fluctuation. - Extreme event attenuation: for stormwater during peak events with 50 to 100 return year period.

Topography strategy

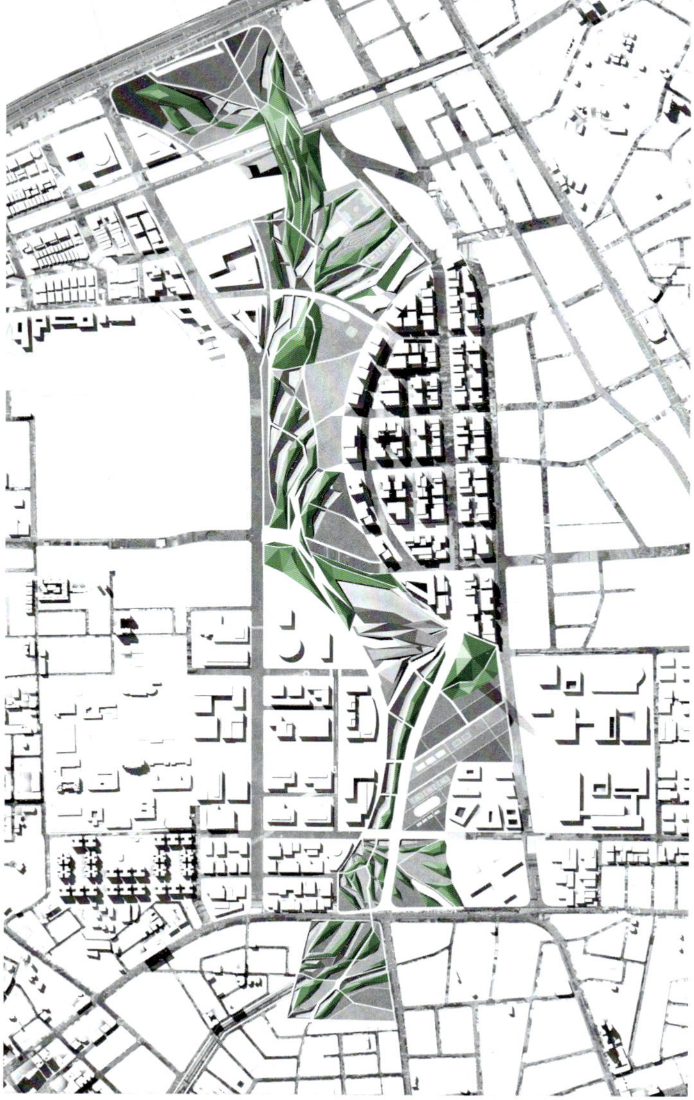

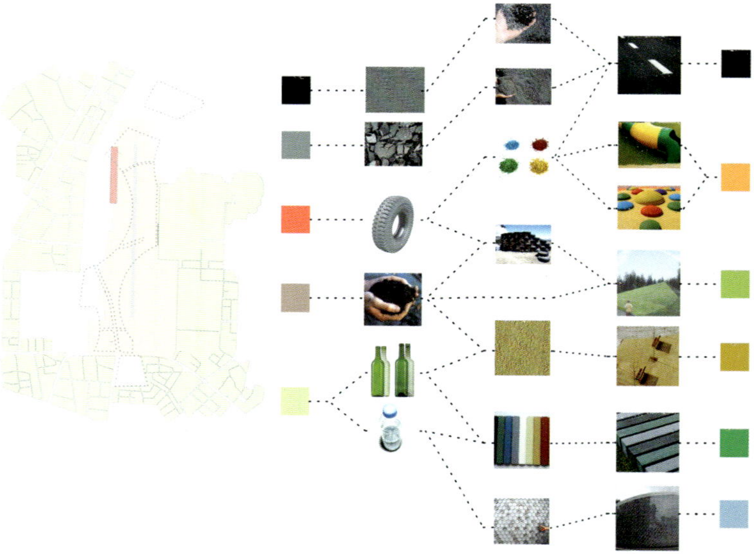

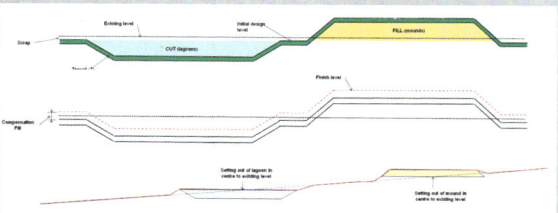

1. Cut and fill operation
2. Different slope types

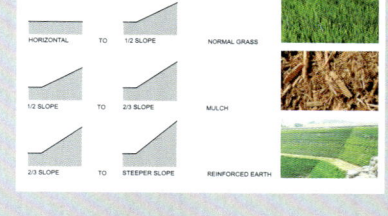

HORIZONTAL TO 1/2 SLOPE — NORMAL GRASS
1/2 SLOPE TO 2/3 SLOPE — MULCH
2/3 SLOPE TO STEEPER SLOPE — REINFORCED EARTH

The braiding process of the water treatment models the topography of the site in a two-fold manner: on the one hand it carves out or 'erodes' the ponds whose terraced levels provide the park with a seasonal character, varying its uses and available areas according to the amount of water collected; on the other hand, as a compensating effect, it piles up 'the sediments' in a set of islands which form a topography that creates different ecosystems and areas throughout the park.

The earthworks strategy of the park has been designed in such a way that there is a NET BALANCE between imports and exports of material. There is a series of sources of cut, as well as areas of fill. The design has managed to avoid import / export of any material (except top soil), thus improving sustainability credentials of the project.

Images Credits

All images by AA Landscape Urbanism, Groundlab, Sarah Majid, Eva Tsouni, Zoe Spiegeli, Eduardo Carranza, Fang Chun-Chien, Alejandra Bosch, Katya Larina, Hossein Kachabi, Wenwen Wang, Cristina Barrios, Karishma Desai, Nicola Saladino. Except p.54 by Google, p.62 by guidokritz, p.70 by Google, p.82 by Luis Montañez and andre m (eye) r vitali, p.97 by Florida Keys, Carmo and NCDOT, p.99 by anaulin, p.112 by Geoff Coupe and Arvid Puschnig, p.113 by Firedesign, p.122 by Google, p.131 by Pricey, mataparda and Google, p. 132 by Keirn, p.133 by Travel Aficionado, Martin Dougiamas, p.137 by twocentsworth, Edwin1710 and Makz, p.138 by Tom Jervis, Tom Olliver and Avius Quovis, p.146 by Soroll and Steven Vance, p.147 by Mathew Oldfield, Wolf Hilbertz and Komang Astika, p.156 by Google, p.166 by Google, p.171 by Google, p.172 by AMT - Agence metropolitaine de transport and Boston Public Library p.183 by Google, p.184 by Federico Novaro and Boston Public Library, p.190 by Google, p.198 by ed37, Gods Child and abjam77, p.199 by liangjinjian and cattoo, p.205 by Google, p.214 by thegreenpages, p.215 by amadej2008, p.239 by sanshifu and cseeman, p.260 by Sam Beebe and feral arts, p.261 by FlickrJunckie and the_mishka p.274 by Google, p.275 by korom, p295 by egorgrebnev, p.296 by Zarrsadus and Wilson Loo, p.307 by Mr & Mrs Stickyfingers, edmundyeo and fung.leo, p.309 by helga tawil souri, p.311 by ...-wink-... and Jim Linwood, p.312 by mischiru, auditopufo0 and chooyutshing, p.313 by phrenologist and Hopkinsii, p.317 by gravity_grave, p.325 by Google, p.326 by Whirling Phoenix, Happy Sleepy and Julius Hibbert, p.328 by County Planning Commission, p.330 by Gerard Dalmond, John Althouse Cohen and Sharon Yeari, p.331 by Wallpaper Osmais and mbgrigby.

Published by
LISt Lab Laboratorio
Internazionale Editoriale
TN, BCN, RTM
Italy-Spain-Nedherland
www.listlab.eu
www.momboo.net

Production
GreenTrenDesign Factory
Piazza Manifattura, 1
38068 Rovereto (TN) - ITALY
T: +39 0464 443427
info@greentrendesign.it

Authors
Eva Castro, Alfredo Ramirez, Eduardo Rico, Douglas Spencer

Editorial and Creative Director
Pino Scaglione

Art Director
Massimiliano Scaglione

Editorial Assistant
Gioia Marana

Editing Collaboration
Marta Postigo Faci
Daniel Portilla

Special Thanks
Sarah Majid (AALU 04/05), Eva Tsouni (AALU 04/05), Zoe Spiegeli (AALU 05/06), Eduardo Carranza (AALU 05/06), Fang Chun-Chien (AALU 06/07), Alejandra Bosch (AALU 06/07), Katya Larina (AALU 07/08), Hossein Kachabi (AALU 07/08), Wenwen Wang (AALU 08/09), Cristina Barrios (AALU 08/09), Karishma Desai (AALU 09/10), Nicola Saladino (AALU 09/10).

Board Scientific
Eve Blau (Harvard GSD), Pepe Barbieri (Università di Chieti), Eva Castro (Architectural Association, London), Maurizio Carta (Università di Palermo), Alberto Clementi (Università di Chieti), Alberto Cecchetto (Università di Venezia), Stefano De Martino (Università di Innsbruck), Corrado Diamantini (Università di Trento), Antonio De Rossi (Università di Torino), Franco Farinelli (Università di Bologna), Carlo Gasparrini (Università di Napoli), Manuel Gausa (Università di Genova), Giovanni Maciocco (Università di Sassari/Alghero), Antonio Paris (Uniroma, Roma La Sapienza), Vanni Pasca (Università di Palermo), Josè Luis Esteban Penelas (Università di Madrid), Mosè Ricci (Università di Genova), Roger Riewe (Università di Graz), Pino Scaglione (Università di Trento).

All rights reserved
© of the edition, LISt Lab
© of the text, the authors
© of the images, the authors; the authors recognize possible rights for the published images.

Printed and bound in the EU, November 2013
by Rubbettino Print

ISBN 9788895623375

Promotion in Italy and International distribution
Messaggerie Libri, Spa, Milano
Numero verde 800.804.900

Actar New York, USA
Inédit Barcelona, ineditllibres.com
Àgora Solucions Logístiques
Tel. 902109431 - Fax 972843168, info@agorallibres.cat

Contact
Italy-Italia , 38122, Trento/Rovereto
tel.T: +39 0464 443427; info@listlab.eu

LISt Lab is an editorial workshop, based in Europe, that works on the contemporary issues. LISt Lab not only publishes, but also researches, proposes, promotes, produces, creates networks.

LISt Lab is a green company committed to respect the environment. Paper, ink, glues and all processings come from short supply chains and aim at limiting pollution. The print run of books and magazines is based on consumption patterns, thus preventing waste of paper and surpluses. LISt Lab aims at the responsibility of the authors and markets, towards the knowledge of a new publishing culture based on an intelligent resource management.

GreenTrenDesign Factory, member of Progetto Manifattura, multiplatform structure, provides advanced design services. In the balance between sustainability and quality, craftsmanship and digital experimentation, the company operates in partnership with LISt Lab.